Jessica Brown-White

About the Author

MARTHA MANNING, PH.D., is a writer, clinical psychologist, and former professor of psychology at George Mason University. After receiving her B.A. with high honors from the University of Maryland, she earned her M.A. and Ph.D. in clinical psychology from the Catholic University of America and focused her postdoctoral work on clinical child psychology at McLean Hospital/Harvard Medical School.

She is the author of *Undercurrents: A Life Beneath the Surface; Chasing Grace: Reflections of a Catholic Girl, Grown Up;* and *All Seasons Pass: Grieving a Miscarriage,* and her writing has been featured in several anthologies. Dr. Manning has been recognized by the National Institute of Mental Health for her work in education and advocacy, she was awarded the American Psychiatric Association's 1996 Presidential Award for Patient Advocacy, and she is listed in *Who's Who of American Women 1997.* Her work has appeared in numerous publications, including the *New York Times Book Review,* the *Washington Post, Health, Ladies' Home Journal,* and *New Woman.*

Dr. Manning has been featured on *NBC Dateline, Good Morning America,* C-SPAN, and *CBS This Morning,* as well as on NPR's *Voice of America* and other radio and television programs. She was profiled (along with William Styron and Mike Wallace) on the Emmy Award–nominated HBO documentary *Dead Blue: Surviving Depression* and in numerous publications, including *People* and *USA Today.*

the

COMMON
THREAD

Mothers and Daughters: The Bond We Never Outgrow

Martha Manning

Quill

An Imprint of HarperCollinsPublishers

A hardcover edition of this book was published in 2002 by William Morrow, an imprint of HarperCollins Publishers.

HarperCollins books may be purchased for educational, business, or sales promotional use. For information please write: Special Markets Department, HarperCollins Publishers Inc., 10 East 53rd Street, New York, NY 10022.

First Quill edition published 2003.

Designed by Nicola Ferguson

Library of Congress Cataloging-in-Publication Data
Manning, Martha.
The common thread : mothers and daughters: the bond we never outgrow / Martha Manning.
p. cm.
Originally published: The common thread : mothers, daughters, and the power of empathy. New York : William Morrow, c2002.
ISBN 0-380-97719-2 (hardcover)
ISBN 0-380-80379-8 (trade)
1. Mothers and daughters. 2. Empathy. I. Title.
HQ755.85 .M258 2003
306.874'3—dc21   2002036799

03 04 05 06 07 ❖/RRD 10 9 8 7 6 5 4 3 2 1

For my daughter,
Keara Manning Depenbrock,
who keeps my feet firmly on the ground,

for my mother,
Mary Louise Manning,
who holds up the sky

CONTENTS

FOREWORD

The Safety Net:
Right Mommies and Baby Birds

ROSIE O'DONNELL

My daughter, Chelsea, cannot stop talking about the dead bird. She was in the park with her brothers and nanny, on her way toward the swings and the sandbox. She saw, in her path on the dirt walkway, a newborn baby bird. A dead newborn baby bird. Chelsea is three, yet she has the vocabulary of a forty-year-old. I think she is like me: When she gets something in her head, it stays there.

"Mama, there was a baby bird, it fell out of its nest, and it was dead. The mommy of this bird must be sad, I bet, 'cause the baby was gone. Forever. Dead. And it must have fallen out of the nest where the mother put it. Maybe the baby bird was looking for something to eat, or trying to see the sky, and it tipped over the edge. And then, it was dead, this baby bird, Mama. And I know the bird's mommy is really, really sad."

So we talked for a long time, about birds and mommies and death. About the fragility of nests as a whole. About sudden sadness, how life can change in a split second. She asked again about my mother, her grandmother, who is, like the baby bird, quite dead. Was she looking for a safety net, something to protect her should she unexpectedly begin to free-fall? I wasn't sure, yet I dug out my stories, the ones I had tucked away especially for occasions like this. She sat on my lap, and I told her of the World's Fair, the boat ride—a story she knew by heart but listened to again, waiting for a new sliver, a hidden gem I had not yet revealed.

We went through our usual Q and A. Why didn't I give my mommy medicine? Was I very sad? Who took care of me? Did I still miss her? I answered, as I always do, slightly amazed at my daughter's rawness, her unending emotional access. Then there was a pause. I knew what was coming. Something my son Parker never asked, something most three-year-olds would not be able to articulate.

"Where is my tummy lady? Is she ever coming to see me?"

I took a breath. I told her I did not know her tummy lady. She was not in our family. She was not going to come visit because she knew Chelsea was with her right mommy now. She was a nice lady, I was sure, and she had listened when God told her of the mix-up, that the baby in her tummy was someone else's. The tummy lady loved Chelsea—a lot, I told her.

"I bet she is sad," she said, a little sad herself.

Real-life parenting is nothing like sitcoms.

I stroked her blond curls. "Yes, Chels, I bet she was sad. I think she is okay now, though. You know, when you are older, Chels, you can go meet her if you want to. I will go with you if you want me to, because I would like to meet her too. I want to look in her eyes and say thank you. Thank you for listening to God. For knowing that Chelsea belonged in our family. For loving my baby girl so much."

There was silence. Nothing. Just air and breath between us.

"It is very sad when a baby falls out of its nest," she told me with authority. I waited for more. "Mama . . . you wanna watch a tape?"

We did, *The Wizard of Oz* as usual. "See, Mama, Dorothy's socks are blue, not white."

This is a fact Chelsea brought up with me last Halloween when I presented her with her Dorothy costume, complete with ruby slippers and white socks. She looked at me perplexed.

"Dorothy wears blue socks in *The Wizard of Oz,* Mama," she said, as if I was a complete moron.

I put in the videotape to check and see, and sure enough she was right.

"Yes, Chelsea, her socks are blue!" I said, as her eyes locked with mine and she nodded. My daughter notices everything.

I realized that night, as I watched her sleep, that we have our own safety net, Chelsea and I. Built of Halloween costumes and rewatched movies, of tummy mommies and baby birds. Of questions allowed, and answers always given.

She is something, my daughter. My mother would have loved her.

INTRODUCTION

The Old Lady and Her Mother

Early in my psychology internship I was assigned the kind of classic case that keeps therapists in business: a mother and daughter in conflict. Before the scheduled appointment, the clinic receptionist handed me the standard chart for intake sessions. The information on the referral sheet was limited to the names, addresses, and phone numbers of potential patients. I reminded the receptionist of my preference for structuring first interviews—I liked to see the daughter first (I'd found that with many girls, this cut down the paranoia about what Mom and the doctor were saying behind their backs), then the mother, then both together.

Several minutes later the receptionist knocked on my half-opened door and began to usher into my office someone who definitely did not look like the patient I expected: a pale little blue-haired woman with bright red lipstick that could only have been applied in the dark and made her look even pastier than she probably was. She wore one of those dresses that, though it was probably made in the 1930s, will never be called "vintage." As she advanced her metal walker, step by agonizing step, I estimated that she had to be at least eighty years old. I considered myself something of a specialist in mother-child conflict, and it took me a second to register the fact that this session might be a bit of a departure from the usual. This woman was much older than any of the mothers I'd worked with.

I introduced myself and, with all the patronizing solicitude of a young woman who believes that she will never be that old, asked her to excuse the receptionist and me for a moment. Annoyed, I repeated to the receptionist my preference for seeing the daughter, *not the mother,* first. The receptionist smirked, barely tolerating yet another upstart intern, and whispered, "Girl, she *is* the daughter." She gestured to the waiting room where an even older-looking woman sat ramrod straight in her chair, still wearing her coat, hat, and gloves and gripping her purse as if she were in immediate danger of having it snatched. She had the look of someone who was badly constipated or just generally displeased.

For the next hour I heard, collectively, 179 years of a mother-daughter relationship that was very connected *and* very conflicted from the start. It was somewhat unnerving to see a ninety-nine-year-old woman point accusingly at her eighty-year-old daughter and complain about what a fussy, demanding baby she'd been. With a one-year-old daughter of my own at home—a baby who'd been very colicky for her first few months—I could identify with the mother. But it was unsettling to think that in seventy-nine years I might still be pissed off about it.

We marched on from there, through childhood defiance and "sassiness," to problems in school, to constant verbal battles over the most minor issues. We covered the preadolescent years, in which the mother had expected—and gotten—nothing but aggravation. In adolescence there had been rebellion—hanging out with the wrong people and general disobedience. In young adulthood there had been an early marriage to a man the mother had disliked on sight—and she had never allowed anything he did to revise her initial impression. The marriage had lasted for about two years, ending with his confession of infidelity. At that point, the daughter had returned to her mother's home, where she remained for fifty-six more years. Fifty-six years of conflict and connection.

The daughter's rendering of their history was considerably different. Her mother had been hard to please, unyielding, and critical, while simultaneously demanding closeness. All of the daughter's attempts to construct a world of her own—making and keeping friends, developing interests outside her home, having boyfriends—were thwarted by a mother who saw any bids for independence as disloyalty. With any risk the daughter took, the mother predicted not only failure but also the inevitable result of that failure: "You'll come running back to me."

When the daughter married and physically left her mother's home, she thought she had achieved the kind of break she'd always hoped for. She assumed that a shift in geography would somehow magically assure her the independence she'd always craved. But she willingly talked to her mother several times a day on the phone. Every Friday her mother took an hourlong bus ride to her daughter's and they cleaned house from top to bottom. Whenever the daughter felt the slightest confusion about anything, she consulted her mother. The number of daily choices and decisions in which she sought out her mother over her husband multiplied and eventually resulted in considerable marital distress.

Finally there was something about which the daughter and her mother could agree: the husband was a disaster. Her mother provided a willing ear and gave freely of her sympathy. In the midst of conflict with her husband, the daughter felt more genuinely and positively connected to her mother than she had in her whole life. The mother felt needed and finally, *finally* felt gratified that she could comfort her daughter and that her daughter could actually accept it. In this scenario it was just a matter of time before the marriage would have to go. The daughter returned with relief to the mother she'd once been so intent on leaving. After a brief "honeymoon," they settled back into the same little dramas they'd been enacting for most of their lives. In her own way, each complained about the same thing: "She doesn't respect me." "She doesn't listen to me." "She's demanding, manipulative, and petty." Some were clearly "mother" complaints—"She doesn't dress right for the weather." (This was rather interesting, since the mother was fully dressed for winter on a rather warm spring day.) "She's sloppy with her chores." "She can be pouty and uncommunicative." "She doesn't respond well to perfectly reasonable advice."

The daughter complained about the mother's constant interference, her control—even over "silly" things, like the time she had "a fit" because the daughter purchased a different denture adhesive from their usual brand. If she failed to load the dishwasher or change a bed in the exact way her mother wanted, ten minutes later she would find her work redone—a silent but resounding reproach.

Listening to the two of them for twenty minutes, all I could think was, "Why in God's name are these two still together?" Fortunately, with four years of clinical training behind me, I was able to phrase it a bit more diplomatically.

"Can you tell me some of the *good* things about your relationship?"

Silence.

"What kinds of things do you like to do together?"

Silence. I forged ahead.

"Okay, forget *liking*. What do you two *do* together?"

Beginning with the list of their "programs"—the soap operas and game shows that punctuated their days—they articulated a number of regular and seemingly pleasant shared activities: bridge with two neighbors; church; the early-bird special every Wednesday at Western Sizzler; visiting their favorite bank clerk, favorite librarian, favorite hairdresser; topped off with their obvious joy in caring for their two cats. Registering the sudden upturn in their mood and connection, I felt totally confused. They seemed relatively content.

"So exactly what is it you want help with?" I asked.

Both of them stared at me blankly, shrugged, and said they had no idea.

"Is it just me," I wondered, "or is something really important missing here?"

"Well," I stammered, "then whose idea was it for you to come?"

"Dr. Randolph," they replied in unison, like that would clear things up for me.

"Who is Dr. Randolph?"

"The doctor at the hospital."

"*What* doctor at *what* hospital?"

"From when I broke my hip," the daughter replied, clearly exasperated that I was taking so long to get it. "Everyone said I was too nervous and that it was my mother's fault."

"No, they didn't say that," argued the mother. "They said that you were nervous and that living with you must be really hard for me."

They bickered as if I were invisible.

I broke in. "Well, exactly what are you nervous about?"

Without hesitation and in almost the same voice, they answered, "Dying."

Now in the last minutes of the session, it became clear that it wasn't so much dying, as in you stop breathing, get put in a box, and buried for all eternity that they feared, but the kind of dying where one person moves on from this world and the other is left behind. And that was the saddest thing—not their marathon conflict but their shared assumption that the death of one of them would signal the other's demise. I told them we could work on the "nervousness" in some joint sessions, and this seemed agreeable. We scheduled the next appointment, spending considerable energy trying to reconcile openings in my schedule with their memory of *TV Guide*. It became very clear that the travails of Luke and Laura would always be more important than their fear of death or my availability.

Getting the two of them out of my office took some time. The daughter groaned softly as she tried to straighten and shift her balance to the walker. Her mother was out of her chair in a shot and stood beside her, so close that their shoulders touched. Silently the mother leaned slightly into her daughter, offering her body as a pillar against which she could pull herself up. As the daughter rose in fits and starts, she whispered, "Okay . . . Yes . . . I think I've got it," as much to herself as to her mother and me. The mother stood solid and straight and echoed with her own encouragements: "You're okay . . . Just a bit more . . . A little more . . . there, you've got it." Someone just looking in might describe the scene as a perfect example of the blind leading the blind. The observer might wonder why the healthy twentysomething in the room wasn't moving an inch to help. But having been immersed in their conflicts and complaints for one very long hour, I saw it differently. To me it was a pure moment. A moment of synchrony. No whining about who was doing too much or too little. There were no criticisms, no "hurry ups," no ultimatums. It was just the small and slow combined effort of two complicated old women—a mother and her daughter—to accomplish the seemingly simple task of standing up, something they had probably done together seventy-eight years before and not given much thought to since.

When the moment passed, they quickly reverted to type. The mother bossed her daughter out the door, instructing her on the correct way to navigate the walker across my carpet and giving me several of those "What would she do without me?" looks. The daughter responded by turning to me repeatedly with raised eyebrows, silently asking, "Do you see what I've been talking about? *Do you?*" I was sure I knew *exactly* what she meant. After they left, I quickly filled up ten pages in their chart, describing their history, their interactions with me and with each other.

I was becoming proficient at glibly rattling off people's problems and cat-
egorizing them using my ever-expanding (and often meaningless) psychological vocabulary. Given the length and breadth of these women's complaints,
and the degree to which their individual patterns of development had gone
awry, there was no shortage of apt psychiatric labels. Terms like "passive-
aggressive," "controlling," "enmeshed," "poor boundaries," "infantile,"
"regressed," and "inappropriate" flowed from my pen. If their relationship
had been an old building, I would have classified it "condemned."

As I dutifully filled out the patient chart, I smiled, already envisioning
my clever presentation at the next staff meeting. Technically, I'd done a good
job of describing what I'd seen. But I'd seen it with such cool distance that I
felt absolutely nothing *with* or *for* them. I had little appreciation for what I'd
missed. And the biggest thing missing was a respectful curiosity for the complexities of *how* their relationship had developed over years and years and
years. Was it possible that behavior I labeled as weird (or, in psychiatric parlance, "pathological") may have "worked" for them? What had they been like
as younger people? What occurred at those natural points in development
when most children become physically and emotionally independent from
their parents? How did the husband/father fit into this equation? What were
the positives they provided each other emotionally? Were there other "standing up" moments in which the old layers of conflict and resentment fell away
and allowed them to be attuned to each other with as much precision as a
mother and infant? And finally, what *would* become of one when the other
died?

My lack of curiosity was less a consequence of limited clinical experience and more an attempt to distance this particular mother-daughter pair
from my own personal experience. I couldn't afford to identify with them
as a mother *or* as a daughter. I didn't want to think of myself as ever being
on *either* side of that walker. I couldn't imagine my mother and I living
alone together on cats and soap operas. And as much as I adored my baby
daughter, one year's sleep deprivation already had me counting down the
seventeen years until she moved in with other people and woke *them* up all
the time.

Yet just below the surface I felt an uncomfortable connection to those
women in a way that was hard to translate into words. Visual images, parts of
stories, fragments of memory, confused me as I tried to understand the rea-

sons this pair didn't leave my consciousness as easily as I'd left them on ten hastily scribbled pages in an intake report.

I recalled stories, given freely or stolen from overheard conversations among my mother, my aunts, my grandmothers, my great-aunts, and my great-grandmother, that had threads in common with the stories of these women. There were stories about bright, formidable mothers—interesting, creative women. Some caved in under an avalanche of babies and children. Others were good with the little ones—free with their energy, interest, and unconditional love but much more limited in the letting-go department. For some, trouble started as their daughters became adolescents and young adults, when the price for all that early love was their mothers' angry sense of betrayal and resentment as daughters began depositing their emotional energy in other people.

My family on both sides is rich with stories of elopements, secret assignations in graveyards, early widowhood and long single lives, younger sisters who move in with older sisters and never leave. An appropriate family crest for us might read "Honor thy generational boundaries." There was my great-grandmother who became furious that her son had broken up with the woman she deemed he would marry. She quickly shoved Cupid aside, confronted the new girlfriend, and announced that she had a gun and was prepared to use it if the woman didn't break off the new romance. In my family there were mother-daughter relationships as symbiotic as that of the two old ladies in my office, if not more so. So symbiotic that when one mother died, her daughter withered and died not long after.

There were stories of daughters who ran like hell away from home and daughters who stayed and suffocated. There were mothers who carried their daughters through adulthood, and daughters who—even as young children—carried their mothers. For some these periods of "carrying" made the relationship stronger and better. But for others it crushed and crippled, engendering a lifetime of exclusive and mutual dependence, which became crises when either the mother or daughter died and a new generation of women was expected to take up the mantle with whoever was left.

But I also learned that there could be humor and strength in numbers, even if that power couldn't be quantified. I recognized that in the midst of long barren stretches in the lives of these women, there were gold mines of creativity and intelligence, and courageous leaps of faith. They were women who liked to tell stories, and daughters who loved to listen—even when they knew the bullshit-to-truth ratio was fairly high. When it came to the women in my own family, as admittedly weird as some of our stories were, I found myself actively resisting turning the *characters* into the kinds of *caricatures* I had made of my patients. My own new motherhood had recently provided a jolting perspective that no psychology course could offer. When it came to the generations of women in my family, I realized that with the craziness there was always rock-solid sanity; with the pettiness there was also tremendous tolerance and integrity; with the anger and rage and frustration there was also wildly generous love. And in only one year, I had become much more humble because I had already experienced them *all*.

ONE

Mothers and Daughters: The Big Deal

Why do we spend hours thinking and talking about our mothers and daughters? Because it's the longest-running show in town and we've had front-row seats for our entire lives. Some of us got our tickets for free, and others paid dearly for them. The plot has endless twists and turns, contradictions, secrets, and surprises. We will never understand it all. We may edge closer to some answers about why our relationships with our mothers and daughters are the way they are, but we'll never make it all the way. We aren't supposed to. Insights? Yes. Answers? Never.

Whenever I tell women that the subject of my writing is mother-daughter relationships, it doesn't matter whether I'm shooting the breeze with two or giving a speech to two hundred, the response is always the same. A collective groan rises up, followed by statements like "Oh, God!" and "You should interview me" and "I have stories you wouldn't believe!" The response is as reflexive as "You're welcome" after "Thank you." It almost seems that we are fulfilling some cultural mandate when we groan about our mothers. Among the multiple dimensions of all mother-daughter relationships, the aspects we are primed to emphasize are those that drive us crazy.

When women say, "Oh my God, I'm turning into my mother!" they don't exactly shout it proudly from the rooftops. We often shudder when we catch ourselves repeating phrases that we swore would never become part of our repertoires, such as "Young lady . . ." or "As long as you live under my roof . . ." or "I don't care if the entire seventh grade is allowed to do it . . ." "Accusing" a woman of turning into her mother is a handy weapon in verbal confrontations for people like spouses and children. When a loved one makes the comparison, a woman's reaction is much closer to "What the hell is that supposed to mean?" than to "Really? What a compliment. Thank you." In a *Salon* "advice" column, Mr. Blue (a.k.a. Garrison Keillor) responds to a letter of urgency—"My wife," writes the troubled husband, is "turning into her mother!" The problem with this transformation becomes instantly clear in the writer's description of his mother-in-law (and, indirectly, his wife): "a wretched, spiteful, miserable martyr, who drives my father-in-law to drink a pint of Canadian whiskey every night."

The irony is that the majority of groaning women admit they have essentially positive relationships with their mothers. The two bickering old women in my office would have said they do, too. If you ask the question "Do you love your mother?" the majority of women will answer, "Yes, of course." Admittedly some will then immediately wish to amend that statement with a list of qualifications. "Yes, I love her, *but* . . ."

THE LONG LIFE OF EARLY EXPECTATIONS

We want our mothers to love us perfectly, completely, and unconditionally. We want them to love us as they did at first sight when we were newborns. At the same time we expect them to treat us with all the adult respect to which we feel entitled by virtue of our age and experience. Unlike our relationships with friends, lovers, or husbands, which have their roots in adolescence and adulthood, the relationship between a mother and daughter is radically different. The sense of loving and being loved—even before birth—carries weighty expectations: that the connection will *forever* be as strong, as connected, as free from boundaries and conditions as it was in the honeymoon stretches of infancy and early childhood.

Mothers can be similarly unrealistic about the ways their daughters should love them. Despite the intensity of the connection, it is rarely ever "equal." For example, an adolescent daughter's "I hate you" usually carries less weight than a mother's use of the same words to her daughter. A mother's scorn over a child's painting packs a far more powerful punch than any rotten thing a child can say to a mother. It's never an even exchange. It's not supposed to be. In most cases, a daughter takes up more space in her mother's mind than her mother does in hers, an insight that can be found even in ancient texts like the Talmud: "A mother is always attached to her daughter but not so a daughter to her mother."

THINKING BACK

In *A Room of One's Own,* her groundbreaking treatise on sexism, society, and art, Virginia Woolf had it right: "We think back through our mothers if we are women." Any attempt to understand ourselves without considering our mothers, and *their* mothers, and *their* mothers, will eventually dead-end in a sign that says "You can't get there from here." To move forward, sometimes we must first move back. My mother and aunt still turn over questions about my grandmother, now dead ten years. "When do you think things changed for the worse?" they ask each other. "Why were you the 'good' daughter and I the 'bad' one?" "What made her so unhappy?" With nine grown daughters between them, my mother and aunt are *still* working out a relationship in which one of the major players is dead. But that doesn't matter. The mother-daughter relationship remains alive for women, long before birth and long after death. It is the lens through which they filter their past, as well as their present and future, experience. "Why don't they just let it go?" my sisters, cousins, and I ask one another. As far as we're concerned, this particular plot of land has been farmed entirely too long. But when it comes right down to it, why *should* they stop talking about their relationship with their mother? As long as they continue to till, seed, and water that soil, their work will unite them as sisters and will further their understanding of a complex and "unfinished" relationship. It will likely influence their relationships with their own daughters and granddaughters, and produce insights, even if appreciated and understood only by them. Despite the many commonalities in their experience, every sister has a different mother. Therefore the pooling of perceptions usually encourages a more nuanced view of a mother than the usual good/bad dichotomy allows.

AMBIVALENCE IS NOT A DIRTY WORD

When women voice the ambivalence they feel about their mothers or daughters, they often express it as if ambivalence is inherently a bad thing. Ambivalence has taken on the status of being an emotion in and of itself, rather than the coexistence of overlapping, possibly conflicting, or inconsistent emotions and reactions. In an interview about influences on her work, rock diva and actress Courtney Love expressed the conviction that she grew up believing that being a girl was absolutely no barrier to anything she wanted to become. As she listed her role models, she gave a wonderful example of ambivalence. "I'll hail my mother as an icon. I can't stand her, but I really was sheltered that way." Human relationships, by nature, involve an amazing array of emotions, thoughts, and behaviors. In most relationships ambivalence is *part and parcel of closeness*. It means having a tossed salad of feelings, like a bunch of noisy siblings who must find a way to coexist. If we weren't meant to bump into one another, we wouldn't have been given parts that stick out, like breasts, butts, elbows, and knees. Growing up involves constantly tolerating and actively working with ambivalence. Whether ambivalence is problematic in a mother-daughter relationship has to do with the degree to which that ambivalence is acknowledged and acted upon.

The typical ambivalence in a parent-child relationship often involves clashes between opposing attributes. For example, the woman who sweetly sings her little girl to sleep and kisses her boo-boos is also the one who won't let her go to preschool in her beautiful Barbie nightgown, gives a time-out when the girl gently shoves her baby brother off the couch, and sometimes loses her temper "for no good reason." In more extreme situations, some girls grow up with tremendous ambivalence about mothers who are so possessed by their own "demons" that they are unpredictable and undependable in their physical and emotional caretaking. Many of these women love their children very much, and their children know it. But in some ways, love makes it harder. No matter how much she loves her daughter, a woman in a full-blown attack of depression, psychosis, or addiction can't care for her—physically or emotionally—the way she can when she's well.

Gloria Steinem recalls a difficult childhood in which her "loving, intelligent, terrorized mother" was "just a fact of life . . . someone to be worried about and cared for." Steinem grew up with love and sympathy for her mother's suffering on the one hand, and frustration with her limitations and embarrassment over her public displays of vulnerability on the other. "In many ways," she wrote, "our roles were reversed: I was the mother and she was the child." A child in that situation often does the loving and the caretaking but doesn't know what to do with the anger, fear, and shame that usually accompany such a role reversal.

Feeling ambivalent doesn't mean we necessarily *act* ambivalently. But often it is only when we, as parents or children, find safe expression for those mixed feelings that we begin to be able to manage them. Love is never completely unconditional. For example, children learn early what can light up their parents like a Christmas tree, and also what can pull the plug out. Many girls learn that a winner is "loved" better than a "loser." Amy Tan's novel *The Joy Luck Club* is a stunning portrayal of generations of Chinese-American women who struggle to balance good daughterhood with authentic womanhood. One character, Waverly Jong, a child chess prodigy, becomes increasingly annoyed with her mother's personal stake in her successes. "Why do you have to use me to show off?" she demands angrily. "If you want to show off, then why don't you learn to play chess?" Needless to say, her mother drops her interest in chess like a hot potato, and Waverly's confidence and career in the game takes a major nosedive.

Ambivalence is the norm, not the exception. Mothers and daughters are eternally and inevitably at different points of development, with different needs, conflicts, pressures, and commitments. At 3 A.M. a sleep-deprived new mother can frighten the hell out of herself with the aggressive feelings she has about the beloved baby at her breast. The brick wall that a mother and her rageful two-year-old slam against in conflict is just awful for each combatant. The mother's job with a toddler is to encourage autonomy while at the same time monitoring and regulating her daughter's behavior. But her daughter never signed that particular contract. Sometimes you can see it in a tantrum—in the supermarket checkout line where the child's desire for Gummi Bears, met by the mother's denial, threatens to become a struggle to the death. Everything in the child's behavior screams, "I hate you! How could you deprive me of something I want and love and that's right here?" In a matter of seconds, however, the hatred comes up against fears of Mom's disapproval, the potential for withdrawal of love, or outright violent retribution. Mothers scarred by their own abuse in childhood are far less able to hold on to adulthood in the face of colicky crying or meltdowns in stores. The volume of a child's distress is turned up so loud for the abused mother that rather than being able to think or say, "This rotten kid's driving me crazy," she falls back into what she "knows." It's not unusual for her to say, "Why are you doing this to *me*?"—a question she probably wondered when she found herself in a similar position as a child.

Another issue between any mother and daughter involves the relationship between love and control. In infancy and childhood, the overlap is usually substantial. The child does what Mom wants, and receives love. The mother experiences her child's compliance as a sign that they are attuned to each other and that mutual and unconditional love abounds. Unfortunately, this gives many mothers the illusion that the marriage of love and control is guaranteed for life. But girls and young women take on more control, exercise more preferences, and depend less on their mothers, even as they remain connected to them, a combination that from the perspective of daughters might seem entirely reasonable. However, mothers who still have some variation of a love-control equation in their heads are often unprepared and frequently hurt when their totally "innocent" comments, like "Yes, but don't you think . . . ?" or "Wouldn't it be better if . . . ?" or "No, you don't think/feel that," make their daughters explode. Growing up, daughters are often much more sensitive to their mothers' attempts at control and make assumptions that the almost totally unconditional acceptance they experienced as children was less a matter of love and more a mother's need for power. In most cases this is a vast overstatement, but it often fuels the heat between the two as they differentiate from each other.

GOOD/BAD MOTHERS, DAUGHTERS,
AND OTHER NONSENSE

One of my favorite scenes from *The Wizard of Oz* occurs when the Munchkins creep out of their hiding places and summon the nerve to ask Dorothy, "Are you a good witch or a bad witch?" They have no way to compute her insistence that she's not a witch at all, and continue to demand that she put herself into one of their categories. As funny as the scene is, I find that when it comes to describing family relationships, we are often as limited as the Munchkins. The terms "good mother" and "bad mother" are relatively meaningless, and yet we use them all the time. Mothers and daughters are easier to pin down at the extremes, especially in the "bad" dimension, like the rotten stepmothers who populate fairy tales. However, the good/bad dichotomy does little to advance our ability to understand the relationship that is typically the longest, the most complicated, and among the most intense connections a woman will ever have.

The Good Mother

When people say that a woman is a "good mother" or a "good daughter," what exactly do they mean? Is it because the good qualities outnumber the bad? Or is it because the mother does no major harm (even though she doesn't do all that much good)? Is a good mother a happy mother, or is happiness irrelevant? It's highly subjective. One girl's dearest mommy turns out to be another's *Mommie Dearest*.

Comparing mothers is a conversation staple. Adolescent and young adult males prefer to insult *other people's mothers*. Insulting the mother of a rival usually ranks at the very top of the hierarchy of things so bad to say that physical assault is the likely payback. It knows no geographic boundaries: From Spain: "I shit on the mother that bore you." Italy: "What a joy, what a joy, to have a slut for a mama." Japan: "Your mother is a protruding navel." South Africa: "You were born out of your mother's ass because her vagina was too busy." And the United States: "Your mama's like a cake, everybody gets a piece." Regardless of the language, the theme of the insults usually involves an indiscriminately promiscuous mother with whom the son and almost every other living male has or will have all different kinds of sex. A recent nightly news broadcast about the outcome of a hotly contested hit-and-run accident highlighted the degree of contentiousness among deliberating jurors. As a reference point for the level to which the discussions sank, one juror exclaimed, "Names were called. People's *mothers* were talked about!"

Young women typically don't disparage the mothers of rivals, particularly around issues of sexual honor, purity, and prowess. They're usually much happier to complain about *their own mothers,* and have plenty to say. There's nothing more annoying than being really angry at one's mother and having a friend say how much she's always liked her. But *her* mother, well, that's a different story altogether. "Islands on the Moon," a short story by Barbara Kingsolver, includes such a conversation between Annemarie and her friend Kay Kay. Annemarie resents her mother, Magda, for her many eccentricities, her attachment to flaky causes, and her refusal to be average and invisible. In the one-upmanship of the game "Who has the worst mother?" Kay Kay offers to trade mothers. Assuming that everyone else's mother must be less strange than *hers,* Annemarie challenges Kay Kay to provide evidence. "For my birthday," she replies, "my mother sent me one of those fold-up things you carry in your purse for covering up the toilet seat." Not to be outdone, Annemarie goes in for the kill: "At least she didn't try to *knit* you a toilet seat cover, like Magda would. . . . She bought it at a store, right?" Point. Match. Game.

The Good Daughter

There's even less to go on in defining a good daughter. Is she the girl her mother can depend on, the good helper, always available and willing when she's needed? For how long is she expected to do these things in order to keep her title? Or is she defined as good based on how closely she reaches her mother's goals in the outside world, even if she's not particularly helpful at home? Is she the girl who smooths things over or shakes things up? Does she fulfill her mother's dreams or squash them? When we call a woman a dutiful daughter, what do we really mean?

Women will always hunger to comprehend the relationships most central to them. The question is not really whether a mother-daughter relationship is good or bad, healthy or screwed up. It has more to do with identifying those factors that are particularly influential at different points in their development—as individuals and as a pair. Motherhood and daughterhood will never be generic concepts, and yet we often treat them that way. There are, of course, common threads woven throughout development that apply to almost everyone. But there are also the many unique results of two closely attached people who will always be at different developmental levels and therefore always dealing with different challenges.

IT TAKES MORE THAN TWO TO TANGO

Historically, examinations of the mother-daughter relationship have focused on it as if it exists in a vacuum. It was assumed that psychological forces predominated and that girls had to accomplish several important things in development: bond with their mothers, identify with their mothers, then separate from, and in many ways repudiate, their mothers. But it's never been that simple. Attachment, identification, and separation are important aspects of all mother-daughter relationships and will remain alive and kicking throughout a lifetime, but insistence on them as the triumvirate of power in women's development has obscured the impact of many other influences.

Mothers and daughters are influenced by powerful forces within them and around them. These forces are reciprocal and in continuous motion, constantly influencing and reinfluencing one another. Anne Frank reflected this basic insight in diary accounts about her conflict-filled relationship with her mother (many of which were expurgated from the original editions of *The Diary of a Young Girl* at the request of Anne's father, in an effort to protect her dead mother; no English translation containing those references was available until 1995). Reflecting on a period of particular tension, Anne ponders not only her mother's influence on her but her influence on her mother: "I was offended, took it far too much to heart and was insolent and beastly to her, which, in turn, made her unhappy. We were caught in a vicious circle of unpleasantness and sorrow."

A similar censorship occurred with the journals of another young writer, Sylvia Plath, whose seething entries about her mother were deleted until their publication in *The New Yorker* in March 2000: "What do I do? I don't imagine time will make me love her. I can pity her; she's had a lousy life; she doesn't know she's a walking vampire. But that is only pity. Not love." Is it taboo for a daughter to publicly explore her ambivalence toward her mother, *especially when she's so articulate about it?*

Windows into Each Other

When I was born I became a new window for my mother to look through to her relationship with *her* mother. My daughter is a window into my relationship with *my* mother. As we experience motherhood and daughterhood over the years, we gain new perspectives, ones that often challenge earlier assumptions. For example, when a girl hits adolescence she may see that some of the conflicts with her mother may not be "typical" in content or degree. Or, as she watches her daughter walk into a future with different choices than she had, a mother might examine the potential choices in her own life that are still open to her.

One House, Many Windows

If you want to get a good look inside a house, peering into one window will yield a small sampling of the overall structure. If that single window shows us the bedroom of a thirteen-year-old who is using every inch of space to make personal statements about her loves and hates and has converted the floor into a closet, the generalizations we make about the entire house will be quite skewed. Alternately, a peek into a living room worthy of a *House Beautiful* spread tells us little about the more private parts of the home. Research into relationships is always limited by the restriction of how many windows we look through. In any study, too many windows yield sloppy research. Narrowing focus has contributed incremental and vital additions to our understanding of human development. The downside is that we often pretend that by knowing about the one or two major windows, we've got the whole picture, when we haven't.

As a psychologist, my natural bias—my window—in examining mother-daughter relationships is toward the emotional and social aspects. This bias is reflected in most popular books about human development. But human relationships are influenced by far more than the feelings and intentions that two people bring to each other. To more fully understand any relationship, we must consider the *contexts* in which it occurs. Each of these contexts, or windows, enriches our view. They are *timing, biology,* and *culture.*

Context Number One: Timing

Timing is everything. A "good" daughter at six months might be a baby who takes several naps a day, has a laid-back disposition, is attached to a pacifier, and prefers to sit on Mom's lap all day. But those criteria applied to the same girl at age five usually aren't cause for celebration. The active sex life of a woman in her thirties is considered normative; at age twelve, however, all sorts of alarms go off. A "good" mother is expected to be watchful with a toddler, but that same degree of vigilance will become a real problem with a preadolescent daughter. The fifty-five-year-old mother who's successfully ruled the roost for thirty years may find that these very same efforts don't go over nearly as well with a grown daughter.

Another aspect of the timing dimension is the dramatic differences in the historical backdrop of mothers' and daughters' lives. Even when a woman passes the very same ages and milestones her mother has, their membership in different generations ensures significant differences in their experience. More than years separate mothers and daughters. In most families, political, economic, social, and moral influences have shifted markedly over the past three or four generations. For example, in contrast to their grandmothers and mothers, young women are marrying later, delaying childbirth, and having smaller families; they have easier access to divorce, more choice regarding education and career, and more money. The terms "Depression baby," "baby boomer," and "Generation Xer" refer to more than just time spans. They are descriptors not so much of women per se but of the social and cultural climate in which they were raised. Whenever a mother tries to justify something to her daughter with the always appreciated "When I was your age . . ." she should probably stop right there, because in many ways, she was *never* her daughter's age.

Context Number Two: Biology

The relationship between a mother and daughter is influenced from the very start by biology. It is the nature of women's lives that they are punctuated throughout by significant biological changes. These changes include the most powerful events through which mothers and daughters identify with each other: birth, menarche, cramps, premenstrual changes, sex, contraception, pregnancy, abortion, childbirth, nursing, tending newborns, postpartum adjustment, terminating reproduction, perimenopause, menopause. The scriptural adage "As is the mother, so is her daughter"(Ezekiel 16:44) may have an element of folk wisdom but has not been totally supported by research. Sharing 50 percent of a mother's genetic material, a daughter stands a chance of resembling *some* of the things her mother most likes about herself and some of those things she's not too crazy about. A woman's height, weight, appearance, cancer risk, and vulnerability to substance abuse and mood disorders can often be traced to her mother's family tree.

The past twenty years have provided overwhelming evidence for another biological contribution: *temperament,* the hardwiring we enter the world with that shapes our reaction to our environment, the environment's reaction to us, our personalities, and the degree of "match" we feel in relationships with others. Several categories of temperament appear to occur consistently in the population and are fairly stable across the life span. Jerome Kagan, the pioneer of research in this area, has found consistently that 15 percent of the population can be categorized as "inhibited." People who fall into this category are often slow to warm to new situations. A loud noise that doesn't faze one baby could register an 8 on the baby Richter scale for the one sitting next to her. Shyness appears to be fairly stable across development with this temperament type. At the other end of the spectrum is the least inhibited group, another 15 percent of the population. These people can tolerate a great deal of stimulation without distress; they are bold and can easily shift from one situation to the next. These "types" are only the substrate upon which personality develops. They are neither inherently good nor bad. American values tend to reward boldness, but a *totally* uninhibited style is likely to leave a person friendless and possibly in jail.

Gender differences, which for a long time feminists and behaviorists

asserted were purely a product of socialization, also appear to have strong biological components. In addition to hormonal variation between the sexes,
imaging studies indicate that men and women actually utilize specific areas
of the brain differently, often for the same exact task. For example, it appears
that in a number of laboratory problem-solving tasks, men tend to "lateral-
ize"—they employ areas in *either* the right or left hemisphere of their brains.
Women, on the other hand, have higher rates of cerebral blood flow, in general, and they are more likely to employ a number of areas in both sides of the
brain when solving problems. The paralimbic cortex, one of the more
recently evolved and "higher level" areas of the brain, goes to work very differently for males and females. When people are instructed, for example, to
try to make their minds a blank, men and women's brains respond differently. The paralimbic cortex, which has been associated with the filtering of
emotional material, doesn't rest easily in a woman. Males are more likely to
"light up" other, older parts of the brain in response to the same instruction.
Males and females are both easily able to register the emotion of happiness on
faces. Women, however, were significantly more adept at identifying *sadness*.
When people were instructed to think about happy and sad experiences, the
PET scans of male and female brains light up like two different pinball
machines. Even when men and women report feeling the same *level* of emotion, their brains differ in the *locations* that deal with feelings. When men and
women are asked to recall something sad, women's brains activate at eight
times the density of men's. These and the many other findings related to gender differences in the brain have major implications for understanding the
unique ways women relate to each other.

For a very long time it was assumed that nature and nurture were opposite
teams in the game called "Why did I turn out like this?" In reality they've
always been on the same team, occupying different positions as the demands
of the game shift and change. For example, the age menstruation begins seems
like a solely biologically determined event. It's not. Certain stressors can con-
spire to launch girls into early menarche. And of the many ways that parents
want their children to develop early, this isn't one. For some time it has been
apparent that girls whose sexual maturity is reached before cognitive, emotional, and social maturity are at risk of being isolated from their same age
peers. They are likely to become depressed and to be involved with older adolescents who engage in behaviors for which these girls are not at all ready,

placing them at risk for decreased academic performance, pregnancy, and sexually transmitted disease.

These are some of the *results* of early menarche. The *determinants* of early menarche represent an array of biological and cultural variables. One fascinating line of research concerns the role of father absence in the timing of early menarche. Recent research suggests that when a girl's natural father is in the home she is likely to begin menstruating within the "average" time frame. In contrast, girls living without a father, or with a male other than the father (stepfather or mother's boyfriend), have a higher probability of early menarche. Researchers speculate on the possible role of the natural father's pheromones (chemical substances that serve as stimuli to other members of the species) in regulating menarche, underscoring the need to consider the complex interplay of nature and nurture, especially when evaluating an event we once understood as purely biological, purely cultural, or purely psychological.

Context Number Three: Culture

The ways in which mothers and daughters relate to each other are highly specific to culture. Many of the behaviors that we consider natural, instinctive, or universal are often more a function of geography and history. For example, parents in the United States agonize over questions related to where the baby should sleep: In her parents' room? In their bed? In her own room? Some compromise of the three? When should a baby be expected to sleep through the night? What must be done to make it happen? How should they fight the urge to pick up a wailing child who has not gotten with the program? The majority of the world's parents live in cultures in which cosleeping is the norm, not the exception. Even people in cultures similar in many other ways to that of the United States would be horrified to see an infant segregated for the night in her own nursery, however well appointed.

American mothers talk to their babies a lot, placing great emphasis on verbal achievement. They also stress autonomy and independence in their children. They are pleased when their children achieve developmental milestones early and when they are able to do things on their own. The claims of being a "big girl" and "I can do it by myself" are not universally valued when they fall from the mouths of babes. In many cultures such statements are antithetical to the prevailing notions of dependence and interdependence. American parents feel pressure to force-feed their children everything their little minds can take in. It's no surprise, then, that they turn to professionals so often in times of trouble, rather than relying on generations of child-rearing wisdom within their families. In contrast to American mothers, Korean mothers tend to see their babies as passive and dependent. They are more likely to be raising their children in extended family systems and relying on family and folk wisdom for advice. Fostering a child's autonomy is considered much less important than helping the child develop a sense of group identity and responsibility.

Mothers' Expectations Maternal expectations of daughters are also highly determined by cultural norms. The long-standing reverence of elders that once characterized many cultures has lost out in youth worshipping Western society. It is still stronger in Eastern cultures, and the painful differences are evident when an older woman is transplanted from Asia to the United States. This is poignantly portrayed in Gish Jen's short story "Who's Irish?" which captures both the loss of stature and the increased expectations of the mother who has come from China to live with her daughter, son-in-law, and granddaughter. She is overwhelmed by reversals she never anticipated. "In China, daughter take care of mother," she complains. "Here it is the other way around. Mother help daughter. Mother ask, 'Anything else I can do?' Otherwise daughter complain mother is not supportive. I tell my daughter, 'We do not have this word in Chinese, 'supportive.' " Other indications suggest ways that the transplant is probably never complete. In a scene in *The Joy Luck Club,* when Waverly complains about her mother to an American friend, the friend matter-of-factly advises that next time she feels troubled she should respond with the very American line "Shut up." Waverly rejects that suggestion with horror, warning her friend that even though it's not technically against the law to tell a Chinese mother to shut up, "You could be charged as an accessory to your own murder."

Daughters' Expectations Culture influences daughters' expectations of mothers as well. In comparisons of adult daughters from different cultures, researchers found that women who emphasize the importance of feeling close to their mothers and the necessity of relying on them often live in cultures where the society is segregated along gender lines, the mother is of practical importance to the daughter, and the family home routinely houses more than two generations. While American women value closeness with their mothers, they also value independence. When women endorse collective rather than individual goals, they are more likely to identify with the needs of the family as a whole and less likely to be reaching for the type of personal autonomy to which most American women aspire. The extent to which women are raised to place their trust in the hierarchy of family and culture (which is almost always patriarchal) varies tremendously across cultures. American women are less likely to trust, for example, that their elders always know better, or that husbands should lead households but not work in them. They are much less likely to defer to their mothers' wisdom in the choosing of a mate or a career or in the rearing of a child.

It's important to remember that in many cultures examining what happens between a mother and her daughter isn't considered necessary or even interesting. Analyzing relationships is, in many ways, a luxury. When I spoke with women in war-ravaged rural El Salvador, it was clear they took their roles as mothers and daughters very seriously, but that didn't mean they wanted to analyze them. These were women who had walked, with children and elders, under the cover of night, to Honduran refugee camps where weeks turned into years. After talking with these women, many of them widowed with children, I couldn't bring myself to ask, "So, how's your relationship with your mother?" It was difficult to ask a woman who had just spent four hours securing the day's water, "What does your mother or daughter do that drives you crazy?"

OLD MODELS

Research on female development has historically either lagged behind the study of male development or just been assumed to be the poor stepchild of research about males. One incredibly persistent area of inquiry across the study of psychological development has focused on identifying the requirements of a successful transition from childhood to adulthood. In the early

years of my training the prevailing notion was that to achieve adult independence, one had to make a clean break from parents, particularly the parent
of the same sex.

While independence and autonomy continue to be crucial themes in
development, in the past twenty years theorists have questioned whether sev-
ering the connection between a mother and her adolescent daughter actually
serves either of them. The hostility between adolescent girls and their mothers is so expected in this culture that its absence is sometimes considered
pathological. I have actually heard women wonder why they aren't having
more conflict with their teenage daughters, as if they are depriving them of
the magic elixir for growing up. Anger is seen as the premier vehicle that
enables the adolescent to pull away from her mother. A recent magazine cartoon pictured a mother holding what are clearly children's toys and senti-
mentally reporting to her husband that their little girl was growing up . . .
because she'd just told her mother she hated her. Anger, disagreement, and
thinking one's mother is a total idiot are all seen as integral to the process by
which early adolescents disengage from their mothers.

Conflict between mothers and daughters does indeed increase in the
early-adolescent years. However, what is rarely considered is that at the very
same time, girls are still talking a great deal to the mothers, especially about
interpersonal issues. Kids who can't yet swim in the deep end may complain
and moan about a parent's warnings, and may even jump in when forbidden
to. But they are highly unlikely to do it if there's no one around to dive in
after them. Conflict and autonomy don't cancel out love, dependence, and
connection, and yet much of our theorizing has made it seem so. In later adolescence the conflict between mother and daughter appears to lessen. Girls
have begun the long process of finding other people in whom to invest emotional energy. Mothers move from the first choice to confide in, and follow
female friends and boyfriends in the lineup. But they are only partially
"replaced" by this reshuffling, even though it may feel like they've been displaced. Girls continue to rely on mothers, but in different ways.

Over the past several decades, many people thinking about girls' development stopped and said the equivalent of "Wait a minute, what's so great
about making 'the Big Break'?" Admittedly, a goal of young adulthood is to
achieve increasing amounts of self-sufficiency. But just because I *can* walk the
ten miles to work every day doesn't mean I've made a lifetime commitment to

doing it. My status as a grown-up suffers nothing by riding a bike, begging a ride on a hot, rainy, or even a no-good-excuse day, or even driving myself. Clearly there are benefits to mothers, daughters, and granddaughters when there are more flexible definitions of attachment and autonomy. I find myself more interested in what binds women together than in how they "separate." There is a difference between independence and interdependence. And within this newer model of interdependence, there appear to be gender differences in the priorities of interests in the "collective" versus the "relational." Are there new threads we can follow over the course of a relationship between a mother and daughter that will illuminate the challenges they face at different stages of development? Are there more useful categories than the good/bad, attached/separated, loved/unloved dichotomies, categories that will enable us to find more original ways of thinking and talking about the essence of mother-daughter relationships?

A NEW WINDOW: EMPATHY

The concept of empathy is one such thread. It winds throughout the lives of generations of women, influencing the quality and intensity of their relationships. To empathize is to try to put oneself in someone else's shoes to get as close a match as possible to the way she feels. The young woman teetering in three-inch heels tries to tune in to the tiny girl in the baby booties. The kid in the size 3 sneakers reads what she can about the woman in the fuzzy pink slippers. The girl in the Air Jordans tries to stretch toward her mother in the Birkenstocks. The middle-aged woman in the hiking boots tries to accommodate her mother in the orthopedic shoes. When it comes to mothers and daughters, no matter how old a woman gets, she and her mother will never be wearing the same shoes at the same time. The two old women in my office both wore flat, tie, sensible shoes. But they weren't the same. As anyone who's broken in a pair of new shoes knows, over time the shoe accommodates to the individuality of its owner as much as the owner adapts to it. The essence of the mother-daughter relationship is the extent to which both players can bridge that gap to reach each other. Every stage of development will offer new challenges and rewards, opportunities for breakthroughs or failures. The process of empathy begins at conception and continues well past death.

The Quilt

In the tapestry of mother-daughter relationships, keeping track of the impact of cultural, historical, psychological, and biological issues is a tall order. But it's worth the effort because these factors can illuminate how successes and failures in empathy (which can be momentary or lifelong) actually occur. For this level of complexity and integration I like the metaphor of the patchwork quilt. A patchwork quilt is the result of hundreds of bits and scraps collected and placed in relation to one another to make an attractive and functional whole. Historically patchwork quilting was one of the few outlets for creativity and fellowship in lives severely challenged by limited economic resources, isolation, and a restricted range of possibilities open to most women. In fact, patchwork quilts have been referred to as the "blues of the American woman." Quilting can be solitary or communal. It can involve a single generation or several at a time. The choices in quilting are as enormous and overwhelming as the twists and turns in relationships; there are patterns, fabrics, hues, textures, shapes, sizes, and design decisions to challenge the novice and experienced quilters alike. Many preconceived notions about making the "perfect quilt" bite the dust as the quilter finds that colors and patterns that work beautifully in a wardrobe or a living room look just awful placed side by side on a quilt. The balance between the objectivity and subjectivity will determine the quality of the finished quilt, as well as the satisfaction of the quilter.

Pregnancy is dedicated to the preparing and protecting of the raw materials that will make up the quilt of motherhood. It's about commitment to a lifelong project without a clear picture of how it will all end up. With the confirmation of conception comes a blank sketchpad upon which a woman projects the designs of motherhood she likes, and tries to erase those she doesn't. She may examine the productions of many generations of her family, taking a color here, borrowing a shape there. As a child she may have assumed that discipline, creative skill, and patience—all central to quilting—came naturally to the elders she observed. As a mother-to-be, she may have a sense of what she wants but lack the conviction that she's a "natural." She knows what she absolutely doesn't want, but she doesn't know how to prevent it. Even though she appears to be the sole architect of the quilt, she will soon be joined by a partner who will make her own profound imprint.

With the birth of the child, the focus shifts away from collecting fabric and thread for the quilt. It is time to learn the intricate ways different shapes, textures, and fabrics interrelate. The quilter must accommodate herself to the task, find a place to work, a comfortable posture, and lighting that enables her to get a good look at what she's got. She may have spent a lot of money on needles that don't seem to be the best match for her fingers or the fabric. On what points is she flexible enough to change strategies or materials before getting in too deep? Where does she find guidance? What does she think of herself as a quilter thus far? Is she having fun yet?

Childhood is the time for getting down to the business of relationships, within and outside the family. It is essentially the work of attaching one piece of fabric to another and then another. Before this is possible, mothers must teach their daughters some of the basics—threading a needle, knotting, making stitches, undoing inevitable mistakes. For young fingers, none of these skills come easily. Motivation comes up against limitations in attention, hand-eye coordination, and fine motor control. It is only with fumbling, pricked fingers, tears, and approximating strong enough stitches that the child can participate in the actual work. A mother's contribution to this process will say a great deal about her willingness to sacrifice time, patience, and perfection so that her daughter can achieve a sense of mastery.

As guides in the process, mothers vary tremendously. An effective guide not only has a fairly good sense of the way for herself, but she knows how to get other, less experienced followers to the designated goal. Mothers may have totally unrealistic expectations about their daughters' skills. One mother is the commandant whose actions communicate to the girl "It's my way or the highway." Another takes a laissez-faire approach, letting her daughter screw up all over the place with little intervention, then redoing the work when the girl isn't around. Yet another strives toward the difficult but noble goal of partnering with her daughter—the hardest work of all. The reciprocity required in this relationship will be the scaffolding upon which so many other interactions will eventually be played out.

Perhaps the essence of this stage is the stitch used so often in hand sewing, especially when durability is critical. It is sometimes called the "sewing machine stitch," and sums up the work for both mother and daughter in childhood. You make a small stitch and then, in what feels counterintuitive, you *don't* proceed forward. You move back—back to the middle of that first stitch, where you insert the needle and make another stitch. Each new stitch reinforces old territory while also claiming more. Forth and back, forth and back: this is the rhythm of relationships. Later there will be time for the fancy topstitching that is purely decorative, but it will be worth nothing atop a quilt with a weak foundation.

Adolescence is a time for assembling squares of fabric and integrating them into a whole design. There is a tremendous payoff in seeing how the project might eventually come together. A long, often painstaking process of mastering skills—cutting, measuring, and sewing—will transfer to many other situations beyond this quilt, while teaching a girl so much about herself—her likes and dislikes, areas in which she feels competent and areas in which she doesn't. It's easy at this point for impatience to set in when she remembers that there are still two more layers to go. And as much as she would like to be finished with the whole project, she knows that a beautiful top layer isn't going to keep her warm at night. This is also a time when a mother may share the task of quilting on a more equal footing with her daughter. If she keeps an open ear, she may hear about the girl's ideas for future projects, some of which may be dramatically different from her own.

Early adulthood is when the quilt is assembled. The three layers mean little without one another. Despite the fact that one is beautiful, one is warm, and one is a sturdy backing, it's only in the integration of these pieces that a quilt is formed. Primary responsibility for the quilt may shift from mother to daughter. As she tries to assemble it, she may find it unwieldy, with some things she can handle alone and others she'll need help with. To whom does she go for assistance? What is the price for admitting she still has gaps in her expertise? How does she make clear what she wants to do on her own? Once the layers are attached, where to go from here? There are intricate quilting stitches in hundreds of patterns. She can make it as simple or as complex as she wants. At this point she will need even *more* skills—mastery of new stitches, working with a thimble, managing different needles and threads. How does she choose to involve her mother, the original designer of the quilt? A daughter who's been sick of the whole quilting business since childhood can, in her new adult freedom, drop it, let her mother do it, or just let it remain unfinished.

When a daughter reaches midlife, the quilt she and her mother began years earlier is almost finished. To complete the stitching patterns, a woman may call upon friends and relatives to gather around a traditional quilting frame and spend the day sewing and sharing stories with one another, and wisdom with the younger participants. Now the quilter must decide what she's going to do with it. Will it be hers? Shall she give it to her own daughter or granddaughter? What does she think of the finished product? Is she gentle in her assessment, or judgmental? Can she celebrate her accomplishment? Is she already planning the next quilt or swearing to never do another again? Does she begin passing on the skills she's amassed since her once-clumsy little fingers first held a needle?

By the time a woman reaches old age, her quilt is complete. Now it can have many purposes, from decorative to functional. Its value is totally dependent upon the vision of its creators and the needs of its owners. As the borders begin to fray, as stitches are lost, the necessary repairs can be made or not. Who has the responsibility for preserving the quilt? A quilt that has several generations of family hands involved with it is like a family portrait, a form of women's history. Does the long life of the quilt add to its value or diminish it? A quilt can be of use even in its most frayed, torn, and faded condition. It can be transformed—becoming the second layer of a brand-new quilt, ensuring warmth, increased texture, and continuity.

I made a quilt once. My youngest sister was getting married, and in some burst of rabid domesticity I decided to make her a quilt for a shower gift. I have a poor track record in the arts-and-crafts area, defying at least four generations of wildly creative women before me. But I was heartened by a book that insisted a person needed next to no ability or, for that matter, imagination to get the job done. I found a quilting store and spent more money than if I'd just driven to Bloomingdale's and bought a quilt. What looked easy wasn't. My hands were clumsy, and I swore my eyes were losing acuity by the day. My back, which has never been the most loyal of body parts, complained every step of the way, and after a while my neck conspired against me too. I began to revise the size of the quilt in my mind, from king, to queen, to full, to tablecloth, to table runner, to one really nice place mat. But then I'd think of my sister and return to the original plan. I felt every stitch of that damn quilt. Piecing it together was a nightmare. I couldn't imagine what had possessed me to choose such ugly fabric, and I started to resent my sister for getting married.

When it was finished I felt strangely ambivalent. The errors (and there were many) screamed at me. The alignment was off. Some fabrics, great by themselves, brought out the worst in one another when placed together. Many stitches had slipped, and it took a day just to repair holes and shore up frayed edges. My mother told me that the Amish have a custom of intention-ally putting an error into each of their quilts because nothing made by mere humans should be perfect. In my case there was absolutely no need to profess my mere humanity. I pictured Amish women giving my quilt the once-over and gripping their sides in hysterical laughter. After I'd fixed all the stuff I could, and made tentative peace with the stuff I couldn't, I fell madly in love with my quilt. I folded and unfolded it, draped it over chairs, tried it over beds. It was the biggest thing I'd ever made, the thing that had taken the longest to do, the first crafts project I'd actually finished.

I can't be a perfect quilter any more than I can be a perfect mother or a perfect daughter. Like the quilt, my history with my daughter is marked by some totally unrealistic expectations at the start and a lot of plunging ahead when I didn't know what I was doing. My years of household projects and object assemblies have always been predicated on the conviction that direc-tions, instructions, and assistance are backups and should be used only at total dead ends. As happened so many times during the quilt making, I often feel with my daughter that I've already invested so much in doing things one way that I can't consider changes. As a quilter, a mother, and a daughter, I am impulsive. I cut corners; I take difficulty personally. I am passionate and grandiose, so focused on the big picture that important details get lost. But even with all that, I appreciate the absolute pleasure of seeing a pile of tiny scraps that are hanging together because of something I did. I know the sat-isfaction of sticking with those pieces over the long haul, and at some point, giving up control and almost allowing the design to complete itself. And more than anything, I know what it's like to send that creation out into the world, crooked seams, sloppy stitching, and all, believing that my good intentions, its unique colors and textures, its singular form and function, are far more important than the inventory of my errors.

The structure of a quilt is very much like the structure of a close relation-ship. The top layer contains the unique patterns, the creativity, the outside face that's shown to the world. The next layer is pure function—necessary for substance and warmth. If a quilt is made correctly, no one ever sees this part. It's usually not particularly attractive, but anyone who pulls the quilt around herself on a cold night will know its value. The bottom layer, usually one long expanse of not particularly interesting fabric, serves as a contrast to the action on the top layer. It encloses the warmth and complements the colorful top. The layers of the quilt are like the unique patterns that biology, culture, psychology, and history contribute to the substance of relationships. But it's the stitching that holds it all together, that introduces new patterns into the material and guarantees durability even with constant wear.

When it comes to mother-daughter relationships, I am convinced that *empathy is that stitching*. The most beautifully patterned top, the warmest stuffing, and the strongest backing are worthless without the sturdy trail of a needle and thread. Without empathy, things can look great from the outside and be awful underneath. But with empathy, even the most modest beginnings can result in something strong and beautiful. The following chapters will focus on empathic connection between mothers and daughters, beginning at conception and extending beyond death. The contributions of timing, biology, psychology, and culture to the development or maintenance of empathy will be addressed at each life stage.

TWO

Empathy: The Strongest Bridge

Let me see my daughter like my mother could not see me. Let her see me too.

REBECCA WELLS,

Divine Secrets of the Ya-Ya Sisterhood

Empathy is the bridge that connects one person to another. It is the sturdy thread, the small stitches painstakingly pulled through yards of patterned cloth to hold it together so well that it will last longer than a lifetime. The word *empathy* comes from the German *Einfühlung,* which literally means the ability to "feel into" someone else's experience. Empathy isn't intuition, magic, mind reading, or pity. It's not the ability to say "I understand" one hundred times a day. Traditionally, empathy was seen as a good thing for a woman to have with children and sick people, but often it constituted little more than the "warm fuzzies." It was not an important quality for males to cultivate. In fact, during the 1970s calling a medical student "empathic" in a letter of recommendation was sometimes "code" meaning that the applicant was a nice but not very bright guy.

We've all been on the receiving end of empathy, and we've all suffered the hollowness when it's missing. We move constantly in and out of people's range of reception, even with those closest to us. Within the field of psychology, empathy is thought about in a number of ways—as a skill, a trait, and a product of the interaction between two people. These are *all* legitimate lenses. The role of empathy at each developmental phase—pregnancy, infancy, childhood, adolescence, young adulthood, middle adulthood, and elder adulthood—is crucial in any exploration of mother-daughter relationship.

WHAT IT'S NOT

Sometimes the best way to define something is to say what it *isn't*. In her memoir, *Are You Somebody?* Irish journalist Nuala O'Faolain describes a total lack of empathy in a mother-daughter communication. During one of her first extended stays away from home, O'Faolain mentioned her loneliness in a letter to her mother, who fired back, "I'm fat, tired, ugly and red, and I have spent all my money and I'm not going to be able to look after my home and family. Contrast these truths with your easily remedied ills and brighten up." This is not a mother to whom I'd be rushing home. Part of what O'Faolain's mother said is evidence of her own bitter unhappiness. But her reply also reflects a cultural—in this case Irish—response to a daughter's "complaining." It's almost formulaic. *Take daughter's complaint, multiply it to the hundredth power, and attach the problem to someone else. Tell it to the child. Watch for guilt and shame. Expect complaints to decrease markedly.* There are strong cultural influences that determine how acceptable it is to have and to express feelings. And not just negative ones.

When Alice McDermott accepted the 1998 National Book Award for her novel *Charming Billy,* she said that the first voice she heard in her head after the announcement was her grandmother's—warning her not to be getting a "big head" about it. When I cite these examples in speeches, I've been assured by women whose ancestors hail from all different countries and continents that there are eerie similarities. Like the grandmother in Alice McDermott's mind, there are voices of particular accents and lilts that can deflate a woman's balloon faster than a pinprick. I've seen numerous women in psychotherapy whose mothers put their daughters' considerable achievements on a par with getting an art degree from a correspondence course advertised on a book of matches. Why? Because the daughter did not meet the mother's definition of "considerable achievement"—marriage and children.

"NO, YOU *DON'T* KNOW EXACTLY WHAT I MEAN"

Empathy is apparent in a number of ways, many of which are relevant to this discussion. Gretel Ehrlich's memoir, *A Match to the Heart,* describes the experience of being struck not once but twice by lightning. The statistical probability of that happening is so low that it is highly unlikely that there is anyone who could honestly say to her, "I know exactly how you feel." The initial trauma extended beyond the many physical insults to a profound sense of emotional loneliness. In the midst of her relentlessly frustrating experiences with the medical establishment, Ehrlich remarks, "You don't have to experience everything life can throw at you—torture or ecstasy—to fuel empathy; just a taste is enough." The ability to use the "tastes" we gain from our own experiences to connect with someone else is a sophisticated skill that is constantly sharpened by experience and reflection. However, it only provides access to one room, never the whole house. It doesn't matter whether you had a kidney stone the size of a marble or a baby the size of a watermelon, you don't know *exactly* how another person feels in a "similar" situation. "I know exactly how you feel" is a lie. It deprives the other person of communicating her experience, which can be one of the most satisfying things women do in good and bad times. Empathy often results in the decision to say nothing. Sometimes the greatest wisdom that people who have come through serious trials have learned is what *not* to say and what *not* to do. They learn how being with someone, sometimes sitting in intolerable silence and discomfort, can be the most empathic connection.

The punctuation marks in women's lives offer them the opportunity to be in the same neighborhood with one another. While these events tend to have specific biological, psychological, and social changes associated with them, they can have as many differences. The conversations in groups of women, even women who don't know one another, are often about these punctuation points, emphasizing the similarities that unite them as well as the qualities that make each woman unique. Women go through puberty with breasts of uncertain growth potential, and menstruation, often not the happy kickoff into adolescence mothers and teachers made it out to be. So many girls experience leakage trauma that girls' magazines often devote entire pages to girls describing the incredible number of ways that menstruation thoroughly humiliated them. Adolescents struggle with questions of what kind and placement of body hair is acceptable. They must reconcile the powerful sexuality they're feeling—and people are responding to—with the onslaught of messages that warn how their sexual bodies could be the death of them. Pregnancy and childbirth are, for every woman, unique stories that overlap only incidentally with other women's. Postpartum adjustments and body changes are typical but never well received with a simple "join the club" response, which is actually more of a dismissal than an invitation. Perimenopause and menopause are events that until recently women and physicians hadn't been falling all over one another to talk about. But it's clear that they, too, bring both the potential for commonality and the certainty of uniqueness.

TYPES OF EMPATHY

Empathy Is a Skill

Psychologist Judith Jordan dismisses the magical, intuitive, or passive characterizations of empathy. Empathy, she insists, is an ability "requiring a complex integration of cognitive and emotional capabilities." There is a body of research supporting the superiority of girls and women in many of the abilities required for empathy. It's more than the capacity to pick up "vibes." Empathy is not the ability to read minds, it's the ability to read situations, facial expressions, body tension and movement, voice modulation and intensity. It is a tremendously active process, one that involves integrating what we know with what we see, hear, smell, taste, and touch. In fact, when a person is very talented at picking up and integrating these "ways of knowing," she is sometimes claimed to have a "sixth sense."

Empathy is fluid, demanding constant monitoring of our interactions with other people. To be able to put yourself in another's shoes doesn't mean you must agree with her, pity her, or take care of her. You may not even understand her. When we think of empathy as a skill, it makes sense that our capacity for it—as mothers or daughters—varies with the range of experiences we've had and what we've extracted from them. We are often unaware of the specific signals we send out that make people see us as empathic and engaging. Without consciously trying, some people change their behavior (facial expression, body language, mannerisms) to "match" another person. To test the impact of "matching," researchers gave pairs of people a problem to solve together. Beforehand they told one of each pair to mimic the other. When one member of the pair mirrored the other, their interactions were rated as "smoother" and members of the pairs reported liking each other more than when there was no mimicry. This "chameleon effect," as they called it, was found to a greater degree in people who rank high on paper-and-pencil measures of empathy as a trait.

Many people are skillful at picking up on the emotions of others and then using that skill for manipulation. Success in the world of business, politics, and some forms of crime often depends on this ability. We are bombarded with messages that "speak" to our fears, our guilt, our vanity, our hunger, our pride, and our insecurities. The fact that there's a "sucker born every minute" has as much to do with the skills of the manipulator as it does with the stupidity and greed of the sucker. During the presidential election I heard pundits talking about the use of empathy as a political tool. They called it "strategic empathy," which on some level is an oxymoron. It represents the attempt to at least *appear* to share the interests and concerns of the voters. Bill Clinton was a master strategist, with the "I feel your pain" approach to the electorate. One of the hallmarks of a sociopath is the ability to zoom in on the exact facial expressions, tone of voice, body language, and what are unscientifically called "vibes" to connect with people. The sociopath's is a pseudoempathy. It represents an *intellectual* understanding of what he needs to do to get another person to do what he wants. Sociopaths are remarkably good at faking it in the absence of any true emotional resonance or connection.

Empathy Is a Trait

Empathy is also thought of as a *trait,* a quality or attribute of a person. People vary along a continuum of empathy, as they do on dimensions such as courage or humor. Highly empathic people (usually determined by paper-and-pencil rating scales) are disproportionately represented in fields like psychology, social work, and teaching. They volunteer to help needy causes more frequently. There is no doubt that there is tremendous variation in the degree of "natural" empathy in the population. Imagine a continuum of people you know, and place them along a range, with "less empathy than a can of paint" on one end and "sees into my very soul on a regular basis" on the other. Some people are probably easy to place. They don't vary much. Others shift a great deal depending on the situation. I am much more sympathetic, interested, and "there" with a friend about a really bad hair day for an important job interview than I am in that same twenty-four-hour period when a graduate student rushes breathless into my seminar half an hour late, announcing, "I'm having a bad hair day!" The problem with thinking about empathy as a trait is that it assumes our personalities are fixed, and fails to consider possible changes when we're in different situational or cultural contexts. There's fairly strong evidence that empathy can be enhanced with training programs or interventions that focus on increasing a person's ability to take the perspective of another person. For example, neglectful teenage mothers and their young children both benefit from programs that support the mothers (that is, are empathic regarding their needs) and help them develop a more realistic perspective of their children so that they can be more effective parents.

Probably the group for whom the general public has the *least* empathy is child molesters. Child molesters get their victims by *faking* empathy. And they are incredibly good at it. The problem with telling our children to be afraid of "strangers" is that molesters know precisely how to transform themselves quickly into "friends." Why are there such high rates of recidivism with this crime? Molesters are not stopped by the experience of punishment, be it jail, estrangement from family, or public derision. Psychotherapy is not particularly useful. One clue into this mess is that child molesters appear to have little empathy for their victims, *even after the fact*. A recent study measured molesters' empathy in three situations. The first involved a child disfigured from a car accident, the second was about a child who had been molested repeatedly by an unknown assailant, and the third involved the molester's own victims. Molesters' responses were compared with those of nonoffending males, and the results yielded some creepy differences. While the molesters and the regular guys had the same level of empathy for the little girl hit by the car, the molesters showed less empathy for the unknown sexually abused child and *significantly less empathy for their own victims than for the unknown victim.* This very selective empathy is a chilling testament to the resistance of molestation to traditional forms of treatment.

A Different Perspective   Human beings aren't born empathic in the way we usually use the term. If we were, we'd sleep through the night and not make such dreadful messes in our diapers. We are, however, born with the necessary equipment. Babies are hardwired to begin making connections to their parents from the start. But to be able to feel for someone else and to act on that feeling, a child requires a number of building blocks. At a very basic level, to become empathic means to move away from the egocentricism with which we are born, in which everything and everyone exists only because *we* experience them. Egocentrism isn't selfishness. In this context it means the true inability to understand the possibility that other realities exist. This is obvious when you try to teach young children games like hide-and-seek. Many of us have had the experience of playing with a toddler who, when it's her turn to hide, just stands still and covers her eyes. If she can't see us, how could anyone see her?

Over time, children's perspective-taking skills increase. They know that the world looks different from different viewpoints. When an object is placed on a table and the child is able to draw it not only from *her* vantage point but also as it appears from the seat *across* from her, she has made tremendous strides. This is some fancy cognitive footwork. As children's vocabulary, especially their *emotional* vocabulary, increases, they become more and more able to use words rather than actions to express happy or painful feelings.

A day's worth of errands at places that parents and children go will yield many chances to hear interactions in which parents try to get kids to think and talk rather than act without consideration. Miranda grabs the stuffed rabbit Richard is holding during story hour. Her mother intervenes to stop the grabbing and then says, "How would you like it if someone walked up and took your Pooh Bear?" Sometimes parents leave this as a rhetorical question, which is a shame. It cuts off the opportunity for the child to say whether or not she actually *does* know how it feels and what beliefs she may have about the situation. It also closes off the chance for the parent to "refine" the child's answer by engaging her in further conversation. Miranda, the little rabbit-grabbing girl, answers her mother's question "How would you like it . . . ?" with a haughty denial. It would not bother her at all, and she would never ever start crying like a big baby like that boy with his stupid stuffed animal. This is a clear move from the *no*-empathy position to the *minus*-empathy column.

The mother, as a repository of Miranda's daily history, needs only to scan her memory of the previous week to find a situation in which her daughter felt wronged. There will always be at least one: someone touched a blanket, a bear, a toy, or a doll, and Miranda lost her composure. As long as Richard gets his rabbit back, the transgression is not severe enough to warrant elaborate outpourings of guilt and remorse. But the work on empathy development with children continues past whatever enforced or insincere apology the child offers. The task is to help the child link up thoughts, feelings, and actions that she has had recently that come close to matching the current situation. Then parallels can be drawn. "You didn't like it when Donnie took your cupcake at snacktime. Remember how much you cried and you were so mad? That wasn't a good thing he did. And how did you feel? What about Vanessa's birthday party when Brittany took your stickers and used them up so you couldn't use them, and you cried, 'It's not fair.' " All the while this rather one-sided conversation goes on, the adult is watching for even the dimmest light-bulb to flick on in the general area of the child's head. With maturation a child becomes more likely to internalize that "How would you like it" question *before* acting, rather than always being forced to reflect about it afterward.

Empathy Is Action

A mother who sits rocking and soothing but never feeding a hunger-screaming infant when there is easy access to food would be labeled neglectful or abusive, no matter how much she loves her baby. Who cares that she has compassion for her baby's hunger? Who cares that she is trying to comfort her? The issue for mothers is not only their capacity for empathy, but their ability to know and carry out *actions* that arise out of empathy and are in the best interests of their daughters. The translation of empathic "feelings" to empathic "actions" is complicated, but several concepts are particularly useful in approaching mother-daughter relationships.

In one of my all-time favorite magazine cartoons, a hip-looking mother and her young child are in an ice-cream store. The scoop of ice cream on the child's cone has just fallen *splat!* on the floor, resulting in massive distress and tears. The mother leans over to the child and asks lovingly, "Would you like to talk about it?" The true empathic response to the crying child is based on the principle that sometimes talk is incredibly cheap. What the solicitous mother needed to do was put her money where her mouth was, and get the kid another ice-cream cone.

A girl comes home from school, slams the door, and throws her books on the kitchen table. She calls her mother at work, reporting in with a petulant and increasingly angry tone. Her mother hears a subtext in her daughter's angry voice. Rather than enter into a combative dance in which her daughter would immediately have a misdirected target for emotional release, leaving her mother totally slimed, the mother remains silent. The daughter begins to sputter and shifts to crying about what is really troubling her—an unrequited love, a bad practice, a tough test. She never really called her mother to fight. She called her mother for comfort. Even without visual clues, her mother knew from the tone of the voice and the edge on each word that the anger in that particular call (unlike many others) didn't ring true. She picked up signals accurately and formed an emotional bridge to her daughter.

Rarely will mothers and daughters approach each other and ask, "May I have some empathy?" Sometimes we go about trying to get it like the frustrated hurt girl who picked the fight with her mother. It reminds me of the courtship rituals of very large animals that never look particularly romantic. Big animals bump up against each other, shove each other out of the way, encroach on each other's space, and make a lot of noise. But in the end they get the job done. Many times, particularly with mothers and daughters, the daughter will engage the mother with anger, then, once she has her hooked (either by getting her to lose her temper, thereby justifying the girl's unhappiness) or not, work down to a more basic feeling, which may be one of vulnerability, fear, hurt, or confusion.

To make things more interesting, these conflicts can move in the other direction, with the daughter at first engaging her mother through need and vulnerability, then moving toward hand-to-hand combat. A girl goes to her mother upset and in search of "cure." When mothers can't kiss boo-boos or make things right in the world, it can be a scary place for a preadolescent to find herself. "What good are you?" "I knew I shouldn't have tried to talk to you." "Don't you understand *anything*?" These and other insults can be incredibly confusing to a mother who thinks she is "helping." In fact the mother is indeed helping—by listening and by showing that she can't be blown off with a couple of insults. In some ways, the girl is offering her mother a chance for 100 percent empathy: "I feel helpless and inept, and now you do too." This is rarely a conscious process, but it is a very powerful inter-action between mothers and daughters. When the heat in the house has decreased, the mother might approach the daughter with some new rules of engagement. For example, "I don't mind having disagreements, but I don't swear at you and I don't want you to swear at me."

Empathy in Relationship: A Two-Person Job

Empathy can also be seen as a *connection between two people* who are constantly building new bridges to each other, in a way that further strengthens the relationship and advances the growth of each person. Feminist researchers and theorists like Jean Baker Miller, Judith Jordan, Irene Stivers, and Carol Gilligan emphasize the mutuality of empathy. It's never a straightforward exchange: "I'll trade you ten minutes of sympathy right now for thirty min-utes of listening later." It is fluid, not static. In a truly mutual relationship, people are energized rather than depleted by their interactions with each other. To experience real connection with a person results in what Jean Baker Miller calls "zest," the almost inspirational sense that something about the interaction has hit precisely the right chord, resonated soundly with both people, and enhanced each of them, as well as the relationship. These can be small moments, brief conversations, no hearts and flowers, no high drama. It's not so much the *content* of what two people share in conversation; all the "right" feeling words could flow from their mouths, and they could walk away feeling emptier than before they came together. Rather, it's the *process* by which they share that conversation, those ideas, those emotions, that is so critical. For a mutually empathic interaction to be possible, both people need to express and receive the authentic experiences and feelings of the oth-ers. These aren't nicey-nice talks. People can be mad at each other, confused, frustrated, and upset. This is an appealing approach because it takes into account the many variations in people and situations. Empathy is not some push-pull, give-get arrangement but a far more complex, interesting, and dynamic way two people relate to each other.

Psychologist Shelley Taylor and colleagues at UCLA reviewed hundreds of studies with animals and humans to determine whether there were gender differences in reaction to stress. In addition to the well-known "fight or flight" mobilization that has been the reigning model for so long, another style became evident and highlighted a distinction between males and females. In the fight-or-flight model, which is common among males, there are two types of reactions to threat or stress: aggression and withdrawal. However, when women are stressed, they tend to cope with a "tend and befriend" style. Women react by "nurturing their children or seeking social contact, especially with other women." The tend-and-befriend reaction appears far more likely to sustain empathy in a situation than a response that is rooted in fight or flight. It is likely that there are strong biochemical underpinnings to these differences. Oxytocin, best known for its role in childbirth, is secreted by males and females in response to stress. It has been associated in humans with lowered anxiety and higher sociability. In the laboratory the maternal behavior of animals has been altered with the introduction or withdrawal of oxytocin.

MAKING SENSE OF FEELINGS

A person who is very empathic is able to "process" a great deal of information simultaneously. She does more than sit back and study a person's words, actions, or expressions. She has to integrate them, resolving any dissonance she picks up along the way. For example, arms crossed over the chest, chin jutted out, facial tension, and tics don't go with the words "What do you mean, I look angry? I'm not angry. I'm fine. What makes you think I'm angry?" A twelve-year-old girl stomps into the kitchen and slams a couple of cabinet doors, huffing and muttering the whole time. Her mother asks, "What's the matter?" The girl turns to her, looks puzzled, and with total sincerity says, "Nothing." Something's going on, but who knows what? Mothers are often frustrated when they pick up something in their daughters that feels like pain, or anger, or rapture, and their daughters totally deny it.

To some extent, empathy is in the eye of the beholder. There is no one "right" empathic response for each situation. The fluidity of empathy has to do not only with the person who feels the empathy but with the one on the receiving end. "You look awful" coming from my mother feels different from "You look awful" coming from my daughter, my husband, or my doctor. And those are just the words. The tone, the intention of the sender, what the receiver picks up and then how she integrates it, will determine how a message is received.

In a previous book I included an account of slapping my five-year-old daughter—a result of a long day's defiance on her part combined with depression and exhaustion on mine. Of the twenty-five essays in the book, this one got more than its fair share of comments. On live radio, during the promotional tour, several male interviewers introduced it as a major topic, saying things like "I can't believe you hit your daughter!" or "I can't believe you *admitted* hitting your daughter." It was a really inviting way to start off an interview. Women interviewers noted it too, but in a totally different way: "I loved the piece about hitting your daughter . . . well, not the hitting . . . you know . . . well, anyway, just the fact that you would admit those feelings. I've been there too."

Even if there was an *Empathy for Dummies* book that was absolutely specific about what to say and how to act, the tremendous variation in what people do when they translate that advice to real life could turn the most supportive statement into an insult, on the basis of tone of voice alone. As onlookers, we often think we know what an empathic response would be in a specific situation. But it's never so simple. A fourteen-year-old girl gets into a typical knock-down-drag-out with her sixteen-year-old brother. Tuning in and out to check for the eruption of major problems, their mother hears her son taunt her daughter about her weight, telling her that he and his friends laugh about her behind her back. The mother, who knows "below the belt" when she hears it, marches into the family room and confronts them. The girl's arms are folded across her chest, her chin is out, her teeth are clenched. The boy is laughing, insisting their fight was "no big deal." The mother demands that her son apologize to his sister. When she hears her mother's command, the daughter looks like she's about to crumble. "I don't want anything from him," she tells her mother. "He's an idiot." The mother is just about to press the point when she notices tears pooling in her daughter's eyes and stops herself. Demanding the apology will make the mother feel better, she realizes, but not her daughter. She understands that every demand for an apology on such sensitive subjects as weight and acceptance by boys will only intensify the original hurt for her daughter. The mother decides to deal with her son later. Before trying to "talk about it" (which parents seem to think adolescents are always *dying* to do in painful situations) with her daughter, she "reads" the situation and decides that the most empathic thing is to back off for a while.

Empathy is not always dependent on actual experience. Sometimes people who have endured great pain are *less* able to identify with situations that are relatively trivial compared with lives of tremendous suffering. The yardstick against which they measure things as worthy of upset can be fairly rigid. These aren't necessarily the "You think you have it bad?" parents. Children are extremely sensitive to fragility in their parents—so much that they might play down average "kid complaints." The children of Holocaust survivors frequently report feeling so much for the agony of their parents that, without being told, they experience the need to spare them many of the typical challenges of childhood and adolescence and to become exceptional people. Likewise, people whose lives were totally ravaged by the Great Depression may have very little patience with a generation that wastes prosperity. Experience may be the best teacher, but certainly not for everyone. For example, it's always interesting how empathy switches when one has passed the hurdles of an especially gruelling initiation. Regardless of the humiliation, danger, exhaustion, or pain a person endured to get in, once he becomes a member he has limited empathy for the next initiate, often putting him at risk when things get out of hand. There's the "I got through it alone, so you should too" mentality or the "You don't have to tell *me*, I went through it too" response. Both are really just polite ways of saying "Shut up."

YOU'RE NOT ALLOWED TO GO, BUT I UNDERSTAND HOW YOU FEEL

A mother becomes embroiled in a battle with her fifteen-year-old daughter over permission to attend a party. When she learns that the party will be unchaperoned, the mother flatly refuses to let her daughter go. The daughter becomes angry and rants against her mother. It is very hard, when a mother's on the receiving end of one of these storms, to have empathy for the person calling her names. Empathy for the daughter's reaction has nothing to do with the validity of the decision to forbid her to go. Being a responsible mother often means pissing kids off. For a mother, overidentifying with a child and allowing those feelings to direct her own behavior is a prescription for disaster. Even when she has to put a lid on her daughter's wishes, empathy allows a mother to reach inside and pull out something that's at least a partial match with her daughter's feelings. She may remember clearly and painfully very similar struggles with her own mother, and the frustration she felt as barriers subverted her right to have fun. She may recall being insulted that her mother didn't trust her enough, or believing that her mother was just unhappy so she didn't want anyone else to be happy either.

Empathy with the daughter means that the mother acknowledges (even silently) that something she's doing in her role as mother is provoking a negative reaction in her daughter. She also acknowledges how lousy it feels as an adolescent to really, really want to do something and not be allowed. She knows what it feels like when "everyone else's" parents are letting them go. She knows the urgency that each one of these social events can have for a fifteen-year-old. It's at *this* party that something incredible might happen, and by not being present, *she will miss out forever*. A mother has to be both coach and referee, which is hard enough. But she's often less prepared to be experienced by her daughter as the captain of the opposing team.

BARRIER TO EMPATHY: PERSONAL DISTRESS

Empathic *feelings* don't necessarily lead to altruistic or caring *behavior*. There is sometimes a dramatic gap between what we say we will do and what we actually do. There are many basic interferences that create barriers to empathic action. I remember being so tired one night I thought I'd cry. My daughter was describing the day's field trip to a petting zoo with the precision of a microbiologist. I couldn't share her enthusiasm. At all. All I could think about was the two hours of work that had to be done before I hit the sack. So I faked it. Distraction, limited resources, and multiple demands on energy can make the road between feelings of empathy and empathic action an impossible trek. Sometimes faking it is the best you can do.

What else gets in the way? Research suggests that *we* do. When researchers told people stories describing a character in terrible crisis and asked them to imagine how that person feels in the situation, their reaction was often quite different from when they were asked to imagine *themselves* in that situation. When people actually projected themselves into the painful scenario, even though it was only in their imaginations, their levels of physiological arousal and stress increased. The response to this kind of stress was typically to withdraw their investment (levels of caring and interest) in the imaginary hero of the story. The way our own personal distress gets tripped off when we get too close to the pain of others isn't just limited to the laboratory. It's one of the most common barriers to empathy in real life as well. One common reason we can't attend to the feelings or needs of another person is that there's a fair amount of static and interference in our own heads. In the annals of mother guilt, many of the five-star infractions are actually failures in empathy. In a family it is normal for there to be continually competing needs, which demand juggling and a Scotch-tape approach to problem solving. There will always be enough empathy lapses in families to go around.

Personal Distress: A Confession

From age two to five, my daughter attended a wonderful preschool in Massachusetts. We moved to Virginia shortly before she began kindergarten. Because kindergarten was only a half-day session, my husband and I enrolled her in an extended day care program at the school. Keara's first day was a bitter pill to swallow. At lunchtime some mothers did an unusual thing. They showed up. Then they collected their lucky kids and took them home. My daughter was furious with me. Only me. Fathers didn't pick kids up in the middle of the day. Only mothers. So the responsibility, as she saw it, lay with me. I tried to explain to her the demands of my new job. She didn't care. I reminded her of the headstands I'd done to manage working Fridays at home. She didn't care. It was as if I had perpetrated a huge lie on her for three years, and it was now my turn to pay. The problem wasn't only that she didn't get to leave at lunch. Even more than that, she despised the extended day care program.

When I allowed myself to think about it, I could understand how she might feel that way. But I couldn't afford to actually slip my feet into her shoes. It was too threatening. The house of cards that my husband and I had constructed to cover family and work hinged on the fact that nothing happened to bump the table it was piled on.

In second grade my daughter came home in tears and told me she had written a play and shown it to one of the counselors, who told her it wasn't a play and she should join the kickball game. Looking back with more honest eyes, I imagine that my daughter probably knew more about plays than most of the counselors. She reported every slight, every unfair limit, every stupid thing that happened. On our rides home I would sigh and say empty things like "Oh, that's not too good." For two years I was unable to be truly empathic with her. I said all the right child-shrink words to her, but they were hollow. I was so afraid that I wouldn't be able to find an alternative to extended day, that my work would be compromised, that I'd never get tenure, and my child would be in therapy before her First Communion. It was all so serious then. So pressured. That, combined with the ongoing acrimony between women who worked inside the home versus those who worked outside, sensitized me to the potential disasters in every area of my life.

Finally an accumulation of painful events forced us to look at the situation from her perspective. And in the final analysis, my daughter was right: extended day "sucked." Only then could I allow myself to remember the sweet relief of coming home from school midafternoon, throwing off my uniform, racing through my chores, then just letting loose with the only part of the day that was really mine. I knew then that things had to change, that my husband and I had to launch into another series of headstands, and that I had to contend with the fact that my distress over recognizing a lousy day care situation had compromised empathy for my daughter and blinded me to what she really needed.

STOP MAKING SENSE: SILENCING THE CHILD

Six-year-old Yolanda had been under considerable stress since the diagnosis and sustained hospitalization of her four-year-old brother, Robert, who was suffering from an aggressive cancer. Despite the rigors of many invasive procedures and medicines, Robert was usually feisty and upbeat, particularly enjoying the playroom and the many visitors. There are many reasons why this is stressful for a sibling. In Robert's case, the diagnosis was swift, followed by immediate hospitalization. Yolanda's mother, single and feeling pressure to spend as much time with her son as possible while keeping her job, was no longer available to Yolanda. Several months into this trial, Yolanda announced to a group of adults that she wished *she* was in the hospital, that she wished *she* had cancer. A dark cloud descended over the room. Some people visibly winced at her unapologetic announcement. "Yolanda, you don't mean that! You take that back right now. Don't you know how sick your brother is? What would make you say such a thing?" These are the times grown-ups get so uncomfortable with the straight talk of kids that they try to silence them with anger or shame. People wanted to know *how* she could say such a thing. No one asked *why*.

Later I asked Yolanda about her hospital wish. She explained that when you get put in the hospital you get toys and balloons and videos and you can go to the playroom whenever you want. People come and bring you presents, and your mom stays with you all the time and sleeps over. Yolanda is lucky. Her mother, though totally overwhelmed, understands this. She tries to "make sense" of the experience as much as she can, then she struggles to find ways of giving Yolanda what she really wants—time with her. Children have one foot in the real world and one in the magic world. It takes a long time to understand that words or feelings (like anger) don't, by themselves, make people sick or cause other bad things to happen. Part of childhood is learning that you aren't as powerful, in good or bad ways, as you may have thought. With a less empathic mother, Yolanda could have been convinced that there was a connection between her "selfish talk" and future downturns in her brother's status.

A CHILD'S-EYE VIEW

It's not just children who must progress through life expanding their viewpoints. Parents must do a variant, except sometimes they need to move backward. My first supervisor of child psychotherapy asked her graduate students to approximate the height of the preschool-aged children we would be treating and try to remain in that position for as long as we could stand it, experiencing the world from a perspective that is very different from our own. It was an illuminating assignment. It's easy to forget how much time in childhood is spent looking up. Parents and children experience time and space differently. When a parent says, "We'll leave in an hour," to young kids, that can be ten minutes or a day. The time-out method of discipline rests upon a common understanding of time between parent and child. Its initial introduction is often met with cries of pain usually reserved for things like being banished to Siberia. Parent and child begin to merge their perspectives on time, using things like a kitchen timer or kids' alarm clock. But it takes a while. I recently spoke with a three-year-old who gave an incredible list of people he'd seen and things he'd done, all "yesterday." For a moment I dismissed his report as the stuff of a rich fantasy life. But then I got it. "Yesterday" fell somewhere in between "when I was a baby" and "right now."

The line between fact and fantasy is blurry in childhood. Many children spin elaborate tales that occasionally include bits and pieces of reality parents can recognize. One child I saw in therapy angered her mother because she "lied" so much. In scheduling the first appointment I envisioned a certain type of lying. "Did you run into the street after I told you not to?" "Did you smack your sister in the head?" "Did you put your toys away?" Those easily verifiable untruths weren't the problem. The mother was distressed by the "lies" her daughter told about things that weren't true and would "never be true." The lies turned out to be a hybrid of wishes, needs, hopes, disappointments, and dreams.

THEN AND NOW: A MOTHER'S PAST, A DAUGHTER'S PRESENT

In trying to connect with her daughter's experience, a mother has an excellent resource: her own memory. The then-versus-now distinction is easy to forget and imperative to remember when dealing with children and adolescents.

The Bad Haircut: Now

When it comes to my hair, my only requirements are that it stay out of my eyes and that it call for absolutely no upkeep. I have a "shake and bake" approach to hair; I don't want anything I can't wash, comb with my fingers, and let dry on its own. Once, with two hours remaining before I had to catch a flight to Florida to give a speech that wasn't yet written, I realized that some of my hair was sticking straight up, in different directions. My husband dropped me off at a cheap (in every way) salon, while he picked up my cleaning (I also wasn't packed). I take my glasses off during haircuts, so I usually have no idea how things are progressing. After ten minutes, the stylist asked me to take a look and decide whether she should stop. With only a glance I could see there was nothing left to cut. When my husband picked me up, he was speechless for a minute and then exclaimed, "Regular Boy's!" "What?" I demanded. "You got a Regular Boy's," which he then explained was a basic barber label for a standard 1950s-type haircut he used to get as a kid. I felt a little self-conscious as he tried to repair the damage his remarks had done by considering my head from different angles, like he'd actually find one that was better. He was clearly more upset than I. In the end, I just shrugged and reassured him with the wisdom of my mother that had been totally meaningless when it was first imparted: it would grow back.

The Bad Haircut: Then

Thirty-five years ago that haircut would have had me throwing myself off some cliff or joining up with the nuns, who wouldn't care what I looked like. I would have cried for at least an entire day, gotten choked up every time I passed a mirror for a week, and required constant reassurance that hair doesn't one day just stop growing. In my angry phase I would have fantasized about marching into the beauty parlor, cursing out the stylist, and demanding my money back. My hair would *never* grow back. *Everyone* would notice my terrible haircut. As a result, they would change their positive opinions about me. It would be *horrible*. And worst of all, it would last *forever*.

In empathizing with their daughters, mothers have a greater chance for success if they can operate from both *now* and *then* perspectives. *Now* has the benefit of experience, the reassurance of ultimate improvement, and a sense of perspective on where bad haircuts actually fit into life's big picture. *Then* has the immediate urgent pain associated with unexpected change. *Then* has the fragile self-confidence, the confusion of appearance with worth, and the catastrophic "domino-effect belief" that one bad event will initiate a slew of others. Until the end of time mothers will feel compelled to state the obvious—that hair grows back, which is a statement of fact, not necessarily of empathy. Holding on to their reassuring authority as grown-ups, mothers have to reach back to places in their adolescence where their thoughts and feelings weren't subject to sense and logic. Allowing themselves the discomfort of sitting in those places for a few seconds helps mothers to realize that events that have become lighter, less important, even amusing with time, *are the exact same things* that are heavy, monumental, and not the slightest bit funny to their daughters.

Total empathy with a daughter is absolutely impossible. It's a series of hits and misses. But for every hit, a mother is allowed a substantial number of misses. She can miss by "making sense" with the practical but totally worthless "It will grow back." She can flat-out lie with "It doesn't look too bad." Or she can minimize her daughter's distress: "It's only hair. Grow up." None of these are likely to score her many empathy points. But mothers can say a lot of dumb, insensitive things to their kids. They can be totally out of touch emotionally from time to time. But they can also do things like agree that yes, it really is a hack job, and that it is an unacceptable haircut that requires fixing or a reduction of the fee. A mother can accompany her daughter as an advocate in improving the situation. With an older girl, a mother can often be an armchair advocate, suggesting moves and letting her daughter try to take care of it on her own. These moments, as long as a mother is cool, collected, and unlikely to embarrass her daughter, forgive hundreds of misconnections.

BARRIERS: WHAT GOES WITH THE TERRITORY?

A prerequisite for making empathic connections with children is some basic understanding that what children need from a parent varies with levels of development. It includes knowledge of children's abilities at those different levels, as well as the limits of those abilities. Maturation proceeds at different paces for different skills. A young boy can be a good runner or even good at football, but in another area requiring coordination—handwriting—he can be a disaster. Gross motor skills (running or knocking people down) tend to develop before fine motor skills (penmanship, helping out with tools, nuts and bolts that require smaller movements). Sometimes an adult takes a child's most proficient area, then sees every area in which the child is less proficient as a problem. For many children uneven development is to be expected. There are a number of highly verbal children who confuse adults because they have the words but nothing behind them. These children are not necessarily immature but do not yet grasp the nuances of language or its many contexts.

A mother wouldn't toss her five-year-old daughter the car keys and ask her to go pick up a quart of milk. She probably wouldn't place a newly frosted cake in front of a two-year-old, tell her not to touch it, and leave the room without expecting to return to find her daughter wearing half a bowl of frosting. However, mothers often expect other things from their children that are almost as ridiculous. One of the most dangerous is a mother's expectation that she and her daughter will magically tune in to each other and then her daughter will give her all the understanding and connection she so badly needs. Children can't give that. They don't have the ability. Plus, it's not their turn. The day-to-day errors that contemporary parents make often stem from a conception of children that reverts to a much earlier historical trend—that they are miniature adults. The empathic bond between mother and daughter can become tenuous as a result of some typical parent errors.

Barrier to Empathy: Talking Too Much

While hearing language from birth is critical to a child's verbal development, the expectation that a child be a real player in "discussions" is fairly naïve. I'm amazed at the frequency of high-level verbal negotiations parents engage in with their young children. Their expectations of what children that age understand—particularly when parents try to approach them on a logical or relationship level—are way out of line with children's actual capabilities. The classic is when parents ask fairly young children *why* they did something. The kid stares back blankly, further testing the strained patience of the parents. Not only may a child be unable to articulate the reason she covered herself in paint and then sat on the new living room couch, she may not even *know* why she did it.

Barrier to Empathy: The Tyranny of Choice

I was sitting in the café section of a chain bookstore on a quiet weekday morning, baking in the sun as it poured through the broad three-story window, drinking my cappuccino and reveling in the quiet pleasures of life. That is, until the Tiny Tot hour let out. Suddenly, the café was swarming with two- and three-year-olds and their mothers. The children crawled all over tables and chairs and constantly bumped into me, always waiting until I had my coffee cup poised at my lips. The mothers sat down and called their children to the tables. Not just once, but on and on. "Zach-AAA-ree, I'm not telling you again . . . Zach-AAA-ree!" Zachary kept running. "Me-lis-saaaa, leave that man alone. Did you hear me?" Melissa didn't leave that man alone. The dialogues continued across the café. As a child psychologist I came really close to offering the mothers some well-thought-out advice: "Get off your asses, go get Zachary and Melissa, sit them on *their* asses, and stop yelling."

Somehow, probably out of fatigue and hunger, the wild children eventually made it back to their mothers, who stupidly had not used the free time to order anything for themselves or their children. What I originally attributed to bad planning was in fact intentional. They hadn't ordered yet because they didn't know what their children wanted. Well, who cared? Presumably the mothers knew their children well enough to predict what they would eat and what they wouldn't. There weren't all that many choices at that hour of the morning—bagels or muffins. At least that's what I thought. Once little Melissa was corralled, her mother started asking her what she wanted. She said she wanted a big cookie. Her mother said no. "Do you want a bagel or a muffin?" "What kind of muffins are there?" Mother gave her a list of eight kinds of muffins. Choosing was torture. Then came something I never anticipated—the juice selection. Once again, mothers were negotiating with their children over what I assumed was only a snack. Zachary had to choose not only among bagels but among bagel *spreads*. Every other possibility his mother read, she immediately retracted, explaining the reason, which instantly made the kid salivate for it.

I am not against giving children choices, but some of the things adults expect from children are unreasonable. We don't expect a four-year-old to read a tenth-grade chemistry text. When children cannot conform to the expectations of the establishment to which their parents are taking them (bookstore, movie theater, restaurant), they should not be brought along. It's a setup for failure. When children are already at the establishment and not complying with the expectations of decent behavior, they need to be taken out. When I mentioned this to a mother whose children were so totally out of control that she hated taking them anywhere, she was horrified. "What would that do," she asked urgently, "to their self-esteem?" Because the job of therapist comes with an expectation of higher-than-usual amounts of empathy, I had to stifle my initial response, which was, "Who cares about their self-esteem?" I tried to explain to her that the concept of self-esteem these days is about as diffuse and useless as the concept of family dysfunction. Presumably, we start out with a sturdy base of unconditional love from both parents. Over time, we have to find ourselves honorable and lovable on our own. Before you have self-esteem, you need to have a self. It is the job of a parent to help this child learn where she begins and ends, how to express her self, how to control her self, and how to connect with people. Before she starts building up the major esteem points, she should find herself feeling and doing things that she associates with being an okay kid.

When I'm working with a child who is difficult to manage, her self-esteem is not at the top of my list of goals. She needs first to feel the safety of parental limits and the reassurance that there are people who care enough not to let her spin out of control. She has to know that her feelings are legitimate but the way she chooses to express them is not. Parents need to learn ways of intervening actively with their children (and this does not mean with power-hungry and punitive behavior) so that, over time, their children will learn how to monitor themselves in a variety of social situations, and begin to develop strategies they can use to comfort or calm themselves when they feel like they're about to lose it.

When I was growing up, my world was divided into door number one and door number one. When my daughter was three, I divided her world into door number one or door number two. That's about as complicated as the world needs to get for most children that age. Cognitively, three-year-olds can only keep two balls in the air, and even then, it's hard to keep them from hitting the ground. The main message of Child Decision Making 101 is "Do you want to wear the red socks or the blue socks?" Unless it's a girl who has a thing for wearing the same pair of socks every day, or whose mother had the forethought to buy hundreds of pairs of socks that are exactly the same, this question gets the mother out of the house a whole lot faster than the potentially deadly "What socks do you want to wear today?" or the even worse "What do you want to *wear* today?" That, on a bad day, could become an eight-hour production.

Barrier to Empathy: Selflessness

The one and only *Star Trek* episode I ever watched had a profound impact on me—so much so that I can't understand why I never watched the show again. A beautiful blond alien was introduced to Captain Kirk and friends. From a stereotyped perspective, this woman was the alpha female—gorgeous and empathic. Not only was she able to tune in to people's pain, she was able to heal it by absorbing it into herself. Captain Kirk, with whom she immediately fell in love, got these killer headaches, which she soaked up like a sponge. Needless to say, Kirk started feeling a lot better. But the "Empath" grew weaker, until, of course, she died.

That episode is a cautionary tale for women who pay the price for being "too empathic." When my daughter is hurting, I can't help but feel a bit of it too. It helps me connect with her, but it doesn't automatically help *her*. When mothers overidentify with their daughters' distress, they may become paralyzed and unable to help them. And we all know where trying to pull off the Empath role eventually leads. If we only absorb people's suffering, we can't help but take in toxic waste that can only do us harm. Without a filtering system, we would be overwhelmed. Mothers who work to spare their daughters troubles by bearing them on their own shoulders deny them something they have to learn—that difficulty is a certainty in life, that there are better and worse ways to handle it, that support from others, including the mother, can be tremendously helpful. In doing this the mother is communicating something essential to the daughter: "I believe you can handle it."

How do we distinguish between being very empathic and being overly empathic? Researchers have applied the distinction between *communion* (having a "positive, caring orientation toward others") and *unmitigated communion* (taking that orientation much further, to the point where the focus is on others "to the exclusion of self"). People who turn toward *only* caring for others (some people call them saints, others call them martyrs) tend to have a more negative perception of themselves. They depend on the reactions of others to determine their identity and worth. This is a recipe for distress. If a woman's self-esteem comes only from other people, she must remain active and highly invested in their lives. She neglects herself even more. She burns out. This is the story of too many women. Born with the belief that their identity is reflected solely in how helpful they are to others, they are set up for lives in which they are constantly physically and emotionally overextended. There is nothing wrong with nurturing and taking care of people. However, when it happens at the total expense of self on a fairly continuous basis, a woman may find herself closer to the role of the *Star Trek* Empath than she'd like.

Barrier to Empathy: Who Owns These Feelings?

I saw a woman in psychotherapy for a depressive reaction to a job setback that had totally undermined her confidence. One morning she began the session with a description of a countywide spelling bee in which her third-grade daughter had participated over the weekend. To qualify for the county competition, the girl had to win in her class and her grade. In the county competition she was able to go several rounds before being eliminated. Her mother was devastated. She wasn't the kind of parent who was always obsessed with her daughter's achievement, so I dismissed the narcissistic injury of watching her daughter lose as the cause of her upset. The little girl, a studious, responsible child, had the typical reaction to losing—temporary disappointment and a little embarrassment, then a growing enthusiasm for enjoying the remainder of the weekend.

Her mother's reaction was *not* typical. She was deeply upset "for her daughter," found herself crying frequently, and searched for things that would make her child "feel better." Over the weekend this mother was trying to feel *for* her daughter, rather than *with* her. Her own losses at her job had so rattled her that she was convinced that her daughter's loss would be similarly awful. When her daughter reacted to the degree of her mother's distress with looks of concern, her mother immediately and mistakenly interpreted those looks as lingering sadness about the spelling bee, which only confused the situation more. The little girl began to think that she had really hurt her mother by losing the spelling bee, and that she must work harder to be a winner.

Such crossed wires cause nothing but trouble. A child needs to know that she can have feelings that are not contagious. She expects that her mother has already been immunized against many of the childhood "viruses." For example, when a girl and her teammates are shedding a few tears after the loss of a soccer championship, it doesn't feel good for her to see her mother sobbing in the stands.

A recent documentary on children's beauty pageants focused on one mother as she applied makeup to her three-year-old, who already had what could only have been called "big hair." The child seemed spectacularly uninvested in the entire endeavor and appeared to take no pleasure as her mother listed her accomplishments using the royal "we." "*We* won this regional pageant. *We* won this national title. That crown was stolen from *us*." When will there be a split in *we*? What will it mean for that relationship? The *we* is not limited to beauty pageants. It exists in any situation where a parent becomes invisibly glued to her child in serious pursuit of unconscious needs or goals in which she is highly invested.

Some mother-daughter relationships are characterized by the mother's constant emotional invasions into the growing girl's private self. Some girls complain that they can't tell where they end and their mothers begin. They have been brought up to think that being out of emotional sync with one's mother is against a major family rule. Mothers often try to tell their daughters that they don't feel *x*, they really feel *y*. The mother puts her own "stuff" on her daughter and doesn't accept no for an answer when her daughter tries to give it back. Daughters report feeling engulfed. "No, I am not furious with my father, *you* are!" "No, I don't like cashmere sweaters, *you* do." Just because a mother can read her daughter like a book at the age of three doesn't mean she can still do it at ten. And as daughters grow they become better able to read their mothers. Sometimes, like the driver picking up radio frequencies from far away, adolescent girls can tune in to stations their mothers forgot existed within themselves. Girls begin to learn very early whether their mothers will really accept them as "players." As a daughter matures, does mutuality fade when she disagrees with her mother? How much does a mother allow her daughter to remain a full-fledged member in the game as the competition becomes more and more even?

Conversations between early-adolescent girls and their mothers are frequent (and often conflicted) and offer one of the first platforms upon which daughters can express opinions, say obvious or dumb things, reformulate ideas and test them out in safety. It's a good setting for learning how to disagree, how to recover, how to balance logic and emotion. It can be a safe setting for getting really heated up about issues, nailing her mother on certain points that she's always hated to concede but also knowing that ultimately the girl forfeited nothing by engaging her mother in verbal duelling. Mothers are in the tricky position of having to remember that no matter how articulate or clever or stinging a daughter's arguments, it's never a fair fight. It's a tricky balance of empathy for the mother. Mothers are expected to be able to take shots much farther below the belt than their daughters.

By adolescence, many girls have tuned in to their mothers—their strengths, preferences, and vulnerabilities—with precision. And they know how to exploit it. Girls can bait their mothers so quickly that women find themselves in deep water before they realize they've been hooked. An angry daughter who's taken the gloves off in a conflict with her mother can often tap into a place so primitive that it can make her mother feel dangerous. These are the moments, whether in the relentless dependency of infancy or the wrenching conflicts of adolescence, when she may have empathy for women who abuse their children. Not that she endorses the abuse. But after a mother has felt that rageful toward a child, whether her daughter is sixteen days or sixteen years old, she realizes that she lives in the same neighborhood as those women, when she'd always assumed they occupied a different planet.

THREE

$\mathcal{B}$

Pregnancy and Childbirth: Raw Materials

I can almost see myself floating in my mother's palm.

Ursula Hegi,
Floating in My Mother's Palm

THE DEVELOPMENTAL TASKS
OF PREGNANCY

Pregnancy is a nine-month-long blind date that culminates dramatically in a lifetime commitment. When it comes to relationships, it's the ultimate in high stakes. Higher than marriage, where at least a couple of million couples who've sworn before God, government, family, and friends to remain together until death don't make it anywhere near it. The no-fault approach to divorce has been a positive or a negative depending on which side of the "no-fault line" a woman finds herself. "It just didn't work out" still gets many nods as a sufficient answer to explain the dissolution of a marriage. "He was demanding, irritable, whiny, and immature." Sounds reasonable. With marriage, people have to make a number of promises, but they can get out of them fairly easily.

In pregnancy a woman makes no formal promises, no public commitments, but God help her if she doesn't hang in over the long haul once she becomes a mother. In contrast to the no-fault approach to marriage, motherhood tends toward the "all-fault" approach. Unless she knows before or shortly after birth that it just isn't going to work out, and gives the child up for adoption, she is responsible for that child, no excuses. "It just didn't work out" is usually translated into harsher language and contained in court orders terminating parental rights. She can get rid of a "demanding, irritable, whiny, and immature" husband, but if she complains about a two-year-old child with those words, very few people will feel sorry for her on that basis alone. No one is going to suggest a trial separation, or that mother and child "give each other a little space," let alone break up.

GROWING INTO A NEW IDENTITY

Pregnancy and childbirth are two of the most defining events in women's lives. Both are times in which so many extraordinarily wonderful and incredibly awful things can happen. Pregnancy is seen as one of life's universal, natural, everyday occurrences. But it is also highly individual, with most of the "action," especially in the first half, being invisible. Many women wait until the beginning of the second trimester, when the pregnancy has a significantly greater potential of survival, to announce their news. However, it is in the *first* trimester that a woman pays a high price for her admission to the "big show." And unless she's ever been stuck for days in a little boat on storm-tossed seas, taking a steady diet of barbiturates and relentlessly tortured by someone using her breasts as punching bags, she can't possibly know what she's in for until she's already there.

These discomforts are not accorded the same attention or empathy as they would be in other contexts. When a woman is vomiting her guts out in the first trimester, she learns quickly that although it feels as bad as any flu she's had, it's not treated the same way. I'm convinced that if nausea and vomiting of that magnitude were due to *any* condition *other* than pregnancy, *or* if men had to endure it, it would be totally legitimate to stay home from work on "pregnancy leave." But because women have been pulling this pregnancy business off for thousands of years and haven't died from the first trimester, it's not considered a particularly big deal. These days a woman would have to be in active labor before anyone would offer up a seat on a crowded bus.

PRENATAL EMPATHY

Far from being a passive process in which a woman slowly loses the ability to see her feet or does everything she's told by anyone who tells her, pregnancy is extremely active. The baby isn't the only one changing by the day. Pregnancy is boot camp for expectant mothers. Labor and childbirth can seem like bizarre, painful hazing rituals for initiation into motherhood. And early infancy *is* commando survival training. I wouldn't sleep too well knowing that the preparation of our military was limited to manuals, advice from friends, families, and the occasional military person. If recruits sign up to protect and defend, then damn it, they need to get *experience* with the tools of protection and defense. I want those soldiers drilled and competent, conditioned and able to perform whatever duty is theirs. I want them committed to their jobs on principle, not just because they need the cash or look good in uniform.

The development of the expectant mother and baby may *appear* to be guided by books and advice, but when it comes to empathy, it is the *experience* of pregnancy that is key. Like the training of new soldiers, pregnancy is a conditioning period in which a woman learns the basics in areas of managing labor, delivery, and infant care. Not only has she rented out her living space to this one baby (or more), she continues to bear all custodial responsibilities. Forget about just keeping the place up. For the first time in her life she may even have to treat her body *better*. She must stop doing things that are bad for her new guest and start doing things that are in her silent partner's best interests. The unique impact of an expectant mother's behavior on her baby becomes more evident as pregnancy advances. For example, she may find that every time she eats spicy food, the baby is restless and neither of them gets a good night's sleep. This is the beginning of reciprocity. (It's also the beginning of years of "I have to eat *that*?") The baby gives the mother feedback about some aspect of her behavior (diet, exertion, posture, stress, noise exposure), and if the mother is "tuned in," she can make connections, and conduct experiments, using the child's response to form a base of information.

Mothers often talk to their unseen babies. In these conversations, for the first time a pregnant woman refers to herself as "Mommy." She tries it on, like possible baby's names, getting used to the "fit." With or without a name, the baby she's carrying becomes her invisible "you"—simultaneously "her" and "not her." Women get to know their babies' rhythms and activity levels. Level of activity in utero appears related to temperament (activity level in utero is similar to infant activity level), suggesting that mothers are learning about some of their babies' basic characteristics even before birth.

In one study mothers-to-be at thirty-two weeks gestation were assessed as they reacted to recordings of babies crying. Cardiac reactivity and pregnant mothers' ratings of the aversiveness of the cries were followed up to determine their relationship to mothers' postnatal reactions to their own babies. The pregnant mothers who had found the recorded baby crying most distressing were more likely postnatally to label their own three-month-old infants as "fussy/difficult and unpredictable."

BEING A GOOD MOTHER BEFORE GIVING BIRTH

When women enter into the world of prospective motherhood they must contend with a dizzying array of contingencies. There are the 357 Commandments of Pregnancy, a list that seems to grow longer with every trip to the doctor, every scan of a pregnancy Web site, or discussion among friends. Some of the major-league "don'ts" are so entrenched as to have assumed the level of religious or legal codes. No cigarettes. No prescription, nonprescription, or illegal drugs. Kiss caffeine and diet drinks good-bye. Tap water, dry cleaning, hair dye, nail salons, computer monitors, and microwaves—all these and more are suspect to some people. Whether these habits were addictions or just very pleasant activities, a thumbs-up on the pregnancy test doesn't magically help women kick them, especially cold turkey. Others who have been under treatment for a variety of serious medical conditions will struggle with the cost versus benefit of continuing to take medicines that have helped manage their conditions but may negatively impact the developing fetus.

Women having children in the fifties and early sixties were far less constrained in the don't department. The rigidity of the rules since that time leads a person to wonder how anyone born before 1965 is capable of walking upright and speaking in complete sentences. In *Little Altars Everywhere,* a wonderful novel by Rebecca Wells about the loves and tensions between generations and the insights that come with friendship and experience, Vivi is infuriated yet again by her daughter Sidda, who has asked for a 1952 photograph of Vivi and her friend Caro, both eight and a half months pregnant, "feet propped up on the table, smoking Luckies, sipping a little bourbon and branch, reading Dr. Benjamin Spock." Vivi angrily insists that she knows the "real reason" her daughter wants the picture—"to bring it to her group, where they all sit around and whine while she tells them lies about the way I raised her." I have pictures of *my* mother and her friends in that very same year, waiting out the terms of their "confinement" with the help of alcohol and nicotine. In addition, my mother was prescribed Dexedrine during most of her pregnancies, which according to those who have married into my family "explains a lot."

DOING PREGNANCY: PLAYING BY THE RULES

The "dos" are somewhat easier: prenatal care, good nutrition, exercise, and vitamins so big they look like they've been stolen from the elephant enclosure at the zoo. Some dos are communicated by books, others by word of mouth. One woman at a baby shower for a mutual friend looked at my protruding abdomen and demanded, "Are you toughening up your nipples?" *"Excuse me?"* All that came to me was the mental image of trying to slap my breasts around or saying mean things to them, which I found pretty funny. The woman leaned over, grabbed one of my nipples, squeezed and rotated it to a hard right, as if it were a stubborn radio knob. Then other, usually normal mothers started demonstrating the procedure on themselves, swearing that a woman can never toughen her nipples enough.

In the sisterhood of motherhood, a certain level of decorum is sacrificed, presumably in the interests of the expectant mother, for whom there is apparently no such thing as too much information. Perhaps because I looked so appalled at the group nipple rotations, they told me that before my baby and I would ever get to those "nursing nirvana" experiences, my breasts, the nipples in particular, were in for it. By the time they finished with stories of nipple cracking, chafing, bleeding, infections, and fevers, I was ready to strip off my bra, get some sandpaper, and start right then and there. These and many other hints during pregnancy are a tremendous "help" in the realization that with pregnancy, a woman crosses over a line and nothing will ever be the same again. These women would have considered the imparting of this wisdom an empathic response to an initiate. From their perspective they were trying to prepare me.

BREAKING THE RULES: LOOKING FOR TROUBLE

To deviate from the Pregnancy Commandments is to play fast and loose with the odds of having a healthy, smart, and beautiful baby. Everything the prospective mother does, or fails to do, is believed to have an impact. And she will be held responsible for her child's development. Women are seen as good or bad mothers, not so much by what they *do* but by the final "product." If a kid turns out okay—good mother. If kid fails school . . . does drugs . . . commits murder—bad mother. Developments in technology have offered us an illusion of control over life. The worldview of baby boomers—that there is a right way to conceive, bear, birth, and raise children—is responsible for an inflated and burdensome sense of control parents think they have on all aspects of their children's development.

When women in my mother's generation lost pregnancies, the most common explanation was that it was the body's way of dealing with a fetus that wouldn't or probably shouldn't survive. In my generation that explanation is probably still the most reasonable. But with more knowledge comes the cruelty of uninvited speculation about what caused a miscarriage. It's proof that information often has little to do with wisdom. I've treated several grieving women who were told a litany of things that they should do differently "next time." In Amy Tan's *The Kitchen God's Wife,* Pearl recalls how her first pregnancy ended in a miscarriage and her mother's contribution was to add insult to injury by commenting about "how much coffee I drank, how it was my jogging that did it, how Phil should make sure I ate more." Needless to say, in her next pregnancy she vowed to wait four months before telling her mother.

When people learned of my two miscarriages, their first question was often "Do they know why?" I wanted to smack them. Miscarriage is such a terrible but frequent occurrence among women that doctors don't launch a full-scale exploration into the why until the third or fourth loss. Pregnancies, labors, and deliveries can go wrong for many reasons, only one of which is a physician's or mother's negligence or incompetence. But we live with the illusion that if we do things by the book, we can insure good things and prevent bad things. If bad things happen, then *someone* must be responsible. If you can't pin it on anyone, it's much scarier to face up to the fact that some things in nature, *and* nurture, are a crapshoot. Probably because of the frequency of miscarriages, women who've suffered a pregnancy loss often deem medical professionals as deficient in empathy.

One way to retain a sense (even if it's an illusion) of personal control is to create psychological distance between oneself and the woman for whom the pregnancy, labor, or delivery went wrong. ("We're not at all alike." "She's much older than I am." "Maybe she's a smoker or a drinker.") The pregnant woman will grasp at whatever will help her feel sufficiently different from the grieving woman, so that the probability of the same thing happening to her is low. It's likely that she feels tremendous empathy for the woman but her distress at the possibility of crisis in her *own* pregnancy leaves her in a kind of "empathy paralysis," in which she's unable to respond. This isn't selfishness or insensitivity. In many ways, it's hypersensitivity. It is an excellent example of the personal-distress barrier discussed in the last chapter. Those shoes are just too scary to stand in. The experience of miscarriage is often as invisible to people as the woman's first trimester of pregnancy. A wanted pregnancy jumps immediately from fertilized egg to baby in the minds of expectant parents. Our cultural ambivalence about the termination of pregnancy has complicated the way we use language to describe the loss of miscarriages.

With my first miscarriage the shift was jarring. "The baby" suddenly became "the pregnancy" or "the fetus." Not only did I have to grieve the loss of the baby, I was also deprived of the language of loss and suffering. Miscarriage and stillbirth are periods of tremendous isolation for women and their partners. They experience the loss very differently and therefore mourn it differently. Others tend to deny or minimize it, thinking that approach provides the most comfort.

INVISIBLE YOU/VISIBLE ME

The nine-month conditioning process of pregnancy is focused as much on the self as it is on the body and the baby. Knowledge of conception requires that a woman make an immediate shift from thinking about herself as a free agent toward always taking into account an additional invisible someone. With a confirmed pregnancy, suddenly many of a woman's automatic decisions, habits, and preferences have to be reexamined. (Many would stress that some behaviors should be cut out even when *anticipating* pregnancy.) These concerns may affect choices about how money is spent or saved. They will influence relationships, particularly with the father of the child, career decisions, and lifestyle changes. Unlike blood, money, or vacation time, expectant mothers can't bank sleep, patience, solitude, or endurance. There are no vaccinations against confusion, fear, inundation, loneliness, or resentment. It's very hard to practice methods of handling those feelings in advance of the actual experience. The addition of an invisible someone else is the beginning of a long lesson on motherhood. That "someone" will become a person to the expectant mother long before anyone else. "Expectant" is a wonderful way to describe the pregnant woman. She could be called a pre-mother, a prospective mother, or a waiting mother. But no, she is "expectant," which means not only does she wait, but her mind is also alive with possibilities, fantasies, and wishes for her child. She is expectant also for the birth of herself as Mother, and the attendant fantasies of how she will fit into this new role. She is in relationship with her child long before he or she appears on the scene.

EVERYBODY'S BUSINESS

As soon as a woman's pregnancy begins to "show," she finds herself entering into a new society, one with different norms and rules. The definition of "comfortable" physical space changes dramatically. Perhaps because a woman in her seventh or eighth month *is* actually encroaching on other people's space, others feel freer to invade hers. Pregnancy is one of the few times in a woman's life when perfect and imperfect strangers feel compelled to offer "empathic public service," by touching, by giving an amazing array of advice. Naomi Wolf, author of *The Beauty Myth* and *Promiscuities,* remembers when her advanced pregnancy became the subject of discussion among several strangers at a swimming pool. One woman predicted that she would have a boy because her abdomen was "pointy." Writer Rita Ciresi remembers being told by a Chinese woman, "Look in mirror. . . . Pretty face, you get girl. Ugly face, boy." In a study titled "Are Women Carrying 'Basketballs' Really Having Boys? Testing Pregnancy Folklore," Johns Hopkins researchers surveyed 104 women who did not yet know the sex of their unborn children. Women were asked to predict the sex of their children and to provide the "data" upon which they based their decisions. Fetal sex was not predicted by abdomen shape, experience of morning sickness, or comparisons with previous pregnancies. For reasons that remain unclear to me, women with more than twelve years of schooling had a 71 percent hit rate on fetal sex prediction, well beyond what we would expect by chance. In a boost for prenatal empathy, women who based their predictions on *dreams* and *feelings* were more accurate than women who relied on folk wisdom.

Most pregnant women don't walk down city streets or grocery aisles searching for answers about the sex of their unborn child or random wisdom about the care of children. And yet strangers are drawn to them as if summoned by sonar. During my first pregnancy, I was approachable in a way I'd never been before and haven't been since. Strangers were more open with me, and because I felt more than just my singular self (I had someone on my team), I found myself more open to them. People were being more protective of me at a time I surprisingly felt the least vulnerable. "I have never since felt so closely accompanied," Isabel Allende wrote of her pregnancy with daughter Paula. Pregnancy turns a woman into a walking affirmation of life, of potential, of hope to other people. What else unites the thousands of people she passes on a busy city street? The fact that all of them were born—under an incredible range of circumstances—and that their mothers at the very same point in their pregnancies looked a lot like her. Many women on those streets have actually trekked to that particular mountaintop. They see a new initiate lugging about the evidence of her future and want to pass on something about the rugged journey before she begins. It often has that kind of urgency to it. Other women, often elder women, made pronouncements with such certainty that they weren't easy to just shake off. In my eighth month an elderly woman leaned over to me in the subway, touched my belly, and whispered confidentially, "They'll break your heart, every one of 'em, but still, you gotta love 'em." She was out the door before I became oriented again to my "condition." "Who's going to break my heart?" I wondered. "And who will I love anyway?"

INFORMATION VERSUS WISDOM

Women have always searched for empathic sources of support in pregnancy and childbirth. Many cultures have established rituals for the transition into maternity, in which community elders guide and support the pregnant woman through childbirth and the postpartum period. In Western industrialized societies it is less likely that pregnant women live in close proximity to their mothers or other female relatives, which often leaves huge gaps in support. And while the involvement of expectant fathers in so many aspects of pregnancy and childbirth has increased, there are limits to what they can provide in the "I've been there" kind of support that is so necessary during many high-definition moments.

Unlike women of my mother's generation who had babies within roughly the same age span, there is now a far greater age range for pregnancy. It is less likely that a primiparous woman and her same-age peers are going through the same thing at the same time. A twenty-two-year-old woman may have no friends who are even *close* to considering children. If four women in their thirties begin their quest for motherhood at the same time, there may be significant variation in the ease with which they conceive, the lengths they are willing to go toward that end, the losses incurred in repeated attempts, and the experience of the physical and emotional aspects of pregnancy.

Daniel Stern, M.D., an expert on the emotional development of mothers and infants, emphasizes the importance of an "affirming matrix" that surrounds a new mother with the security and confidence she'll need to find her way as a parent. Mothers, grandmothers, aunts, friends, acquaintances, sometimes even strangers, can offer that support. Christina Baker Kline, editor of *Child of Mine,* a collection of essays about motherhood, recalls the simultaneous assistance and oppression of the printed word, which was a lackluster substitute for human wisdom. Motherhood was presented "as a how-to chore, a connect-the-dots task that is pragmatic, rational, task-oriented and forward-progressing." While she admits appreciating the "rules" approach, with its structure and promise of progress, she "kept wanting to read between the lines." There is more to motherhood than *doing*. The contributors to her book demonstrate in essay after essay the critical role of empathic connections with women, particularly during the early months of motherhood.

MOTHERS' EMPATHY WITH DAUGHTERS

A daughter's pregnancy can take her mother to a number of places—to her *experience of motherhood in the past and present*. She might think back to her pregnancy with her daughter, or other pregnancies before and after. It may take her to memories of herself before motherhood and lead her to reflect on her life as a mother. The mother's capacity to empathize with her daughter will also be related to the experience of her own mother. Memories of the past are altered by events that have occurred between the *then* we are remembering and the *now* we are experiencing. There's no such thing as a perfect, correct memory. It's the difference between the memory of our computers and the memory in our minds. We input data into a computer, and unless some freak event occurs, when we go back for it it will be exactly as we left it. It is inflexible and relentless in that way, but also comfortable and dependable. The emotionally charged memories of people undergo instant transformation as they occur, even *before* we input them into our memories. The way we encode or input our experience will strongly influence what it's like when we retrieve it, which is why parents and children rarely remember even the most basic details of certain events the same way.

Leveling the Playing Field

Pregnancy (the usual but not exclusive prerequisite for Motherhood 101) places a daughter in her mother's territory. Unlike education, career paths, marriage, or other areas where mother and daughter may share similarities and differences, pregnancy is so potent because it pushes each woman into a powerful new role while she simultaneously retains the old one. A daughter steps up and assumes a mother's role, but she is still *her* mother's daughter.

Her mother steps up to the grandmother role, but she is still her mother's daughter and her daughter's mother.

A mother's empathy for her pregnant daughter depends a great deal on the quality of their relationship before the pregnancy. She may see her daughter's pregnancy as the magic salve that will heal all past wounds, setting a mutually hostile or estranged relationship back on track. The expectations of women who feel they've been judged unfairly by their daughters in the motherhood department may, with their daughter's first pregnancy, anticipate a happier circumstance, once their daughters understand what motherhood is *really* like. Unfortunately these expectations are usually totally unrealistic. Rotten relationships, particularly when mothers haven't demonstrated much empathy for their daughters before, are not likely to get much better with the happy event. Novelist Carolyn See recounts years of hostility from her mother, who railed against her in drunken and sober states with accusations that she was "slow on the uptake" and a "moron." See was, in fact, a very bright girl who was only "slow on the uptake" when it came to her mother. In a letter to her mother she wrote, "It took me forty-one years after my father left us when I was eleven to get it through my head that it just wasn't working out. You couldn't stand me." It was only in the experience of strong positive relationships with her own daughters that she finally had a healthy yardstick. See could find validation that having a mother almost totally deficient in empathy was no predictor of her capacity to be empathic with her daughters. Anticipating a pregnancy and new baby, as well as seeing how *other* mothers support their daughters, can be an additional reminder of the way the loss of a parent resounds at every milestone. Loss of a *living* parent, particularly in times that emphasize mother-daughter relationships, can be particularly hard to take.

In her memoir, *Giving Away Simone,* a story of five generations of abandonment, Jan Waldron recalls the impact of her mother's leaving on her subsequent teenage pregnancy. Her mother had been extremely inconsistent, angry, and emotionally troubled from the start. She walked out on Jan and her brother when they were both adolescents. One of the few "motherly" things Jan's mother did before she left was to take her daughter to a gynecologist for birth control pills. Several weeks later, as Jan herself prepared to leave the house, she looked at the several months' supply of pills on the shelf and very deliberately left them behind. They were one of the few things about her mother that she could reject. "If my mother was going to walk," she wrote, "I for one was not going to collude with her easy exit. I stared at those pills as if they were my mother's stand-in, resented, lousy baby-sitter." This act of defiance resulted in pregnancy and her mother's return, if only temporarily.

Hidden Motivations in Pregnancy

There are many motivations for getting pregnant, some having little resemblance to the most straightforward one—having a child to raise. Some women hope that children will revive a failing marriage, solidify a flagging relationship, or patch an awful wound from which they've suffered since childhood. Perhaps it will serve as an anchor to keep an errant husband from straying too far. Some women look to babies as "antidepressants," something that will turn their lives around and provide them with the joy and purpose currently missing from their lives. To other women daughters represent a security for the future that sons don't. The old saying "A son is a son till he takes a wife. A daughter's a daughter for the rest of her life" isn't entirely empty.

Women who especially want daughters sometimes long for an idealized mother-daughter relationship that will "undo" an unsatisfying relationship with their own mothers. In Frank McCourt's stirring memoir, *Angela's Ashes,* his mother, Angela, longs, after four boys, for a girl. She expects a daughter to provide something in her life that her husband and sons can't. But she also craves a closeness that she and her mother never had. Her mother is depicted as the kind of woman whose only chance at warmth would have been if someone had set her on fire. One example says it all. The day after she has lost a third child to death, Angela is desolate and in bed. Her mother marches in, all business. What she says is ultimately true, but thoroughly lacking in empathy. "Grandma comes and tells Mam she has to get up," writes McCourt. "There are children dead . . . but there are children alive and they need their mother."

From the moment of her birth, baby Margaret McCourt was seen as special. "There was a holiday in heaven the day this child was made," commented a family friend. In her seven weeks on earth, Margaret was able to accomplish something her mother never could. She had a stabilizing effect on her father, whose wandering, erratic work, and drinking left the family only a couple of steps away from homelessness and starvation. Angela proudly described to a friend her husband's reaction to Margaret: "He's in heaven over that child. He hasn't touched a drop since she was born. I should've had a little girl a long time ago." When Margaret died, her magic spell over her father evaporated as well.

Mothers carry their dream children within them, long before they are conceived. Those dreams influence their choices—of names, clothes, schools, hobbies, friends, and expectations for those children. Children are given job descriptions long before they can read. With increasing age, daughters get tangled up in, and then try to differentiate their reality from, their mothers' dreams. Sometimes it means rejecting what their mothers most hoped would take root in their daughters and flourish over a lifetime, and dealing with the fallout that comes as a result.

Been There, Done That, and Beyond

For better or worse, with her first pregnancy a woman enters a new club, one in which her mother has been a member—happily or unhappily—for a long time. A sympathetic mother does several things to introduce her daughter to that club. She reflects upon her own first pregnancy, identifying the mixture of feelings she had. She recalls her mother's treatment of her—supportive, belittling, competitive, fearful—and remembers what she would have preferred. If she stops here, as many mothers do, feeling confident that, *from her own experience,* she knows what her daughter is going through and precisely what will be helpful to her, she won't be going far enough. Then she will be confused and hurt if her daughter doesn't respond as she'd hoped.

It's the second step that differentiates "been there, done that" from true empathy. An empathic response requires the acknowledgment that when it comes to pregnancy, in its universality, a mother has lived in the same general neighborhood her daughter now inhabits. However, because each pregnancy is also unique, her daughter's pregnancy may have her living in a different house on a different street. To be truly empathic with her daughter, she must come to terms with the fact that she is, at once, the veteran expert and the novice guide. It's a bit of a trick to lead the way and admit you need frequent instructions along the journey. And yet that paradoxical combination is the stuff of true empathy. A woman's experience of pregnancy and childbirth, as well as the experience of motherhood in general, will influence her empathy for her daughter's pregnancy. For some women, pregnancy represents the beginning of the end. This is definitely the case for Vivienne, from *Little Altars Everywhere*, who laments all she lost through pregnancy and childbirth, compounded by the fact that her daughter doesn't feel the slightest bit guilty about it. "I lost my waist for her," she complains. "My feet grew from size six to seven-and-a-half." And then the bitterest of all: "I lost my potential for her."

Many mothers feel compelled to point out the many things their daughters "won't be able to do anymore, once the baby comes." It was with this "you're in the army now" mentality that the mother of Susan, a newly pregnant patient of mine, took every opportunity to point out the many doors that would close once the baby was born. She thought her daughter should "practice" sacrifice while she was pregnant so it wouldn't be such a shock when the baby came. According to her mother, Susan needed a new, no-fuss hairstyle and more practical clothes. She might as well cancel her magazine subscriptions because she was never going to have time to read. It was never too soon (Susan was only two months pregnant) to start making meals and freezing them for later. If Susan reported some fun activity, like going out to dinner or a movie, her mother always delivered the same doom-and-gloom reminders. This mother approached pregnancy preparation as if her daughter were entering a convent or a bomb shelter.

Susan was thoroughly annoyed with her mother's attitude. She felt that her mother was taking all the fun out of the whole thing and that she didn't care at all about *her*. I encouraged Susan to take all of her mother's advice and turn up its volume in her head until the actual words were distorted and almost seemed to merge into one tone.

"If you can't make out the words," I told her, "find the feelings under the words." Susan persisted with her sense of her mother's meaning: "You are incompetent" and "Motherhood is a drag."

"No," I said, "those are just more words. You get pregnant and what *feelings* do you hear in your mother's voice? How is her voice different when she talks about the pregnancy from when she talks about other important events in your life?"

Susan had trouble getting past the words to the feelings, so I became more structured.

"Was she unhappy at the news?"

"No, not exactly. It was like she was happy but . . ."

"What else?"

"She got all nervous."

"Is she a nervous person?"

"No, she was nervous for me."

"Why is she nervous for you?"

"It's like she's afraid I won't be ready."

"And if you aren't ready?"

"I don't know. It's like I'll lose my life or something."

"Lose your life . . . as in die?"

"No, like lose myself."

"Why might she have that particular worry?"

This opened up a whole different way of perceiving her mother's attitudes and comments, which had much more to do with her mother's own experience of pregnancy and motherhood than any feelings about her daughter's competence or right to be happy. Then Susan did basic things like asking her mother what she would have done differently in her pregnancy and early motherhood, and found that the main theme of the advice concerned being totally unprepared, psychologically more than physically, for motherhood. In a clumsy way, she was trying to spare her daughter that pain, yet unknowingly she was creating new distress. Fortunately this was a pair who could talk to each other, even if it wasn't on the deep levels that psychologists like. With seven months to spare, they had plenty of time.

A mother whose unplanned pregnancy resulted in a forced, rushed, and ultimately unhappy marriage, or a difficult journey of single parenthood, adoption, or abortion, may be sensitized to the same risk for her daughter. In fact, she may be so concerned with preventing a repetition of her experience that she becomes hypervigilant about her daughter's sexual behavior, sometimes long before the girl even thinks about having sex. I know of several cases where mothers dragged their rather bewildered daughters to gynecologists, insisting that the daughters be prescribed birth control pills. This is clearly appropriate when a girl appears on the verge of becoming sexually active or there is evidence that she is already having unprotected sex. But when a sexually inactive girl is swallowing hormones just to reassure her mother, it suggests anxiety in the mother that needs some attention, and conveys a very confusing message to the girl. A woman's sense that pregnancy, whether planned or unplanned, ruined her life is unlikely to communicate positive images of sex, commitment in relationships, and marriage in a way that fosters healthy discussion on subjects like sexuality, personal control, and contraception.

Bliss

Mothers can also approach their daughters' pregnancies with blissful and somewhat sanitized memories of the years they spent having and caring for children. They look forward to their part in the raising of grandchildren and expect their daughters to find motherhood equally rewarding. This can introduce an unintentional burden, as new mother Elissa Schappell recounts in her refreshing essay "In Search of the Maternal Instinct," when she compares herself to her mother, for whom "pregnancy had been a breeze, birthing . . . a joy, and raising children . . . a marvelous adventure." She finds her view of her future littered with pictures of millions of miles of car pools, batches and batches of brownies, and "chaperoning all those field trips to terminally dull places like the Franklin Mint."

Women who are honest with themselves about the heights and the depths of all phases of motherhood may be more accessible to their daughters than those who can only be 100 percent positive or 100 percent negative. Mothers who received the message that ambivalence is a *normal* part of being a parent, and not an aberration, have a far easier time dealing with their daughters' conflicted emotions. *"Yes,"* they can tell their daughters, "you are brave and competent. You climb mountains and you make tons of money, and you can *still* be very fearful about childbirth." "*Yes,* you may have done *everything* that the books say, but you can still worry about your baby." "*Yes,* you tried for three years to conceive this baby, but no, it's not horrible, strange, or predictive that there are times during your pregnancy when you want to be unpregnant." Sometimes this is when mothers share confidences with their daughters more openly than they have before, which can put them on the most solid footing they've had since preadolescence.

Barrier to Empathy: But You're Supposed to Take Care of Me!

Women who transferred their dependency on their mothers to their young daughters quickly reverse roles. They "parentify" their daughters as early as childhood, and play it out through adolescence and adulthood. There are many situations in which a mother is truly impaired and has difficulty caring for herself and her children. In other situations the mother, despite her age, is emotionally immature and dependent.

Often mothers and daughters find a relationship that works for them. Theirs becomes a collusion of sorts. The mother says, "What would I do without you?" which at first feels like a big gold star to a little girl. But over time, the daughter comes to believe that her mother's well-being rests entirely with her. Maybe she sees herself as her mother's emotional protector against a father who is cruel or "just doesn't understand." Perhaps she is the substitute for an adult social life. If there are younger children, she often becomes the "real" mother, with her own mother as figurehead. In situations like these, one hopes that the daughter has developed an "outside" life that gives her other information about her "self." When the daughter upsets the applecart, even in ways that are developmentally appropriate for her, all hell can really break loose.

"Upsetting the applecart" can include such things as having a best friend, a boyfriend, a part-time job, going away to college, choosing to live away from home, working, marrying—or having children. The two old women who presented with their concerns about dying are an excellent example of how sticky these relationships can get. At some point the mother and daughter communicated to each other that they couldn't make it without that tight, exclusive relationship. The language varies: "How can I live without you?" or "How can you live without *me*?" Sometimes it's hard to tell where the mother ends and her daughter begins.

Barrier to Empathy: Fear and Concern

Mothers can have difficulty being empathic with their pregnant daughters because they are so afraid for them. Many women are high-risk, either because they have a medical condition that might complicate their pregnancies and their general health or because they will have difficulty providing for the child. These are often heart-wrenching concerns. In the movie *Steel Magnolias,* a story about the enduring relationships among an unlikely group of women in Louisiana, M'lynn learns that her recently married daughter, Shelby, is pregnant. In sharp contrast to everyone else's celebration, she is furious and terrified. Shelby has diabetes that is very difficult to control under the best of circumstances. She'd been warned very clearly that pregnancy would be extremely dangerous, but she conceived anyway. Shelby expects her mother to do the impossible—to simultaneously understand the joy that she feels at the prospect of a child as well as the sickening fear that *her* joy may result in her mother's greatest sorrow.

Barrier to Empathy: Hexes, Prophecies, and Pronouncements

One aspect of a mother's complex response to her daughter's pregnancy can include, in varying degrees, the "paybacks are hell" phenomenon, in which many of the "Just wait till you have children" warnings, pronounced over years and years, finally have the potential of happening. From the discomforts and horrors of pregnancy and childbirth to the sleeplessness and selflessness demanded in infant care, mothers have woven narratives about what their children "put them through" in one way or another, and they often don't hesitate, throughout their children's growing years, to mention one or two of them. Tone is critical here. Sometimes this information is given as fact with little emotion. "You gave me one scare after another. It seemed like we were in the emergency room every week with a break or a sprain or a tear." But there are combination accusation and retribution statements such as "You treated me like dirt when you were in high school, and you won't even know how hurtful you were until you have a daughter and she does it to you."

Number of hours in childbirth, number of episiotomy stitches required, and the delineation of the many shades of pain are among the instruments of guilt induction. My personal favorite, when I've been in some minor conflict with my daughter, is to display my six-inch vertical C-section scar.

Barrier to Empathy: How Could You Not Want Children?

Women who can't have children get sympathy. Women who choose not to have children get scorn. It's seen as a fundamental rejection of one's basic reason for being. Selfishness is the major attribution given to couples who choose not to procreate. Women, for whom motherhood has seemed the central life task for so long, are judged more harshly than men for their decisions. People offer predictions that they'll be sorry, that they will lose out on the fulfillment of extending the generations. This can be a particular point of contention between mothers and daughters. A daughter's decision to forgo motherhood can be taken by some mothers as rejection—of themselves and their choices. Another mother may see it as a devaluation of everything she did for her children.

There are many reasons people forgo parenthood, and most of them are articulated by other people as pathological. The first is that some couples just don't want kids. That's it. Some couples are committed to not bringing children into the world as they currently see this one. Others enter relationships with partners who already have children and want no more. With family histories of genetically linked illnesses, some women decide against the risks. Many women look back to their own childhoods, identify with their suffering mothers, and have no desire to go through anything like what they did. Some women who were traumatized by abuse and neglect can decide against children because they dread the possibility that, no matter how well they're doing in their adult lives, the instant they become mothers themselves, they will do to their children what was done to them. And some people simply know they don't want to sacrifice work they love, travel, and freedom.

Barrier to Empathy: Really Bad Timing—
Adolescent Pregnancy

Women who know the difficulty of raising children even under supportive circumstances see their daughters' futures in ways that adolescents can't possibly anticipate. A woman who's been a single mother herself knows the tremendous challenges that come with being immature and on her own with a helpless baby who needs a grown-up mother. As one mother learning about her daughter's unplanned pregnancy commented in dismay, "I have to drag her out of bed every morning. How does she think she'll be able to deal with baby schedules?"

The restricted financial resources associated with single-mother families leave pregnant girls and their mothers with limited alternatives. Abortion and adoption are available, but in the exaggerated invincibility of adolescence, many girls decide to keep their babies, with no idea what it will entail. In most cases the pregnancy does not result in a shotgun wedding. Instead the young mother stays pregnant and single, and her prospects for completing her education and gaining fulfilling employment that can support her and her baby are slim. Research has shown her prospects of a later marriage also diminish. Mothers' lifelong dreams for their daughters—high school, college, job, travel, marriage, and *then* children—can be dashed as quickly as it takes the pink line to form on the pregnancy-test stick.

Sometimes, if a mother is very upset by her daughter's behavior, particularly if she perceives it as resulting in shame and humiliation, she'll respond with, "How could you do this to me?" On its face, this is a rather narcissistic lament. If, in a psychotherapy session, a mother who is furious with her daughter for quitting cheerleading yells, "How can you do that to me?" I know my work is with the *mother*. If, however, the daughter, without permission, took her mother's car and totaled it, then the question "How could you do that to me?" makes more sense. In the case of a young pregnant daughter of a relatively young mother, "How could you do this to me?" is a valid question. The likelihood is that the daughter's pregnancy will result in another mouth for this mother to feed, and often another child to care for. The number of children being raised by their grandparents, who are already limited by health and financial concerns, is increasing yearly. How many grandparents look at the prospect of raising a second generation of children by themselves and call that future the "golden years"?

Barrier to Empathy: "Look, Ma! No Man!"

There are many pivotal events that are experienced so differently by women on either side of generational fault lines. They present excellent opportunities for discussion, but we are often so tenacious about our own positions, and so disrespectful of women much older than ourselves, that we don't make room for such potentially rich exchanges. For example, the proliferation of fertility treatments and conception techniques has accelerated amazingly over the course of only one or two generations. What is familiar territory for the woman undergoing fertility treatment can seem very strange to her mother. Some of these techniques have enabled women to conceive without a partner, without a live-in father for the child. When young Maya Angelou informed her mother of her pregnancy and the fact that she didn't want to marry the father, her mother agreed and replied philosophically, "There's no use ruining three lives."

I often wonder what I will say to my daughter if she reaches her thirties and isn't married. From my own experience, I will want her to be able to be a mother, if that's what she really wants. I will ache for her as the clock begins to wind down. Will I encourage her to have a child whose father is nothing more than a sperm donor? Selfishly, I'd really, really want to. It's my only shot at a grandchild. But I think about how hard it was to raise her even with equal input from her father. Is it being empathic to encourage her in something that will be difficult in ways she can't possibly know? What about her unborn child? Many women are highly ambivalent about what they expect in the father department. Women who proclaim their equality with men in the workplace and at home seem to fade when it comes to parenthood, where most fathers still play the role of understudy. Frustrated by the difficulty of getting men to commit to long-term relationships, more and more white middle- to upper-middle-class women have been saying the equivalent of "Screw them" and taking care of business themselves. By choice or by default, the number of children living in fatherless households is growing.

There is a building body of research suggesting that fathers are important in the development of girls as well as boys, and that sometimes a mother can be most attuned to a girl when she facilitates interaction between father and daughter. The father of an early-adolescent girl can validate her in ways her mother cannot. All dressed up for a dance, a girl looks to her mother for the basic inspection: no food in the teeth, hair combed in the back, all price tags off, the *Good Housekeeping* Seal of Approval. The mother says, "You look beautiful/pretty/lovely/nice." And that's all right, but because her mother said it, the exchange rate is lower, as with Canadian versus U.S. dollars. Mothers' compliments on appearance are necessary but not worth as much on the open market. But if a girl has a father who is not a sleazeball, who's a regular guy, and she comes down the stairs and he looks up from the newspaper or TV and says, "Wow!" or "You look great," or just smiles sincerely, he has just made a significant deposit in his daughter's account. When he does that about her academics, her ability to debate something at the dinner table, or her soccer game, he offers a unique and gratifying perspective.

If I cavalierly encourage my daughter to go ahead and have a child on her own when her window of opportunity starts closing, I will be something of a hypocrite. My experience of motherhood isn't restricted to the interactions between my daughter and me. It is intricately tied to my husband's experience of fatherhood. From the beginning, child care was a shared responsibility, which was complicated and costly. It meant working and reworking schedules. It meant earning less money. It meant that he chose jobs in which he could have a flexible schedule to accommodate a young child. And we were lucky to even have those choices. I really can't tell my daughter *anything* about becoming a single mother, because I wouldn't know what I was talking about. The only thing I *do* know is that it's hard to raise a child, even with a partner. Responding to women who glibly tell him that they can raise their kids without men, comedian Chris Rock quipped in a recent concert, "Yeah, and you could drive your car with your feet if you want to, but that don't mean it's a good idea."

Empathic Confusion: Between the Needing and the Getting

When Mara was preparing for the birth of her first child, she was delighted with the many choices: labor rooms and birthing rooms, visitors during labor and delivery, husbands' participation in labor and delivery, an approach to pain control that would accommodate patients' original wishes but also support them if they needed medication. Mara called and invited her mother to be with her during labor and delivery. Her husband was the designated coach, so her mother's duties would be in the nonspecific, cheering-squad category. This was a major step for Mara. A vibrant, emotional young woman, she was very different from her mother, who had always been uncomfortable with the expression of strong feelings. Despite the fact that they spent a fair amount of time together, Mara never felt "connected." It was not a conflict-filled relationship. There were rare disagreements and no fights. But there was that painful distance that happens when two people who have every reason to be very close to each other couldn't be farther apart.

Every interaction becomes evidence of this failure, a failure they can't even name but that clouds the air around them whenever they are together. Mara saw this impending birth as a watershed moment. It was something so intense, so personal, that sharing it with her mother would forever move them in a different direction. She would need her mother. Her mother would be able to help her in a way no one else could. And when it was all over, her mother would have her first grandchild.

When Mara went into labor, her mother dutifully arrived, as grim as if she were going off to war. Her presence gave Mara pain beyond labor. Instead of joining her daughter at her bedside, to comfort her, calm her, amuse her, or just keep her company, Mara's mother hung back, frozen. Mara was devastated. That tableau represented so much of what she had felt throughout her life with her mother. In terms of empathy, there was a lot that needed to go around in this situation. Mara had constructed a beautiful if unrealistic fantasy, and saw its failure as the crystallization of thirty years of an empty relationship with her mother. Her mother was asked into a situation that was probably alien to her, and she said yes anyway. She showed up and actually stayed despite her discomfort. She saw her daughter's disappointment and hadn't a clue why it was there and what she could have done to prevent it.

It's painful to see two people trying so hard but completely missing each other. These gaps become magnified during significant life events. Mother and daughter were each trying to give the best to each other, and these very efforts were pushing them apart. The empathic emptiness they felt had more to do with their preconceptions of what should be felt or shown or done. Both women needed to understand that a person's feelings aren't limited to the ones they clearly express. And in this case, Mara had to understand that as far as her mother was concerned, "frozen" did not mean cold.

Nobody Does It Better

For many women, the usual ways in which their mothers get on their nerves are eclipsed by their capacity to comfort, soothe, and understand them as they advance through pregnancy and await birth. In any strong mother-daughter relationship, it's often a good idea to return to the source and, if the well isn't poisoned, to fill up for the journey. Novelist Barbara Kingsolver recalls her second pregnancy, at the age of forty, when she was almost a month overdue. Her mother reassured her that ten-month-long pregnancies ran in the family, but still, as time passed, her concern for her daughter grew. She began to call daily to check in. Kingsolver's husband intercepted one call and hesitated before handing the phone over to his wife, worried that her mother was badgering her. But what may have felt like badgering to King-solver weeks before had become the greatest of comforts, as she reflected in a moving letter to her mother: "I am a woman lost in the weary sea of waiting and you are the only one who really knows where I am. Somewhere I'm sure I have my own things to do and a hundred opinions you would not want to paste in the family album, but at the same time you and I are sisters and daughters and mothers and your voice is keeping me afloat."

DAUGHTERS' EMPATHY WITH MOTHERS
A New Look

A friend, after hours and hours of major labor pain, slow progress, and no anes-thestics, grabbed her husband by his collar and gasped, "Tell my mother I understand now and I'm sorry for every lousy thing I ever said or did. Promise me!" The husband promised. Later that week, when my friend's mother arrived and immediately began making a number of "suggestions," my friend panicked. "Please," she whispered to her husband, "tell me you didn't tell her what I said in labor."

"Why?" he asked.

"Because I have a feeling that in about twenty-four hours I'm going to be taking it all back."

Once the shine or the shame wears off the news of conception and daughters begin to experience the roller coaster of emotional, physical, and social changes associated with pregnancy, many women have the unsettling experience at some point of thinking or saying, "Oh my God, my mother did this six times?" or "I can't believe my mother got through this when she was only twenty" . . . or "with no husband" or "gave me up for adoption."

In Light of New Evidence: Reevaluating Mother

In pregnancy, a daughter often begins the long process of reevaluating her mother. As she begins to travel the same road that her mother walked with her, it's hard *not* to wonder about her mother's experience. This is one of the first points at which women can experience *retrospective empathy*. A woman's experience in the present can lead to a revision of history with her mother. With daughters, pregnancy often has the impact of superimposing new insight on the images of *her mother then and her mother now*. It's a time when many mothers get a booster shot of respect from their daughters. As she traverses roughly the same course her mother did, a pregnant woman finds that there are numerous things she may never have been curious about before. She wonders about her mother's relationship with her own mother. She may learn family secrets—pregnancies before marriage, adoptions, deaths of children. A daughter's pregnancy can advance her to a higher standing than the fact that she is married. It may be that with the pregnancy, the daughter sees her mother's life as more interesting. Each time she asks her mother for information or personal disclosure the connection for both people is affirmed.

Experience Never Guarantees Empathy: A Legacy of Loss

Sandra, a thirty-five-year-old woman I saw in therapy, was crushed by a recent miscarriage. Since she already had three children, she felt that people totally discounted her pain. Her husband, an optimistic and loving man, said plainly, "We'll just start trying again." He was obviously a little off track, but she didn't mind. She was more disappointed with her mother's response—or in this case, nonresponse. As her mother's only child, Sandra expected a lot more. After a good bit of anger on both sides, it became clear that (1) the mother's distance was a result of not wanting to "fan the flames" of her daughter's distress (sympathy would just prolong or intensify her grief), and (2) she had to confront her long-held but silent resentment over her daughter's ability to produce three children without a hitch, when she herself had suffered three miscarriages and one stillbirth before Sandra's birth.

Sandra's mother had always been helpful to her daughter. In fact, she had been very responsive to the birth of each grandchild, flying fifteen hundred miles and staying to help out for three weeks after each birth. The problem was that with this miscarriage, she expected her daughter to feel bad for a couple of days, which was her idea of the appropriate mourning period for a woman with three healthy children and only one miscarriage. The underlying message was that the couple of days were over and it was now time to "get on with it." Given the acute pain Sandra was experiencing, and the chronic, though previously unexpressed aching that must have haunted her mother, I did not consider this a time for a major confrontation about who wasn't giving what to whom. Instead, I proposed to my grieving patient that perhaps one way to get an empathic response from her mother was to *offer her empathy*. Sandra knew relatively little about the circumstances surrounding her mother's stillbirth and miscarriages, especially about what happened immediately after her losses and what kinds of support her mother had received. We discussed ways she might communicate to her mother that her own miscarriage had made her wonder what it had been like for *her* all those years ago.

Through an exchange of letters, each woman gained a greater appreciation of the other's experience. It turned out that Sandra's mother had had next to no support with her miscarriages and was deeply traumatized by the stillbirth. After a normal pregnancy but a long and difficult labor, the baby was whisked away, without her having the opportunity to see or hold it. She spent the next twenty-four hours highly sedated and awoke to the realization that no one had even told her whether she'd had a girl or a boy. People around her acted upon the assumption that the less said, the better. They encouraged her to start trying to conceive again right away, and minimized her fears and her grief. At that time, few stillbirths were afforded the comforting rituals that occur around other deaths. Surrounded by people, Sandra's mother felt completely alone.

Even now, she confided to Sandra, when people ask how many children she has, she feels the loss acutely when her head says two, but her lips say, "One." Now that Sandra was a mother who had also suffered loss, she could empathize with her mother's pain at the time of the stillbirth. She understood how powerfully the grief haunted her mother and how it had affected their entire relationship. She wondered what might have been different if she had known about her mother's losses much earlier. In finally acknowledging and affirming her own suffering, Sandra's mother was able to be more supportive of her daughter's feelings. Both women knew that the feelings related to these losses weren't "over and done with." But the bond they shared provoked a more honest and equal relationship between the two. When Sandra miscarried a year later, in what was to be her final pregnancy, her mother immediately flew the fifteen hundred miles. This time she contributed to more than the running of the household. She was there to help, but more than anything, she was there to support her daughter.

Insight: An Empathy Boost

Sometimes a lightbulb goes on over a daughter's head when she comes to a bump in the road that precipitates an empathic insight, a connection between herself and her mother. Often it involves going through an event (like divorce) or an age (like forty) and rethinking the mother through lenses of finer magnification. Writer Marge Piercy communicates this to her mother: "You had me at age forty-four. When I was that age and considered that face, I was filled with sympathy. I realized what it would be like to have a child in middle age, how much harder those incessant demands would prove to be." When daughters are in situations that invite identification with their mothers, their curiosity about the women they thought they knew soars. As these women become mothers, their mothers often seem more "real" to them.

The experience of pregnancy and childbirth leads some women to reevaluate their mothers in a more *negative* light. As they have experiences that challenge their mothers' advice or behavior, they begin to understand for the first time some of the reasons for long-standing problems with their mothers. Maureen, a teacher in her early thirties, consulted me for therapy during her pregnancy. Contrary to the horrible picture her mother had painted of pregnancy, Maureen found that she actually enjoyed it. However, her mother was quick to comment on the amount of weight she was gaining, clipping out articles about preventing stretch marks, and trying to brace her for the fact that her body would never be the same. These are not helpful things to say. Maureen was able to deflect her mother's comments, but the frequent concentration on preserving and losing her looks disturbed her. She recalled her mother's excessive preoccupation with appearance. When Maureen was still in that preadolescent place where baby fat and the blossoming of breasts and hips collide with perceptions about what is beautiful, she remembered feeling like she'd done something very bad, but she wasn't ever sure what it was. Her mother's reaction to the changes in her pregnant body resurrected memories of earlier disapprovals that had more impact on her than she'd realized.

Putting Mom in the Hot Seat

Most women, with very little prompting, could give a litany of all the lousy, mean, stupid, and embarrassing things their mothers ever inflicted upon them. "Remember when you . . . ?" "How could you have . . . ?" often are preludes to specific shameful accusations that their mothers might not even remember. In these situations the questions are rhetorical. A daughter doesn't want to know why her mother always insisted on wearing ugly red plaid shorts that showed her varicose veins and sang show tunes loudly when driving car pools. She just wants to see her mother squirm. The worst things are often the haunting unasked questions: "Why didn't you stop him from hurting me?" "Why were you so constantly critical of everything I did?"

"Why didn't you let me have friends?" "How could you have confided all that stuff to a kid?" "How did you become an alcoholic? How could you love alcohol more than me?" "Why did you let Dad hit you like that?" "Why did you keep leaving?" "Why didn't you take care of me?" "Why didn't you love me?"

Giving Mothers a New Name: Understanding the Transition to "Grandmother"

Most young women don't initially compute the fact that their prospective motherhood is also a powerful point in the lives of their mothers (especially if the birth will launch the mother into her first experience of grandmotherhood). Mothers' feelings about their daughters having children can be different from their feelings about their new roles as grandmothers. Unlike the timing of other roles involving career, marriage, or motherhood, grandmotherhood is one over which mothers have *absolutely no control*.

Sometimes women feel they have waited so long for their daughters to have children they don't care if Grandmother becomes their legal name. Women with larger families may still have children at home when their first adult daughter gives birth, making them both "high-maintenance" mothers. For other mothers, the pregnancy of their adolescent daughters, particularly if they had their daughters young, can make them very youthful grandmothers. If the daughter remains single and stays with her mother, the lines between the generations can become quite blurred, and grandmothers have to stretch their energy and resources to cover their own children still living at home and a new generation with immediate and substantial needs.

I thought my mother was being ridiculous when she expressed her happiness at the news of my pregnancy but didn't want the "title." Now that I'm three years away from the age at which my mother became a grandmother, I think I see what she means. I could be saddled with the label "grandmother" years before I can cash in on any kind of senior-citizen perk. I love the idea of having a grandchild. I hate the idea of being called someone's grandmother. Now I wince when I hear a familiar handle for describing the victim of a crime or victor in some laudable event. "Grandmother attacked in the park." "Grandmother runs in New York City Marathon." "Grandmother" here is a qualifier, worsening the impact of the crime, inflating the value of the achievement. "Grandfather" is rarely used this way. It is no surprise, then, that many women like the baby but hate the name.

❦ FOLDING CLOTHES ❧

The final month of pregnancy was fairly thankless. There was so much—having nothing to do with becoming a mother—that I had to accomplish to "clear the decks" before the baby. Then, when everything was finished, it was time to wait. We lived in a small one-bedroom apartment, with two old (as in clunky, not antique) desks claiming the majority of the living room. There was no nursery to decorate, no adorable crib and curtains and everything matching in the pristine and peaceful ways they do before a baby comes and messes them all up. We had a treasured cradle built by my great-great-grandfather and a white wicker changing table with drawers. It was brand-new and stood out strong against a backdrop of cluttered desks and piles of textbooks. It was the sure sign that our hectic lives would soon have something different at their center.

It was June. I was hot and swollen. I'd just finished an internship with children where several of them reacted to my advanced pregnancy departure with angry fantasies like: "Hey, I got a great idea. Why don't we take the new baby high up on the Ferris wheel? And we'll sit together, you and me. And the baby will sit by himself. And y'know what? Let's not put his seat belt on. Don't you think that's a great idea? Don't you think that would be fun for the baby?" In my nonpregnant days, I'd had little trouble listening to the incredible range of children's fantasies and feelings about me. They could be pretty astounding. But when they started having thoughts about an area in which I was already feeling a bit apprehensive, finishing up with time to spare was a blessing.

For the few weeks before her birth, as I cleared away all the debris associated with academic achievement, I ended each day with the same ritual—taking an inventory of the changing table. It was the only place in my life and my house where everything was new and perfect. Every single thing had its place. There were stacks of baby undershirts, the kind that wrap around and snap. There were piles of gender-neutral jumpers, smooth and fuzzy cotton. More snaps. There were baby blankets, with lambs and bunnies, perfectly folded, towels with hoods for baby heads, piles of diapers. There were sunhats and booties, bibs and diapers.

I am not a smoother of fabrics, or a smeller or folder, for that matter. Neither am I in the habit of conducting a regular inventory of my holdings. In fact, I am careless with my belongings. The childbirth classes we'd just finished were fine, but they taught us nothing about entering into a relationship with the mysterious creature who'd been with me twenty-four hours a day for nine months. Playing with the piles of her things was as close as I could get to knowing her. Every night before bed, I refolded each undershirt, each blanket, each jumper. I'd hold them up to the soft living room light and pretend to see my baby in them. I'd lay my favorites on my belly. I'd inhale the new-baby-stuff smell like it was a mind-altering drug. The sweet smell that disappears the instant the baby's bodily fluids make contact with it. But I didn't know that then. I'd count and stack, admiring an order that I'd never known in my own life and swearing to maintain it in hers.

Twenty years later I stare at my daughter's clothes, emptied carelessly onto the floor of our rented cottage in Maine. She is visiting for the weekend, and somehow it seemed to her a good idea to bring along several weeks' worth of dirty laundry on vacation, rather than do it at home. Laundry was one of the first tasks my daughter took on independently in early adolescence. I guess the thought of her stuff commingling with her mother's boring white cotton briefs and her father's black socks became a picture she'd rather not deal with.

So much of growing up is figuring out where and how you want to intersect with your parents. As a child, my daughter was an open book, ready to share any thought, question, fear, fantasy, or protestation that occurred to her. And as an only child she had the whole stage. Even in early adolescence, when she became more circumspect, I could still bring up a subject and, after she denied interest in discussing it, use one of my best shrink tools: outsilencing her. It actually yielded a great deal for about a year, until she figured out what I was doing. Now when my daughter doesn't want me to know something about her, I remain in the dark. I miss the mutually permeable membrane between us.

Sometimes I want to turn her upside down and shake her by the feet until all those hidden pieces of her fall out like spare change upon the floor. But since she's become the monitor of her own borders, there are many guards stationed at the crossings. Sometimes it's as difficult as crossing in illegally from Mexico. If I'm very lucky, I can still find the occasional opening in Canada. This, of course, is exactly as it should be. But I feel a bit displaced.

As I bend to transfer a load of my wash into the dryer, there is a warm pile of hers already there. I scoop it out and survey the contents. There are the usual suspects (she hasn't made much progress in remembering to empty pockets before washing): a ticket from a midnight movie in the city, a barely readable card for an Ethiopian restaurant, a shopping list, and a fifty-dollar speeding ticket from the state of Connecticut. Some members of the pile are old friends: her high school field-hockey sweatshirt, a favorite band T-shirt. And the one constant, over all these years: a green-and-white-checked blanket she received before she was born, the only survivor from the white wicker changing table. For years the blanket covered her. Now she smushes it together and buries her face in it to fall asleep. It looks exactly the same.

There are clothes I've probably paid for but never seen—a zippered tan sweater, a two-piece bathing suit, tank tops, and jeans. There are adorable cotton A-line skirts with childhood prints on them. Then there is the underwear. My God, the underwear! Where do I start? First of all, it matches. There are colors like midnight blue and plum. These things are so nice a person could walk around her backyard in them. They're from Victoria's Secret and other places I've never been because I don't believe in paying full price for underwear. I try not to think too long about the implications of my daughter's sexy underwear and instead find myself falling back into an old ritual, moving without thinking, folding her clothes. Not in the haphazard ways of her youth when clean laundry could wait in unfolded piles so long we'd have to do a quick smell check to see if they were wearable. No, I fold these clothes while they are still warm, while the scent of fabric softener perfumes the breeze as I shake each piece of clothing. I take a moment to pick up each of her things and hold it to the light so it can be examined, appreciated, and remembered. I fluff and I fold and I stack. When my daughter comes in she'll be clueless about who's done her laundry because her clothes look almost professionally cleaned. She's certainly never seen this part of me. The mother who looks for clues to her daughter wherever she can get them. The one who will always smooth and smell and fold and stack just to know a little more about who she is and who she's on her way to becoming.

FOUR

~

Infancy: Mutual Attachment and Synchrony

As long as I live I will be redefining my daughterhood in light of my motherhood.

ERICA JONG,
"My Mother, My Daughter, and Me," The Source of the Spring

THE DEVELOPMENTAL TASKS OF INFANCY

During infancy mother and daughter are laying down the foundations of attachment and empathy. Each will learn from the other. They must learn to accommodate to each other's rhythms. The tasks of infancy involve the necessary prerequisites to what we think of as empathy—"reading" each other using a variety of sensory cues (visual, auditory, olfactory, and tactile) that become sharper over time. The new mother is working within a powerful new role that will inevitably alter and enrich her identity. It is a transition in which she will look to her mother and other women for empathy. She may have to find new sources of support for this new role. For a couple, the introduction of a child into a marriage often demands a redefinition of roles.

Within the space of a year the experiences of mother and father often diverge dramatically, even though both were going through pregnancy, labor, and childbirth together. This in itself can be stressful, since it can conflict with the expectations they entered marriage and pregnancy with. Many women, accomplished in their professions, comfortable with an equitable division of labor between spouses, find that with a baby everything is up for grabs. There are frequent reexaminations of who does what, often placing husband and wife in new roles they may not understand or appreciate.

In a study provocatively titled "The Perils of Love, or Why Wives Adapt to Husbands During the Transition to Parenthood," researchers Elizabeth Johnson and Ted Huston assessed couples' feelings toward each other and their attitudes about who should be responsible for specific tasks in marriage and child rearing. Researchers made these assessments three months before the couple married, then in one- and two-year follow-ups. At each point they "measured" each spouse's reported love for the other, focusing on such feelings as closeness and attachment. First, it was noteworthy that the attitudes of engaged couples about who should do what in child care weren't related to each other. Men and women had very different expectations of child-care roles. But *after* the birth of their first child, husbands' and wives' preferences were strongly correlated. The more wives reported loving their husbands, the more likely they were to adapt their preferences about child-care responsibilities to those of their husbands.

In addition to love, there are other reasons for the divergence between men's and women's attitudes that can make a new mother feel overburdened and isolated. Before marriage money can be pooled, chores assigned, consequences agreed upon.

If one person doesn't make dinner, the other can call out for a pizza. Adults can go for long periods without clean laundry or with overgrown weeds. But a baby is a nonnegotiable item. Once she arrives at her new home it's a little late to begin figuring out who does what. In situations like this it's easy to fall into familiar gender stereotypes. Since the mothers of new mothers are often of a different mind-set than their daughters, they may have trouble understanding their daughters' distress over husbands' less-than-hoped-for involvement. I don't think it was just hormones that made me want to murder anyone who said how "cute" my husband was with our baby, or called his time with her "baby-sitting."

MOTHERHOOD IN ITS INFANCY

The birth of a child begins the long process of discovering what it *really* means to be a mother, as well as what it means to be a *particular child's* mother. It's a process that often stands a woman's previous sense of herself on its head. As an individual and as a female, she feels different than she used to, and many of her relationships are profoundly altered. As woman takes on the mantle of motherhood, it's natural that she reflect upon her relationship with her *own* mother, past, present, and future. And, as a mother of a female, she is strongly influenced in her attitudes and behavior by gender-specific perceptions and misperceptions, products of the present and past generations, only to be challenged all along the way by her daughter's redefinitions of what *she* think it means to be female.

With childbirth, a new mother must absorb the jarring impact that is inevitable whenever fantasy crashes into reality. The boy she expected turns out to be a girl. The baby has medical complications. What she expected to feel, she doesn't. What she never expected a good mother would feel, she does. A continual theme in the comments of women after the birth of their first children is the feeling that they must have skipped a couple of *really* important pages in their childbirth bibles, or that women they trusted as mentors withheld crucial information. Anne Lamott, who writes frequently and frankly about motherhood, sums it up perfectly: "No one tells you, for instance, that your life is effectively over; that you're never going to draw another complacent breath again. No one learns that whatever level of hypochondria and rage you'd learned to repress and live with is going to seem like the good old days about three weeks after your baby's arrival."

Very few women report that the first weeks of their first child's lives go as expected. They never expect that motherhood could be so hard, so exhausting, so intimidating. At other times they are overcome with the intensity of the fierce connection and love they feel for their babies. After one week of caring for her infant, a woman knows that there are dimensions of fear, love, anger, exhaustion, and ecstasy she never knew existed. No matter how many younger siblings she has, no matter how many hundreds of hours of baby-sitting she's done, no matter how many dolls she owned that sniffled, pooped, peed, or cried, no matter how many books she memorized, *nothing* and *nobody* can prepare a mother for the early months with an infant until that baby is *on the scene*. It's the difference between reading romance novels and falling madly in love. It's the difference between disaster drills with rescue workers practicing on victims with fake blood and actually being a victim of a terrorist bombing. Practice is very important, but it never fully prepares a person for the real thing. And the more emotionally powerful the situation, the less one is ever completely ready for it.

When they describe the first weeks and months of new motherhood, women commonly use images of fluctuation to describe the dramatic heights and depths of its emotional terrain. Seesaws and roller coasters appear frequently in mothers' commentaries, suggesting their growing recognition that they have much less control in the mothering process than they expected. Being hit by a train, flattened by a bulldozer, or pushed from a plane without a parachute offers other powerful images. New motherhood can be like finding great rooms in the funhouse and then getting lost in the little shop of horrors, over and over again. "Motherhood," writes Janet Maloney Franze, "dissolves bones and explodes brain cells and utterly disintegrates hearts. Sleep deprivation, comic relief, towering rages and bittersweet tears, wave after wave of unexpected emotion, are all part and parcel of the motherhood routine, its never-ending responsibilities are stifling, its salvations are so thick with love that sometimes you can't breathe."

MADE FOR EACH OTHER

Whether they know it or not, mother and newborn are outfitted with ultrasensitive powers that make attachment highly likely. A superwoman who can leap tall buildings in a single bound is incredible. But I'm much more impressed by the woman who is able to sniff her newborn's dirty T-shirt out of a pile of newborns' dirty T-shirts. The infant who prefers Mozart at two weeks is less of a big deal than the average baby in utero who knows the voice of her mother and prefers it to the voices of others. I admire the average newborn whose nostrils know her mother's scent, and who is primed to reject the more artistic renderings of the human face by Picasso or Miró for a chance to gaze at shapes that most closely resemble the basic human (and some research suggests female) face.

Baby Building Blocks

Infants are born with incredible skills that insure their survival and bond them to their caregivers. Parents have sensitivities that they don't even know about that "kick in" as they interact with their babies. The relationship between mother and infant is much more reciprocal than was believed even twenty years ago. The infant is also much more of a "player" from birth. We can see it in the ways she gets and keeps her mother's gaze, in the way she alters the tone and frequency of her vocalizations in time with her mother's movements. A newborn can recognize her mother's voice among those of other women. Infants are talkers, right from the start, even though the sounds they make aren't crystallized into their culture's language. They love speech, especially when it's directed toward them and accompanied by eye contact. The adult voice is of great interest, and within seconds infants synchronize their movements, which on the surface appear like random flailing, to the rhythm of the speaker's voice. Mothers and fathers speak at higher pitch, vary high and low pitches, use repetitions, and ask a lot of questions when they address their infants. Their speech is accompanied by exaggerated facial gestures that serve to keep the child's attention.

In experimental conditions, an infant will do the equivalent of a pigeon pressing on a bar—suck hard enough on a pacifierlike nipple to get and keep a picture of her mother's face in front of her. She can discriminate her mother's voice and will suck vigorously to keep her recorded voice playing. She moves her body in time with the voices around her. When she loses her mother's attention, she works hard to regain it. Babies also learn their mothers' smell very early and make associations to comfort and feeding. Infants invite touching, which appears related to their health and well-being. Parents have an unconscious but near-universal approach to touching an infant, starting with the fingers and palms, moving to arms, legs, and trunk. There is more and more evidence that premature infants, who by virtue of the fact that they need so much machinery to stay alive, benefit greatly from human touch.

Maternal Instinct?

To some women, the "maternal instinct" is what makes them attracted to children, ready to nurture, ready to become pregnant. Other women think of this instinct as a form of "automatic pilot"—motherhood with cruise control, as natural as breathing. Most women, however, are certain that they were bypassed when it was conferred, and that their babies will suffer the consequences. It seems that we carry some vague standard of what a "high-maternal-instinct" woman is, even though we can't articulate the observations and beliefs upon which it's based.

In her hilarious and moving essay, "In Search of the Maternal Instinct," Elissa Schappell admits to being sure she'd been passed over. When she announced her pregnancy, a number of friends seemed to agree. " 'Are you going to keep it?' someone inquired in gentle horror. Some joked, 'Are you serious?' Others were more blatant: 'Are you scared? Aren't you worried about your depression? Aren't you afraid of becoming like an Anne Sexton mom?' The answer to all these was, *You bet.*" Schappell was definitely a woman who needed to find other sources of support during her pregnancy. In the days after her daughter's birth, she was still afraid, and still uncertain about how to do basic things like comfort her baby when nothing seemed to work. Feeling she had hit the depths of ineptitude, she finally *stopped* thinking and just started rocking her daughter "back and forth, back and forth," the way she'd seen chimpanzee mothers hold their babies at the zoo. As she became more adept at comforting her daughter, she let go of the elevated idea of the maternal instinct, an idea that had done nothing but make her feel bad. "I had no maternal instinct, but the animal instinct seemed to be alive in me. Perhaps I couldn't raise Isadora properly, but I could protect her should our neighborhood ever be overrun by wild dingoes."

Love Potions

The hormone oxytocin was indirectly responsible for my only remotely "maternal instinct." I was in the middle of Sears, still barely able to stand up straight from my C-section incision, trying to make the most of the two-hour window of opportunity between feedings. I was checking out curtain rods when an infant cried in Housewares. Before I was even aware that it was an infant and that it was a cry, I found myself in the midst of a mammary explosion. It was, of course, a letdown response, totally out of my control and, once I got cleaned up, rather awe-inspiring. All I could think of was Maurice Sendak's strange and wonderful book *In the Night Kitchen.* "I'm in the milk and the milk's in me. God Bless Milk and God Bless Me." I was a victim of remote control, and my daughter held the clicker. I felt connected to something primal, something I shared with mothers and infants of many species. I also felt very wet.

Powerful physiological influences operate in pregnancy, childbirth, and the postpartum period. In the days following childbirth, estrogen and progesterone, critical to the maintenance of pregnancy, take a nosedive. And unlike the many biochemical changes that go unnoticed, this one is felt by a majority of women. It has to be one of nature's meanest jokes that several days after childbirth, while women are "recovering" from pregnancy and childbirth and happily anticipating their changed lives, already beginning to cope with sleep disruption, stitches, and nipple pain, they also get the emotional rug pulled out from under them. As estrogen and progesterone levels fall, they get a taste of the "baby blues," which are a milder and shorter version of depression. Some of the symptoms poison the same thoughts and feelings that are *already* vulnerable in the new mother.

Shall We Dance?

I'm old enough to remember Dick Clark from *American Bandstand,* a teenager's entrée into the world of music, dancing, and kids who had miraculously sidestepped acne, bad hair, baby fat, and clothes catastrophes. My favorite part of the show was the introduction of a new record. Dick would spin the disc, the kids would dance, and then a lucky few would be asked to give it a rating. I always loved one of the most common criticisms best: "Well, Dick, I gave it a six. It had a nice tune and cool lyrics, *but you can't dance to it.*"

What does this have to do with mothers and newborn daughters? Everything. Embodied in these two strangers is the equipment necessary to start and maintain a lifelong relationship. Mother and infant each come with a nice tune and cool lyrics. The question is: Can they dance to it? Learning to dance involves some of life's simplest and most complex maneuvers. Remember those first awkward moments, when you wondered how something that looks so easy could be so hard? A good dancer paired with a klutz who can't differentiate feet from floor knows quickly how her enjoyment will be limited. Two very clumsy people, however, can agree on their own flexible definition of dancing and have a ball. On the other hand, two excellent dancers can have tremendous difficulty getting in sync with each other. They push and pull, fail to pick up on the intentions of the other. Their dancing is uninspired and flat. A ballerina can be brilliant by herself but a disaster when she shares the stage with others. It isn't just a matter of learning one dance. There are unlimited turns and lyrics, thousands of dances to be learned and adapted across development and partners.

Synchrony

A mother's early interaction with her baby is all about *synchrony,* about the capacity to recognize and respond to rhythms. It is the very foundation of empathy. The absolute resonance with another person, the ability to "zone in" on the same frequency and remain tuned in despite the many distractions, vulnerabilities, and challenges that threaten to disrupt it. When mother and child tune in to each other, the experience is mutually pleasurable, which increases the potential for more interaction. Mary Catherine Bateson remembers how her mother, anthropologist Margaret Mead, used to quote a line in a letter written by Harriet Beecher Stowe in which she complains that she is not getting on very well with her novel, "because the baby cries so much." "My mother's comment," says Bateson, "was that the reason the novel goes slowly is not because the baby cries so much, but because the baby smiles so much."

Taking Turns   Getting in tune with a baby involves fairly simple but important adaptations. Several years ago, in a restaurant, I overheard a young woman with a two-month-old baby talking with her older sister. The baby was in an infant seat on the table. The mother leaned in to the baby and talked, in both "motherese" and regular adult speech. She talked and talked and talked. Then she turned away from the baby, looked at her sister, and said with exasperation, "See? She doesn't respond to me!" In a tone that only sisters can get away with, the older sister said, "She would if you could just shut up for more than five seconds!" To illustrate her point she directed the sister's attention to the baby, who, "with a whole lot of shakin' going on," was registering the transfer of her mother's attentions. Her arms and legs moved and she was working her way up to vocalizing. As with people of all ages, the "your-turn, my-turn" exchanges between mothers and infants are frequently derailed. It's a part of daily life. At issue is the length of time two people remain off track, their flexibility in getting back in tune, and ways to avoid the predictable interferences with synchrony.

Regulation

In the previous section, the emphasis was on the way mothers and their infants engage and stimulate each other, how they keep the ball in play. Mother engages baby and baby engages mother with a rich and varied supply of techniques that, in favorable circumstances, evolve over time and keep them in an extended conversation that becomes quite sophisticated. But if that was all a mother did, within a couple of days her baby would short-circuit, go into meltdown from so much stimulation. There is tremendous variation in the amount of stimulation *adults* can tolerate. The video arcades that kids love so much would, within one minute, get on my last nerve. It's a basic example of temperamental differences. I've worked with hyperactive or anxious kids who can only focus on their homework if they have music blaring in their ears. Other children can't read beyond two lines with that level of distraction. For some children with psychiatric problems, headphones help them work because the music balances the blasting internal "noise" that distracts them far more. As we grow up, we gain more and more control over choosing the kinds of environments we want for home and work. The way we organize our homes, our cars, our free time is dictated by the kind and amount of stimulation that is most comfortable for us. My first reaction to having my own apartment was that I couldn't believe such quiet existed.

Coming from a house with eight people, most of them still young and noisy, I had no idea how much the quiet actually promoted relaxation and concentration. I do now. Two days in New York and I succumb to what I call the "Times Square syndrome," which assaults my every sense. In cabs, on streets, in hotel lobbies, I want to scream, "Shut up!" "Turn it off!" and "Leave me alone!" I can feel the city on my skin. My idea of heaven is a silent retreat in a monastery, which to many people would be torture. Overstimulation is relative. The noise that steals my sleep is someone else's warm milk.

As adults we can usually find ways to protect ourselves from being overwhelmed by stimulation and emotion. I can leave Times Square. We can adapt our lives so that we have certain types of arousal at certain times. For example, most people who exercise regularly and vigorously don't do it right before bedtime. Caffeine may be great in the morning but trouble at night. The loose, disinhibiting impact of alcohol may be appropriate for a party but not for a high-intensity meeting with new clients. It is possible to walk into a person's home and get a sense of the levels of stimulation she creates for her own space. Are the colors muted or bold? Is the place full of piles, with things spilling over into every corner? Or is it sleek and well organized? How many electronic devices are there? How many are on at one time or another? How many people are in and out of her place in a week?

An infant has no control or escape. Internal factors (hunger, pain) and external ones (Mom's face, noise) arouse an infant in ways she can't yet regulate. One of the major tasks of childhood is to learn how to control our emotions and our behavior. An infant is all raw nerve endings and must be protected from being constantly overwhelmed. Inundation can be a continual experience for an infant. Early on, the mother's task is to identify her child's comfort zone, to learn what sets her particular child off and the best ways to calm her. In doing that, she begins teaching her how to comfort herself.

Take three infants and expose each to the same quick, unanticipated loud noise. It's likely that they will all startle in response. However, from then on we will see variability. One kid may quickly return to her resting state. Maybe two minutes later she'll be sound asleep. A second child cries at the noise and kicks her legs in distress. When one of her parents comes, she is soothed easily and within a minute or two has been distracted by a toy. The third child all-out loses it. She cries loudly, seeming to upset herself more. She can't calm herself down. Perhaps at lower levels of distress the child might suck on her hand, but she can't initiate anything. This kind of upset is a runaway train. It is often not amenable to a nipple or a pacifier or to verbal or visual comfort.

Parents become experimenters. They find that the first thing they need to do is "turn the volume" down everywhere around the child. Voices go softer, speech slows. Bright lights may dim or darken, depending on time of day. The baby will be held, walked, or rocked, and the parents will use the pressure of touching that works the best. (By this time they'll also want to murder the person who made the original loud noise.) The trick with a kid like this is to control exposure to potentially distressing things in the hope of desensitizing her over time.

A mother can never totally rid her child's life of noise. But she can introduce her child to the hundreds of *gradations* of sudden noise, and the infant learns to tolerate some of the discomfort and to find ways of soothing herself. She may always be more of a startler than other kids. But she can find ways of keeping her emotional temperature at a tolerable level and use an adult's support in the process. Mothers act as buffers through which their babies encounter the world. At a neighborhood fireworks display, a woman was practically standing on her head, trying to comfort her wailing baby. She seemed to have absolutely no awareness of what fireworks sound like in the eardrums of babies. She did not adequately "filter" the experience for the child, and they both suffered as a result. The seeds of emotional regulation, one of the central aspects of human development, are sown in infancy. Mothers and fathers help their infants, first by turning down the volume, pulling down the shades, and second by encouraging the development of self-regulation. The ability to pull back, to comfort herself, to control some of her environment is the work of infancy.

Barriers to Synchrony and Regulation

Unfortunately, many things can interfere with the synchrony and emotion regulation between mother and daughter. Attributes of the mother, the daughter, or the context may influence their ability to click. Synchrony and regulation are the scaffolding for cognitive, emotional, and social development to come, so any barriers warrant considerable attention. An infant who cries excessively, a premature baby, an ill or developmentally disabled infant each brings unique challenges to establishing a synchronous relationship with her mother. A colicky infant can unsettle an entire household and has the potential to make the mother feel that what she does makes no difference. This can lead her to emotionally disengage from the child, which is terribly premature, since colic tends to resolve after several months. The infant gets pegged as "trouble," or the parent personalizes the child's behavior as rejection.

Adolescent Motherhood   Adolescent motherhood can be a pressure that severely taxes the foundations of an empathic bond between mother and daughter. By virtue of her developmental status and an environment that is not particularly supportive of adolescent pregnancies, the average teenaged girl lacks the maturity required for motherhood. The very same adolescent who is not ready for motherhood at fifteen can make a great mother at twenty-one. It's a matter of timing.

Adolescence is a time for so much growth, change, experimentation, development, and planning for the future. In our culture it is *not* a time for motherhood. So much of an adolescent girl's development is foreclosed with early motherhood. Any woman who has a child knows that it demands maturity. Teenage girls don't have maturity. They aren't supposed to. Despite the declining rate of teen pregnancy in the United States (18 percent since 1991), it is still a major issue. Nearly half a million unmarried girls gave birth in 1998. Fewer and fewer of these new mothers are giving their babies up for adoption. This represents a dramatic change over fifty years. In the 1950s and 1960s the "relinquishment rate" was estimated at 40 to 50 percent. Fewer than 9 percent of unmarried teen mothers gave children up for adoption in 1973. In 1995 it plummeted to 1 percent, leading the author of a recent *Washington Post* article to conclude, "U.S. women have virtually stopped placing babies for adoption." Most girls keep and raise their children with the help of their mothers and grandmothers. They are less likely to graduate from high school than their nonpregnant peers and more likely to be on welfare. They are likely to become stuck in poverty with limited means of climbing out. Children born to teenage mothers are at high risk for neglect, delayed development, poor school performance, behavioral problems, substance abuse, and premature parenthood themselves. There is some encouraging evidence that early intervention with young mothers that "hangs in there" with them over the course of their baby's development helps tremendously. Offering girls a way out of what looks like an educational or vocational dead end is critical. Encouraging the prevention of further pregnancies and involving the baby's father in financial and emotional support of the child also makes a difference.

The bond between the teenage mother and *her* mother is very important in an infant's development. Maya Angelou's mother was able to help her frightened daughter become a mother. Unfortunately, it often doesn't go like that. Jan Waldron gave up her daughter, Simone, after coming to the devastating but accurate conclusion that her mother would be of absolutely no help to her. For her, it was abandonment times two. Jan's mother had abandoned her. Jan had purposefully gotten pregnant shortly thereafter so that her mother would return. But even that didn't pull her mother any closer. Waldron describes the heartbreaking defining moment when two mothers let go of their daughters. Simone was cared for primarily by Jan's grandmother, with Jan more in the role of baby-sitter. One Sunday, while her grandmother was at church and Jan was left in charge of baby Simone, she became inundated by her daughter's seemingly endless hungry crying. At that moment she came face-to-face with the fact that more than anything else she felt "mad" toward her daughter, and that maybe she was not ready to be a mother.

When her mother called and Jan vented about the day's experience with Simone, her mother responded with yet another abdication: "We can't do this." And Jan, as hungry as her own screaming Simone, knew that what she longed for from her mother neither she nor her daughter was ever going to get. "I listened with my life to her," she laments, "to the mother words of my lost parent. Like a gambler running out of money, hoping for high returns, I had mortgaged my youth, anted up my newborn, bet on my mother's return; and I was losing bigger by the minute. I was still too much of a daughter to be a mother."

Postpartum Depression Postpartum depression can take a woman who possesses the skills and the maturity for motherhood and render her unable to access them. The depression influences the way she perceives her child as well as her energy to bond with her baby and form a strong attachment. Another barrier to the empathic bond between mother and daughter is postpartum depression. Because twice as many women suffer from depression as men, and because it has such deleterious effects on relationships, maternal depression is a serious problem. While some women become depressed *during* pregnancy, they are at greater risk in the postpartum period. According to Deborah Sichel and Jeanne Watson Driscoll in their book *Women's Moods,* "The postpartum period is a time of immense hormonal shifts, psychological impacts, and developmental demands—all of which can impinge on [the] brain simultaneously." This isn't the temporary and self-limiting experience of the "baby blues" described earlier. The incidence of postpartum depressive and anxiety disorders is conservatively estimated at 10 to 15 percent. Symptoms such as crying and irritability, alterations in sleep and appetite, hopelessness, feelings of unworthiness and guilt, and suicidal thoughts and plans can no longer be brushed off as the blues, if they last longer than two weeks. Sometimes diagnosis is tricky, because some things on the list of symptoms (like alterations in sleep) are a byproduct of high maintenance infant caretaking. But it's the constellation of symptoms and the degree to which they create prolonged pain for the mother that are important.

While the baby blues kick in several days after delivery and wind down within ten to twelve, postpartum depressions can begin weeks or months after delivery and stretch across the baby's first year of life. It is a frequently missed diagnosis, and one for which there are so many euphemisms that cloud its significance. When new mothers express their concerns to their mothers, they often get cheerleading and denial ("Just be glad for the beautiful baby you have!"), dismissals ("It's only temporary. You'll get over it"), or uncomfortable silence. It's likely that many of the women who suffer postpartum depressions have mothers who suffered similarly but without recognition, labels, or treatment. This can make a mother more or decidedly less empathic with her daughter, depending upon how much she has come to terms with the pain of those early years.

A woman who has experienced an episode of depression prior to her pregnancy is at a 25 percent greater risk for developing postpartum depression than a woman with no history of mood or anxiety disorders. Suffering one postpartum depression means a woman has a 50 percent chance of having another following the birth of her next child. A family history of depression can make a woman four times more likely to develop depression than a woman whose close family members have not been depressed. Women who have been physically or sexually abused have a very high rate of depression. A large proportion of adolescent mothers also suffer from depression. Those who have better support networks (Maya Angelou versus Jan Waldron) are less likely to be depressed.

Depression blunts emotion. People who are depressed don't pick up cues from others accurately. They often think they're projecting one emotion (for example, sadness) when to other people they appear to be feeling another (for example, anger). Forget initiative. Depressed people are reactive. They often talk less, move more slowly, and do the minimum to get by. When people become very depressed they actually appear to lose muscle tone in their faces. The mask of depression makes it very difficult to express a variety of cues for an infant to read and respond to. The psychic pain of depression makes a person emotionally unavailable to others. Relatives often comment that the person has become self-centered, or selfish. On the contrary, self-preoccupation is almost necessary to keep going. A woman doesn't think about her thumb in the ordinary course of a day—until she slams it in a door. Then she experiences everything through the lens of that pain. It pervades all aspects of her functioning.

Maternal depression has far-reaching effects that can continue throughout the life span. It has been underestimated as a health problem and underfunded in terms of prevention. Even in a culture that doesn't care about children nearly as much as it professes, the bottom line is that it is best to treat depression early, because (1) treatment works, and (2) untreated maternal depression leaves a legacy of problems. Observations of depressed mothers and infants demonstrate early obstacles to harmony and synchrony. Depressed mothers are less attuned to their infants. Their timing is off. They tend to be either intrusive or withdrawn, neither of which helps them flexibly respond to their babies. Infants of depressed mothers lack emotional regulation. Physiologically, they demonstrate the stress of their situations with heightened levels of the stress hormone cortisol, as well as variability in heart rate. Sleeping, crying, and eating are also affected. These babies may fall behind in intellectual and emotional development.

The good news about postpartum depression is that it is highly treatable.

Psychotherapy, medication, and support groups are effective in helping mothers feel better. Additionally, since some of the behaviors and ways of interacting between mother and baby may have already become habitual, technical help that emphasizes building skills for engaging, stimulating, comforting, and regulating is recommended. These techniques have been demonstrated effective with outcomes such as catch-ups in developmental delays and declines in irritability. Social support is consistently cited as mediating the harsh effects of maternal depression on infant development. In cases of severe depression, mothers in the United States may be hospitalized, separating them from their infants. Reflecting the very basic need for infants to remain with their depressed mothers, many hospitals in England have psychiatric mother/infant units, where the focus is not only the resolution of the mother's depression but the development of a secure connection between her and her baby.

MOTHERS' EMPATHY WITH DAUGHTERS

The challenge for a new mother is that she's at a major turning point in her own life just when she has to take on responsibility for someone else's life. She has all this "stuff" to work out—new role, new understanding of herself, her life direction, reevaluation of her relationship with her mate, and new perspectives on her relationship with her mother. All of this—and she's really tired. Sounds like a perfect time to find a cabin in the mountains for a private retreat. But at this very time, when she has so much going on inside herself, she must provide for another needy person. She has no choice but to take care of baby business and hope she figures *herself* out as she goes along.

Concerns about competence are the stuff of new-mother anxiety. The ways to screw up seem endless and the consequences eternal. Mistakes can't be undone. The baby slips in the bathtub; she automatically drowns. The formula is too hot; she'll never speak. The mother lets her baby cry for a while, probably provoking the need for at least one year of psychotherapy. The antibiotics the doctor prescribed for mastitis will wreak havoc on her poor infant's little neurotransmitters, some research study will probably report *five years from now*. The common denominator in each is often the unspoken, but loudly experienced mothers' anthem: "AND IT'S ALL MY FAULT!"

Faultfinding is partially the product of the technology of child rearing, which says that parenthood is very complicated, requires numerous skills, and has dire consequences for screwing up. Even though everyone says all they *really* care about is having a healthy baby, it's usually not true. Once the relief about health is over, there are strong cultural influences about what parents set as their next goals. Independence is not only an American governmental ideal; it is a goal for each of its little citizens. It is essential to parents that they help their children along the road to self-sufficiency. On that road, autonomy, confidence, and individual achievement are central. Doing things "all by yourself" (with no intervention) is highly prized. Doing them before everybody else is extra good. One of the complications of raising a baby in a culture that values self-sufficiency and confidence is that all babies start out far away from that goal. They can't do anything for themselves. Instead of seeing this as the natural state of early development, we often see dependency, in all its forms, as a problem in need of a remedy. When some parents voice concerns about their children's behavior, it sounds like they're afraid they have little addicts on their hands. When should she stop using her pacifier? Sucking her thumb? When do I take her off the breast? The bottle? What do I do about her blankie? Why is she still in diapers? Why won't she stop crawling and just walk?

When a new mother is in the midst of it, it all seems so critically important. The only laughs are in retrospect, when she acknowledges that yes, despite her concerns, her daughter did surrender her pacifier before she reached the legal drinking age. Mothers are major players in bolstering and undermining their daughters' sense of competence. After young Maya Angelou gave birth, she was terrified about caring for her baby and didn't want much to do with him. Her mother, whom she described so beautifully as "a hurricane in its perfect power," knew she had to break through her daughter's avoidance. She brought the three-week-old baby to Maya's bed and insisted that he would sleep with her that night. No matter how much the frightened Maya protested, her mother stood firm. Maya resolved to remain awake all night, a promise that her fatigue wouldn't let her keep. Later, her mother gently woke her, told her not to move, and instructed her to look at the baby. "I found that I was lying on my stomach with my arm bent at a right angle. Under the tent of the blanket, which was poled by my elbow and forearm, the baby slept touching my side. Mother whispered, 'See, you don't have to think about doing the right thing. If you're for the right thing, then you do it without thinking.' "

Empathy 101: "Poor Baby"

To my mind, reassurance is consistently underrated. People often don't want information, they don't want advice, they don't want to be told how they should or shouldn't feel. They just want to be told they're basically okay. And if they aren't okay, if they're hurting or tired or scared or sick, they want to be soothed, to have someone say to them "Poor baby." They want the relationship equivalent of chicken soup. Mothers can be good at that, in person or on the phone. Whenever I throw up, or run a temperature over 100, I call my mother. My basement could flood, I could bounce ten checks in a row, the kitchen ceiling could fall in, and I wouldn't think to call her. Generally I don't even call with my "dental and mental" highlights, which are often substantial. Why fevers and vomiting? Maybe because they go back as far I remember. Maybe because my mother was great when I was sick. And I was sick a lot. Now I call my mother like I'm registering some important piece of information in the family almanac. My mother is one of those women who wouldn't say "Poor baby" if someone held a gun to her head. But she sighs, asks several mother questions—the whens, whys, whats, and hows of the situation. I have no expectation that she should do anything but listen to the gory details of my maladies and say things like, "Oh, no . . . Yes, you always did vomit a lot . . . Remember the hundred-and-five-degree fever you had?" My mother tells me I will feel better, and I know she'll call the next day to see how I am. She'll tell my father I'm sick and maybe a brother or sister if they happen to call. That's it. It's more than enough. Maybe it comes from memories of being taken care of: the clean sheets, the smell of rubbing alcohol, the cool cloths, the alone time. Maybe it's the memory of running home from school so sick to my stomach, finally getting to my door, knocking, and when my mother opened the door, instantly vomiting all over her and the new rug in the hall—and still being welcomed in. Who knows?

When my daughter was a baby, her projectile vomiting could have landed her the starring role in an *Exorcist* movie. I couldn't stand being puked on. But I also could not have loved my puking daughter more. I loved her out of control, vulnerable, and suffering. I loved her because if your mother doesn't love you when you're puking all over her, it might be hard to find someone who will. Part of growing up is taking that "you're puking all over me, but I still love you" feeling that someone gave you as a child, offering it to yourself as an adult, and being able to offer it to your child.

My twenty-three-year-old now lives in Sweden. She plunges into situations I could only tiptoe around. But with the first wave of queasiness, the first rush of nausea, she is dialing my number. At first I always get a little anxious in my long-distance helplessness and then annoyed to be reminded of it. "What do you expect me to do about it?" I want to say. But then I remember my mother and dismiss the phone bill. I know exactly what to do. "Poor baby," I tell her. "You poor baby."

Cease-Fire Agreements

Even fractious relationships sometimes allow for time-outs when things are harder than usual, for whatever reason. It is possible for a mother to be her daughter's greatest comfort and greatest irritant at the same time. Some mothers who were not particularly nurturing or close to their daughters "redeem" themselves with a grandchild. Skipping a generation appears to be of great benefit in many family relationships. However, when the daughter has been a "parent" to her mother, this transition can become quite strained. The new mother has a finite amount of energy and investment, and the person in the most immediate need is the baby. Mothers who have always felt competitive with their daughters can throw down the gauntlet, yelling the child-rearing equivalent of "Let the games begin!" They can revel in the ways in which they feel superior to their temporarily vulnerable daughters.

Some mothers are well intentioned when they visit after the birth to help out. There is, however, a broad range of what can actually be construed as helping. Mothers and daughters who have both been satisfied with a calm, somewhat emotionally distant relationship may be quite happy when the mother arrives after the delivery and takes care of "business"—cooking, cleaning, answering the phone, and helping with the baby. There are no deep talks about the nature of motherhood or reminiscences of the past. If both women are satisfied with this, even though "experts" might say there's not much of an empathic connection there, they are in sync with each other. Contrast that with the mother who keeps foisting things on her daughter that she doesn't want. It could be advice: "It's getting cold; you need to put on your bathrobe," or "Hold her up a little higher when she's nursing; she's not getting enough." It could be wearing down the bedroom carpet by compulsive vacuuming, or trying to force-feed her soup. Or, because her daughter is basically a sitting duck, for at least a few days or weeks, it could be the perfect time to tell her things she may never have confided before—about her own motherhood, about her marriage, or about her mother.

When we say something is "natural," we often assume it should be easy. A hurricane is just as natural as a sunset, but it's a lot harder to take. Even when we say that a particular ability "comes naturally" to someone, exercising and developing that ability is a matter of choice, determination, discipline, and experience. It's not at all automatic. A mother who empathizes with her daughter helps to refocus reality for her by letting her know that whatever difficulty she's having is probably fairly common, not the single exception. There's a great moment in Julia Alvarez's *How the Garcia Girls Lost Their Accents* when Yolanda, in a series of dreams, wakes up, terrified that she has seen the ghost of a mother cat, from whom she stole a kitten. Her mother tries, albeit unsuccessfully, to normalize her daughter's terrifyingly real visions. " 'A phase,' Mami said, worried. 'A perfectly normal nightmare phase.' "

A new mother with a screaming infant may feel first relieved but then incompetent when her mother is able to calm the baby. Her mother can let her success with the baby stand as evidence of her general maternal superiority, which leaves her daughter out in the cold. Or she can attribute it to some *action* she performed—jiggling, rocking, swaddling—something she *learned* from having babies herself that she can pass on to her daughter. In this scenario, the daughter doesn't need to suffer by comparison. Writer Sarah Bird, who had a real screamer on her hands, was demoralized about her inability to quiet her fussy newborn but, as she said, "perversely comforted by the fact that even my mom can't seem to calm him down." But her comfort is short-lived. She confesses her fears that she shouldn't have become a mother, and when her mother reassures her that she's doing fine, she feels even more alone. "I know what is in my heart and feel even more of a fraud that I could fool the person I'm closest to in the world."

Power Renegotiations

Sometimes we figure out who we are by bumping up against someone else. For the new mother, that person is often *her* mother. In some ways a mother has to dethrone her mother to be able to step into the crown herself. This doesn't necessarily involve banishment from the kingdom. It just means that like the British monarch, she has to be able to see herself as queen, and her mother as the queen mother. It's mostly a psychological exercise but very important in relationships in which mothers have continued to exert tremendous power over their adult daughters. For all the help women can give their daughters with new babies, there can also be tremendous friction, arising from the fact that mother and daughter see the world differently. For mothers and daughters who never reached a point in their relationship where they could comfortably "agree to disagree," the introduction of children can become a major battlefield. Many women admit that they feel a regressive pull back to their adolescence, childhood, or even toddlerhood, when the stakes in the mother-daughter shoot-out seem so high. I have heard my voice turn petulant in response to some simple piece of advice from my mother about my daughter. There are times when it's not even a bad idea, but I need to resist anyway. *I rebel, therefore I am.*

In her memoir, *Riding in Cars with Boys,* Beverly Donofrio describes a wonderful interaction that occurred when she was seventeen, two months after she brought her son home from the hospital. I've heard this kind of exchange between *grown* women. After the six-week period her mother had deemed necessary for the baby to remain in the house, Beverly was extremely restless and decided to take the baby out to the library. Her mother forbade her to go, becoming increasingly forceful until she backed herself into a corner. "You can't take him," she told Beverly, "and that's the end of it." Beverly then drew a new boundary in the sand, one that redefined her identity and her mother's and altered their relationship. "He's my baby," she declared, wrapped him up warmly, and went to the library. "I checked out *David Cop-*

perfield," she recalls with satisfaction, "and when I returned, my mother had lost her stand as big chief the baby expert."

DAUGHTERS' EMPATHY WITH MOTHERS

Women are often flooded with thoughts and questions about their own mothers at this time. As a new mother rocks her inconsolable daughter in the middle of the night, she wonders, "Did my mother go through this with me?" In those moments when all is righter with the world than it's ever been, and she and her baby share a gaze that surpasses any possible dollar value, she tries to remember, "Were my mother and I like this once?" "If we weren't, why not?" "If we were, what happened to us?" It's amazing how little most women know about their mother's postpartum experiences.

At some point a woman realizes that the ambivalence she feels in her relationship with her mother isn't just some big fluke that happened to strike the two of them. She understands, often with some horror, "Maybe this sweet angel suckling contentedly at my breast and bathing me in pure love is going to think I'm a moron/bitch/hypocrite!" Just when she is putting so much energy into becoming a good mother, she realizes that her daughter may never see her that way. Her daughter isn't even going to *remember* any of what she's doing during infancy. Then it occurs to her that *her* mother probably thought the same thing as she contemplated *her* motherhood experiences. What did her mother think and feel when she learned she had a daughter? What kind of support did she get? Did she breast-feed? For how long? How did becoming a mother change her relationship with her husband? Did her mother like her new role? If not, what did she dislike? What did she like? What did she see in her daughter then that she still sees today? What would her mother have done differently?

Many fruitful conversations with mothers, aunts, grandmothers, and sisters emerge from these questions, providing a springboard for building or rebuilding the empathic bond between mother and daughter. It always amazes me how much older women emphasize the positive aspects of having a new baby, and deemphasize or ignore the negative aspects. We often have the idea that talking about something bad increases the likelihood that it will actually happen. If we talk to kids about sex, they'll start fornicating in homeroom. If we ask someone who appears depressed whether she's considered killing herself, we'll give her the idea. And if mothers tell their daughters about their run-ins with the baby blues or serious and long-lasting postpartum depressions, they'll be responsible for inducing them. In the end, what daughters want from their mothers in situations like these is honesty. Because of their vulnerability, perhaps the sharp edges of truth could be smoothed a bit. "I felt so bad after I had you that I didn't get dressed for three months," or "Yes, sometimes I hated you so much I fantasized about smothering you with a pillow," might lose a bit of their honest brutality with, "Oh, you should have seen me. There were a lot of days I didn't have time to get dressed." Or, "Honey, lots of women have scary thoughts about their babies. Believe me, it comes from being absolutely exhausted and totally overwhelmed."

HENRI MATISSE SAVED MY LIFE

I just opened a birthday card from my daughter. It was a print of the Matisse cutouts, and it made me cry. My daughter doesn't remember exactly; it was twenty-three years ago. But she's the only one I've ever told about how Henri Matisse saved my life. The first year of motherhood was hard on me. There's no clever way to say it. I was not a natural. When I was pregnant, I truly thought that I had timed things perfectly. I'd passed my Ph.D. comprehensives a few weeks before my due date, and I planned to work on my dissertation while the baby slept. This turned out to be the most delusional thought I've ever had. After only a few weeks, I was way past tired, living in a *zone* where it's hard to know the difference between exhausted, sick, and crazy. No longer pregnant, my body still didn't feel like mine. It was heavy and slow. My hair was weird and my feet were too big.

In the space of weeks, I'd gone from the intellectual intensity of a rigorous doctoral program to the constant company of someone who cried a lot and never said a word. My husband was at work and my friends were in graduate school or jobs. My mother still had three kids at home. I didn't know anyone with a new baby. What I felt went way beyond lonely. I'd never been in such close contact with anyone for so long and felt so totally alone.

I longed for the kind of natural community of women my mother had when she was my age. Everyone had babies at the same time, and they congregated at one house almost every day, while their children raised hell in the yard or basement. A mother who was ready to lose it could pass her kids off to someone else for a few hours. If one mother got sick, another would drive over, pack up her kids in the already crowded station wagon, and bring them home for the night. I loved that system as a kid. It was women's built-in backup plan. Not only could other mothers take care of you, they could also yell at you. Even now, I take pleasure in the number of friends' and siblings' children to whom I feel closest, based solely on the ease with which I can yell at them. When people quote the line about it taking a village to raise a child, I always think of the women in my growing-up neighborhood and think that it also takes a village to raise a mother.

At three months my daughter was thriving, and I was withering. I stopped wearing a watch because time had become irrelevant. Sometimes I fantasized about designing a whacked-out abstract clock that would speed up, then slow down at random intervals to approximate the way time passes for mothers with infants. Never having been particularly fussy about how I appeared in public, I was used to waking up, throwing on clothes, hopping in the car, and swallowing my first gulp of diet Coke in a span of ten minutes. But with a baby, it took more than ten minutes to get one eye open. All of a sudden, making it to the car was this huge deal, and usually hardly worth the effort.

Long before she got into her two-year-old habit of changing outfits twenty times a day, she had me doing it for her. Her timing was almost malicious. No sooner would I have her buttoned up in some little dress, with white tights, and the little bows on her tiny white shoes tied, than the sounds of abdominal thunder signaled impending disaster. Her productivity always demanded a complete change of clothing (including shoes). She could wear two completely different outfits before she was lifted off the changing table. Ten minutes later the other end would explode, and although baby puke could usually be wiped off, the smell was bound to be there till the next washing. If I'd just erupted from both ends, the last thing I'd want is a meal. But not her. To her, I was a baby drive-thru, open 24/7. A human Big Gulp dispenser.

In retrospect I see that I was suffering from more than the general displacement most new mothers feel. It was clearly a postpartum depression, but I never admitted it to myself or anyone else. I was determined to recover from feeling like I'd made the biggest mistake of my life. My baby and I had to get to know and like each other. The way to do this, I thought, would be to share pleasurable activities together. But this assumes that there actually *are* activities that are mutually attractive to a gassy three-month-old and her twenty-five-year-old depressed mother.

I'd always loved the National Gallery of Art, particularly the newer East Wing. It had generous open spaces, startling sunlight, and huge Calder mobiles I thought she might like. It was hard to be depressed in the East Wing. I would take the baby there. We would have a real outing. I'd also heard it was never too early to expose a child to the arts. Three months was pushing it, but I needed a reason to get dressed, leave the house, and visit a place from my former life, where I had felt like a normal, happy person. We'd take in some of the exhibits and then have lunch at one of the tables lining the magnificent glass-enclosed cascade in the cafeteria. She would love the water.

Not only did she *not* love the water, she didn't like a single thing about the entire place. The light I loved was too sharp for her. She squinted and whined. She hated being in the Snugli, so I took her out, leaving only one arm to hold the collapsible stroller, baby bag, and purse. She was totally off schedule and demanded to be fed. When your kid screams in a public place, time slows down, the noise is magnified by ten, and everything seems impossibly urgent. These are always the times it takes forever to find a bathroom or an exit. The stress of a screaming child can make you stupid.

This was before the time when anyone gave a damn about nursing mothers, so the ladies' room was not particularly inviting. I sat on the cold tile floor and nursed her, surrounded by all of her junk, trying to move out of the way as normal, unencumbered women attempted to pass. An older woman admired her but advised me that it was too early to have my daughter out in a public place. I didn't know if she was speaking on behalf of my child or the general public, but I felt terrible either way.

I pulled "ourselves" together and ventured back to the exhibits. Maybe she'd already been ruined by television, because she definitely wasn't into art. She was squirmy and working up to what would definitely become a major outburst. It took everything I had not to cry out loud. I had to keep wiping my eyes, because they were stinging with tears. I used a baby wipe on my runny nose. I tried to put her in her stroller. She screamed. I tried to put her in the Snugli. She screamed. I gathered up everything and, with the most tenuous hold, headed out, dreading the long stairs. Around a corner I spotted an elevator and pushed a button without even determining its destination.

When it stopped, I stepped out into a much quieter hallway. The lighting was dimmer. The first entryway opened without fanfare into the Matisse cutouts exhibit. In his old age, Henri Matisse suffered from duodenal cancer that restricted him to a wheelchair for years. Painting the way he was used to, with similar results, became difficult. But he couldn't let go. He began new projects. Big, bold, abstract, primary-color cutouts of flowers, hearts, people, and all kinds of forms and designs. The work must have been tremendously painstaking. I wondered if bending over the cutouts served as a constant reminder of his limits and losses. Or, did the cutouts somehow liberate him from being preoccupied with his reversals? The wheelchair must have made placing the huge cutouts so hard. How did he do it?

I had seen the cutouts once before. I loved their vibrance, their fluidity, the relatedness of one to another. I wanted to go in, but the baby's edginess was escalating, so I decided to cut my losses and just find the damn exit. As I passed the entry, with her slung over my shoulder, she spotted the cutouts and immediately stopped crying. It wasn't just the noise that stopped. Her usually tense body relaxed against me. Her little head popped up, as she craned her neck for a better view.

"Want to go in?" I asked, as I made my way into the large room, empty except for a single guard. All four white walls were lined with cutouts. A rope prevented touching, but it was possible to get quite close. We made our way slowly around the room. I pointed at things, named colors. Her gaze was as intense as I'd ever seen it. She strained her body toward the ones she particularly liked. When her little arms and legs fluttered, I knew to linger longer. Halfway around the room, I realized we were having a time—a good time—together.

The guard smiled and said, "Looks like you two are art lovers." He said, "You two," meaning "us." Before then, I hadn't really thought of the combination of my baby and me as "us." I thought we were a "unit." I loved her. I took care of her. But I didn't identify with her. I didn't share things with her. She was there to have needs, and I was there to fill them. But the man said "you two" like we were a pair, companions, a couple of girls out for the day. I told the guard he was right. We two were art lovers. Then, because no one else was around, we chatted about babies, their terrible sleep habits, and the fact that this was our first real "outing." "Looks like you picked the right place." "Yeah," I answered, "looks like we did."

I slung all the stuff over my shoulders, got my sleepy baby back in the Snugli, and finally found the exit. Immediately, I pulled out my sunglasses, because I was sure I was going to cry, and this time I wasn't going to stop myself. The tears I couldn't catch with my hands landed on her little bald head as she slept against my body. The tears were part loneliness and fatigue, part confusion, part fear and frustration. They were the kind of tears that have been there so long, you feel them in your throat and chest when they finally come. But they were also tears of relief and, quite possibly, joy. My daughter and I . . . just the sound of it . . . we went to a museum together, and yes, it was something of a disaster. But at the last moment, it was redeemed by a man who took the restrictions life handed him and still made big, bold things. He dared to go in a completely different direction from that of his earlier work. The cutouts were more than stand-ins, poor substitutes for an earlier brilliance. One small admirer had seen other paintings that day. They did nothing for her. But Matisse totally captivated her with the cutouts. Through her reaction to his work, I experienced the pleasure—which would be repeated thousands of times over the next twenty-three years—of watching my child fall in love with something I loved. Ultimately she would introduce me to new things and would know the joy of being "on the money" about my pleasure.

I wish there had been a fairy godmother that day, or maybe just an older docent, who would have said, "Honey, the poop and the puke, the gas, the shrill screaming during the arsenic hours, the body lost to you, the self you think is gone, it will all get better. Matisse is just the beginning with this kid. I promise. There is so much to come." But I probably wouldn't have believed it. I wish I had known Matisse's own words, which so perfectly described my situation: "In art, truth and reality begin when one no longer understands what one is doing or what one knows, and when there remains an energy that is all the stronger for being constrained, controlled and compressed."

For another few months, our timing was still off. I was still depressed. My dissertation wasn't getting done. I was lonely. But my daughter and I—those incredible words—had visited a museum. My daughter and I loved Henri Matisse. And most important, my daughter and I were eventually going to be all right.

That's why I cried over my birthday card today.

Sometimes my daughter understands without knowing.

That's why I cry sometimes, still.

FIVE

Childhood: Learning the Language of Feeling; "I Can, Therefore I Am"

> Intuition is the guardian of childhood.
>
> MAXINE CLAIR,
> *Rattlebone*

THE DEVELOPMENTAL TASKS OF CHILDHOOD

During childhood girls are becoming more and more proficient in the use of language. They begin to be able to differentiate and label the emotions they feel and those they observe in other people. They are learning how to modulate these feelings, particularly in their expression, and they are coming up against many social expectations. Relationships with adults and peers present new opportunities for learning and feedback. A girl and her mother must develop a way of relating to each other that takes into account their differences in temperament, comfort with emotional intensity, and such things as conversational styles. The roles that they fulfill for each other will become clearer over time. Childhood is also a time when really rotten things can happen, from physical and sexual abuse, to the death of a parent, to family estrangements. There is no doubt that these events will impact the child's present and future. However, there are things that will mediate how *much* a child's emotional development may be compromised. For example, when a girl confides an accusation of sexual abuse to her mother, and her mother believes and supports her in dealing with it, the girl's ultimate risk for many of the pervasive adult consequences of child abuse can be mitigated.

With a talking, feeling, doing child, a mother has more to contend with than she did with basic baby maintenance. For many women this is a terrific thing; for others it isn't. Being the repository of love, anger, frustration, and confusion can be quite taxing, particularly if the mother has little experience of that from her own childhood. A willful two-year-old digging in her heels against her mother on some point is, in some ways, a good thing. The child is experiencing her self. She is differentiating that self from her mother's self. The bad news is that she's inflicting that self on her mother. A mother of more than one child must deal with the often impossible task of being in sync with very different children at the same time. Becoming comfortable with sometimes being perceived as the mean mother, the unobservant mother, or the distracted mother is one route to sanity maintenance.

MANAGING BIG FEELINGS

Six-year-old Anna was referred for psychotherapy because she was having enormous temper tantrums at home. She had difficulty falling and staying asleep. The range of foods she ate was very limited. Her clothes irritated her. Like the insomniac princess pestered by the pea, she was acutely sensitive, even to minor changes in her environment. Not surprisingly, this child also had significant allergies, which further impinged upon her life. After an initial meeting with her parents, I expected Anna to be hell on wheels at her first appointment. In my office, however, she was somber, reserved, and cooperative. Unlike many kids her age, Anna seemed to have some insight into the reasons for her referral, but she had difficulty translating her ideas into words. This is not at all unusual with bright children, who may precociously understand something before they can fully express it in language. As Anna became more frustrated, I could see her distress simmering. Finally, she gave up and announced with frustration, "I just don't know how to tell it." I assured her that it was okay. But she couldn't let it go. I began to show her around my office and explain the toys, games, and rules, when she blurted out, "Dr. Manning, the problem is I've got all these big feelings, but I'm just a *little* girl!"

While Anna's difficulties fell in the more extreme category, *all* little kids have to figure out how to deal with their big feelings. The ability to regulate our selves and our emotions begins in infancy and increases from there. To know what you're feeling, understand how it affects your behavior, and have some influence over its expression is a lifetime assignment. Fortunately it is advanced greatly by the maturation of cognitive skills. Before you can be empathic to someone, you need to know how to "decode" the signals they give out. When a person frowns in a certain way, does that mean she is sick, hurt, tired, or mad? A young child who sees her mother crying assumes, from her own experience, that she is probably physically hurt. As she searches her mother for boo-boos, she might hear, "Mommy doesn't have a boo-boo. Mommy's sad." The continual refinement of the connection between emotion and language occurs in the hundreds of thousands of small interactions between mothers and daughters.

INCREASING A MOTHER'S PERSPECTIVES

A mother who can reconstruct the "feeling" part of her childhood has more tools to work with than one who can't. These aren't the memories of her fourth Christmas, or her first baby tooth falling out. They are the qualitative memories of *what it was like to be a little girl*. It has absolutely nothing to do with getting in touch with one's inner child, a phrase that is essentially meaningless. It has to do with the ability to approximate the unique perspective of childhood.

During my training I worked in a therapeutic nursery school for emotionally disturbed children. The clinical supervisor suggested that my classmates and I try to experience the world from a child's vantage point, forcing us to experience a different perspective. Unlike poor Alice, who had to alternate "Drink Me" bottles until she became the right size for her new surroundings, most of us just had to observe the world from our knees or lower to get a good picture of a three-year-old's world. From that vantage point, stairs became individual Mount Everests, each step a small act of faith. The toilet seat suited perfectly to grown-ups became high, wide, and deep. And if you stop to think about it, the concept of being flushed is a scary thought for a little girl, who has to deal with all of this *and* urinate in the right place. It was also clear how much time babies and young children have to spend looking up if they are going to have meaningful human contact. Children's stories and movies in which size and perspective shift dramatically are very popular, probably for this reason. Somehow, the "littles" struggle to gain advantage over the "bigs." From *The Borrowers* to *Honey, I Blew Up the Kids,* children are delighted with stories in which the perspective of size shifts—in their favor. On your knees, it was easier to remember: you had fears and trembling uncertainties. Sometimes you felt that you were the only child not let in on some big secret that was known to the rest of the world. You felt small, helpless, and vulnerable. There was so much you didn't understand. And this was in a *good* childhood. If a mother is unable to get some access to her *own* childhood emotions, she will have more difficulty being empathic with her daughter.

Mothers' experiences don't have to be the same as their daughters' to enable them to be empathic. A mother who was outgoing and instantly popular in school initially can have trouble recognizing that socializing can be difficult for many girls. If she has a daughter who happens to be shy and unpopular, she may not have a clue as to what her child feels. She can, however, reach back to something else in childhood that didn't come easily to her, and build a bridge to her daughter with that. A mother who was academically indifferent in school laughs off her high-achieving daughter's tears over a B on a spelling test. But before laughing it off and telling her daughter to "chill out," she can look for a source of similar pain in her own adolescence and try to make a connection through that.

Daughters have no need to know the specific details of these events in their mothers' lives. When a mother says things like "Well, I know just how you're feeling, because once I didn't get invited to a birthday party and I cried all night," as if that should take care of it, the daughter, who may have been excluded from the last ten parties, may give her mother one of those "What planet did you come from?" looks and find absolutely no comfort in her mother's intimate disclosure. It is the work of the mother to see if she can step into her daughter's shoes before she dismisses her sorrow or joy, anger or pride as inconsequential. No mother can be empathic to her daughter 100 percent of the time. Mothers have other children with similar needs. They have jobs. They have lives. And even if it was humanly possible, daughters benefit from learning emotional flexibility and resourcefulness when they find gaps between themselves and their mothers. From an early age, it's good for girls to diversify at least a bit of their emotional investment. Part of growing up is learning who will be empathic to you in what circumstances. Many girls, for example, find that their fathers, grandmothers, aunts, and older sisters can sometimes be more sympathetic in certain situations than their mothers. Sometimes mothers are most attuned to their daughters when they realize that they are not and should not be the only source of empathy in their children's lives, and encourage them to branch out.

A PIECE OF CAKE: TAKING THE ROMANCE OUT OF CHILDHOOD

Many people look back on childhood as a piece of cake compared with adulthood. They idealize it as a time when little was expected of them, and much given. On Mother's and Father's Days, my siblings and I used to demand to know the date of "Children's Day." My parents always gave the same answer: *"Every day is children's day."* But unless you grew up on the good ship *Lollipop,* your childhood had challenges, pain, and obstacles to overcome.

From early childhood, girls begin to define themselves by what they can do. Children are expected to master so many different types of skills within specific windows of time. Think how far a little girl has come just to be able to put on a sock. There's the fine motor control needed to open the sock, then learning which end is for the heel and which end is for the toe. She then must be able to get in a stable position so that she can pull the sock on without falling over. Balance is increasing with age, but in so many activities falling remains a definite probability. Then the shoe. Making the distinctions between right and left. Then there's the fastening: Velcro, buckles, and the inevitable shoelaces all require more fine motor control, as well as mastery of the sequence steps so things turn out all right. There is tremendous variability in the level of frustration kids can tolerate before breaking down. Some girls are extremely invested in mastering the many "big girl" possibilities in their worlds. Other girls appear content to let their mothers continue tying their shoes till they leave for college. Still other girls may develop the determination before the fine motor control and need support waiting for the catch-up.

But shoes and socks are a tiny fraction of it. A little girl has to learn how to sustain herself for periods of time without her mother or father. She has to deal with the new baby-sitter, preschool teacher, other girls' mothers. She is expected to gain more and more control over her body. She must become increasingly attentive to internal body cues, such as the need to urinate. Girls are learning to dress themselves and discovering what they like. Some decide they like one, and only one, outfit, often creating major uproars when it disappears into the washing machine or is banished for a time-out in the closet. It can also be very hard for a little girl to understand why a frilly pink party dress that her cousin gave her (that her mother hates) wouldn't be great to wear to preschool with her Barbie high heels and the rhinestone tiara from her grandma. From her position, Mom's decisions are incredibly arbitrary and blind to beauty. From the ages of three to five girls often go through periods of wanting to change their clothes frequently, choosing one incredibly awful combination after the next. There can be major struggles during this time for girls who suddenly want to wear dresses all the time when it is much more practical for them to wear pants. Then some friend or aunt who has no experience with children gives her "cute" things like nail polish and makeup. The daughter is then launched into the "Junior Miss" phase of development, overdosing on traditional femininity until it becomes clear that Barbie shoes are nice, but she can't really run in them. The tiara gets kind of heavy after a while and messes up her hair. And a dress and tights seriously limit her fun on the monkey bars and slides.

Because so many mothers have been sensitized to the problems associated with traditional female stereotypes, they are often alarmed at this turn of events and have very little desire to give their daughters what they want: admiration of their beauty and assistance with it. A mother can empathize with her daughter in her wish to be pretty and experiment with looks. Her participation in some of the girl's dress-up games will not condemn her daughter to a life of cheap perfume, glitter nails, and plastic high heels. The strategy of trying to convince a girl that what she says she wants isn't what she *really* wants is going to fail as badly at four as it will at sixteen.

MOVING IN WIDER CIRCLES

Between the ages three and five, a child takes on a more public life. Now there are places she goes that her mother doesn't. She has experiences that she can choose to share or not. She is now measured by different people with different standards. Her mother may think she's swell, but that means nothing if she annoys the hell out of every little girl she plays with. When she entrusts her daughter to the care of others, a mother can feel a good bit of insecurity about judgments of how she's done so far. A parent's basic nightmare in this regard was depicted in a recent *New Yorker* cartoon that featured two earnest parents sitting in those little kid chairs preparing to hear what the new teacher thinks of their little darling. The teacher cuts right to the chase. "Your daughter," she says solemnly, "is a pain in the ass."

Not making it with any peers or at school, even if everything is going beautifully at home, can be a concern. We know that a girl's self-confidence is partially related to her ability to form and maintain stable, satisfying friendships. Having a mutual best friend, for example, is a "protection" against being victimized by one's peers, a situation that happens all too often, usually out of a parent's view. Mothers can facilitate getting two girls together, but they can't make them enjoy playing together. In these situations it's not enough to sympathize with a daughter who already feels like an outcast.

Mothers of socially skilled girls "coach" their daughters in the art of friendship. Coaching involves giving guidance about peer relationships. "Maybe it would be better if you gave Amanda a little more notice when you invite her over." "Tell Susan that you like to play with her but you want her to help you clean up." "Find something that you both like to do." "Show her that you're interested in what *she* has to say, before telling all of your stuff." Mothers coach by giving feedback. To a daughter crying over the abrupt departure of a friend following a disagreement, a mother might say, "Just picking up your game and walking away doesn't usually solve anything. Maybe that's why she called you a quitter." The tone can be gentle or judgmental and, more than the actual words, will determine the way the guidance is received. To engage a child in trying to comprehend how some social situation self-destructed, the daughter and mother have to "rewind" the events, pinpointing the trouble spots and then spinning several scenarios in which things may have turned out differently.

Certain combinations are combustible no matter how deftly they're handled. Many women learn early to bang their heads against the relationship wall, overestimating their power to change another person or relationship, then blaming themselves when it doesn't go well. It's never too early to learn when to fold up one's tent or Barbie Dream House and go home. It can be very painful for a mother who felt like an outsider in childhood to see her daughter experiencing the same thing. Her anxiety can easily spill over, resulting in a daughter's sense that she has failed her mother, as well as the relationship.

STICKS AND STONES: TAKING IT ON THE CHIN

One of the hardest things for a parent to watch is the social rejection or even persistent teasing of her daughter. Let's face it. "Sticks and stones may break my bones, but names will never hurt me" is one of the most amazingly disingenuous pieces of parental propaganda to persist over time. A consistent theme in many of the multiple shootings at schools was the perpetrator's sense of being verbally tormented by his peers. For girls too names can be as bad as, if not worse than, sticks and stones. Daughters have to learn to deal with names throughout their lives. Being called "baby" at the age of five feels awful. Being called "baby" at twenty-five by a bunch of leering strangers is no picnic either. Mothers can say things like "Well, just find some new friends," a statement that belongs in the "Just say no to drugs" junk pile of useless inspiration. Then there's "Honey, if you don't stand up for yourself and let them know you don't like it, they're going to keep doing it," a statement that's probably true but not particularly useful in helping the child form friendships. The empathic response is not necessarily the "all-feeling" one. Girls can feel hurt or sad or bad and still act. Painful feelings are no reason to avoid or shut down.

Dealing with teasing is tough because letting people know you really don't like it is the equivalent of an engraved invitation to them to continue. Flirting a bit with teasing, giving a bit of it right back, is a complicated skill but one that girls learn over time. It's especially important, since children can be incredibly cruel to one another in different ways. Boys usually face cruelty in terms of physical consequences to themselves or their property; girls are more often victims of relational cruelty. Relational victimization is less obvious than physical victimization. It occurs in whispers, in passed notes, in quiet but awful pranks, in exclusion. Often the victimized girl feels lonely and socially anxious. She's also likely to become more submissive than her peers. She is at risk for a number of adjustment problems, including impulsivity and poor self-control.

The evidence is fairly clear that girls see themselves, and are seen by others, as more empathic than boys. A girl's empathy is strongly related to her mother's behavior toward her. Empathic girls have mothers who are able to take the perspectives of other people ("It must be sad for her to move away") and who use problem solving and discussion when their daughters are distressed or anxious ("Let's try to think about what would make it better between you and Rachel," "Sometimes when I'm nervous, I take really deep breaths and it calms me down a little"). They reinforce sympathetic expressions and behavior in their daughters ("You were very generous with your little sister when you let her use your markers") and restrict their displays of hurtful negative emotion ("You can tell your sister you're mad at her, but you can't call her ugly"). They rely less on power plays ("You will sit in that chair and eat every bite and you won't get up until you do") and more on reciprocity in discipline ("This eating thing is getting to be a real problem. I can't understand it unless you tell me what's going on"). Ratings of mothers' empathy when their children were only five years old predicted their *children's* empathy at age thirty-one. Mothers who were tolerant of the expectable dependent behavior in their five-year-olds, who effectively inhibited their children's aggression, and who were satisfied with the role of mother were more likely to raise kids who became empathic adults.

MOTHERS' EMPATHY WITH DAUGHTERS
Reciprocity Begins at Home

In childhood, a daughter learns best about empathy when she is on the receiving end of it with her mother. One of the clearest lessons I learned as a therapist is that when it comes to empathy, it's often very hard to give what you never got. Contrary to some stereotypes, girls aren't born completely outfitted with empathy. Certainly, there are biological factors that can influence how easy or difficult it is for her to make emotional connections to people, but empathy has to be seen and felt before it can be learned.

A girl has numerous opportunities to watch her mother interact with other people, then model that behavior in other settings. As her mother displays her emotional range, her daughter tries to understand what precipitates and transforms each emotion. Mothers vary tremendously in how much they display or disclose their feelings to their young girls. When the mother makes statements that begin with "I feel," "I think," "I wonder," and "When I was your age I," she is inviting her daughter into her world. Inviting a daughter into your emotional life doesn't mean she's welcome in every room of the house. In fact, if the mother is totally open, it's probably better for the child to wait outside a bit longer. It may be authentic to say, "I hate your father. I wish he was dead," but it's the difference between tossing the daughter a ball and hurling her a boulder.

Making the Passive Active

During the play of young girls who take on the role of mommy, doctor, or teacher—all jobs that require the exercise of authority with considerable empathy—children often make the passive active. They transform the "one down" position in which they usually find themselves into one in which a doll, a smaller sibling, or a generous therapist becomes the child and they become the adult. One of the staples of any child psychotherapy room is a doctor's kit, with the full complement of instruments—from stethoscopes and blood-pressure cuffs, to the dreaded shots. You can tell a lot about how a child has *experienced* a visit to the doctor when you watch her *become* the doctor and let the doll become *her*. Occasionally what you see will be an enactment of an actual event. But in children's play, it's more likely that what you see will be the merging of images from the event itself with the way the child *experienced* the event, which can be very different. A mixture of helplessness, fear, and rage often kicks into action the minute the child gets her hands on the toy "shot." Dolls get smacked around a good bit and receive brutal shots in all kinds of places.

As a therapist, I often play the voice of the doll who echoes what the child probably felt at the time. When the doll voice says, "Oh, no, I'm scared. What are you going to do with that thing? No, no shots. No!" (I really ham it up), the girl's response as "doctor" is always interesting. It may be an empathic response ("Don't worry, baby, it will be over before you know it. Here, squeeze my hand really tight") or a factual one ("If you don't get the shot, you could get very sick"). There's the punitive ("Be quiet and stop crying. Do you want even more shots?") or the comparative ("Do you want people to think you're a baby? I didn't hear any other kids crying"). No responsible mother watches her daughter lose it at the prospect of a booster shot and decides, "Well, maybe you don't need it after all. Let's just go home." Empathy is not the same thing as keeping children comfortable. It doesn't mean giving in to children's distress. At issue in empathy development is "How do I help my daughter get through this difficult thing?" With a shot, she will learn that repeated exposure doesn't kill her, even though she continues to hate it. Some of the most intensely painful scenes I've witnessed have been on pediatric oncology units where children have had no time to warm up to the many procedures. I've seen parents, already devastated by the child's diagnosis, crumble after having to hold down their screaming children as something is done that would be tough for a grown-up to take. When the child cries out, "Mommy!" it is a plea, a question, *and* an accusation.

An empathic approach is one that recognizes that yes, shots are hard for a second, and yes, most kids don't like them, but they still have to be done. Suggestions for coping, like counting to ten, imagining a scene, or thinking about a small reward, can give the child a chance to experiment with ways to keep herself together in stressful situations. The concepts of bravery and courage often get off to a confusing start in situations like these. Children often get the message that bravery and courage are the opposite of fear. When they're facing the sharp end of a needle or the meanest girl in class, fear is normal. It's the *reaction* to the fear that's important. Girls and boys are treated differently in this area, to the benefit of neither. A girl's fear is given more room for expression and so is accepted as a valid reason to avoid the object of her fear.

The good news is that a girl can admit she's afraid without the disapproval that boys get. The bad news is that she is often let off the hook too soon because of it. Expressions of fear—trembling, clinging, and crying—are just that, expressions. Girls need more help in "accepting" the fear, finding ways to meet it, and moving on. I'm not talking here about big-game hunting. I'm talking about a willingness to risk being wrong, in the minority, socially rejected, or seen as a junior ball buster. Being fearful is often seen as "consistent" with being female but dissonant with maleness. This dichotomy serves neither gender. Boys are discouraged subtly and directly from expressing their very normal fears. To be fearful is to be a "wuss," a "pussy," a "mama's boy." "Be a man!" some boys are told. We all know what that means. What does "Be a woman!" mean? It's amazing how many of the disparagements that males inflict upon one another have to do with resembling women. Girls don't miss those messages. And many mothers are at a loss to explain to their daughters why males say those things and why those accusations are as powerful now as they were twenty years ago. Fear alerts us to situations of high risk. To deny fear is to discount cues necessary for a child's safety and survival. It is an area in which gender expectations are suffocatingly powerful and interfere with a child's self-confidence and self-protection.

You Say "Potato": Tolerating Differences

In childhood, a girl becomes increasingly sophisticated in differentiating between her own feelings and those of other people. Mother and daughter begin to more openly acknowledge that they don't always have the same reactions to the same things. Babies and toddlers, whose identities are so tied up with their mothers, don't see themselves as separate players. This is obvious on a basic level, for example, with food preferences. A toddler who likes vanilla ice cream can't comprehend or accept the fact that it nauseates her mother. She will be confused when the mother turns down her generous offer of a bite. When a girl begins to see her mother as separate from herself, she comes to enjoy accumulating knowledge about how they are alike and different. "Mom's favorite color is blue, but mine is pink." "Mom gets Chicken McNuggets. I think Chicken McNuggets are nasty!" a three-year-old little girl leaned over and confided as I sat alone at McDonald's. She was so pleased with herself. When girls notice that they have different preferences from their mothers, it paves the way for the acceptance that they also can have different *feelings*. This is a long road, one that has no end. It is a lifetime challenge and constant source of friction in mother-daughter relationships. "How can you *possibly* feel so differently about this than I do?" "How can you be so mean just because I don't share your feelings?" "Why weren't *my* feelings ever factored into the equation?" "Did you ever stop and think how *I* might feel?" "You never felt like that *before*!"

Words for Feelings

Infants' communication is confined to crying, facial grimaces, and body movements. Mothers' comprehension of various physical and emotional states is at first limited to good/bad. As a mother becomes more skilled at interpretation, she can make differentiations *within* the "bad" category—hungry, sleepy, wet, or bored. In "good," she can see satiated, interested, or playful. Over time, infants begin to give clearer signals that refine the readout their mothers are getting. They try to connect their mothers' expressions to behaviors. "Mom's frowning and yawning equals low probability that she wants to play." Some of the best advice my daughter's pediatrician gave for dealing with my night-owl infant was to attend to my own behavior—avoid all "fun" signals such as smiling, eye contact, brandishing toys—reinforcing that nighttime feedings were "all business."

In childhood girls become more confident in their ever-expanding "feeling" vocabulary. As mothers use a greater diversity of emotional labels, girls become more skilled in using words that hit the emotional nail on the head to express or explain an experience. Megan, an extremely bright five-year-old I evaluated for possible placement in an accelerated academic program, told me about how much she hated kindergarten. When I said something about her being angry at having to color "within the lines" for an hour when she wanted to read a book, she corrected me immediately. "No, Dr. Manning, it's not *quite* angry . . . it's *actually* closer to frustrated and bored." It didn't take intelligence testing to realize this child needed more stimulation than what she got in a typical kindergarten classroom. Her use of modifiers like "quite" and "actually," not to mention her wish to find a word that combined the feelings of frustration and boredom, was evidence of precocious verbal skills.

Emotional labels are like crayons. Little kids get the big ones, but only a few—basically the primary colors, plus black and white. They know they're headed for the big leagues with the double-decker Crayola box—the one with twenty-four. Then there's the major leap to sixty-four—three long rows, on three levels, with a built-in crayon sharpener. Oh, the beautiful order of it! A place for everything and everything in its place. (You can tell a lot about a kid by her investment in preserving that order over time.) Now primary colors just aren't enough. Hues, hints, and shades enable the young artist to more richly express her ideas. There's no such thing as "red" anymore. There's violet red, scarlet, red violet, wild strawberry, magenta.

"No, Gracie, that's *not* purple," my five-year-old niece, Tori, says insistently. "It's *lilac*." Gracie, at three, spends a great deal of her day naming, reciting, singing, and counting. She is proud of her progress, sure in her knowledge and unappreciative of her sister's input. As much as Gracie wants to please Tori, she also knows what she knows and is not about to give it up. This is the stuff of sibling squabbles, one of the many things that can transform a perfectly harmonious coloring moment into a pitched battle in which no one can possibly win. Tori is correct for a five-year-old. Gracie is correct for a three-year-old. When my sister intervenes with her judgment that they're both right, Tori has no respect for her mother's relativism. There *is* a right answer, she has it, and she's going into meltdown if it is not acknowledged immediately. Can a time-out be far behind?

Which Messengers Should Be Killed?

One of the best places to explore portrayals of daughters and mothers is in popular literature aimed at girls. There are many fairy tales in which a kind and pretty young woman—usually tormented by a totally unsympathetic older woman—is rescued by a prince or other male "good guy." The message is that good things happen to good girls—girls who are beautiful, sweet, and passive. Good girls are good daughters. They do what they're told. Their bravery is more in their stoicism than their assertiveness or risk taking. In many tales daughters must be isolated to keep them safe, especially from sex.

Then, in some unguarded moment, they prick their fingers on roses and bite into apples, and years of protection go down the drain. As popular as these fairy tales have remained, reinforced by their mass distribution by Disney, there is a parallel body of literature in which the conflicts between good daughter/good girl and real girl are the stuff of bestsellers. The young heroines in many of these well-loved books are simultaneously good daughters *and* real girls. Madeline, Eloise, Pippi Longstocking, Anne of Green Gables, and *Little Women*'s Jo are plucky, feisty, and unabashedly imperfect. They speak their minds, even when it gets them in hot water. A real girl is rich in imagination. She's a girl who makes mistakes, occasionally hurts people and herself. She gets mad and is committed (often a bit rigidly) to the absolute fairness of things. She is openly competitive with boys. These girls don't have the stereotyped beauty of their fairy-tale counterparts. They look fine, but their appearance neither promotes nor constrains them.

When a mother can accept mixed feelings about herself, she is better able to allow her child to be both "real girl" and "good daughter." As a kid, when I did really "bad things" (intentional cruelty to siblings, lying, stealing) and clearly made my mother mad, I often asked for the reassurance that I hadn't landed myself in the Jeffrey Dahmer ballpark. My mother always answered, "I love you and I like you. Nothing you can ever do will ever stop me from loving you, but right now I don't like you very much." On one hand, it was a relief to know that I wasn't cast forever into the cold night. At the same time, I wasn't exactly warming my hands by the fire either.

What Can I Do, and Where?

Mika, a seven-year-old, comes home from school with a note from her teacher that must be signed and returned the next day. She is quaking in anger and fear. There was a dispute in the classroom that day. While the teacher was out of the room for several minutes, two boys took their dusty, dirty, disgusting shoes and made footprints on the backpacks and book bags of several girls *on purpose*. The girls got into a yelling match with the unapologetic perpetrators. As the teacher walked in, it was Mika and her friend who were making all the noise. Despite their protestations about being provoked, they, not the boys, had to stay in during recess. It could have stopped there, but Mika, who was very much into justice, insisted loudly, "It wasn't our fault." When the teacher announced that the discussion was over, Mika, worked up over the boys' transgressions *and* the usually nice teacher's bad call, reached her breaking point. She burst into angry tears and sputtered loudly, "It's not fair! You're not being fair!" The teacher then increased Mika's punishment to no recess in the afternoon, at which point Mika yelled, "I hate you! I hate you!" Hence, the note sent home. A mother whose daughter comes home from school with a note describing these circumstances can respond in a number of ways.

Teaching Moments   A mother can try to deal with the behaviors that got her daughter into trouble, particularly if the girl's actions really *shouldn't* occur in a school setting. She tries to support a school setting that she knows to be very fair, *most of the time* (if this is true), and tries not to undermine the teacher. Even so, sometimes teachers make mistakes, just like parents, and her daughter has to learn to cope with them. It's so easy for a parent to be seduced by the blow-by-blow descriptions of "he said, she said" that the emotional part can be easily missed. An empathic mother can comfort her daughter without endorsing her course of action. But if she's going to take it to the level of a "teaching moment," she needs to address her daughter's *emotional* reaction, as well as her actions. How did she feel when the boys were kicking her stuff? How did it feel to be blamed and punished in front of the whole class? How did she feel when she yelled at the teacher? How might the teacher have felt to be yelled at? What led the teacher to see things so differently? How does she feel about those events in the present? What does she want to do about them?

Many parents are perfectly content to bypass this step. There are as many possible responses to a note home about a verbal outburst in school as there are children. When I was in grade school, a girl never amplified to her parents the reasons a nun rapped her knuckles with a ruler. In Catholic school, double jeopardy did not apply. If a woman of God thought a kid was bad enough to punish her, she must have been evil incarnate and therefore deserved to be smacked again by her parents. It's safe to say that this reaction is fairly low on the empathy scale. It may not stop the bad behavior itself, but it will surely cut down on complaints about school punishment.

A mother who generally has difficulty keeping clear the differentiation between herself as an adult and her daughter as a child may have a totally different reaction. As a child, she may have had constant trouble with her teachers and as a result now overidentifies with her daughter. The mother thinks she's connecting with her daughter about the mean teacher when she impulsively states, "What a bitch!" or "You know, I never liked that woman." These are not good things for a seven-year-old to hear. The mother may quickly launch into tales of similar insults she endured when she was young. This mother has responded to *some* of her daughter's feelings, but she's crossed an adult-child boundary by undermining the teacher. And even though she may *appear* more understanding, she actually hasn't heard any more of the girl's version of events than the "hit first, ask later" mother.

A mother can be so distressed by the "rudeness" of her daughter's behavior that she emphasizes her daughter's angry *feeling* as bad, inseparable from the angry *behaviors*. For many mothers, daughters are reflections of themselves, and women often don't like to see the angry-outburst part reflected back to them. "You should be ashamed of yourself!" "Who *cares* what the conflict was about? No daughter of mine should ever behave that way! What are people going to think?" "You've embarrassed the whole family." This approach can easily lead a girl to think that the best way to handle difficult feelings is to swallow them—in psychological parlance, to internalize. They preclude the possibility of working with the problem in a way that will foster anything but shame.

Helping a Girl to Tell Her Story   Probably the most effective and empathic response to the note from Mika's school is to give the girl a chance to tell her story, interrupting to help her elaborate. As she listens, the mother can try to identify exactly what set her daughter off. The justice issue is a big one for children, and despite the hundred millions of times the phrase "*Life* isn't fair" is spoken to a child, it is as worthless now as it was when it was painted on the walls of caves several thousand years ago. I have yet to hear a kid respond to that brilliant intervention as if she's had a lightbulb go off over her head with the sudden and much appreciated revelation of truth. The issue for a child is how to deal with "big feelings" without totally losing control. The *hate* Mika expressed to her teacher had more to do with being disillusioned, disappointed, embarrassed, and misunderstood. She was really angry. And her anger "fit" the situation. "I can see how you would feel" in no way endorses the behavior but says to the girl that her feelings are valid. Her mother could discuss with her other ways of handling unfairness at school. Rather than say to her daughter, "Don't have those feelings," she needs to ask, "What do you do with them?" Maybe the daughter could write the teacher a short note about the incident. Or the mother might help the girl think about ways to direct the anger when she's in school. Perhaps she can write a note to her mother that she can share with her at the end of the school day.

A child of six or seven is still figuring out which behaviors are appropriate for which settings. A sophisticated task throughout childhood is to learn how to express emotions safely, appropriately (not necessarily politely), and in the right context. As a girl comes to understand what "feeling words" means, she also learns when and how to use them. To embrace a perfect stranger on a crowded street just because you're having a particularly good day will earn you strange looks. An impulsive embrace at home might not raise an eyebrow. A girl in the midst of a close soccer game between major rivals may mutter with her teammates about how stupid a referee's call was, but she definitely does not want to hear her mother's sobbing voice from the stands. A mother can tell her daughter that, when it comes to expressing herself, school is different from home. In Mika's case, school was a place with less tolerance of emotional expression and stricter rules than home. After dealing with her daughter's behavior, her mother might share an "unfair" personal experience from her own childhood or adulthood, describing how she felt about it and what she did.

"I Know a Girl Named Mary": An All-Purpose Story

Stories are often the glue that keeps maternal wisdoms together and helps them to stick in the mind of a child. With a girl who is denying an emotional reaction that she is most likely having, another kind of story often works well, especially if the girl is younger. The story can be true or it can be total fiction. For example, a four-year-old may be absolutely furious at the arrival of a baby brother. Somehow she had it in her head that the kid stayed at the hospital, or went anyplace other than her home. In response to this unwelcome and encroaching stranger, the little girl stomps around, whines, throws tantrums at the blink of an eye, and demands more of her mother's attention than she has since she was much younger. She is rough with the baby in those jealous-child ways—she "pats" his head with a bit too much enthusiasm, she cannonballs onto her mother's bed while her brother is being fed. In a quiet moment together, the mother may try to bring up the issue of the daughter's hostile feelings toward her baby brother.

> *Mother:* It's hard to have a new baby in the house.
> *Daughter:* No, it isn't.
> *Mother:* Well, I was thinking that sometimes a girl can feel like her parents don't love her as much as they used to and she can feel mad.
> *Daughter:* I don't.

This can go on and on. At some point a child therapist would go into "displacement." It's the equivalent of eliciting advice "for a friend." The "Yes, you do," "No, I don't," becomes unproductive and "stuck," with mother and daughter feeling that they understand each other even less than they did when the conversation began. What to do? Back up. Distance the conflict. Tell what my clinical supervisor called "Mary and John" stories.

> *Mother:* It's interesting that you don't feel that way. I thought a lot of kids get pretty upset when a new baby comes home. In fact, I knew a girl named Mary [or heard about a girl named Mary or was friends growing up with a girl named Mary]. She lived with her mother and father, alone, until she was about three or four. They lived in a nice house. Mary's mom and dad loved her very much, and she loved them. She loved the way her mom would _____ [fill in something appropriate] and her dad would _____. And then, one night, her mom and dad went to the hospital and her mom had a baby. I can't remember if it was a boy or a girl. Anyway, everyone was really happy. Even Mary was, at first. But when the

baby came home it was different. Mary's mom and dad were busy with the baby and didn't have time to do stuff that Mary wanted. Grown-ups kept telling her to be careful with the new baby. It was all baby, baby, baby. Mary got sick of it.

This "feeling statement" may be the first introduction of opposition.

Daughter: I never felt like that.
Mother: Well, that's fine, but this is a story about Mary and what *she* felt. Anyway, Mary felt mad, mad, mad. It was like she wished she was a baby again. She was afraid that things would never be the same as they used to, and it made her sad . . . and afraid.

This story can get spun out many different ways. Unlike children's books on the same subject, Mary stories don't have to end on some moral high note. In fact, it's often better when they don't. Their purpose is empathic connection, not the transmission of information or values. Stories need to reflect both sides of a girl's ambivalence and stay distant enough that she can hear her mother's acceptance of Mary's feelings as "normal," when she can't address them yet for herself. This is not like reading a colorful children's book in which the ending is always fast and happy. The goal is not immediate resolution but letting a child know that her mother remains emotionally resonant with her, even as situations change.

If the story is a good one, the girl may jump into it with questions: "Did she have brown hair?" "What was the baby's name?" This is an excellent sign. The point is that Mary and John stories offer the opportunity to explore feelings, normalize them, recognize how they can get tangled up in relationships, along with things grown-ups and kids try that succeed or fail in making the kid feel better. Mary can become a *mother's* best imaginary friend.

Barrier to Empathy: Don't Feel

Women are acutely vulnerable in the "bad feeling" department, and very likely to pass this vulnerability on to their daughters. While women are generally "allowed" to be more expressive of emotion than males, "bad" feelings—

anger, fury, sexual arousal, boldness, pride, and desire—are the exceptions. Many women come into psychotherapy totally disconnected from these emotions. They can "talk the talk," but in terms of identifying with the "negative" feeling, they deny. Women are also very good at taking a feeling they have about someone or something external to themselves and "swallowing it." They internalize the emotions that often keep them from acting in their own best interest.

Women are ruminators, probably the result of both socialization and biology. From childhood, they are taught to "understand." Some of this is social and some is biological. If we can find the *reasons* behind someone's lousy treatment of us, we make the mistake of thinking the pain somehow shouldn't count. A woman finds out that her husband has been unfaithful to her. When confronted, he may tell her that it was because of her preoccupation with the kids, he felt shut out, he was under a lot of pressure at work, blah, blah, blah. All of those factors may be valid, but that man is no less of a dog than if he had *no* reason.

One of the greatest—and most common—emotional cruelties we can commit against our daughters is to deny their intuition, to teach them to distrust their own wisdom and defer to adults' perceptions. "No, honey, you don't hate your sister/teacher/me." "Nice girls don't hate their daddies." "Mommy's girls don't yell at or hate each other." "You want to be nice to her." "What kind of a thing is that to say?" "Don't use that tone with me." "Get that look off your face." "You have your ugly face on!" And my personal favorite, to a child who is *already* crying about something, "Stop crying, or I'll give you something to *really* cry about!" Outside the home, challenging authority is even less expected from girls, therefore it's more obvious and seems more problematic when it occurs. Good girls learn to stuff anger, resentment, jealousy, and rage.

Barrier to Empathy: Neglecting Privacy and Integrity

Beverly Cleary's *Ramona* series depicts a normal girl from a regular family who, in the course of an average day, can have ten significant things happen to her that grown-ups won't understand. The long-standing popularity of this character is due to Cleary's ability to see life through the eyes of a young girl—the emotional bumps and bruises, the personal triumphs, the confusion, the constant vulnerability of childhood that coexists with enormous strength. One anecdote from *Ramona and Her Mother* helps illustrate the differences in the ways adults and children view the world. It is about Ramona's embarrassment over a parent's "minor" disclosure at a party: "Mrs. Quimby said with amusement, 'I remember when Ramona named one of her dolls Chevrolet after the car.' Everyone laughed. 'She didn't have to go and tell that,' thought Ramona, feeling that her mother had betrayed her by telling. . . . She still thought Chevrolet was a beautiful name, even though she was old enough to know that dolls were not usually named after cars."

Parents constantly do this kind of thing with no intention of hurting their children. It is defended as "harmless" and "cute," and most kids have to just put up with it occasionally. Children don't like it, but blabbing about your adorable kid is one of the perks of parenthood. However, it crosses the line when it becomes public teasing and taunting. Sometimes it is an invasion of a child's privacy, no matter how priceless the comment or behavior. When it happens a lot, especially when the child has protested, it demonstrates a failure of empathy and a lack of respect.

In a *Ladies' Home Journal* mail-in survey in which twenty thousand mothers and teenaged girls replied, both mothers and daughters admitted invading each other's privacy. We need to be careful about making generalizations on the basis of totally self-selected populations. This one is a primarily white, middle- to upper-middle-class group. One might also expect that readers of *Ladies' Home Journal* who are able to get their daughters to reply to a questionnaire probably start out with a more positive relationship overall. It wouldn't be surprising, therefore, to see idealized representations of parenthood and late childhood/adolescence. Some of the results are quite interesting, because even though they represent a group of mothers and daughters who probably get along, there were still some striking admissions, which are likely to underestimate the incidence in the general population.

Even though 84 percent of mothers endorsed the idea that their daughters deserved their privacy, 60 percent admitted to reading their E-mail, listening in on phone calls, or reading their journals. Forty-four percent of daughters reported eavesdropping on their mothers' phone calls and opening their mail; 72 percent admitted to going through purses, closets, or drawers.

My mother was respectful of personal privacy. She didn't open mail addressed to her kids, read diaries, or listen in on phone calls. I understood privacy as a right of childhood. Then, as my friends and I edged toward preadolescence, I realized that it wasn't. Other mothers routinely read my friends' diaries, or notes written in school. I was caught totally off guard when, at age eleven, I was visiting my grandmother and overheard her telling several friends about a letter I'd written to a boy I really liked. I still remember hearing one of her friends laughing and saying that it was "precious." I felt naked in front of strangers, and I hated it. I began to understand why the word *protect* is mentioned so often with the word *privacy*. How could this woman I loved so much not only breach my privacy, but also make my deepest feelings the subject of light luncheon chatter? Was this the reason my mother was so observant of her children's privacy? Had she been burnt? I have had to call that memory to mind over the years as I spotted my daughter's diaries or journals open on her desk or thrown on the floor. There are the E-mails from when she's used my computer, and the folded notes I removed from pants pockets before washing. Even when her SAT scores or letters from colleges arrived, I had to wait it out until she returned home. It killed me. On more than one occasion I found myself holding things up to the light, which I learned, in the case of "yes" or "no" or letter grades, is a highly unreliable detective tool. Access to her private musings was so compelling and so seductive. But the memory of my own betrayal years ago kept my hands off.

Clinically this issue sometimes arises when a mother has read her daughter's diary and found accounts of dangerous behaviors, growing alienation, and possible suicidal thinking. There are many instances of girls leaving their writing out so that it will be found. One of my early-maturing preadolescent patients who was hanging out with people much older, experimenting with drugs, and having unprotected and somewhat random sex faithfully wrote journal entries in a loose-leaf binder. She "accidentally" left some explosive pages folded in the pocket of her jeans and threw them in the hamper. Several days later, when her mother, who was the one in the family who did the wash and who was always careful to empty out pockets, found and read the entries, the girl was outraged. Despite her protestations, I believe she wanted to be found out. She was going down the drain, and on some level she knew she needed to communicate it.

Children are often less direct, communicating distress through drawings, a sentence here, a remark there. The question of how much a writer should reveal about her children is somewhat controversial in this age of memoirs. However, the issue is not limited to those people who put their ideas down on paper. "Who owns the story?" is a question mothers need to ask themselves. In mothers' relationships with their daughters, what information is shared with friends and relatives? What is respected as private between mother and daughter? It's not up to the mother alone to make this decision. Some girls are extremely sensitive about wanting what they confide to their mothers (even though adults would say it was "trivial") to stay there. It's a matter of trust. And once a mother loses her daughter's confidence, it can be very hard to regain it. What are the "rules" about confidences? What are the rules about secrets, especially when they involve specifically leaving another family in the dark?

Barrier to Empathy: Disruptions in Service

An essential aspect of every close relationship involves a realization that "close" does not mean absolutely perfect, totally generous, or selfless. It is in the connections to people we love the most that we have the highest potential for pain, for feeling totally misunderstood and rejected. A strong relationship is ultimately self-correcting. Differences need not be erased but must find a way to coexist. This is one of the major dramas in mother-daughter relationships. "Whether or not one wants to change lies at the bottom of most quarrels between mothers and daughters," writes poet Carol Bly. Children are very forgiving creatures. They're rooting for their mothers to succeed, to finally get it right. Mothers get a lot of second chances.

How can a mother be empathic to a child's expression of feelings when she doesn't understand them? In her refreshingly honest article "Girly Girl" Mona Gable relates the story of pulling duty at her daughter's nursery school and having to confront, once again, the fact that her daughter is very sensitive and prone to crying. Following a crayon dispute, her daughter begins sobbing. Instead of feeling empathy for her, and anger at the blonde in short pants who has driven her daughter to tears, Gable admits, "I feel irritated by [my daughter]. Why is she so damned helpless and thin-skinned?" Gable bravely takes the question further, wondering, in essence, "Why does it bother me so?" With three older brothers, Gable learned fast to toughen up, scramble to protect herself, and demonstrate her competence. Tears were not an option if she wanted to survive. So she shelved her sensitivity and eventually even came to have contempt for girls who didn't do things like boys. After winning a sixth-grade girls' pentathlon, for example, she was happier about not being "just a girl in a training bra and pleated pastel skirts" than about actually winning. It's no mystery, then, that having a very sensitive daughter would take Gable back to feelings she had long since rejected and buried. As she begins to see her daughter for who she really is, she confronts the real feeling behind her irritation: "The truth is I can't bear to see my daughter going through childhood like I did, suffering from too gentle and loving a heart. The world has precious little space for people like her, and I worry that I will not be able to be the patient, wise mother she needs." By virtue of that type of self-examination, I'd put money on the fact that she probably will.

Barrier to Empathy: Developmental Dumbness

One of the main tasks of parenthood is to shelter children from things for which they are not yet prepared. We are at a point in time in this country when many are wondering aloud about the impact of relentless media violence and sex on children's behavior. Children are inundated by too many things they are often powerless to escape. One seven-year-old girl I had been seeing in therapy for fearfulness suddenly seemed to regress. Melissa had difficulty falling asleep, demanded the lights be left on, and often sought the comfort of her parents in the middle of the night. Nothing in the therapy or the parents' memory pinpointed a cause. After getting a sense of when the sleeplessness began, I asked Melissa to describe the scary images. They were exceedingly well organized and recounted in a plotlike way, which isn't all that common with six- and seven-year-olds' dreams. Finally, it became clear that Melissa's dreams began after a slumber party at which very scary movies were shown. Judging from the titles, some of them would have scared *me*. What were the parents of the party girl thinking? Were they thinking at all?

When I asked Melissa why she didn't speak up and say that she didn't want to watch, she replied that the other girls would have thought she was a baby. She didn't even feel comfortable telling one of the parents or leaving the family room and finding an alternate activity. She even rejected the last resort—calling her parents to get her. She was frozen, as children often are, in situations where they don't realize they have any power, and resign themselves to conditions that cause them unnecessary pain. Melissa needed some basic assertiveness training. As a temperamentally sensitive and fearful child, she would encounter this kind of situation again and again. I coached her in a series of things to say when she didn't feel comfortable with what was going on. So that Melissa felt her mother's support, I encouraged the mother to call ahead before slumber parties to pave the way for her daughter; this way Melissa would know what to expect and not feel ambushed when she went to a party. Fortunately, this was a woman who had considerable social skills and would be able to do it discreetly. (Most parents can learn the skill of appropriately running interference for their children.) We also worked together to expand the inclusion rules for times it's okay *not* to "obey" adults, and how to pull that off without getting into trouble. We set up an understanding that without negative consequences as a final backup, the parents would always come to get her. Often just articulating the possibility of rescue can help fearful children challenge their concerns. Later on, in adolescence, there may be similar conditions (like picking up an adolescent in the midst of a heavy drinking party where all drivers and designated drivers are plastered) made in families for when kids find themselves in a situation at odds with their parents' expectations or judge themselves at risk for getting into trouble or danger.

Around the time I was treating Melissa, I was engaged in some major developmental dumbness of my own. At the age of four, my daughter really wanted to go to the movies. This was in the era before Disney videos, so when *Bambi* came to a local theater it was a big deal. In my excitement, I conveniently forgot that movies like *Bambi* and *Dumbo* are sentimental Disney classics to adults and the equivalent of disaster flicks for young children. My husband and I took her to an evening showing at a wonderful old theater, with a balcony that she thought was incredibly cool. After a bit of well-founded anxiety about the seat closing up on her, we settled in to watch the movie. She loved it, until the part that I had totally forgotten (translation: probably blocked out because it was too threatening for *me* to deal with), when Bambi's mother gets shot and then she's not there anymore. I hoped maybe my daughter hadn't noticed. She began to shift in her seat. She gripped my arm and whispered urgently and loudly, "Where's Bambi's mother?"

I replied something vague: "Oh, she's probably just in a different part of the forest." My daughter wasn't buying it.

"What happened to her?"

"Well, she may have gotten shot by the hunter."

"Did she get dead?"

I paused.

"Did she?" She was alarmed.

"Yes, honey, she did."

"We have to go!"

"But sweetie, don't you want to stay and—"

"No, we have to go RIGHT NOW!" It was as if seeing any more would make Bambi's mother even deader. We made a hasty exit. I wanted her to stay. I wanted her to see that it all worked out in the end. But that's an adult point of view. To a four-year-old, a mother's death couldn't possibly be redeemed by any happy ending. For months she dogged us with Bambi questions. "Why did the man shoot Bambi's mother?" "Did Bambi's mother come back from being dead to take care of him?" "What happened to Bambi?" She is now old enough to vote. She can legally consume alcohol. And she *still* hasn't seen the second half of *Bambi*.

Barrier to Empathy: Emotional Poverty

Women for whom motherhood was probably *not* the wisest choice sometimes don't even grow into the role until their children outgrow childhood, if at all. Motherhood tests every inch of sanity, patience, and strength a woman has. A woman who lacks emotional resilience, who has little to give to anyone, is going to have a very tough time with children. A child's sometimes glomming dependency, which can get on a sturdy mother's last nerve, can feel like drowning to a vulnerable or brittle woman. Lois Gould, in *Mommy Dressing,* her memoir about her mother, fashion designer Jo Copeland, painted a heartbreaking portrait of a professionally successful and relationally empty woman who could not deal with the basic emotional needs of her child. As a child, Lois went through a phase of nightmares and fears about gypsies kidnapping her from her bed (probably as much a wish as a fear). One night, when her mother was entertaining, Lois had a particularly scary time and cried out loudly. She heard heels echo down the hall toward her room. "I stammered and sobbed my preposterous explanation," Gould recalls. "She did not enter the room but stood poised in helpless silence for a moment, in the shaft of harsh yellow light. Then she closed the door firmly and made her escape, back to the safe world of her bright living room, her bewildered guests. What would she have told them? 'My daughter saw gypsies, and she thought she belonged to them?' Probably not. Perhaps she only shrugged her gleaming shoulders and apologized for the commotion."

Barrier to Empathy: Vulnerability

A mother can be so burdened by her own problems that no matter how much she loves her daughter, she is unable to sustain empathic connection with her. Some girls will have always known their mothers as suffering and distant in ways they don't understand but have grown used to. But for others there is often a sudden break that divides the healthy, happy mother of the past and the withdrawn, suffering mother of the present. Depression and grief, particularly over the loss of a child or spouse, can steal a mother away.

Ellen Glasgow wrote in her autobiography, *The Woman Within,* about an idyllic early life, when her mother was the "center of my childhood's world, the sun in my universe." Following the death of a son, Glasgow's mother "changed from a source of radiant happiness into a chronic invalid whose nervous equilibrium was permanently damaged." Ellen and her sister shared a bedroom that adjoined their mother's, with the door between them left open. "Night after night, we would lie awake, listening to mother's voice as she walked the floor in anguish, to and fro, back and forth. . . . I would draw the sheet over my head, holding it fast to the pillow in a fruitless effort to shut out the sound of her voice." As mystified as she was by her mother's torment, Ellen also couldn't understand why her mother didn't at least shield her from it. "I have never understood why my mother, who had never known a selfish thought in her life, whose nature was composed of pure goodness, could have kept her two youngest children, beside her, day and night, in her period of melancholy."

Barrier to Empathy: "If Mama Ain't Happy . . ."

Many women are so dissatisfied with their own lives that they poison the well their daughters drink from. They emphasize their daughters' failures and trivialize their successes. Their daughters have not "succeeded" in rescuing them from their unhappiness and will be held culpable as a result. With these mothers, daughters often feel that they can't catch a break, that everything they do is wrong. These women are less likely to be suffering from grief or depression, and much more likely to have childhood histories of neglect, deprivation, distress, and abuse. From a clinical standpoint, they are much more likely to be diagnosed with personality disorders, lacking stable, consistent "selves" that are solid enough to keep to appropriate boundaries between themselves and others, or flexible enough to roll with fluctuation in relationships. Their children are little more than narcissistic extensions of themselves, powerless to defy them. Writer Carolyn See directs these words to the mother who used her children for verbal target practice: "When Sister Edith down at St. Dominic's Elementary said I had a 165 IQ, you made sure to tell me that 'genius' in the third grade was actually a moron in adult life!" These are the mothers who make it unlikely that the practice of psychotherapy will dry up anytime soon.

When a wave of mother's all-encompassing anger breaks, it is very difficult for a girl to know what part is her responsibility and what part is her mother's. Many times girls will take personal responsibility for their bad treatment because it's easier to think that *they* did something to deserve it than that their mothers knocked them around for no good reason and that their lives are totally out of control. Sometimes one girl is the designated scapegoat, while other siblings are treated fairly well. And a woman looking back on being scapegoated as a child may never get a satisfactory answer to the question "Why me?"

Barrier to Empathy: Mirror, Mirror

A different type of narcissism in a mother results in allowing her daughter a very narrow range of acceptable behavior. A daughter must be very pretty, very popular, and very smart. These accomplishments are jewels in the mother's crown, not the daughter's. The mother is approving and may even seem empathic, until the daughter shows her imperfections or makes a bid for independence. Then the daughter gets slammed, often for something over which she has little control. Preadolescent girls get into this bind frequently. One mother made frequent comments at the family dinner table to her nine-year-old daughter, insisting that she watch what she eats, cautioning against gaining "any more weight." The daughter felt tremendously self-conscious, hurt, and "fat." When she brought it up with her mother in the next therapy session, the mother dismissed the negative impact of the comment by saying it was because she "cared," and she knew "what happened with overweight girls." This was said in front of the daughter, who was of perfectly normal weight. The mother who said it was about fifty pounds overweight and felt stuck in a relationship with a chronically unfaithful husband.

Poet Carol Bly recalls what turned out to be her final conversation with her mother. She and her siblings visited their mother, who was hospitalized for tuberculosis. Her mother's first words to the child she hadn't seen for quite a while addressed a change in Carol's appearance. "Oh, no, Carol! Not glasses! You don't wear those glasses all the time, do you?" Carol replied that she was supposed to wear them all the time. To which her mother said, "But you don't really have to wear them, do you? No one in our family has ever had to wear glasses! It must be a mistake!"

Barrier to Empathy: Terminal Lack of Humor

One of the least acknowledged keys to solid relationships is a shared sense of humor. There are numerous ways humor can be used to belittle, wound, or nullify another person. People can hide behind humor, and they can discount children's serious concerns with it. But for every time it is used to place a wedge between people, it is also used to grease the wheels for a smoother ride. Sharing one's sense of humor with a child is an important component of emotional growth. There are so many times in life when the only two choices are to roll over and die or to see the perversity, the outrageousness, or the irony that can take a bit of the edge off painful reality. Children love to see their parents doing goofy things, inviting them to join along. In reports of family activities it is often the father who is perceived as the fun one, but that in no way limits the importance of the mother.

Humor is a great tool for showing a kid that there is always more than one way to look at a situation, and that the way you look at it may affect how you deal with it. Sharing jokes, inviting the inevitable imitations and mimicry that children get so good at with their parents, are invitations to accept humor as an important component of the relationship, one a mother hopes her daughter can generalize to new situations. A mother doesn't have to have the skills of a stand-up comedian to be adept with her own daughter. She just has to demonstrate her own ability to enjoy, to laugh, to be silly, and to show that humor enhances pleasure and soothes sorrow. There is built-in reciprocity with humor, indicated in expressions like "sharing a laugh" or "telling a joke." They imply that a joke is relational—it requires two people for the loop to be completed. One of the saving graces of many families is that along with their list of "dysfunctions," they can still join together in the rituals of telling tales and relishing the dark and often perverse chapters in their history.

One of the best examples, occurring against an extremely challenging backdrop, comes from writer Dorothy Allison. Young Dorothy, who still doesn't quite have a handle on how totally screwed-up her family is, comes home from school with an assignment. Her teacher has focused on genealogy and has encouraged her students to look for documentation in their homes of the generations before them. Dorothy decides to begin her archival work with a look at the family Bible. She asks her aunts and mother, "Where's our family Bible?" Her aunt Dot is amused and challenges, "Our what? Lord. Lord. . . . Girl is definitely not from around here." "We don't have a family Bible?" Dorothy asks incredulously. And her aunt's reply pretty well sums up the state of things: "Child, some days we don't even have a family."

Barrier to Empathy: Displacement

Immigration to this country from almost any other requires major adjustment—not just to language and exchange rates but to new and often different cultural expectations and strictures. Intergenerational conflict is rampant as children who immigrated young or were born to immigrant parents adopt more of an American identity than that of their parents' culture. This is highly relevant for women, since many of the differences involve women's freedom.

The conflict between the generations is clear in many of the memoirs written by immigrant and first-generation women whose families represent other cultures. M. Elaine Mar recounts her rocky journey from Hong Kong to Kansas and ultimately to Harvard in *Paper Daughter*. In her early years, while she and her mother lived in Hong Kong, they enjoyed a loving, even permissive relationship. But everything changed with their move to a sister-in-law's basement in Kansas. As Elaine struggled to make it in a new school, with a new language, in an atmosphere that was not at all inviting to Asians, her mother sank into despair and anger. Elaine was in the impossible position of having to bridge two worlds. If she was to be as successful academically as her parents wanted, she had to jump into the American world. But whenever she did it, she was perceived as rejecting her mother. One of many poignant scenes involves the loneliness of not being able to express to her mother her sorrow at never being "it" in school-yard games. "The Chinese don't ask their children, 'How was school today?'" she explains. "They say, 'What did you learn?' and 'Do you understand your lessons?' In Cantonese I could only describe the equations we'd solved that day. I was able to show her my spelling list. It was harder to explain that kids groaned when I was chosen to be 'it,' that I hated dodgeball, and that I was largely mute."

Barriers to Empathy: Competing Loyalties

A mother has a number of relationships, some of which may interfere directly with her capacity to empathize with her daughter. Unfortunately, this can lead to a scenario in which the mother's conflicted motivations actually place her daughter at risk. The most blatant and painful example is a woman who tries to preserve her relationship with her husband or boyfriend at the expense of her daughter. These women live in denial or explain away the possibility that their daughters are being physically or sexually abused. One of the most excruciating recountings in literature of this destructive triangle is described by Dorothy Allison, best known for the award-winning *Bastard Out of Carolina*. She portrays a mother-daughter relationship between Anney and Bone that starts out strong and empathic. However, with the introduction of a new husband, the mother's loyalties shift. During an unprovoked and brutal beating of her daughter Bone at the hands of her husband, Anney screams outside the closed door. When she finally reaches her battered daughter, she holds her in her arms and tries to comfort her. She swears to leave the man and to protect her daughter. But in repeated episodes, Bone was to learn that this was the beginning of surface empathy—all feeling, no action. " 'Baby,' she called me. 'Oh, girl. Oh, honey. Baby, what did you do? What did you do?' What had I done? I had run in the house. What was she asking? I wanted her to go on talking and understand without saying anything. I wanted her to love me enough to leave him, to pack us up and take us away from him, to kill him if need be."

However, a short time later, she hears her mother and stepfather having sex, with her mother clearly a willing participant. No one was leaving. And in choice after choice, when it comes down to protecting her beloved daughter from her slimy husband, Anney's commitment to Bone always falters. Mothers in this situation perpetrate an additional violence on their daughters, by inducting them into the sisterhood of silence. "Push it down. Don't show it. Don't tell anyone what is really going on. We are not safe, I learned from my mama. There are people in the world who are, but they are not us. Don't show your stuff to anyone. Tell no one that your stepfather beats you. The things that would happen are too terrible to name."

DAUGHTERS' EMPATHY WITH MOTHERS

Empathy between a mother and daughter is reciprocal, if not equal. The burden of trying to make empathic connections falls naturally on the mother; when mothers expect their young daughters to tune in to *them,* there's usually trouble. Most girls, as they grow, want to figure their mothers out. At some point girls begin to realize that their mothers exist as people, outside of the role of "mom." In *Rattlebone,* Maxine Clair describes young Irene Wilson's microscopic interest in her mother. "Gradually, a curiosity set in that kept me studying my mother. If her hand hesitated in the middle of an ironing stroke, as if something had occurred to her, I wondered what it was. . . . Sometimes she closed off everything in the outside world and appeared to be looking at nothing."

Marking the Moment

Via Revere, an eight-year-old in Eliza Minot's novel *The Tiny One,* suddenly loses her mother in a car accident and then struggles to assemble memories of the woman who was the center of her childhood universe. She recalls, with the fullness of the senses that her mother had helped her appreciate, the many wonderful moments her mother taught her to embrace with her memory. Via remembers a sunset boat ride with her mother: the blue water, her mother's arms around her, the taste of a juicy peach. "Take a bite of this," Via tells her mother. She wants to encapsulate for her mother the words that will define the perfection of the moment, but she "doesn't know how." Her mother attends to the gap between the beauty of the experience and her daughter's difficulty matching it with language. "Mum smiles at me," Via recounts. "She's smiling at me because she sees how I feel. She lowers her head toward my ear. . . . 'You must always remember, my pumpkin, that there will always be days like this.' She's smiling. 'Always,' she says again."

Reconciling Competing Images

Other daughters are aware that their mothers have dark moods, or fall into deep holes from which it takes a long time to emerge. These holes have different names: alcoholism, mental illness, cancer, trauma, abuse, grief, and the many other conditions that flatten grown-ups. Often these are the kinds of situations in which children are lacking many of the important facts and adults aren't rushing to fill in the blanks. But children are exquisitely attuned to their mothers and can pick up changes, even when they can't explain them or have any idea how to help.

It Was Never as Bad as You Said Sometimes there are things that daughters think they'll understand and excuse more easily when they become women, perhaps even when they are mothers themselves. But their mothers' destructive behavior is sometimes *harder* to reason away with the perspective of increasing age. The girl who accepted the many reasons her mother constantly offered for bitterness, unhappiness, and inattentiveness as a parent learns from her own experience of motherhood that the old excuses don't hold up as well. Carolyn See, in an adult voice that still echoes the plaintiveness of an abused little girl and the hard-won wisdom of a woman with daughters of her own, writes to her mother in words that ache out loud with wisdom and resignation: "All the time you were tearing your hair and breaking dishes and whaling away at us and screaming until your throat got hoarse and tottering and staggering and flailing and howling, all around you there was a beautiful world. A beautiful world, and two little girls, who wanted you for a mother, believed you were their mother."

In Your Eyes   Even very little girls can be uniquely intuitive and responsive to their mothers. The combination of love and closeness with a child's new eyes on the world can help a mother see herself from a completely different vantage point. Little girls are free from so many of the dark filters that women impose upon themselves. Guiding a girl through childhood provides the mother the opportunity to go along for the ride, perhaps experiencing things as an adult that she missed as a child. To their little girls, loving mothers are always beautiful and smart and powerful. In her relationship with her daughter a mother can learn a great deal about herself. Through her daughter she is exposed to a wide range of experiences that she wouldn't get any other way. To feel herself as playful and silly, the source of comfort and calm, wise and clueless is to know herself in ways the adult world doesn't necessarily allow. Poet and novelist Alice Walker, who suffered a traumatic eye injury as a child, worried that her three-year-old daughter would someday be embarrassed by her mother's different eye. "Every day," she wrote, "she watches a television program called the 'The Big Blue Marble.' It begins with a picture of the earth as it appears from the moon. It is bluish, a little battered-looking, but full of light, with whitish clouds twirling around." When Walker puts her daughter down for a nap one day, the child stares into her mother's eye and Walker braces for the moment she's feared for so long. The little girl takes her mother's face in her hands and redeems years of pain when she says, "Mommy, there's a world in your eye. . . . Mommy, where did you get that world in your eye?"

✌ THE STANDOFF ✌

One of the first major public standoffs I experienced with my two-and-a-half-year-old daughter—excluding the typical bedtime, food, coloring on walls, and general disobedience problems—was over a dress. I was shopping for a big family reunion, and because she was still fairly deficient in the hair department, and because I was sick of people telling me what a cute little boy she was, I was determined to dress her so there would be no doubt about her gender. I found the most adorable white-and-blue sailor dress. It even had a little white hat that matched. I held it up to her to do a quick check on the length.

By the time she was two my daughter was usually a good-natured, easygoing child, but there was something about that dress, I still don't know what it was, that made her react. She folded her little arms across her chest and issued her declaration. "No! Baby dress!" I couldn't believe she actually cared.

"It's not a baby dress," I told her, and started to walk toward the cashier.

She stood her ground, saying more loudly, "No! Baby dress! No! No! No!" Was I really having a disagreement about fashion with a two-year-old? I don't remember mouthing off to my mother about clothes until preadolescence. I was in a tough position. Should her clothing, within certain limits, be a negotiable issue? Or was this an area in which I should flex my muscle?

"Well, she *is* the one who has to wear it," I thought to myself. "Maybe we can compromise."

I told her she didn't have to wear the hat. She was unmoved. I didn't know how to come out of this without looking like a wimp or a witch. I tried to get her to tell me what exactly made it a "baby dress," as if a two-year-old can really articulate such things. I knew in my heart that this purchase was going to be a total waste of money if she thought the dress reflected some underestimate of her vast maturity.

"Well, what do *you* like?" I asked, hoping that no one was over-hearing our fashion negotiations.

"Big-girl dress. I want a big-girl dress."

A big-girl dress. I had no idea what that was, but I was beginning to understand its importance. My husband and I had been using the Big Girl phrase indiscriminately for a few months. Every habit needing kicking, every new behavior needing to be learned was defined in terms of "When you're a big girl you won't need to have a pacifier on twenty-four-hour call/you'll put your blankie 'someplace special' forever/you'll pee in the potty," and so on. We'd really built up this Big Girl business, like it was some great thing. (In reality there is no automatic, intrinsic reward in changing, except that it reassures your parents about your development and makes them proud of you in a way that you don't totally understand yet but you've already developed an addiction to.)

"Well, what is a big-girl dress?" I asked.

She walked around and around the rack of dresses for girls her age. She seemed to be making her judgments based on the dresses' hemlines. As she moved slowly around the circular rack of thirty or so dresses without finding anything, I started worrying that what she really wanted were big clothes (as in clothes that are way too big for her), which I couldn't possibly get. I began to fear a major public struggle.

She jumped up and tried to reach for a dress. I hoped she wasn't pointing to the one I was afraid she was pointing to.

"Mama, get that. No, not that one. No, not that one. *That* one."

She reached up, and her little fingers grazed the bottom of the dress that would have been my absolute last choice. It was incredibly red, not ugly exactly, but not anything near what I had in mind. It had sort of a Little Orphan Annie thing going on and I just couldn't picture her wearing it. She grabbed for it as I took it down and pronounced proudly and in a somewhat deeper voice, "THE COLOR RED," at which point I decided we would no longer continue to support *Sesame Street* in particular and public television in general. I didn't want to be rigid, but we just weren't a red-wearing family.

"Keara, honey, this doesn't really go with your red hair, which isn't really red, but more orange, and orange and red don't really go together."

"Why?"

"Well, I don't know . . . it's a matter of taste."

"What taste?"

I could tell we were about to fall off the communication deep end—where my ability to verbalize something and her ability to understand it would sink us. This was the child who, several weeks before when I was bemoaning the fact that we were out of milk for our cereal, shrugged and said, "Just put juice on it." She made me feel rigid, but no way was I ever putting orange juice on Raisin Bran.

"We can buy the red dress," she said, as if I needed her permission. I checked the size and the price—neither gave me an out. Had I been watching this interaction between another mother and young daughter, I would have been amused. But there was nothing funny about it with my own little girl. I knew exactly how I wanted her to look for that reunion. And I knew exactly how much of a kick I got out of all the compliments about my adorable child. I knew, but didn't understand, how hungry I was for my child to shine at the reunion. I thought these early years were the time when you molded children—presumably to your own tastes. My adorable child was now my formidable child, which made me uneasy about our future.

We bought the red dress. She was thrilled and tried it on over and over, always needing help with the buttons. She modeled it for her father, "See my big-girl dress. Mommy wanted a baby dress. But I said no." I could see my husband looking over her at me, mouthing silently, "Red?" I shrugged.

At the reunion I looked over at her many times in that incredibly red dress and pictured how much better she would have looked in the little sailor dress, especially with the hat. The red dress was technically the right size, but it was too big and hung below her knees. It made her skin look even paler than it already was. And, as I had pointed out to her in the store, it didn't do her hair any favors either. At every opportunity I was quick to point out that I wasn't responsible for the dress. And polite relatives who never would have dressed their daughters in that red getup reassured me that she looked good, "in spite of it." But Keara didn't hear those people. She walked around that party like she was Queen of the Reunion. She didn't need the nod from anyone. She had already crowned herself.

All week before the party I kept hearing in my head those vague conditional statements mothers make to their daughters about their appearance. "Humor me." "You would look so much better if . . ." "Why can't you give on a simple thing like this?" "Do it for your mother." This experience was my first taste of a kind of wisdom that took me a long time to really understand—that inevitably your mother's approval of your appearance should come in a distant second to your own. But I still saw my daughter as a walking representation of me, and that was going to be very hard to give up.

Told from the perspective of parental foolishness, this is a silly story. But what went on wasn't silly at all. It was one of the moments—and in this case, one of the first moments—in which my daughter clearly articulated, "I see things differently from you." "What you think is pretty, I don't." "Sometimes I know what I want more than you do." "This is important enough to me to make a scene, to tolerate your displeasure." "We may both be girls, but I know, even this young, that we are very different."

This moment in the life of a mother-daughter relationship is the introduction to a parade of requests, denials, and negotiations—in which the mother declares to her daughter that something is absolutely forbidden (like tinting her hair) until the girl wants a tattoo, which makes the mother want to offer to color her daughter's hair pink herself. From that day on, my daughter declared herself a player in every clothes purchase. She had very specific and definite opinions, sometimes involving major departures from the mainstream, but never to the point where I told her she had to change her clothes before she went out. (Not that she would have.) Other than the junior-prostitute look, which I did not allow, she had a great deal of flexibility.

She lives in New York now, a poster girl for Goodwill and other thrift shops who can also name every designer and accurately predict fashion trends. I am relieved that so far she has refused to yield to the funereal black that seems de rigueur for young women in Manhattan. It continues to be absolutely impossible for me to choose anything wearable—with the possible exception of heavy winter socks—that she will like.

She just turned twenty-two, way past "baby girl," past "big girl," on her way to young-adult girl, whatever that means. Recently she flew home for her birthday dressed in a way that 99 percent of Americans would say was weird but the other 1 percent would say was incredibly cool. She had on a denim jumper ($3.00 from Goodwill) and a print cotton blouse ($7.50, Salvation Army). Below her jumper hung six inches of a pale blue silk slip ($0—my mother gave it to her when she was in a high school play). She carried a square red leather bag with a long shoulder strap ($150, Saks) and red clogs ($95) to match. As she emerged from the plane, my husband leaned over and asked with alarm, "Do you think we should tell her that her slip is showing?"

"No," I whispered, feeling slightly superior, at least to him, in fashion sense.

I saw my girl emerge from the gate and felt a surge of something I still can't name. It went beyond love; it was a split second of ecstasy, like I had felt twenty-two years earlier when I saw her for the first time. I'd waited nine months, and in many ways my whole life, for the moment when I would first see her. I watched her negotiate her way through the crowd, and for a second I flashed on that strong-willed two-year-old who, in the beginnings of her "differentness," stated her position and held her ground. Her constant capacity to reinvent herself has invited (sometimes forced) me to do the same. She made her way toward us, beaming her hellos. As she circled my neck in one of her unself-conscious hugs, I realized that it had taken me twenty-two years to see something I should have recognized in an instant with the two-year-old in the department store: my daughter is beautiful, *because* she wears red.

SIX

➶

Adolescence: Identity, Differentiation, and the Door That Swings Both Ways

An adult woman can hunt for and find her own value. She can graduate herself into importance. But during the shaky span from childhood to womanhood, a girl needs help in determining her worth—and no one can anoint her like her mother.

JAN WALDRON,

Giving Away Simone

THE DEVELOPMENTAL TASKS OF ADOLESCENCE

The adolescent girl faces the prospect of becoming more individuated while still preserving connections to her mother. While these may seem like contradictory goals, in many ways they are entwined. It's easier to set out on an uncertain journey knowing that the home fires will remain burning than leaving a cold and empty hearth. A daughter's healthy connection to her mother is the fuel that enables her to travel distances but also to return home. Developmentally, girls are confronted with changing bodies and shifting relationships. They must negotiate the labyrinthine network of peers, getting the lay of the social landscape, zeroing in more closely on the people with whom they would most like to be. Despite continued guidance from parents, adolescents themselves must begin to look at their futures and take responsibility for making the steps that reach toward that future. Adolescent girls need to become comfortable in their own skins—even though they are bombarded with input that tells them to be eternally unhappy in those skins and grab (and pay) for anything that promises improvement.

MY GIRL

In the middle of a weekday, the subway car I was riding emptied out, leaving a mother, her daughter, and me. At first the daughter, who was about ten or eleven, sat close to her mother, who was trying, unsuccessfully, to read a paperback. The girl was thoroughly enjoying her mother's company. She leaned her head on her mother's shoulder and teased her with silly jokes and funny faces. She was right on the cusp of adolescence—breast buds poking out of her pink T-shirt, new braces, and feet and hands that seemed to be growing faster than the rest of her body. She was becoming gawky but was not yet self-conscious about it. She kept her mother's attention by pulling every single thing out of her small backpack and making a great display of deciding whether to show it. She always ended up dangling it in front of her mother with a flourish, reveling in the amused or admiring response.

Slowly, she moved away from her mother. She stood and staggered against the motion of the train to reach the closest pole, seeming intrigued by the challenge of keeping her balance as the train lurched forward after each stop. At first she put on an exaggerated display of shakiness, inviting her mother's cautions about falling. "You need to be careful," her mother warned on cue. "You could fall." This emboldened the girl, who began letting go of the pole and maintaining her balance on her own. As she became more confident, she sang out, "Look, Mom! Look! I'm Metrosurfing!"

Once again, her mother smiled, shook her head, and said in a teasing voice, "I don't know you." The girl scooped up her mother's sunglasses and hat, slapped them on, and gave the show of her life—pretending she was dodging waves, calling again and again for her mother to look at her, to share in the delicious moment.

Her mother alternated between obvious pleasure and, conscious of my presence, slight embarrassment. But they were both living "in the moment," totally attuned to each other. I knew nothing about the girl or her mother. I didn't need to. Once upon a time, I had enjoyed my own Metrosurfer, who loved testing the powers of gravity, motion, and speed. Who knew the potential of falling but never seemed to care. It was a time when she thought that the worst consequence of falling was scraping an elbow or landing on her butt. And even those possibilities weren't enough to prevent her from taking risks. With puberty, my Metrosurfer became preoccupied with a new liability: the remotest chance of appearing foolish—even in front of me, even in front of herself. For the next several years, protection against humiliation became a prime motivator in her decisions. And Metrosurfing just wasn't worth it anymore.

Maybe I was once a Metrosurfer too. I can't remember. I see my past filtered through eyes that are so much more critical than they were when I was ten. I certainly recall those "Look at me, Mom" needs, the exhilaration when they were filled, the resentment when they weren't. But I see the child "me" in home movies, and when I watch that girl wildly swinging upside down on monkey bars or taking repeated hits on the ice, awkwardly flopping around and trying to get back up on her skates, only to land on her ass again, she is a total stranger. I wince as I watch her swing and fall. I want to tell her, "That's enough." Although she looks silly at least 75 percent of the time, her cheeks are flushed with pleasure and her crooked smile has a radiance that I "outgrew" somewhere in adolescence.

I guess that's why I got such a kick out of the girl on the subway. She was so full of herself. Not in the way we describe self-centered people who are so taken with their own reflections that they can't see anyone else. This girl was cocky and confident. She looked absolutely secure in her mother's affection and respect and was perfectly willing to look foolish, just to have fun and put on a good show. And audiences don't get much friendlier than her mother. The few times she said "I don't know you" were the only indications that she felt obliged to slip in the possibility of embarrassment. However, her voice was full of humor, not admonition.

Those words—"Be careful!" and "I don't know you!"—will echo later in their lives, in a different tone, with an altogether different impact: wounding, accusing, confused. In a moment of frustration, the mother may say to her daughter, "I don't know you anymore." And the girl could turn right around and repeat it to her mother. "I don't know you!" becomes a statement of confusion about change, and fears about where it will lead. The problem is that in the heat of the moment, those feelings often get expressed as betrayal. "You've changed!"—certainly one of the most universal experiences of living beings—is usually not delivered or received as a fact or a compliment. It becomes an accusation, with the implication that the old "you" was better than the current "you." These expressions of disappointment tend to place the fault for the estrangement solely at the feet of the other.

The award-winning television series *My So-Called Life,* an account of fifteen-year-old Angela Chase, accurately portrayed a multifaceted mother-daughter relationship. In a scene from the series pilot, Angela dyes her hair red. Her mother, Patty, seethes. "She did it to get me to react," she tells Angela's father. "It's so hard to look at her. She looks like a stranger!" The intensity between adolescent girls and their mothers often leads to verbal explosions in which one or both of them, upon reflection, can't believe what came out of their mouths. This happens frequently when a mother hears words emanating from the general vicinity of her mouth, in a tone she vaguely remembers but can't quite place. Within seconds she realizes that she's just been possessed by the "demon mother"—the one she swore she'd never be, the one who says, "As long as you live under my roof," and "Wipe that look off your face." The mother is shadowed by the "ghost of mother past" in the play that features her in the debut performance as the unenlightened Jacob Marley and her daughter as Tiny Tim, with attitude. When Patty hears herself yelling at Angela, she is appalled at what she thinks she heard herself say. "Do you think I ever *dreamed* I would sound like this?" she asks an empty kitchen.

On that subway I had a ringside seat from which to observe a moment in the evening of a girl's childhood, when one of her greatest contentments is basking in the glow of her mother's undivided attention, without giving a damn who else sees it. It's a time for preening and pushing the limits, engaging her mother boldly with the direct command "Look at me." She could flail her arms, bend her body, and shift her feet, flash her silly hat, sunglasses, and a smile full of braces with little concern about how she might be perceived. She was so free.

I gave it six months before this scene disappeared from their repertoire. The risk of humiliation would skyrocket with the onset of adolescence, and the cost of getting her mother's attention in the old ways will seem way too high. An adolescent girl rarely courts her mother as she did when she was younger. It's not just a matter of the foolishness that adolescents associate with public goofiness and mistakes. "Look at me, Mom!" is such an outright statement of need, of connection. As a girl gets older, the need for connection and attention remains, but she's no longer willing to state it as directly. As a result, her mother may not receive or interpret her daughter's signals correctly. "Mom, look at me!" becomes "What are you looking at *me* for?"

IDENTITY: HELP ME SEE MYSELF, HELP ME LIKE WHAT I SEE

Long before girls seek approval in the mirror, they see themselves reflected in their mothers' eyes. Mothers of adolescent girls often require a fine-tuning of the senses. In order to create an empathic bridge over the sometimes choppy waters between childhood and adolescence, they need sharper acuity to hear the little girl's voice hidden under muttered frustrations, whispered conflicts, and unflattering family portrayals overheard on the phone or down the stairs. Sometimes mothers need X-ray vision to penetrate the disturbing shifts in clothing, the beginnings of awful makeup, strange hair and nail color, suspicious changes in their daughters' rooms, and questionable choices of friends. They need to notice more but appear to be watching less.

It's like Halloween. An adolescent girl adopts a number of temporary selves. She can be wickedly scary, incredibly capable, stunningly beautiful, wretchedly disheveled, smolderingly sexual, and absolutely vulnerable within the space of a day. She can be bitchy and brilliant. In the same breath she can use her continually honed verbal skills to reduce her younger sister to tears, while passing up the roast beef and launching into a diatribe about cruelty to animals, without a nod to irony. Early adolescence *is* Halloween, every day. An empathic mother tries to answer the door at every knock, recognize her daughter somewhere underneath the costume, invite her in or at least drop a sweet in her bag, and resign herself to the fact that it may be a long time before Thanksgiving. She also must remember that although *she* thinks of herself as a fairy godmother, her daughter may look at her and see the Wicked Witch of the West.

Adolescents try on identities like clothes. They see what works, what doesn't, when, and with whom. Psychologist Susan Harter calls this a time of a "proliferation of selves." They aren't necessarily false or fake selves. All of us have some variability of "self" that is dependent on context. We act differently at work than we do at home, one way with a romantic interest, another with a lifelong best friend. Contrary to earlier thinking that identity was basically the diploma you received when you graduated from adolescence, identity has the potential for change over our entire lives, especially if we remain open to new experience and learning. There's usually enough overlap that, even with the inconsistencies and experimentation, there's still a fairly cohesive "self." Sometimes a girl can only feel a sense of separateness by deliberately making almost everything into a contest: "I disagree, therefore I am." *My So-Called Life*'s Angela confesses, "I cannot bring myself to eat a well-balanced meal. It means too much to my mother."

Girls can spend a great deal of money to look like they just came from a final clearance sale at the Salvation Army. They can also easily find expensive clothes in any major department store that will help them look like apprentice hookers. Makeup, hair, piercings, and tattoos are potential minefields for mothers and daughters to negotiate. A mother wonders what's become of the sweet girl she once knew, who now looks like she'd sooner bite her on the neck than shake her hand. "She obviously has some secret life apart from us!" Patty Chase complains to her husband—*as if that's not the whole point*.

Experimentation in almost every aspect of thinking, looking, and behaving is the norm. A girl can fall in love with an idea, an ideal, or a goal. She may follow it with a passion or give it up when it receives no peer support or something better comes along. She can hunger for membership in a certain group, only to find that once she's in it she feels far away from her true "self."

FRICTION

Early adolescence is clearly the time of the greatest uproar in the journey toward adulthood, when almost everything in the adolescent is pushing for redefinition. Research consistently demonstrates that it is the time of the greatest conflict between many girls and their mothers. It is also, however, a time when the girl needs her mother very much. In the early teens, girls usually still rate their mothers as their most frequent confidantes. This will change over the stretch of adolescence and young adulthood, when young women "diversify" intimacy beyond their mothers. From childhood mothers form the bridge to their daughters' social lives and friendships. That connection, even when it is loudly protested, is incredibly important in the twelve-to-fifteen-year-old range. Early adolescence can, for mothers and daughters, feel like one of those bad dreams about showing up for a final exam and realizing that you never took the course. Yet so many aspects of development continue along even though no one is particularly happy.

NEW WAYS OF THINKING

From birth until puberty, a girl's development is mostly linear and vertical. Childhood requires that she develop *more* of everything: physical growth, emotional, cognitive, and social skills. There are steps and stages. When a young girl grows up, she does so literally. But in adolescence the emphasis becomes nonlinear, and along with the vertical action, changes are also horizontal. Quality (how you think) becomes more important than sheer quantity (how much you know). The adolescent's ability to think abstractly—about those things she cannot touch, see, smell, or hear—allows her to engage in discussions of ideas, concepts, and principles. She is developing the capacity to consider an issue from several perspectives at once. She is becoming more skilled at playing "mind games." Essentially, she moves from the fill-in-the-blanks kind of knowledge to "compare-and-contrast essay questions." Adolescent girls are able to spend more time in the gray areas, where answers are complex and often subjective. They become very interested in discussing their feelings, and begin to understand the concept of ambivalence.

This is by no means a smooth process. Sometimes a girl can become so paralyzed by the lack of structure in the gray areas, and by the overwhelming number of possibilities, that she suffers an attack of "temporary stupidity," which can account for brief decrements in academic performance. It also occurs in moments of debate with her mother when her language and abstract skills hit the wall and bring the conversation to a dead stop with comments like "This is stupid. I don't want to talk about it anymore," or the wonderful, all-purpose "What*ever*." This can be incredibly confusing to a parent who's so delighted about engaging in meaningful conversation with her daughter on any topic *other* than themselves. They each make attributions that will explain why the conversation went south. And they'll both be half right and half wrong.

> *Mother:* "I thought we were having a great talk. She is totally unpredictable."
> *Daughter:* "How was *I* supposed to know what that word meant? She's just trying to make me look stupid."

MOTHERS' EMPATHY WITH DAUGHTERS
Teflon Mom: Fair Fights?

Adolescents often assume that their mothers are made of Teflon: slings and arrows bounce right off them. They automatically discount the power of any pain they inflict, as if their mothers have a built-in antidote for venom. When a girl says she hates her mother, even when she really feels like she does, she wants to wound, not to kill. It will *never* be a fair fight. She can wheel out an arsenal of automatic weapons, and her mother has to try to make do with her wits. Even when women reach adulthood and begin to have much more empathy with their mothers, many find it hard to revise those Teflon attitudes. As with a therapist, no matter how much a patient rails against her, criticizes clothes, intelligence, choice of words, hitting back is not allowed. Of course the therapist is getting paid to deal with the abuse, whereas for the mother it's more or less volunteer work.

Mothers need not stand and take it like the early Christian martyrs. It's a good thing for a girl to hear (often after the heat dies down) how her words and behavior affect her mother. The goal here is not to inspire an instant outpouring of guilt and apology. It's to remind the girl that she's dealing with another *person,* not a brick wall. In giving her feedback—straightforward and nonblaming—the mother is modeling empathy. She is showing her daughter how to respond under fire. She is teaching her that there are gradations of wounding, and she needs to learn where her arrows tend to land, even when they aren't intended to do much harm. The other important message is that a girl's feelings can hurt but not kill her mother, that even her scariest, most out-of-control anger isn't capable of closing and locking up access to her mother. The security of attachment in a mother-daughter relationship is a lot like the framework and foundation of a house. In good times, no one thinks too much about them. But in the hard times, when the storms hit, strong frameworks and foundations are put to the test. It's easy to see how mothers who have poor control of their own feelings, who are easily wounded and quick to anger, will find this very difficult and damaging.

Mourning the Lost Child: Where Did My Sweet Girl Go?

These negative reactions can be confusing for mothers who once enjoyed strong, mutually empathic connections with their daughters. Confronted with their changing daughters, they often feel betrayed. They remember the "good old days" with the child, not the adolescent, and often make it clear that they prefer the child. Mother and daughter both struggle with the disconnection between the person who used to occupy that place at the table and the one who does now. The mother can remember the girl's chubby little legs as she kicked and wiggled in her high chair, banging a spoon, babbling and playing. She may remember her daughter sitting in a "big girl" chair, having to kneel to reach the table, always wanting the next instrument up—the fork when her mother only wanted her to have the spoon, the knife once she graduated to the fork. She may remember how her daughter wouldn't eat without companionship, demanding that she stop whatever she was doing and pay attention. Visions of the child swinging her legs under that table, perhaps making contact with a sibling, sharp disagreements about hated foods, give-and-take conversation, major silliness, bad-but-getting-better manners—all in the past.

How can the two of them have shared that small piece of geography for more than a decade and now experience everything so differently? The answer is that they really *never* saw things the same way, from the same perspective. It's just that the differences never seemed so dramatic, and they rarely resulted in as much confusion, anger, fear, and pain. It's not that a mother is really dealing with a new person; she has to be empathic in the old ways *plus new ones*. She has to work to find new ways to make an empathic connection to her daughter. It's easy to reach out her arms to a tearful, long-legged prepubescent daughter, who still finds private comfort in her lap and embrace. The daughter may be on her way to outgrowing this particular physical comfort, but it still satisfies on an emotional level. It's fine to get this nurturance in private, although she wouldn't want her friends to see it. But by early adolescence many daughters, unless they are feeling especially precarious, find direct physical displays of support and physical affection uncomfortable. "I can't help it. Now that I have, y'know, breasts, it is just too weird to have to hug my mother and smush up against hers," an adolescent patient once told me. But she still wanted the "essence" of that closeness.

Mothers make the mistake of thinking that because the old ways are rejected, the daughters don't still want, or need, to have bridges built to them. This is a major error. The fact that the Brooklyn Bridge is temporarily closed for reconstruction is no excuse for missing work. If you have a job in the city, you have to find an alternate route. Despite all of a daughter's warnings that say, essentially, "You can't get there from here," a mother's job is to try.

Hot Spot: Sexuality

Mothers continually get messages about what they aren't doing to reduce the risks of sex and drugs for their children. Very effective ads portray parents and their adolescents in prolonged silences, chomping on cereal or driving in the car. The punch line labels these situations as yet another missed opportunity to talk to a child about drugs. Although I support the goals of these ads, the implication is always that it's the uptight parents who don't want to deal with their kids directly on the tough questions. But there's another element here. There are a lot of kids who aren't eagerly awaiting these exchanges. I remember laughing with my friends about the pathetic "sex talks" that were inflicted upon us when we hit double digits. In the words of My So-Called Life's Angela Chase, "When I was twelve my mother gave me my sex talk. I'm not sure either of us has fully recovered."

Our mothers and teachers were so earnest, so serious. They acted like they were passing out classified information as they welcomed us to womanhood, which in the early 1960s didn't look like a particularly exciting prospect. We were willing to accept that perhaps there were perks we just didn't know about yet. But they never told us about those. Becoming a woman, as best as we could figure, involved "feminine hygiene"—a concept, like "nervous breakdown," that I still don't entirely understand. There were sanitary napkins and sanitary belts. There were things called cramps. And all that blood. Given the choice, I would have been happy to forgo womanhood. The adolescent girl is not only growing up but also growing out. Breasts, hips, hair, acne, sweat, and blood emerge, requiring major physical and emotional adjustments for the girl and her parents. The body, over which she spent her childhood getting control, all of a sudden changes its "mind." A physical plan unfolds in which the girl has had no input. And there is precious little she can do about it. For some girls, the timing or momentum of these changes is unacceptable. They may lie to their friends about menstruation, wear baggy shirts and pants to hide hips, breasts, and axillary hair. They may learn that there's one way to resist the "developmental express": If she severely restricts her intake of food and amount of exercise, a girl can prevent herself from reaching the critical weight level for menstruation to begin, or reverse it once it's begun.

The most empathic approach for a mother is to accept the ambivalence, to normalize it. If a daughter feels that she doesn't have the same level of enthusiasm her mother has for the whole process, how much can she believe about the beauty of joining the great sisterhood? Let's face it, there are demands on women that begin in adolescence and don't let up until we're pretty damn old. Women vary in the extent to which they want to live up to societal expectations of appearance and hygiene. But if they dip below a certain level, their negligence is protested loudly. Actress Julia Roberts's appearance in public with unshaven armpits was treated with a level of alarm befitting "armed" robbery. And if Julia Roberts is scorned for the decision to let her razor have a couple of days' vacation, what about the rest of us when we "let ourselves go"?

In the span of a year, many changes hit at once. Most girls get an introduction to cramps and premenstrual cycling that can make them feel tired, grouchy, or tearful. They can bump up against unseen ovulations with an appendicitislike pain that is then dismissed as "mittelschmerz," like *that's* supposed to make them feel better. Upkeep turns out to be a lot of work. There's the leg and underarm shaving or waxing and dealing with the unruly pubic hair that bathing-suit makers pretend doesn't exist. There's sweating and deodorant. There's "feminine odor" and trying to figure out what "that fresh feeling" means. There's oily skin and acne, and a head of hair that won't behave. Toenails and fingernails to manicure. For some, there are glasses and braces. Beyond just basic upkeep, all the makeup and clothes responsibilities can put a girl over the edge.

These physical and psychological changes inevitably influence a girl's relationship with her mother. A mother is supposed to be a guide on the circuitous journey toward sexual identity and experience. But this particular trek is fairly difficult. Only seasoned guides with years of experience under conditions of great risk qualify to lead ascents of Mount Everest. Being a guide is more than just having a good sense of direction. It means having traveled the route, knowing the vulnerable places, the conditions that put a party at risk. It means screening the participants and not allowing them to participate in expeditions for which they aren't prepared. It means knowing when to say "Stop" for the day, and when to say "Get going." It's knowing the climber's strengths and vulnerabilities. The articulated goal is to make it to the top. In the process, how much is the leader willing to sacrifice the climbers? Many times mothers have their own "peaks" already designated for their daughters. Anything that doesn't edge the girl closer is considered a waste of time. It's a bit like the current preoccupation with combining fun *and* learning.

"The Talk"   If, in the spirit of athletic competition, we were to rate mother/daughter interactions according to difficulty, negotiating about room cleanliness would probably rate about a 2, while talking about sex would be a 9 or 10. As with so many other milestones, mothers and daughters often emerge from these shared experiences with very different reactions. Mothers may report that they had an open talk in which they covered all the relevant topics. Adolescent girls will say, "Was I asleep when that happened?" For many mothers and daughters the perfunctory sex talk is basically about the plumbing and how to protect it; there's very little discussion of sexual desire and activity. It's a bit like trying to teach someone about tennis by giving detailed descriptions of rackets, nets, and balls and a pep talk about the greatness of the game and good sportsmanship—hoping she'll draw the necessary inferences about: (1) how to play the game, (2) when and why she should and shouldn't play the game, (3) how to choose a partner, (4) how to protect herself from getting hurt, (5) how to keep score, and (6) how to learn more.

Most mothers give daughters the racket and ball, but they don't teach them how to play. Even at the level of introducing her daughter to puberty and plumbing, a mother's perceptions can differ markedly from her daughter's. A frequent theme in women's writing is the experience of being caught off guard by menarche. The spot of blood, discovered in the bathroom, the bed, or worse, in a public place, convinces many unprepared young girls that they are seriously ill or dying. Many mothers start out straining their credibility by emphasizing all the wonderful future possibilities that womanhood will bring, without acknowledging that menarche, breasts, and all the other stuff represent a huge change, which will take a while to get used to. Girls are more likely to feel the uncomfortable and inconvenient aspects first, way before they get to the transcendent part.

In Elizabeth Strout's novel *Amy and Isabelle,* the clash between a mother's words and a daughter's experience is painfully clear. Upon learning that Amy had begun to menstruate, her mother proclaimed, "This is a very exciting day." Amy didn't see it that way. "She felt loathsome and frightened as she walked to school, her abdomen heavy, odd pains in her thighs, and an extra sanitary napkin packed in a brown lunch bag. And she had been asked to stand in front of the classroom to diagram a sentence on the blackboard. She thought she would faint standing there, pass out from the shame, as if the whole class could see through her corduroy skirt to the bulky monstrous thing pressed between her legs."

Then there's the protection department. What kind of birth control? Pills, sponges, unwieldy diaphragms and jelly. Then the STD protection. Condoms? What kind? Do you get prepared before anything is even remotely on the horizon, or wait till sex is imminent? How do you bring up the subject? Given the fact that 20 percent of all unprotected teenage pregnancies happen in the first month of intercourse, and that STDs don't care if it's your first or hundredth encounter, early preparation is probably wiser. It's a lot to deal with.

Other cultures have integrated menarche into the social fabric, deeming it an event requiring at least a passing ritual observance. A Jewish mother, in what may initially seem an insensitive response, slaps her newly menstruating daughter on the cheek. And as the redness rises and spreads across the girl's face, the mother wishes that this be the worst pain she knows (which as far as I'm concerned falls into the "fat chance" level of probability). But it's a nice thought. In her epic novel about a family of women that spans Africa and America, *The River Where Blood Is Born,* Sandra Jackson-Opoku creates a powerful figure called Big Momma, who holds fast to the old rituals and wisdoms so that she can share them with young girls coming up. Little Daughter, who has just begun to menstruate, asks Big Momma about the "doubled rope of discolored beads" that she wears around her waist. Although Big Momma doesn't know the exact reason for the beads, she knows their important history, all the way back to Africa. Big Momma's beautiful prayer at the time of Little Daughter's menarche is silently echoed by many mothers: "God Jesus. . . . We want you to look after our Little Daughter here. Let her come into love in her own time. Allow her to know the gift of birth, but not before she's blessed to receive it. Don't let her be a mother 'fore she knows what it is to be a woman."

Sex talks deal not so much with sexuality but with its potentially awful outcomes: teenage pregnancy, sexually transmitted diseases, and social disapproval. "When I was sixteen," says the narrator in Barbara Kingsolver's short story "Stone Dreams," "my mother found birth-control pills in my sock drawer and declared that early promiscuity would ruin me psychologically. She said I'd been turned loose too young in the candy store and would go spoiled, that later in life I'd be unable to hold down a monogamous relationship. She said many things, but that one stayed with me."

When adolescent girls who had menstruated for at least a year were asked how to best prepare younger girls for menarche, they stressed the need for emotional assurance that menstruation was normal and healthy. Emphasis should shift from the abstract connection between menstruation and womanhood to a more pragmatic approach that downplays the biology of the whole thing. Information about hygiene as well as the subjective experience of menstruation (what it actually feels like) were underscored. Girls saw their mothers as being extremely important but not always very effective in preparing them for menarche. Fathers, on the other hand, should be "supportive but silent" or "excluded completely."

The Rules Mothers are anxious to impress several ideas upon their adolescent daughters. They want them to know *about* sex but not to *do* anything about it, resulting in advice like "(1) Don't ever run after boys, and (2) Keep your pants up and your skirt down." They want them to know that a premature pregnancy gets a girl's life off track, sometimes forever. They want their daughters to know about HIV, AIDS, genital warts, herpes, chlamydia, and all the other consequences of unprotected sex. They want them to know about date rape. Many of them want girls to know that boys and men "only have one thing on their minds" and should not be trusted. The unspoken part that many mothers *intend* to communicate—that sex in the right relationship is absolutely terrific and will be one of the highlights of her life—somehow gets lost in the fear. Other mothers *can't* talk to their daughters about the pleasure because it hasn't ever been part of their experience.

To be fair, many adolescent girls are threatened by the idea that their mothers are sexual beings. In Maxine Clair's *Rattlebone,* when Irene's mother defends an affair by saying, "Women have needs," Irene complains, "I hated to hear her say women have needs. I hated that dark sea of mysterious passions women were supposed to have, that apparently made them act in uncontrollable ways." And in *Amy and Isabelle,* Amy's best and pregnant friend, Stacy, is much more direct: "You're lucky your mother's not married. You don't have to picture her doing it." Anne Sexton thoroughly embarrassed her daughter Linda by asking her about her masturbation habits and then telling her that she "had to masturbate."

The main themes of advice from mothers to their adolescent girls involved being fearful of their own sexuality and the constant threat of males. Writer bell hooks describes the climate of her household growing up, with her mother watching her sisters and her like a hawk. It's a good example of the ways in which mothers' cautions about the negative consequences of sexual behavior can overshadow the positive aspects of sexuality. "A major issue around sexuality in our household was the issue of pregnancy. We were constantly told by Mama's raging didactic voice not to bring any babies into this house for me to take care of. Our mother had been pregnant as a teenager. She wanted us to do life differently. Yet that was never what she said. Instead she made us see our bodies as this site of shame and betrayal. Any day now those feeling, sensual, sexual bodies could lead us away from ourselves into a shame so powerful we could not come home."

The message is presumably the same ones their mothers had to contend with: don't trust your sexual instincts and urges. In all the discussions about sex, pleasure is usually the least mentioned aspect. There is little consideration of relationships outside the boy-girl model. Masturbation, which these days is the closest thing there is to safe sex, is shadowed by a deep and long-standing distrust of sexuality, particularly when it is not for reproduction. In *Dreaming in Cuban,* Cristina Garcia's feisty adolescent character complains of being forced to work for next to nothing at the bakery where her mother works, as a punishment for her "filthy" mind. This mother, like bell hooks's, feels compelled to be hypervigilant about her daughter, unapologetically invading her privacy to protect her from herself. "My mother reads my diary. . . . She says it's her responsibility to know my private thoughts, that I'll understand when I have my own kids. That's how she knows about me in the tub. I like to lie on my back and let the shower rain down on me full force. If I move my hips to just the right positions, it feels great. . . . Now, whenever I'm in the bath-room, my mother knocks on the door like President Nixon's here and needs to use the john. . . . When Mom first found out about me in the tub, she beat me in the face and pulled my hair out in big clumps."

Timing Is Everything One of the things that can complicate a mother's empathy for her daughter is the girl's relatively early entry into puberty. Even though the mother of an early-developing girl is likely to have matured earlier than *her* peers, she can be unprepared to shepherd her daughter through puberty. A leading pediatric journal recently asserted that with the increasing number of seven- and eight-year-old girls who are showing early signs of puberty (such as breast buds), it was no longer appropriate to see it as a developmental aberration necessarily in need of medical intervention. There are a variety of factors that contribute to early menarche. Genetics is one. From a nutritional standpoint, body weight is related to the onset of puberty, and the growing trend of childhood obesity has been offered as one contributor. Early menarche has also been associated with a history of family stress, divorce, and anxiety in late childhood. It is likely that the timing of menarche is the product of a complex blend of genetic, environmental, and psychological influences.

Early Puberty Early puberty starts a girl off on a rougher road and has consequences that last well beyond the time her peers catch up to her. She had less "rehearsal" time to prepare for the demands of adolescence. Compared with her male classmates, who generally lag two years behind the average girl, the early developer is very far ahead. Socially, both adults and adolescents may treat her as if she is older. She may be ostracized by girls her age who are threatened by the changes they know are coming their way, leading her to groups of older kids who are engaged in activities for which she is not at all prepared. Fathers of early-developing girls report more hostility toward their daughters than fathers of girls developing at age norms.

An early-developing girl is trapped in a woman's body, and unlike other times when she just dressed up like Mommy, this time she's stuck with the whole costume. The most consistent and disturbing research finding is that early-maturing adolescent girls are at significantly greater risk for psychopathology, especially depression and anxiety, than their "on-time" counterparts. Some girls may show the nosedive in self-confidence in adolescence that has been documented in the work of Gilligan, Jordan, and Baker-Miller. However, since early-maturing girls *aren't even in adolescence* (teens) yet, it appears that what puts a girl at risk isn't only hitting a certain age or grade, it's also the *timing of menarche.* During childhood, the rates of depression are relatively equal in girls and boys. However, with puberty, the rate rises quickly for girls and levels out at two to one throughout the childbearing years through to menopause.

Early bloomers need mothers who can help them deal with the ambivalence about being "different," and monitor their activity significantly, forestalling premature sexual involvement and the other high-risk behaviors that older adolescents get into. It is important that a mother appreciate the crookedness of her daughter's development—that while she looks just like a woman, to quote Bob Dylan, "she breaks just like a little girl"—which, in this case, she is. The sense of this uncontrollable force bearing down and changing her can make a girl excruciatingly self-conscious. Her differentness isn't just in her imagination. Insults about sexual development, or the lack of it, are a theme of adolescent cruelty. In *Amy and Isabelle,* this is evident in Amy's desperation to forestall the inevitable. "She couldn't tell her mother how her breasts had grown so much earlier than the other girls', how she had slept on her stomach to try to keep it from happening, but it happened anyway, and how her mother, pretending to be casual about this, had wrapped a tape measure around her chest and ordered a bra from Sears. And when the bra came it made her breasts look bigger, stupidly grown-up. There had been some kind of game at school where the boys would sneeze when they walked by her. 'Anyone have a Kleenex?' they'd say. 'Oh, forget them,' her mother said. 'Just forget them, who cares?' "

When parents dismiss adolescents' worries about the reaction of their peers, they might as well tell them to just stop breathing. Few girls are sturdy enough to shake off that kind of teasing. From the vantage point of adulthood, we know that boys' teasing about breast size is irrelevant in the big scheme of things. And yet that differentness, that sense of being mocked for something over which she has no control, at a time when she longs for sameness, is acutely painful for a girl in the midst of it. In a wonderfully titled article, "What Is Victoria's Secret?" a mother and her seven-year-old daughter drop in to the popular store to take advantage of a bra sale. Curious about the whole bra business, the girl asks a number of questions that her mother thought she wouldn't have to deal with for a few more years. Noticing the letters denoting cup size, she asks her mother why breasts get grades. The discussion pulls the mother back to a place she thought she had deservedly relegated to the "no longer painful" section of her mind's attic. "Suddenly, out of nowhere," she recalls, "I heard the taunting male voices from my seventh-grade algebra class: Hey, you're a carpenter's dream—flat as a board! You're a pirate's dream—sunken chest! Ha ha ha ha ha ha!" Later the mother wondered about those boys, now grown-ups. "Have they turned into nice men who respect women's bodies?" she reflected. "Do they occasionally flash back to their seventh grade behavior and flinch in embarrassment?"

Late Puberty Despite the short-term anxieties about whether they will *ever* develop, late-blooming girls don't suffer the same long-term consequences as early-maturing girls. A late-maturing girl is probably still in step, at least, with the development of most boys her age. More than anything, she needs reassurance that she will, in fact, become a woman, and support against teasing or a sense of exclusion from girls who are already into bras and boyfriends. Berie Carr, a character in Lorrie Moore's *Who Will Run the Frog Hospital?*, describes the late bloomer's dilemma. "I was flat, my breasts two wiener-hued puffs, and I had to avoid all dresses with darts, all nylon shirts and plunging bathing suits. Though I pretended otherwise, I hadn't even menstruated yet, though I was already fifteen. The words 'developed' and 'undeveloped' filled me with dread and loathing. 'When you develop,' my mother might begin a long, embarrassing prophecy, or the school nurse would come by and talk to us in Science, and I would freeze in my chair, not moving a muscle, trying to disappear."

Hot Spot: Body Image

Girls get very strong messages very early about the absolute importance of physical attractiveness. In Rebecca Wells's novel *Little Altars Everywhere,* the messages about weight are not the least bit subtle. "Mama looks in the rearview mirror and says, 'Lulu, put that donut back in the bag this instant.' Lulu protests, 'Oh, Mama, why?' Mama says, 'Just do what I say. Trust me, you will live to regret that donut if you eat it. I am only trying to save you from growing up to be a lard-ass like the women on your daddy's side of the family.' "

Although most interactions are not as direct, body image is one of the great minefields of women's development. Despite the amount of conflict it can generate between mothers and daughters, the issue is experienced similarly across generations. Dissatisfaction with one's body is handed down from woman to woman like family recipes or silver tea services. Women often can see themselves as beautiful only in retrospect. While we may be more generous in evaluating other women than ourselves, the yardstick we use for *all* women (even when we don't like to admit it aloud) tends to be fairly punitive. We are told that we should love our bodies, but there is a stronger undertow that tells us that if our bodies aren't perfect, they don't deserve to be loved. Most are more gracious about the bodies of mangy, smelly old house pets than about their own bodies.

Pimples at thirteen, breasts that are too large or small at fifteen, the constant awareness of the presence and perceptions of one's buttocks at seventeen, then cellulite, fat, varicose veins, stretch marks, lines, and wrinkles—at every point in development there's something we can look forward to—another thing to hate about ourselves. We need look no further than the large percentage of prepubertal elementary school girls who make the assessment that there already is "too much" of them and commence the long road of food restriction. Within the women's magazines with enlightened articles about self-esteem and health are contradictory—and more powerful—images that insist that most women need to change. When she was nine my daughter didn't have much of an idea who Elizabeth Taylor was, but every time we waited in the checkout line and she perused the tabloids she couldn't figure out why so many people were so upset about her weight. It was as if Taylor had committed icon treason. When we watched MTV or network award shows, my daughter and I both absorbed the catty things people said about young actresses who'd put on a few pounds. The one that really got to us was a rather lengthy debate about whether actress Kate Winslet, from the films *Sense and Sensibility* and *Titanic,* was "fat."

The self-hatred that is cultivated in women is so woven into the fabric of the culture that even when a mother swears that she will protect her daughter from it, she is instantly outnumbered and outgunned. Ethnic differences in body image have been fairly consistent, at least for several generations. African-American girls have been more accepting of their own bodies and more approving of their mothers' looks than white girls. However, there is more research to suggest that the gap is narrowing, with African-American and Hispanic girls expressing more dissatisfaction with weight, in particular. It will be interesting to see, now that there are more ultrathin women of color in fashion magazines, whether girls' identification with them will lead to greater dissatisfaction with themselves.

An adage that has had a long life in the wisdom of women is, "You have to suffer to be beautiful." We remember or are reminded of the lengths our mothers went to for their looks. Lois Gould's memoir, *Mommy Dressing,* revolves around the fact that her mother's greatest accessibility was when she was sitting at her vanity, in preparation for an evening out. "One day," Gould writes,

> I found myself at age eleven studying my mother's naked body, appraising it, comparing it to mine. "What's the crease?" I suddenly asked, pointing. It was a deep indentation in her back, on the right side . . . the crease was nearly a foot long.
> "I had a rib taken out," she said. Matter of fact. She with her horror of doctors, of hospitals?
> "Why?"
> "To make my waist narrower. Young women had to do that."

"Is That a Zit?" and Other Stupid Questions   Some of the worst, dumbest, and most painful things mothers say to their daughters about their appearance fall under the guise of "helpful" comments. They assume that the girl has absolutely no idea of the apparent flaw and feel compelled to point it out. My husband and his siblings wrestled with severe acne as teenagers. I was probably average when it came to breakouts. Average in this case is still awful, since anything over zero zits is generally experienced as a disaster. Admittedly, I was anxious about my daughter's skin when she hit puberty. From infancy, it had been translucent and smooth. The first pimple on the horizon threw me into a quiet panic. Given my husband's teenage suffering, should I take a proactive step and schedule an emergency dermatologist visit? That felt a bit silly. I remembered in high school when my most beautiful friend unintentionally overdosed on vitamin C, which her mother had liberally administered at the sight of her first, and only, zit. I didn't want to go overboard. But in the end, I also couldn't help myself.

My daughter sits at the breakfast table. She is reading the paper and gets grouchy when she's interrupted. And today she's in a lousy mood. I want to help. I really do.

"Is that a zit?" I ask gently.

"Thanks, Mom. Thanks a lot!" She slams down the newspaper.

"Are you mad at me? I'm just trying to help. You can hardly tell it's there."

"Why don't you just draw a bull's-eye around it?"

"Honey, I didn't mean to hurt your feelings—"

"You *didn't* hurt my feelings. God, I can't believe you!"

As soon as she left for school, I smacked myself upside my head. "Is that a zit?" *What was I thinking?* It would have been kinder to *hit* her than say that. How was she supposed to answer? "Why, yes, it is, Mom. Do you have any suggestions?" Or, "No, I think it's a deposit of volcanic ash." It felt like an empathic thing to do at the time. I wanted to reach out to my daughter in an area of vulnerability. But it's a great example of the many ways in which "helpful" can be perceived as intrusive and cruel, despite every good intention. Physical imperfections in adolescence (perceived or real) are magnified a hundred times. Adolescents carry the heavy burden of an "imaginary audience" that goes with them everywhere and reflects back every mistake, every flaw as if it were being flashed on one of those huge screens at concerts, so thousands can see every detail. Struggling with a breakout, *My So Called Life*'s Angela Chase said it all: "The zit had become the truth about me." She railed against her mother for making a suggestion about how to deal with it. Finally her mother demanded to know why that was so upsetting to her. "Looking at you," Angela cries, "at the way you look at me. The way you instruct me to wash my face so I don't get zits. Like you have to fix me. Like you are ashamed of me. You expect me to be beautiful."

When mothers recognize the zit, or the weight gain, or the frizzed-out hair, they are not only trying to be helpful. They are dealing with their own ambivalence about their daughter's imperfections. The daughter whom a mother thought would surely bypass the weight problems *she* had in adolescence starts to gain weight. The mother is quietly freaked. But she doesn't say it. Instead, as the girl reaches for the second serving of potatoes, the mother asks, "Are you sure you want to eat those?" Those caring suggestions are stealth-bomber attacks, because the girl can never defend against them. She is probably already feeling the weight gain in her clothes and seeing it on the scale, and undoubtedly she has feelings about it. If she defies her mother and takes another helping, she is inviting an even more direct attack, spelling out the reasons why she *really* shouldn't be having those seconds. The only thing she can do to turn the discussion off is to put the potatoes down and swallow a hefty serving of shame instead. Our memories are so short. When it comes to our bodies, I think it has something to do with our own pain having such a long and sturdy life.

Hot Spot: Males

The subject of men is the stuff of many pieces of advice from mothers to daughters. Men are generally viewed as worthy of suspicion until proven otherwise, at least when it comes to sex. In Mei Ng's funny and endearing novel, *Eating Chinese Food Naked,* the mother advises her daughter: "Be careful of men, and boys too. You know if a guy asks you what time it is, he just wants to know what time you want to fool around. He has his own watch in his pocket."

Hopefully, a mother will take a step beyond the "men are dogs" approach and help her daughter learn to differentiate the men who will treat her well from the men who won't. Given the number of women who are abused emotionally, physically, and sexually in relationships, it's a point that needs to be made strongly. Unfortunately, by the time a woman reaches adulthood, if she has sexual or physical abuse in her past, she is already at high risk for alcohol abuse, depression, eating disorders, early-onset sex, unprotected sex, teenage pregnancy, sexually transmitted diseases, and future sexual victimization.

Sensitizing daughters to make good judgments about men involves more than a list of cardinal sins against women. Mothers want to convey the need for respect, which is easily undermined when their daughters see them accepting less for themselves. There's a wonderful passage from Kaye Gibbons's novel *A Cure for Dreams* in which the mother gives her daughter advice derived not only from her own experience with men, but from what she observes in other couples. The daughter asks her mother how she can look at her friends and tell who's well loved. "Listen and hear what the men call their wives when they come to the store to fetch them," she instructs her. "Listen. 'Old squaw.' This sounds bad but it's truly sweet. No name. Just, 'Come on!' This is what your father says, so that should tell you something. Rarely, rarely, though, will you hear a woman called from the store by her name, which is best. So listen for each time Richard Bethune comes to the door and calls, 'Amanda!' so nicely. And watch how gladly she goes to him. A woman's name will always suffice, but if you'll keep your ears open in a room with men and women, you'll hear it's the call used least often."

The tradition of men disrespecting women is a theme in so many women's stories. The names, races, and economic classes change, but the wisdom of one generation to the next emphasizes the need to toughen up, capitulate, or resign oneself to the meanness of men. In her autobiography, *Two or Three Things I Know for Sure,* Dorothy Allison recalls "comfort" from one of her aunts after she'd confided being teased by boys. "Men and boys, they all the same. Talk about us like we dogs, bitches sprung full-grown on the world, like we were never girls, never little babies in our daddy's arms. Turn us into jokes 'cause we get worn down and ugly. Never look at themselves. Never think about what they're doing to girls they've loved, girls they wore out. Their girls."

A New Attitude

Sometimes establishing connections to adolescent daughters is like trying to feed strained green vegetables to an infant. She usually spits most of it out. It lands on you, the floor, and herself, but if you keep shoveling it in, *some* of it will eventually make its way down her digestive tract. Mothers' expressions of concern, caring, understanding, and sympathy, which in childhood were the equivalent of strained peaches, become, in adolescence, mashed peas. Still nutritious, but definitely not as delicious. It's not the responsibility of the child to accommodate. Kids don't say to themselves, "Let's see, I hate the green stuff, so maybe if we play 'airplane in the hangar,' it will make it easier." That's just not the deal. It's the job of the parent to figure out how to get the nourishment in. It takes trial and error. Lots of spitting. Awful messes. Months later the baby will probably like peas no more, maybe even less, than she did before. But, by then, the mother will have learned techniques to get the peas in, and expanded her child's exposure to a full range of vegetables.

A New Mantra

When their daughters hit adolescence, mothers need to adopt a new mantra: "I can't win." It sounds defeatist, but it isn't. In what often feels like a competition of wits, power, and attention, mother and daughter can easily feel like opponents. But empathy requires that the mother divest herself of the entire win/lose mind-set. If she thinks her adolescent daughter is going to give her gold stars in the motherhood department, she's in for major disappointment. It's unfortunate but true that the goodness or badness of mothering does not immediately translate to the kid. In the short run, mothers are good and cool, to the extent that they facilitate, rather than frustrate, their daughters' desires. It's foolish to wait around for the daughter to say, "I realize that not letting me go to the biggest house party of the year is in my best interest. It must be really tough to say no to something I want so much. Motherhood must be really hard sometimes."

Rewind the Interaction

For a mother, trying to judge her effectiveness based upon her adolescent's assessment is like trying to judge how tasty a cake might be before it's baked. The process of making it delicious involves a necessary "sticky, lumpy, yucky phase" in which you couldn't *give* the thing away. While you're waiting to see how the cake turns out, there are things to do—check the ingredients and the steps in the recipe. Did I listen to what she said? Did I give her my full attention? Did I recognize out loud my recognition of how strongly she felt? Did I let her "have" her feelings? Did I show her the same respect I would show a friend or colleague? One deserved "I'm sorry" from a mother is worth at least five "I love yous." They have to be "clean" apologies—no "I'm sorry, *but* you really made me mad when you wore my dress without asking *and*. . ." Those "apologies" are actually blaming using different words. "I'm sorry" or "I was wrong," standing alone, without qualifiers, is so hard to say for anyone. But in pitched battles between mothers and daughters, apologizing means sacrificing hard-won territory. Adolescent girls tend to apologize more, probably because they're in the one-down position and they know what can be withheld if they don't cave in.

My father was always quick to snap or yell. But I could go to my room, count down from ten, and he'd be knocking on the door: "Listen, I didn't need to yell like that. I'm tired" or "I'm frustrated." My mother was not liberal with the apologies, first, because she didn't have emotional blowups like my father, and second, because she was pretty well convinced that she was right. That's why the times she said she was sorry or wrong during my adolescence stand out. They were gifts. I'm not saying mothers need to offer mea culpas for every time they screw up with their daughters. They'd be on their knees all day. But moments when mothers admit, without sacrificing any authority or credibility, that they were hurtful or careless or selfish, or just plain wrong about something, are duly noted and valued by their daughters.

Las Vegas School of Mothering

Over time I've come to appreciate what I think of as the Las Vegas approach to mothering. Walking into a casino, you know that even though you would love to win big, the chances of that actually happening are quite slim. If winning the big bucks is your only motivation for playing, you're going to be very unhappy. When you lose, you can blame the machines, the casinos, yourself, or the person who convinced you to go. However, the truth is that you went to the casino with only one guarantee—that you would be a player, not necessarily a winner. And for many people, playing with even the remotest chance of winning is enough. Many routinely leave casinos with the curious combination of lighter spirits *and* pockets. Winning is great, but it's the playing and the *possibility* that keeps them coming back. An adolescent girl is like a slot machine. You can put a lot of money into her and get very little back. There's no payoff schedule. Even when you win, you don't have a clue how it happened, so it doesn't help you with your next bet. Passively feeding her nickels isn't going to get you far. You're better off sampling other games, particularly ones that involve some level of skill. You never lay all your resources on one deal or one game. It's dangerous and often leads to ultimatums, threats, and lines in the sand that are hard to recover from once they're out there.

Points of No Return

Girls and their mothers can push each other to high-stakes extremes—"If you leave this house, don't bother coming back." The mother in Fae Myenne Ng's novel, *Bone,* rejects a daughter because of her defiance with the chilling words, "I have no eyes for you." When an adolescent's identity is coming together in ways that upset her mother, there can be explosive moments that set off years of estrangement. Sexual orientation, moral/ethical choices, attachment to friends, lovers, and decisions that reverse something the parent thought had been "decided" all have the potential for creating high-register tremors on the emotional Richter scale. Anger, frustration, or anxiety can ignite ugly scenarios in which mother and daughter pay dearly for the ensuing disaster. Apart from the very explosive ultimatum ("Leave my house!") scenarios, it's always fascinating to see how some of the low-down moments that daughters describe are scarcely memorable to their mothers. High-impact moments of childhood and adolescence often don't mature like memory for less emotional events. That is, factual information, empathy, and insight don't necessarily nurse the memory of these events into a more mature perspective. Painful events in particular can remain stuck at the age they happened, becoming an emotional burden that interferes with relationships later in life. Recent research suggests that even adults have as much of a chance of being incorrect in memories of their past as they do of being right.

For writer Joanne Meschery, the daughter of a minister and his very controlled, proper wife, an exchange with her mother blew the roof off their relationship. In a letter to her mother she recalls the interaction. " 'Joanne Marie,' you said, your voice rough behind the bedroom door I'd slammed in your face, 'someday I'll be dying—just mark my words.' 'Well, I wish you would,' I shot back. 'Just go ahead and die!' 'Mark my words,' you said loud through the door, 'I'll be dying, and you'll come and ask my forgiveness, but I won't forgive you. I will never forgive you. Never!' " There are mother-daughter pairs for whom such high-volume exchanges are an almost daily occurrence— most of it garbage in/garbage out; intense emotional expression is the norm. However, in Meschery's case, this was something that had bubbled under a very tidy surface for quite a while. With the unspoken demand of cultivating the impression of a gentle, loving family, she violated the peace-at-all-costs rule. In contrast with constantly bickering relationships, moments in an emotionally unexpressive family in which a single insult, threat, or inappropriate confidence will stand out starkly are all the more significant. Meschery's mother's words sounded like hexes, haunting her, for twenty-seven years. Much later, confronted by her *own* children who complained about the lousy things she'd said or done, Meschery responded with exasperation: "Why do you always, always only remember the bad things?"

Barrier to Empathy: Feeling with Her, Not for Her

Empathy is relatively easy when a tearful daughter recounts a rotten day and spills her pain about a fight with her best friend. Most mothers can remember how the senses of perspective, proportion, and time shift dramatically in early adolescence. What a girl feels right now she is convinced she will always feel. The event of the moment is the very best or worst thing to ever happen. Bad things cancel out all the good that has preceded them. Heartbreak is a late-stage, terminal condition. In any of these states, it is worthless to start off with logic. To remind a fifteen-year-old that she felt exactly this bad when the last two boyfriends broke up with her is not a particularly helpful intervention. Information and advice are great when a girl wants to know how to lift a stain from her shirt or parallel-park a car. Mothers are used to giving wisdom and structure, two things the adolescent girl isn't looking for. She wants to vent, in a safe place, to a person who won't dismiss her feelings as trivial or weird.

A mother's empathic attunement to her daughter's pain can lead her to *act on* her daughter, rather than *feel with* her. My daughter's tears are so much harder for me to bear than my own. I want to tell her what to do and how to do it, or just do it for her. If I could carry the pain for her, I would. A child's pain exposes more than just *her* vulnerability. It is a stark reminder to her mother of the limits of love. Sometimes I torture myself, thinking that a better mother would be able to find the right way to ease my daughter's pain. I know it's nonsense, but in those dark early-morning hours when I answer the phone, first to my daughter's sad silence, and then to crying that has been going on so long it sounds like gulping, I would do anything for it.

There are some sorrows mothers cannot bear for their daughters. In many ways, it's almost disrespectful to try, insinuating distrust in the girl's ability to do a lot of the work on her own. Sometimes I'm sure I know detours that can cut miles from the rocky, rugged portions of my daughter's journeys. I want to save her those miles. She could get "there" faster, and she wouldn't get lost. But direction and speed aren't as important as the journey itself. Unlike earlier times in a girl's life when maternal interventions could dramatically erase pain and divert distress, now the right thing to do is rarely clear. Mothers who once ministered to their daughters' physical and emotional wounds now mourn their fading magic. In the good old days it seemed so easy to pull the rabbit out of the hat. In adolescence a mother can't find the rabbit, and she's lucky to get her hands on the hat. The things that help aren't even consistent over time. At one point, a gentle teasing reminder of a similar "life and death" situation two days earlier might do the trick, but a day later, when the mother tries it again, she's perceived as callous and mean.

Barrier to Empathy: Emotional Constriction

Empathy is also an issue with positive emotions like pride, pleasure, and love. It is as much a failure of empathy for a mother to discount, explain, or restrict her daughter's exuberance as it is her anger or tears. When I watched that girl on the subway, I knew that the constraints that would enter the picture in six months would cut both ways. If the girl didn't settle down herself, the mother would instruct her that behavior that was once adorable is now inappropriate. What happens to mothers at this stage, when they collude with daughters to "behave"? Perhaps it's a reflexive wish to inoculate girls against the shame of falling, of looking foolish, of people looking on with disapproval. Perhaps it's just time for a girl to begin to transfer her capacity for silliness to her peers. One has only to be in the same subway car, fast-food restaurant, or, God help us, movie theater with a group of preadolescent girls to know their capacity to be boisterous, giggly, full of stage-whispered secrets and exaggerated reactions. I was just like that with my friends, giddy to be out without parents, who were always on guard for bad behavior. I try to remember those times now when the dialogue of the film I'm watching is in direct competition with the voices of those exuberant young girls and I want to deposit my buttered popcorn on their heads.

It's important for mothers to protect those "full of themselves" girls from emptying out, bit by bit. But that means competing with very strong messages: "Don't strut your stuff." "Don't wear your love on your sleeve." "Don't let people see how competitive you are and just how much you want to win." "Don't do a victory dance over the win today because you'll likely lose in the future and then what?" "Be safe." "Be polite." "Don't take a chance on making others feel bad." The problem is, if you can't crow about your successes, your conquests, and your pride at home, where can you?

Barrier to Empathy: "I Told You So!"

One of the risks a mother runs when she gives her daughter unsolicited advice is that occasionally she'll actually be right. Being right usually feels good. But if the original advice had anything to do with predicting pain, an empathic mother will take little pleasure in her accuracy. There's a moving passage toward the end of Amy Tan's novel *The Kitchen God's Wife* in which a mother and her adult daughter, Pearl, face up to decades of misunderstanding each other, following her mother's disclosure of an important family secret that finally put their difficulties in perspective. Pearl had always experienced her mother as controlling, competitive, rigid, and disapproving. In their first really honest conversation, Pearl's mother looks back to her daughter's adolescence with an example of unintentional distance. She reminds Pearl about a boy she thought she "could not live without," who'd come for dinner. She'd been distressed by how much the boy took for granted about her daughter, and had warned her: "Be careful . . . that man considers himself first, you second, and maybe later you will be third or fourth, then never. And later, you did not mention his name anymore. But I saw your broken heart, your good heart, trying to keep all the pieces together. . . . I wasn't going to tell you, 'I told you so.' . . . My heart was breaking for you." Unfortunately all Pearl heard was the disapproval. The mother's identification with her daughter and the vicarious pain she felt was never articulated.

The urge to draw a nice box around certain events and highlight them as "teaching moments" is natural for any mother. It may have been effective in childhood. "You know I told you never to stand in front of someone on a swing." "Now you see why it's important to brush your teeth really well every single day." "Aren't you glad you stayed home to study? You'd never have done so well on the test if you'd gone to your friend's house after school." "Now look what you've done." Each statement implies that the mother's way is, was, and always will be best, and the current consequences are a direct result of the mother's advice being heeded or ignored. These ideas don't go over nearly as well in adolescence. Now they aren't teaching moments but exercises in humiliation. Adding insult to obvious injury, these are just a few of the non-empathic ways to address a painful situation. "I never liked that girl. I told you that, remember?" "I told you if you left things till the last minute, this would happen." "What did I tell you? That salon is overpriced and does a lousy job." "Didn't I tell you to always have extra pads with you?"

Mothers want to reinforce what they think are important points, and unfortunately, the only way they think they can accomplish this is by having their daughters acknowledge (even just by squirming) that their mothers were right and they were wrong. In many relationships that involves giving up way too much power. A girl's self-confidence takes a direct hit. And yet many mothers' "I told you sos" arise from their own vulnerability and shaky confidence. Mothers of adolescents strike out so frequently that when they actually hit one out of the park, they want to see the scoreboard light up. It's the part *after* the "I told you so" that is perhaps most important. A girl's feelings are bruised by her best friend, she faces failure on an important school project, she failed to block the winning team's goal, she has to live with a wretched haircut that ate up several weeks' allowance or obsess about what people saw through her flimsy dress. Does she really need her mother's punctuation point to finish the sentence?

"I told you sos" in adolescence don't even have to be verbalized. For a daughter to confide in her mother, she has to feel certain that her mother won't be too judgmental. The feeling of being judged can have little to do with whether the mother *actually* judges or not. An adolescent girl has *two* mothers. There's the flesh-and-bones one she sees every day, the mother she eats with, talks to, drives with to the mall. The other mother is the inner voice that has developed over the course of their relationship. The internalized mother is a collage of feelings, memories, and impressions dating from early childhood. They are not necessarily even conscious. When something happens, even if the flesh-and-blood mother responds calmly or not at all, the internalized mother can be disapproving or controlling. It's not unusual for a mother and daughter to be in an adversarial discussion, one in which the daughter accuses the mother of being angry when she really isn't. In situations like this the daughter is fighting her internalized mother. When the smoke clears and the distortions are corrected, mother and daughter can find that they've actually been "locked in violent agreement." A mother is a particularly good screen upon which a daughter may project feelings that are unacceptable to her. "You think I'm fat/ugly/stupid/untrustworthy."

Barrier to Empathy: Narcissism

Many women (and men) look like successful grown-ups on the outside but on the inside they have an emotional age of about four. They relate to the world from an egocentric perspective. As long as things go the way they want, fine. But the temper tantrums that follow frustration of any need can rival a toddler's. While they may on the surface seem "in touch" with people, they can only make it work when others are kept at an emotional distance. Marriage to such an individual would be possible only for someone who was willing to indulge her and circulate in her orbit. This narcissism puts a woman at a great disadvantage, however, in the mother department.

Lois Gould's memoir, *Mommy Dressing,* describes such a situation. Her narrative succeeds so much because, unlike her fashion-designer mother, who was emotionally quite limited, she can describe the awful things without whining and look at the good things without having to tear them all down. When early-adolescent Lois prepares for a dance, she asks to borrow one of her mother's many beautiful creations. Her mother gave with one hand and took away with the other when she adjusted the dress "around the baby fat of my midsection. She then delivered her instructions for the evening. 'Don't perspire in this dress,' she warned me. 'I never perspire. Why must you?' This was a typical non-question, unanswerable but exquisitely painful. . . . I did, of course, perspire in the silk repp dress. She never wore it again, and I never asked to borrow anything of hers I couldn't live up to."

Barriers to Empathy: Rigid Expectations

Some women have a fixed worldview that permits their daughters little "wiggle room." Their rigid expectations aren't always directly stated but come through loud and clear anyway. The price of deviating goes way beyond the normal friction that occurs when a daughter decides to go her own way. Most mothers get royally pissed off when they perceive their daughters rejecting their goals and values. But being angry is not the same as rejecting. Conversations between mothers and daughters are often at cross-purposes. These "double monologues" happen constantly, often with one or both parties even realizing it. Mary Mebane describes a mother-daughter interaction about conflicting values that is likely to go nowhere but down over time. Inherent in this volley is the threat that Mary's literary, musical, and academic interests are worthless.

> "And my teacher said that I could go far in life, Mama."
>
> "Marguerita makes all of her own clothes."
>
> "And my teacher said that I was smart. You know I can't sew, Mama."
>
> "And Miss Pear says that Ida Mae does all of her washing and ironing."
>
> "I'm going to play a piece at Mrs. Shearin's piano recital."
>
> "You keep your head in a book all the time. What is the matter with you, girl?"
>
> "Mama, I'm sorry that I can't do anything right. I'm sorry."

In this climate only a very resilient child would be able to create an internal voice strong enough to block the defeatist, disapproving parental one. Mebane was such a child.

Her early education began in pre-integration North Carolina, and culminated in a Ph.D. and professorship in English.

Weight is often a very touchy issue between adolescent girls and their mothers. Ellen Gilchrist's wonderful character Rhoda Manning returns home from her first year of college, very pleased with her academic and athletic accomplishments. Her mother greets her:

> "My goodness, honey," she said. "You've gained so much weight. I thought you were on the swimming team."
>
> "I won the freshman writing contest, Momma. I didn't even enter it. I won first place."
>
> "We'll take you to the doctor tomorrow and get you some of those new pills. We'll go in the morning."

With the help of the family doctor's liberal prescription of Dexedrine, Rhoda speeds through the summer on a diet carefully supervised by her mother. She only comes to question her mother's criticism of her weight when she meets a woman she immediately admires who is surprised that anyone thinks she should be on a diet. The writing prize never comes up again.

Things go more easily when a girl, at least temporarily, is 100 percent with the mother's program. Sidda, in Rebecca Wells's *Little Altars Everywhere,* knows exactly what her mother expects of her, and is ready to sign on. "You have to start early if you plan to be popular," she says. "Mama was extremely popular when she was growing up. She was elected Most Well-Liked, she was head cheerleader, captain of the girls tennis team, and assistant editor of the yearbook. Even though it sometimes wore her out she said Hi! to every single soul she passed in the hall. It was a lot of work, but that is how her reputation was built. Mama understands the gospel of popularity and she is passing it along to me so that I won't be left out on the fringes."

Barrier to Empathy: An Eye for an Eye

Because the teenage girl looks more like an adult, it is easy to slip into expectations that she act like one. The parent often expects a level of reciprocity that is far too high and can overpersonalize and punish a daughter for her "selfishness." In a PBS special on mothers an elderly woman recalled early years with her children when she differentiated between her children's toys and her things. The rule was simple: "You break one of Mommy's things, Mommy breaks one of your toys." Her children must have been either exceedingly well behaved or very attached to their toys, because they never broke a thing.

Later, in an adolescent version of this quid pro quo nightmare, a perfectly nice-looking woman in her late seventies calmly described how she successfully shaped her daughter's behavior. It made me shiver. The daughter had been told about a dentist appointment and the need to be out of school on time. She forgot and went for a soda. When she realized what she'd done, she rushed to her mother, full of apologies. The mother matter-of-factly took her daughter to the dentist. Several days later the daughter told her mother about a dance at school and asked her mother to make her a dress. They went shopping together, chose the material, and made the dress. On the night of the dance the mother left the house as her daughter was getting dressed. She sat in her car down the street and cried. She insisted to her concerned husband that he not take the daughter to the dance. She arrived home when it "was too late to take her to the dance." The mother looked at her crying daughter and said, "Huh. Remember three or four weeks ago I asked you to be outside and we were late for the dentist? You *forgot*? OOPS! I *forgot*. When you can remember to do for Mother, Mother will remember to do for you."

In the heat of frustration and anger mothers sometimes respond to their daughters in kind. But as discussed earlier, the weight of an "I hate you!" from a daughter isn't close to an "I hate you!" from a mother. It's not a fair fight. In some ways, it never will be. The novel *Amy and Isabelle* is an excellent treatment of a single mother, Isabelle, whose promising future was foreclosed by a pregnancy at the end of high school. Unbeknownst to her daughter, Amy, Isabelle never married the father, an already married man. As Amy moves through adolescence, so much is reawakened in Isabelle. In a very common adolescent-mother scenario, Isabelle gets angrier and angrier as Amy dismisses her basic attempts just to make plain conversation. "Such moments alarmed Isabelle. It alarmed her that anger could erupt from her so easily, provoked by a simple glance from her adolescent daughter. . . . Was she a shrew simply because she would like a pleasant hello from her daughter? Was she some beast because she longed for a pleasant 'Hi, Mom, how was your day?' from a girl who virtually owned her life?"

Their relationship deteriorates over several months and then explodes when Isabelle discovers Amy's sexual involvement with her math teacher. She tries to convince Amy of the absolute inappropriateness of the situation, but Amy rejects her mother's appraisal. Her mother insists that Amy doesn't know enough about "what the world is like" to even grasp the gravity of the relationship. Amy replies, "No! *You* don't know what the world is like! You never go anywhere or talk to anyone! You never read anything . . . you never even go to the movies. How do *you* know what the world is like?"

This is the kind of moment that separates the women from the girls. Adolescent daughters have a radarlike ability to pick up their mother's vulnerabilities and either exploit or protect them. Amy had, without knowing it on a conscious level, kicked her mother in the tenderest of spots. Isabelle responded angrily, saying that Amy had no idea what it took to raise a child alone. But as angry as she was, she stopped herself from saying more. "What she did not do, and wanted to do so badly she could almost feel the shape of the words in her mouth already formed, was to shout, *You weren't supposed to even be born!* Whenever she went over the dreadful scene in her mind, the way she was now in the darkness of her room, she allowed herself a moment of approval, because it was, really, very good of her not to have said such a thing." And it really, really was. Those cats are very difficult to get back into the bag.

DAUGHTERS' EMPATHY WITH MOTHERS

There's a short-but-sweet line from *My So-Called Life* that sums up the challenges to adolescent girls' capacity for empathy toward their mothers. The mother, Patty, has just had her long hair cut quite short, to the surprise of her family and she is particularly interested in what her daughter, Angela, thinks. Angela shakes her head and refuses to tell her. "Pretend I'm not your mother," Patty insists. And Angela replies, with a basic truth: "I can't."

A girl makes her own judgments about her mother—some articulated passionately, others kept to herself. How could she have failed to notice her mother's hideous taste in clothes, her ineptitude with makeup, the way she blathers on and on to people she doesn't even know? How can her mother humiliate her by singing along to the oldies station when driving the car pool? How can she not understand the crucial importance of things she casually dismisses as "out of the question"? How can she act one way with her friends and so totally different at home? When did her mother become hypocritical or weak or mean? How can her mother have such a short memory? Is this a woman who should lead the way into adulthood?

Attunement

Despite the appearance of insensitivity to their mothers, girls are actually acutely attuned to them. They've had a long time to study the strengths, vulnerabilities, and inconsistencies in their mothers. Girls see the way their mothers act with husbands or lovers, the connection they have to their work, their satisfaction with family, the kinds of friends they make, and their involvement in the community at large. Adolescent girls are quite astute at knowing how comfortable mothers are in their own skin. They are beginning to see their mothers not just as people but as women. A girl uses her mother as a template against which she decides who she wants to be. Vocalized the loudest are the negative proclamations: "I will never let a man treat me like she lets my father treat her." "I will never let myself go like that." "I will never get sloppy drunk." They don't usually declare things like "I hope I have my mother's patience," or "I am going to pursue my intellectual interests throughout my life, just like my mom." When I was an adolescent, I had a long list of the "nevers": "I will never have six children." "I will never drive a station wagon." "I will never have so many rules." "I would never wear my hair in a French twist." "I will never say 'Hell's bells!' or 'Jesus, Mary, and Joseph!' instead of real curse words."

Although I never admitted it out loud, I was also filing away other things. These were the things I kept private, for which I wasn't sure I wanted to yield her credit. Whatever it was that my mother did to have such close, fun, loving, and long-lasting friendships, I wanted to do. She knew how to observe every holiday, birthday, or other special occasion really well. I was determined that I would do that too. I wanted to talk right back to my future husband like she talked to my father. And I wanted to marry a man who loved me as much as my father loved her.

Missing Pieces

Adolescent girls begin to see their mothers as women, but it's often harder to see them as ever having been young women or teenagers. They hear their mothers' stories, they see the photographs, but it's often difficult to imagine that they had the same tremendous insecurities, great adventures, jagged conflicts with *their* mothers, painful loves, close friends. They often know very little about the risks their mothers took. It can be jarring when they are given pieces of information that do not compute with the mother they experience. In a haunting memoir about growing up as the daughter of Holocaust survivors, Helen Epstein describes knowing her mother only as a woman who wanted to die. She was totally taken aback to hear that her mother had, at one time, danced a terrific tango. It didn't fit. "The words ricocheted wildly in my head. 'Mother! Tango!' Where had that tango woman gone? Was she hiding out for safety, or just erased? Was she always there, but I never saw it? Why did my mother keep that part of herself from me?"

A girl can love her mother and still want to be very different from her. It's a painful truth that daughters are easily confounded by mothers who tell them to "grow up" and then get furious and wounded when they do, leaving them feeling simultaneously overmothered *and* motherless. Novelist Barbara Kingsolver describes that time in late adolescence in a letter to her mother. "We didn't exactly fight. Whenever we were together, you kept telling me you loved me. And behaving as if you wished I were someone else entirely. I did the same—minus the part about telling you I love you."

The exchanges with her mother echo in hundreds of thousands of relationships in which the daughter stakes a claim for herself and her mother can't reconcile herself to the choice. Adolescents can't afford to spend too much psychic energy on their mothers' pain. If they did, they wouldn't be able to keep moving. In late adolescence a girl isn't aware that her mother can feel like her daughter is "breaking up" with her. Some daughters are swearing that they want to be the best of friends. Others aren't making any promises.

Barrier to Empathy: Just Because I Love You Doesn't Mean I Have to Be You

Mothers and daughters often struggle to differentiate their love and attachment to each other, on the one hand, from their individual differences, on the other. In their anxiety, mothers often see love and rebellion as mutually exclusive. They can't exist together; one will always cancel out the other. This is the source of continual, and often unintentional, wounding. Barbara Kingsolver describes the pain and sense of betrayal mothers so often experience when their daughters are in adolescence:

"How can you hurt me so, by turning out so different from me?"

"Who says I have to be just like you? What does that have to do with love?"

"It has everything to do with love. I'm your mother. Who else should you be just like?"

Barrier to Empathy: An Added Burden

Daughters of emotionally vulnerable or impaired mothers have more of a challenge in differentiating from their mothers in adolescence. While most adolescents are "renegotiating" new relationships with their mothers, daughters of troubled mothers often feel stuck. As scary as it is to claim more independence and strike out on their own, most adolescents only have to worry about themselves. For many girls, however, the greatest worry has to do with leaving their mothers behind. They get conflicting messages from their mothers: "You should go away to college" in the same breath as "I don't know what I'll do without you." "Moving into that apartment sounds like a good deal" alongside "Who will keep me in line about my drinking?" Sometimes the conflicts aren't verbal. Perhaps the mother relapses or loses ground. A crisis arises that only the daughter can handle.

How do girls from difficult backgrounds flourish, clouded by their mothers' instability, health problems, psychiatric illnesses, substance abuse, and cruelty, particularly when these factors are likely to be accompanied by increased parentification, limited financial resources, and nowhere near the level of social support that we know increases the resilience of troubled families? In some cases it requires the girl to create psychological distance, a firewall that lets the heat come only so far. Children and adolescents are incredibly resourceful in using fantasy to maintain their personal power and hold on to hope.

Gloria Steinem writes movingly about living alone with her mother, who was tormented and paralyzed by intense anxiety and depression. She describes the relationship as one where "our roles were reversed: I was the mother and she was the child. . . . That's why our lives, my mother's from forty-six to fifty-three, and my own from ten to seventeen, were spent alone together." Her mother's fragility weighed heavily on her. Despite her deep love and empathy for her mother, Steinem often felt resentful, or embarrassed by her mother's unpredictable disorientation in public. Her ultimate protection was the thought "I was just passing through, a guest in the house; perhaps this wasn't my mother at all. Though I knew very well that I was her daughter, I sometimes imagined that I'd been adopted and my real parents would find me."

The response to cruelty and unpredictability requires more than just the fantasy of escape. Sometimes it involves continuing a practice that began in childhood, when the child was forced to deal with situations that children are never meant to endure. As her mother was literally making a bonfire of the family's possessions and coming at her daughters with a knife, young Mary Karr, author of *The Liars' Club,* turned the whole situation into an imaginary cartoon, with her family as stick figures, safe and removed from their frightening surroundings. Carolyn See, who had to manage years of a mother who had deep and serious limitations in the basic fabric of her personality, found another way to deal with the barrage of invectives. "From the time I was twelve to when I was sixteen my whole purpose was to turn myself into a rock, a stone, an army tank. When my mother said I was like my father—I said nothing. When she said if I wanted clothes I'd have to work for them, I borrowed clothes from my rich friends. When she said men would know I was an easy lay because of my birthmark, I duly noted it. Scorn was my career."

A girl in these situations has a high likelihood of paying the intergenerational price for her stressful childhood. She can internalize the pain and become one of the walking wounded who keeps emotional or physical distance from everyone to guarantee her safety. She can run from herself and start looking for love in all the wrong places—poisonous relationships, drugs, and booze. She can be so frozen that she is ultimately unable to leave her mother. She is convinced that her mother will die without her. Or, worse, that she will die without her mother. The daughters of abusive mothers have a significant likelihood of making the passive active, and abusing their own children. They are also likely to choose abusive partners. Abuse, like love and attachment, is a gift that keeps on giving.

The resilient women are those who can distance themselves psychologically from their mothers' problems. They are adept at connecting with people who will fill in the blanks in mothering. They find interests and abilities that become for them a safe haven, something that is theirs alone. Often these interests are their vehicles to situations that will foster their healthier development. With the control that comes with age, they begin to call the shots as far as their mothers go. Some reach a limited understanding. Other mothers continue to be so toxic that distance is imperative.

Stories of horrible childhoods fill the hours of therapists. It's awful to hear the incredible array of weapons that adults use against children. But at the same time it's astounding to sit with some of those women and realize their amazing accomplishments—not getting pregnant young, being able to make friends and keep them, to find and sustain romantic love. These are women who've been beaten and didn't strike their children; neglected women who've fended for themselves and siblings from a very young age and still been able to deal with the demands of child rearing; women who have found meaning in work and creative expression of their pain. They often belittle these accomplishments as the most minimal a woman can claim.

Barrier to Empathy: If Your Feet Hurt, Get New Shoes

Just because you can put yourself in someone else's shoes doesn't mean you have to walk around in them. And it certainly doesn't make you responsible for their upkeep. Sometimes adolescents and adults who have survived rocky relationships with demanding mothers, the kind who were never pleased, for whom perfection wasn't good enough, have to be able to say, "Yes, I can put myself in my mother's shoes. I can try to see the world from her perspective." But maybe her mother's shoes are five-inch heels, uncomfortable as hell, with no protection or support. The daughter might have to learn to believe and articulate, "Yes, Mom, those *are* uncomfortable five-inch heels, and no, I *don't* know how you do it and how your feet *must* suffer. But you know what? It's not like you don't have other shoes. It's your choice. I will help you patch them up, or choose alternatives from your closet, or even buy you a new pair. But Mom, if you decide to stay in those shoes, the calluses, the blisters, and the feeling of being constantly off balance are all yours, not mine."

❧ PERIOD ❧

When I was twelve, still mortally embarrassed by my body's bloody betrayal, I ran out of sanitary pads. My mother was pregnant at the time, so my guess is she wasn't adding them to the shopping list as automatically as before. Rather than asking her for more, I tried to make my own by wadding up rolls of toilet paper. They worked all right, as long as I remained perfectly still. I used up a lot of toilet paper that day and probably stained some clothes. My father was doing some laundry and found the stained clothes. He told my mother. I didn't know fathers knew about menstruation in general, and I certainly didn't want my father to know about mine. My mother demanded to know what was going on. When I explained, she was angry that I hadn't told her, since it was such a simple thing to take care of. Thousands of pads and tampons later, I can't get to that scared, humiliated, alone place from here. I don't know why I couldn't have told my mother. I don't know why she was so angry. "First thing tomorrow morning," she told me, "you're going to go next door and ask for several pads." Next door was a family with a lot of girls, who were older than me.

I couldn't believe it. She made it sound like going over to borrow a loaf of bread. I didn't sleep that night. I wanted to run away. I couldn't imagine doing what my mother commanded. She was not a cruel person. And yet this was the cruellest punishment, especially since I'd never asked for all this period business anyway. My mother had no idea. And I couldn't tell her. In those books and movies about menstruation, they always tell you how it's not dangerous, that you're not dying. But anticipating the next morning, I wanted to die, preferably immediately.

I must have fallen asleep toward morning. When I woke up, at the foot of my bed was a small brown paper bag with several pads inside. Perhaps there was a menstruation fairy who visited needy girls in the night. I knew, however, that it was my mother, who upon reflection must have found some belated empathy for me and taken care of the situation. I am still grateful for that deliverance, even with the distance of so many years.

When I became a mother, I had a long list of things that I would do "right." I was determined not to use silly euphemisms for anatomy. We were open and honest, creating what we thought was a solid foundation on which we could guide my daughter's sexual knowledge and development. That was, until my mother-in-law came for a visit. We took her for a drive to admire the spectacular New England foliage. Apropos of absolutely nothing, my darling three-year-old piped up,

"Grandma, guess what? My mom has hair on her vagina!" In moments like these, I always wish there was an ejector button that could jettison a person far from the source of her embarrassment. In this situation I couldn't tell who'd benefit more—my mother-in-law, who was appalled, my daughter, who was very pleased with herself and had God knows what other anatomical tidbits to disclose, or my husband, who was about to lose control of the car or his bladder from trying to contain his laughter. It was then that I realized that even though I could curse like a sailor and correctly identify the names of reproductive organs, I was not the slightest bit enlightened.

From the age of four, it became clear that my daughter may have been interested in basic anatomy but was totally uninterested in its function. I kept waiting for her to ask where babies come from. She didn't. When I spotted a woman in the Stop & Shop with a big belly and used it as an entrée into a baby discussion, Keara started scanning the shelves for different kinds of toilet bowl cleaners or other things she cared nothing about.

Committed to my duty, I became more assertive. A clinical supervisor at my postdoctoral fellowship had written a charmingly illustrated book that was perfect for her age. I got him to sign it personally for her. "Look what I got for you," I said when I got home from work. With her lust for books, she rushed over. But after a quick look at the cover, she stepped back.

"I don't want that book."

"What do you mean? You haven't even read it yet. I thought we could read it before bed."

"I want *Willy Wonka and the Chocolate Factory,* not that stupid book."

"Okay, we'll just put it in your bookcase and you can read it when you want."

"I don't want it in my bookcase," she insisted, like it would somehow contaminate her other books.

"Well, where should I put it?"

"Your room."

Over the next few weeks, I'd cleverly leave the book next to her bed, or on top of her bookcase only to find it back on the pile of books in my bedroom the next day. It was all silence and subterfuge. I knew I must be doing something wrong, but I had no idea what it was. Over the next few years I bought other books—lots of them. There was one really nice one about the whole human body and how it works. She was fascinated with the liver, heart, even the salivary glands, but whenever we got close to the pages that had the naked man and woman with all the parts labeled, she slammed the book shut and announced that it was past her bedtime. I kept asking why she didn't want to look at those parts of the book. No answer. I was good at getting kids to open up to me. It was, after all, my job. She and I had always been able to speak easily. But I was coming up against a wall that was growing higher. I'd look at her and ask silently, "Why won't you let me be a good mother? I have to do this now. I don't want to spring it all on you when you're ten or eleven." No dice.

Books began to disappear. Her casual excuses—she brought them in to share at school or lent them to a friend—belied the fact that she'd stashed them somewhere. If we were watching a television show in which a character happily announced a pregnancy, she'd be out of the room before I could comment. Peaceful passive resistance is indeed a powerful tool. I couldn't force her to talk about sex. In fourth or fifth grade, when I was volunteering at her school, a teacher mentioned that she was a bit surprised that I refused permission for Keara to participate in the "health" program in which the menstruation/where-babies-come-from movie was shown. Keara was the only girl who didn't return the signed permission slip, so she had to sit alone in a separate room and do math problems. She hated math.

I thought it was about sex. It was, but it was about much more. She was becoming more of *herself* and less of me. As her self became more defined, so did her ability to protect the permeability of that self. Not everything is let in, and there's much more control about what goes on.

It's amusing now that we are safely on the other side of it, but we were both so tangled up in something we didn't understand. She couldn't bear the information. And I couldn't bear failing her. To see a problem between you and your daughter or you and your mother and to feel totally powerless in the face of it is one of the most excruciatingly painful experiences I've known. Being a psychologist was not only worthless in the situation, it was actually a burden. I kept looking us up in the psychiatric diagnosis handbook. I already had a couple of pages bookmarked for myself, but I had to consider that maybe I was even worse off than I'd thought. And my daughter, God only knew what was or would be wrong with her.

When she hit the age of ten, I decided that I didn't care if she knew about sex or pregnancy—she had to know about menstruation. Every time I thought about the possibility of her discovering her period in school without understanding what was happening, I wanted to cry. A friend lent me a book titled *Period* that her daughter had liked. I left it on her bed. It disappeared. Years later, presumably after the statute of limitations passed on retribution for defiling books—a mortal sin in our house—she told me that she had totally bypassed the indoor wastebaskets and taken it directly to the garbage cans in the yard.

Around this time I was seeing an adolescent in therapy. She was a delightful girl who had hit a couple of developmental ruts in the road but was in pretty good shape. One afternoon she was complaining about how it felt when her mother really wanted to "talk" and she didn't. "I feel like she's trying to invade me." I made an empathic face. "You know what she does?" she asked. "She gets me in the car. We're driving along and her face gets all serious. She turns down the radio and I know we're going to have a talk."

I tried to respond empathetically. "That must make you feel pretty trapped." As she nodded in appreciation for the fact that I, at least, understood her, I thought to myself, "That's a great idea! I'll trap Keara in the car!"

The next time we were alone in the car, I turned down the radio. She tensed. "Keara, listen, it's finally getting through to me that you don't want to talk about all this sex stuff." No answer. "Well, we don't have to. There's just one thing that you need to know that could happen soon." No response. "Keara, I swear to God you don't have to say more than one word, but I'd be a really crappy mother if I didn't ask. Do you understand about getting your period?"

She looked straight ahead and mumbled, "Yes," then immediately leaned over to adjust the radio dial. End of conversation.

After that I worried that she wouldn't tell me when she actually got her first period. In my anxiety, every time I went to the store, I bought a package of pads. I'd put them on her bed without comment. Seven years later, when we were packing her up for college and cleaning out her closet, there were at least twenty unopened packages of pads. When we pulled out the boxes under her bed, there were another fifteen. "A little anxious there, Mom?" she teased me. "Went a little overboard, did you?"

She got her period at school and didn't tell me. However, I knew something was up shortly after that. I asked, "Did you get your period?" trying to keep the tone in the neighborhood of "Did you have macaroni and cheese for lunch?"

"Yeah."

"Do you know what to do?"

"Yeah. I hate those things." This was definitely not time for one of those "isn't womanhood wonderful" proclamations.

"Well, when you want, you can try Tampax."

"Why do you call them Tampax?" she corrected me haughtily. "They're tampons."

The shadow of New Age feminism overtook me, and I said, "Y'know, sometimes when girls get their periods, they do something special with their mothers to mark the occasion."

"Let's go to the mall," she suggested. "You can buy me something."

We ended up getting a green sweater from L'Express. It had some French phrases on it that I thought might be "significant." But with my broken high school French, the most I could make out was that it was possibly about a bunch of herbs.

"Mom, let's keep this to ourselves." Translation: don't tell family, friends, or even her father.

"Okay," I promised. We finally had our meaningful, albeit brief, exchange.

Things worked out. I don't know how. Over time, she became direct and comfortable with discussing all kinds of topics, sometimes teaching me a great deal. She and I laugh now about how strange we both were. But afterward, there is a quarter second of silence that marks the isolation of that time, the sadness of it. Neither of us can explain why it was so hard or how it got so much better. It was a lesson to me about the temporary nature of so many problems between parents and children. In the bad times, we often underestimate good intentions, the power of love, and the passage of time. Over the course of adolescence and adulthood, unbearable situations actually become tolerable. Rage can give way to forgiveness, and estrangement can transform to approximate closeness. And much of it happens in untold ways that no book or expert has yet to explain.

SEVEN

Young Adulthood: Turning Out and Turning Into

Because if everyone just turns out like their mother, then what's the rat's ass point?

ELIZABETH STROUT,
Amy and Isabelle

For most women, adulthood spans a very long time. The expanse is so vast that it makes sense, for the purposes of this discussion, to divide it into three stages: early, middle, and late. Each phase contains the threads of earlier times and introduces unique characteristics of its own. A twenty-five-year-old and her forty-eight-year-old mother, or a thirty-five-year-old and her sixty-five-year-old mother, or a seventy-year-old woman with a ninety-year-old mother may interact with each other in some ways that haven't changed much since the daughter's childhood. However, since each phase of adulthood presents different challenges, we can expect to see variation in how mothers and daughters handle these challenges, how their relationships continue to develop or stagnate, and how the relationships contribute to women's sense of competence and well-being, no matter how old they are.

THE DEVELOPMENTAL TASKS OF
YOUNG ADULTHOOD

Young adulthood is the time for a young woman to discover who she wants to be and what she has to do to become it. It's a time for establishing self-sufficiency in some areas, like financial stability and taking responsibility for one's actions. It's also a time for continued development in the areas of interdependence—reevaluating relationships with family and friends. The young woman faces the empathic task of looking through the new lenses of adulthood to gain new perspectives on her mother. She begins formulating her ideas about marriage and children, and may take on the roles of wife and/or mother. Young adulthood is the time for claiming one's desired work and interests and making the efforts to attain them. It's a time that usually calls for mother and daughter to reach a new understanding of their relationship and their wishes for how it should proceed.

DECLINE

Jacquelyn Mitchard, author of *The Rest of Us: Dispatches from the Mother Ship,* writes about watching as her adolescent daughter strains against the bonds that hold her back from the "good life" she envisions when she grows up. Mitchard notices, however, that many women believe that the window for the "good life" is fairly limited. "I wish there was a serum I could give Jocelyn (and perhaps I could use a dose of it, too) that would imbue her with the understanding that life is not a steady upward progress towards college and then a steep decline." Her wish for a "serum" is interesting, and somewhat depressing; it's clear that she doubts the power of words or actions in changing the perception that a woman peaks at twenty-one. It's so entrenched that only a major, almost magical intervention will change the belief that everything after early adulthood is a vast wasteland, a greenroom for obsolescence. I know exactly what she means. Most adolescents and adults, male and female, have in their minds some benchmark, some event that will represent the pinnacle of their goals and wishes, after which everything will be downhill.

Unless a woman identifies that pinnacle as death, she's bound to live part of her life in her own definition of "decline." To some extent, her expectations are culturally determined. An eighty-year-old woman living in a very traditional Asian family can reasonably expect that in the wisdom and authority department, she will improve with age. However, if an American woman, on the basis of age alone, anticipates automatically garnering increasing respect with increasing years, her expectations will inevitably hit the wall. She will learn at a young age that societal and family respect for her authority and wisdom tend to be inversely related to age, and that both take a dive much earlier. Many immigrants to this country are horrified to see how quickly their power diminishes, rather than increases, with age, as their families become more and more acculturated to American ways and the honor of their seniority evaporates.

Women's perceptions of steep declines are set at various points along adult development and have a powerful hold over emotions and behavior. Therefore, how a woman defines *decline* tells a great deal about what she values and dreads in her own development. It should predict her expectations of satisfaction and happiness over the course of her life, as well as her sense of self as a major player in her world. One woman may look to the "mountain-top" and see a sign that says MARRIAGE. Another might see ADVANCED DEGREE or she may climb the peak in pursuit of UNDER 105 POUNDS, NO CELLULITE, STRETCH MARKS, OR WRINKLES. The beckoning sign might spell out career accomplishments and creative dreams. Some women see the bearing and rearing of children as the ultimate accomplishments, with a steep decline coinciding with their children's departure. Other women's signs say MENOPAUSE, GRANDCHILDREN, or RETIREMENT.

Often it's a specific age that holds special meaning to a woman as specific ages may have meaning for the generations of women before her. Is it the age of her mother's death? Is it the age at which she perceived her mother or grandmother "going downhill"? Is it a reflection of overwhelming cultural expectations? Witness the booming business of party paraphernalia that "celebrates" a fortieth birthday as symbolizing one foot in the grave, a fiftieth as both feet, and absolutely nothing at the sixtieth, possibly because by then people don't find age humor even remotely funny anymore. The proliferation of ads for cosmetic surgery underscore the pervasive attitude that young adulthood is as good as it's going to get. It's not enough to *feel* youthful. You have to *look* it.

The *actual* experience of decline is, fortunately, for many women, one of constant revision. Many of the points I once thought would be the ultimate peaks weren't. They were just preludes to pinnacles much more exhilarating to climb and savor at the top. Getting married neither begins nor ends a woman's life. Neither does the "empty nest," a concept so pervasive that many women whisper guilty confessions to their friends that, yes, they miss their kids, but it's great to have the freedom that comes with a switch from high- to low-maintenance motherhood.

CHANGES

One of the most dramatic shifts in understanding human development involves abandoning the idea that an individual's cement sets, to a great extent, in the first few years of life. With increasing knowledge about genetics comes the awesome recognition that from the time of fertilization on, genetics and environment will have powerful and reciprocal influence over each other. There is far greater plasticity in human development than was assumed even twenty years ago. And that plasticity extends into the adult years, when women continue to grow and change. To some extent, a young adult is able to create an environment that may be a better fit for her than the one in which she's grown up. The values, activities, and expectations of young adult women have shifted constantly over the past century. Before that, a mother in the nineteenth-century American West, for example, could predict with accuracy the type of life her daughter, by virtue of being adult and female, would have. Unless there was some powerful intervention (for example, her daughter's marriage to an upper-class man, or a shift from rural life to city life), things didn't change much for women from generation to generation. But with dramatic changes in the rights and lives of women, mothers are less able to peer into the cultural crystal ball and predict, or for that matter understand, their daughters' futures. Shared experience is of great benefit in increasing empathy between a mother and daughter. Regardless of cultural shifts, there will always be continuity in many of the important aspects of being a female. But empathy is also aided when mothers and daughters, admit, rather than accuse, that their experience is different.

FROM SEEING TO DOING

With her entry into early adulthood, a woman begins to consider roles for herself that she has seen her mother perform—marriage, career, motherhood, pursuit of interests, and involvement in the community. In addition to being able to legally split a six-pack, a young woman and her mother make conscious and unconscious steps about taking their relationship to the next level, moving from a girl-to-woman relationship to a woman-to-woman relationship. By virtue of having a young adult daughter, a mother (unless she was very young when she gave birth) is facing the probability that she now qualifies for what many consider the long purgatory of adulthood labeled middle age.

EMPATHIC ATTACHMENT AND EMPATHIC AUTONOMY

Unlike the beginning of adolescence, marked by the physical manifestations of puberty, the end of adolescence and beginning of adulthood has no clear biological markers. Achieving financial independence, establishing one's own household, making new friends, developing and pursuing new interests, completing one's education, maintaining gainful employment, marriage, and parenthood were at one time fairly clear signals of the onset of adulthood. Today the increasing technology of the workplace demands longer periods of training and education. The availability of birth control and the increasing expense of living independently each contribute to a lengthened adolescence.

A twenty-five-year-old who is receiving financial support from her parents for medical school, living expenses, and all unanticipated costs is in some ways an adult and in others an adolescent. Autonomy is rarely an all-or-nothing quality. It's possible to be autonomous in one area of functioning and not another. A young woman can be financially independent, make more money than both parents combined, live in a great house, and have good friends but be unable to make even minor decisions without her mother's approval. Her paralysis in pursuing anything her mother condemns is a signal that while financial independence is important, it does not guarantee confidence, self-sufficiency, or maturity.

Differentiating from her mother is something that a young woman began doing at birth. One of the few useful things I remember from high school math is the Venn diagram, in which two or more circles intersect at some point, demonstrating the space they share. In pregnancy and infancy the two circles representing mother and daughter overlap almost completely. Over time, both mother and daughter enlarge their separate spheres, ideally maintaining significant overlap. In late adolescence and early adulthood, one of the challenges is to determine how increased geographical separateness and greater freedom impact the overlap of those mother-daughter circles. The part of the daughter's circle that does not overlap with her mother's is one indication of increasing differentiation. But two entirely separate circles don't indicate healthy adult separation or autonomy, unless one of the pair is total poison for the other. It's much more likely to signal estrangement or a rupture in the relationship.

A near-total overlap of circles, which is expected in infancy, becomes a sign of big trouble by early adulthood. One of the most difficult challenges to a daughter's autonomy is a history of blurry boundaries between herself and her mother. Helen Epstein, daughter of two Holocaust survivors, haunted by the legacy of suicidal women in previous generations, gives voice to this dilemma. "My relationship with my mother was the most passionate and complicated of all. So intense was our bond that I was never sure what belonged to whom, where I ended, and she began." There are similar threads of mother-daughter entanglement in Meg Wolitzer's novel, *Surrender, Dorothy,* about two women who confided to each other every intimate detail of their lives. "Mother and daughter hitched their stars to each other," Wolitzer writes, "for there was no one else." The essence of the growing daughter's increasing ambivalence about the lack of boundaries between her and her mother is beautifully summed up in one sentence: "Her mother, though an extremely intrusive person, was also a source of comfort." There's the rub!

Differentiating is not the same as leaving, rejecting, or even separating, in the way the word is commonly used. The word *separation* is often associated with negative experiences, like *separation anxiety* and *marital separation*. Anyone who has tried to comfort a screaming toddler convinced that she has been left forever by the only woman she trusts in the entire world knows the intensity of real or imagined separation in the life of a child. Marital separation is consistently judged as one of the most stressful events in an adult's life. These are extremely powerful and often traumatic events in anyone's life. Many researchers and theorists believe that the traditional model of development, in which identity is the "prize" for cutting the cord to one's mother, is certainly not helpful to growing-up girls, and probably not to boys either. For too long, the concepts of separate and attached have been viewed as mutually exclusive. Separateness, in a society in which the individual is much more highly valued than the group, is seen as a necessary precondition for success and maturity. A child's dependency on her mother has historically been identified as a major blockade to her independence.

But there is no expiration date on mothers. The need for empathy from one's mother remains strong, even if the way it's expressed will change from childhood and adolescence. To leave the nest, most girls need much more than a good strong push. Like Dumbo with the magic feather, or the Little Engine That Could facing the upward climb, they need fuel for the journey and the encouraging voice that whispers, "I think you can. I think you can"—along with the reassurance that the track runs both ways.

Connected and Individual

A young woman can be "separate"—have a strong sense of self, clear purpose, and satisfying relationships—*and* remain very connected to her mother. Attachment to her mother is not the ransom a girl pays for her adult identity. In fact, from a very early age, a healthy attachment promotes the sustenance and courage to venture forth into the world. The street games I loved as a child, no matter how rough and dirty, always had a "home base" or other safe place where a kid could have a time-out. With all the bickering over rules, never once did anyone ever propose that we up the ante of our games by getting rid of "home." In fact it was the very existence of "home" that helped us take the risks, to rest, all sweaty and out of breath, so that we could return to battle. It was "home" where we could check out the game and catch up on the strategies of our teammates and opponents. Getting "home" might take some doing, but once a kid was standing on the plate, or the crooked square drawn in the dirt, or under the designated tree, home was as sacrosanct as if it were surrounded by an armed fortress.

Vulnerability and dependence are rarely acknowledged as natural parts of adulthood. "Running home" is considered the behavior of children and definitely something to be outgrown (like bottles and braces), either through the passage of time, years of psychotherapy, or a stint in the Marines. But even big, bad professional ballplayers need home base. Because a mother is the person usually associated with nurturing children in their neediness and dependency, leaving childhood has come to mean cutting the threads that connect to her.

By adolescence, boys have diminished their attachment to their mothers by internalizing a yardstick, which identifies anything female as ANTI-MALE, something to be avoided at all costs. He is no longer on "the Girls' Team." A solid connection between a mother and daughter can remain quite stable over the course of a lifetime and be a source of strength for both women. A woman who has a strong connection with her mother is also more likely to have a similarly stable attachment to her own daughter. It's important to remember that empathic attachment doesn't mean that things are automatically rosy or mellow. Mother and daughter can be securely attached and disagree on absolutely everything. They can get angry and have major falling-outs. They can be totally different in temperament, values, and goals. The true question is when the young woman dusts off all the leaves, litter, and dirt, can she still find home base somewhere under there? And can home base be stable and sturdy enough to be found?

Passports

Attachment is not a locked gate, it's a launchpad. A secure and empathic connection to her mother makes it more likely that a young woman will develop a strong identity of her own. It's interesting that the two primary forms of identification (ID) that verify the basics of our identity both involve travel. A driver's license and a passport—"we don't leave home without them." When I leave the country, my passport certifies, rather than diminishes, my identity. At the very point of leaving, I have to declare who I am and where I come from, or I won't be able to proceed. Without the backing of my homeland, I am stuck at the border. It is only by claiming my identity (picture and name) and my connection (USA) that I am allowed almost unrestricted access to the world. I don't have to renounce my citizenship to explore beyond U.S. boundaries. Belonging to one place helps me go other places, with the knowledge that "home" will always let me back in. Over time my passport will need updating. The face in the photo will look older; a name might change. My passport carries a record of my travels. If I run out of pages, there are always more. As long as I retain a connection to my country, I can travel as far as I like. For many people, the country of their birth suffocates or threatens their adult lives. Like many resilient young adults, they will then seek asylum in other countries, perhaps even become citizens over time. For many, even the remote possibility of becoming a part of another country, or another family, is what saves them from a life sentence in destructive situations that have trapped them for years. For example, a woman can make a "maternal" connection to a woman other than her biological mother, or find her own "good family" among a group of friends. Many women never realize that the most encouraging settings for growth may not be at the addresses they started out in.

Redefinition

Early adulthood is a time when women reevaluate their relationships with their mothers. With more independence and geographical distance, a mother and daughter may find that without some shared interest, structure, and effort, long stretches of time can go by without contact. For some women, this represents the realization of a lifelong dream. Others will have to figure out what it is they want from their mothers, what they want to give them, and the contexts and circumstances in which they'd like the contact to occur.

Daughters are typically the "leavers," setting out for new homes and experiences. Mothers are typically the "stayers," remaining in the same situations they've been in for a long time, minus one daughter. A mother of many daughters will feel the differences in the ways she responds to each girl's leaving and each girl's continued connection to her. The leaving of the first child can present an entirely different situation from the departure of the last. There is also the possibility that the first leaving will not be the last.

It's not uncommon for a young adult to leave home—for school, marriage, or career—and then return, when those things are finished or didn't work out. This presents mothers and daughters with the need to again redefine the relationship. In the interim between the first leaving and the subsequent coming home, daughters have established their own rhythms, habits, priorities, and preferences, and will have difficulty surrendering them just because they are back under the roof of their parents. It can begin during a daughter's college years, where school offers almost unlimited freedom. With semester breaks and summers, there can be tremendous tension about how many of the old rules still apply. Curfews, expectations about contributing to chores and errands, and attendance at meals are just some of the many sticking points between parents and daughters. As a newly proclaimed vegan, the daughter can ruin her family's dinner by enumerating the many reasons that every bite they swallow contributes to the suffering of animals, and doesn't promote human health either. Since one of the major shifts during the first leaving home is that the control parents have had over their children's daily lives is dramatically reduced, reentry problems are inevitable.

Some daughters have tremendous difficulty adjusting to being on their own. It's no surprise that the college years are ones of potential vulnerability for some young adults. It's common for the first episode of depression, anxiety disorder, and even schizophrenia to occur during this period. Young adulthood may be the dream many kids hold out for, but it is not without its minefields. Despite the fact that our society has identified the ages between eighteen and twenty-one as the time for leaving, not everyone is ready to make that transition then. The tough task for a mother of a homesick, over-whelmed, anxious college freshman is to know how much to let her tough it out with long-distance encouragement and support from the school, and when to accept the fact that she is not ready and should perhaps return home and go to a school nearby.

This is one of the basic conflicts of motherhood. On the one hand, the mother can have tremendous empathy for her daughter in her unhappiness and discomfort. Perhaps she has known that feeling herself. At the same time, just as with earlier painful situations, she must judge how long she can allow her daughter the safety of home and when it's appropriate to give her a push from the nest. In many clinical cases and in several generations of my own family, it appears that this period is often critical in establishing a sense of self as a capable individual. Women who never leave, typically in some unspoken collusion with their mothers, or who leave and return fol-lowing any kind of hurt or failure, have a high likelihood of not leaving again.

Many people find it easier to leave than to be left. During my daughter's first two years of college, she was in a dorm during the semesters and then she was back "home." Now she lives in an apartment that she loves, in a city that she adores. The last time she swept into town, she casually mentioned some-thing about when she planned to "go home." "Hel-lo," I corrected her. "You *are* home." She flushed and answered a bit too slowly, "Oh, yeah." My heart began to register the weight of what my mind has known for a while. Soon, when my daughter and I say "home," we will picture completely different places, probably for the rest of our lives.

Same Game, New Rules

Many women wonder what they should feel or do in this new phase of the relationship. How much are you supposed to miss your mother/daughter? How acceptable is it to acknowledge the things you won't miss at all? What do you have to do and be for your mother to see you as a good daughter? What is long-distance mothering? What do you have to do and be for your daughter to see you as a good mother? Who bears the weight of relationship? What are the rules of engagement? It's an uncertain time between mothers and daughters. Mothers can feel left behind as daughters experiment with new freedoms. Missing a child can be expressed with more hostility than is intended, giving the message that a mother disapproves of her autonomy, rather than just communicating normal ambivalence about change, and the loss that comes with more miles between them than they're used to.

Daughters who have always assumed that their mothers lived and breathed for them can get their noses out of joint when it becomes clear that their mothers are not nearly as bereft as they expected after they've left. My husband and I laugh each time our daughter leaves this message: "Hi, guys . . . Anyone home? Pick up . . . Hel-lo . . . Mom . . . Dad . . . *Where are you guys?*" It's still a bit hard for her to imagine that "us guys" actually have lives. Writer June Bingham described a similar time when a daughter in her twenties "once hesitantly confessed that whole days go by without her thinking of me. She was startled when I burst out laughing. "Whole days go by without my thinking about you."

Geography exerts a powerful influence over relationships. It's hard to act like a grown-up in your old bedroom. "I am never so full of contradictions as when I'm in my mother's house," writes Hannah, the adult daughter in Katie Singer's novel *The Wholeness of a Broken Heart,* which tells the story of three generations of women dealing with complexities of being separate but not separated. The places we spent our growing-up years hold powerful associations that get set off like trip wires once we cross the thresholds of our old homes. The moldy smell of the basement, the muffled downstairs noises of your mother making dinner. The precision of food placement in the refrigerator, the piles of *Life* magazines in the corner, the radio tuned to the same somnolent station that only your grandmother and your childhood dentist used to listen to. The bickering, teasing, or silence between your parents. The comings and goings. The house's creaks and moans. They can take a thirty-year-old back to age six or twelve or sixteen. Those ages can have good or terrible memories and can kick daughters back into thoughts, feelings, and behavior that aren't usually part of the adult "us" we like to show the world. When an adult daughter reenters the space that witnessed her childhood and adolescence, it can also touch off new feelings, ignite old conflicts and concerns, and encourage regression.

You Can Never Have Too Much Heat and Light

My parents have begun going to Florida for two months every winter, prompting my daughter to blurt out, "Oh God, my grandparents are turning into clichés!" They rent a two-bedroom apartment and always invite me to visit for a week. I'm lucky. I like my parents, and by the time February drags itself around, I'm happy to accept their invitation. However, after twenty-four hours, I remember several things I'd conveniently forgotten from the last visit. First of all, a two-bedroom apartment isn't very big. Second, all the attention I thought I'd missed out on as the oldest of six kids comes to me in spades during these visits. So much so that I've had to reevaluate my early assessment that I never got enough. My parents are so solicitous and interested in me that I find myself wanting to go to a place where people will be mean to me for a little while, just so I can feel justifiably hostile. Their questions haven't changed much over the years. Growing up there were always two major preoccupations: heat and light. ("Are you warm enough?" "Are you sure you can see in that light?") Something in my parents' generation made them concerned about freezing to death and going blind.

Scenario: It is early evening. I sit reading a book. My father walks into the room, stares at me, waits for me to look up. I don't.

Dad: Do you have enough light?

Me: Uh-huh.

Dad: Are you sure?

Me: Uh-huh. I'm fine.

Dad: Because I can move this floor lamp over there if you need it.

Me: No, really, I'm okay.

He leaves. Comes back and fools with the different light settings. I hear him ask my mother, "Can she see like that?" I try to pay no attention.

Mom: John, if she *said* she can see, she can see.

Dad [*wounded*]: I was just trying to help. [*Goes into other room.*]

Mom [*conspiratorial tone*]: He always does that to me when I'm reading. He just doesn't understand that some people like silence.

I remain silent, hoping the irony of her words will become clear.

Two minutes later.

Mom: Why are you holding the book so close to your face?

Me: That's the way I see best.

Mom: Maybe you need bifocals.

Me: I already have them.

Mom: Maybe you need better ones. When did you have your eyes checked? Did I tell you where I get mine?

Me: Yeah. [*only about a million times.*] I'd just lose them.

Mom: No you won't.

Me: Yes I will.

Mom: No. You just get one of these chains. Look, like the one I have.

Me: I don't want to wear a chain.

Mom: Why?

Me: I'm just not ready for that look yet.

Mom: What look?

Me: You know, that old-lady look.

Mom: This is *not* an old-lady look. John, come here, show her *your* glasses holder.

[*Dad obligingly demonstrates his sportier version.*]

Me: I'm just not comfortable with them.

Mom: That's nonsense. It just helps you keep your glasses nearby. Here, try mine on.

Me: I don't want to.

Mom: Oh, come on. [*She takes off her glasses with chain and starts putting them on me.*] John, doesn't this look okay on her?

Dad [*preoccupied*]: It looks fine, dear, but there's still the problem with this light. I just don't think she can see.

It's now time for a long, brisk walk on the beach, because I am about to scream. It's a "reserved for parents only" type of feeling. As we dance around concern and control, I fall back in time, knowing that only a total cave-in, an explosion of anger, or a quick retreat will break my fall. We have done this dance thousands of times, and it is almost exactly like it was when I was fourteen. Except that now I don't take it as an indictment of my ability to take care of myself. Even though being interrupted while reading is one of my pet peeves, I know that those heat and light questions are my parents' expressions of nurturance—code for "I still care about you."

Since my daughter's adolescence, I too have become increasingly concerned about the adequacy of light, heat, and so many other things in her life. I inflict the same exact thing on her, when I'm convinced that I know what's best for her and I'm determined to drum it into her *for her own good*. I'm always deluded into thinking that at some point she'll actually come to me and say, "You know, Mom, you are absolutely right about keeping my ears covered up in the cold. It doesn't matter if I look like a total dweeb in those pink earmuffs you bought me. All that matters is that my ears stay warm." But that's about as likely as me wearing bifocals on a chain.

For a long time in a child's life, the parent is assumed to be the person who knows what's best. It's not a power trip. It's the truth. For the most part, *mothers do know best*. The problem is that parents never get any notice in the mail saying that perhaps in Situation X or Y, they're not hitting the bull's-eye as often as they used to. And even though the dartboard will *always* hang in the basement, sometimes it's best to let the daughter play her *own* game, with her *own* rules, in the company of *other* people.

But it takes a long time to get it. I find myself driven to rephrase a suggestion that my daughter has just shot down, which is a lot like compensating for not knowing a person's language by speaking louder and more slowly. It always takes me a while to understand that there is *no* possible wording of my wisdom on that particular subject that she's going to accept. My second error is to assume that it was my timing that was bad, so I find ways to introduce it into the conversation every now and then. It's not so much a lack of empathy for her as it is my inability to accept the fact that when it comes to advice, she's gone on to greener pastures. The little girl who loved collecting my random opinions and insight is gone, and I'll probably never totally get it.

MOTHERS' EMPATHY WITH DAUGHTERS
Going to the Source

The farther away one gets from childhood, the "better" one is expected to tolerate hurt and sorrow, and the fewer places exist where a girl or woman can safely bring those same deep feelings of pain, the ones that require, more than anything, simple recognition and comfort. In *The Bean Trees,* Barbara Kingsolver introduces the characters Alice, her daughter, Taylor, and Taylor's adopted daughter, Turtle. Kingsolver writes with exceptional clarity about all kinds of mother-daughter relationships that transcend boundaries of income, education, or race. Taylor, who is traveling across the country with Turtle, is heartbroken over losing Estevan, a man she deeply loved. Hundreds of miles from home, she knows that there is only one person who can make her feel better, and she calls her mother from a phone booth. After explaining the basics, she gets to the real reason for the call: "Mama, I feel like, I don't know what. Like I've died." Alice, her empathic mother, replies, "I know. You feel like you'll never run into another one that's worth turning your head around for, but you will, you'll see."

In a subsequent novel, *Pigs in Heaven,* when Taylor calls again in distress from the road, her mother has an experience similar to that of many mothers who try to maintain long-distance relationships with their daughters. She "feels the familiar deep frustration of loving someone by telephone. She wants to hug Taylor more than anything, and can't. So much voice and so little touch seems unnatural, like it could turn your skin inside out if you're not careful."

Common Ground

Over the course of the early-adult years, young women will begin to enter the arenas in which their mothers continue to function. Completing education, finding work, selecting partners for long-term relationships, marriage, and children are concentrated in a fairly short period. Many of the skills needed to take on these roles require on-the-job training. A young woman learns early that it's going to take more than a shiny college transcript to pay her rent.

There comes a time when she has to make the distinction between the work she loves and the work that pays the bills. It's wonderful if they are one and the same. But especially early on, young women find themselves in jobs they could have gotten out of high school. The challenge of finding work that is more than a job is often uneasy in early adulthood, but if the inherent anxiety can be tolerated, it is better than foreclosing too early on a career choice just because it's a parent's wish or was a college major.

Bookstore shelves are packed with tomes on every way a woman can possibly screw up her relationships with men. Women are too nice, too bitchy. They're too moralistic, they're amoral. They play games, they don't play at all. They are from different planets, they're different types. They can learn how to twist themselves into the shapes of pretzels to make men happy. They can follow step-by-step guides to bagging a husband. But none of them tell a woman how to *be* a wife, how to *be in a marriage*. Things are tremendously more complicated in the getting-married business today than even ten years ago. The market is flooded with bride magazines, wedding consultants, and marriage expos. After that kind of buildup, marriage itself often seems anticlimactic. The preparation for *being* married (as compared with getting married) is haphazard and often leaves vast expanses of important issues unexplored.

A woman can take classes to learn how to feed a baby and how to resuscitate her if she happens to get it wrong. But she can't take a class that will teach her how to *become* a mother. Any mother who has a halfway decent relationship with her daughter can be of tremendous comfort, support, and empathy as her daughter tries to get a footing in each of these new areas. Particularly with a daughter's first child, a mother has an excellent opportunity to strengthen the relationship. A grandchild is the living, breathing link between mother and daughter. No matter how much they drive each other crazy, that baby is proof that they are now bound together by something more than their own history. A mother who picks up on her daughter's fatigue or restlessness and gently but firmly sends her out to be alone for a few hours is being empathic in one way. Another mother's empathic response may be allowing her daughter the time and space to vent her frustration, without feeling the need to do something about it. When new mothers watch their mothers handle their new grandchildren, they may be seeing a repetition of what was given to them but not remembered. A new grandmother who was an overwhelmed and less-than-giving mother may surprise her daughter with the degree to which she invests in the baby, and the pleasure she derives from her. In nurturing a daughter's child, the mother is vicariously forming connections with her own daughter.

One of the unfortunate byproducts of 1970s early-feminist thinking was the devaluation and demonization of motherhood. The presumption of some was that any woman who thought she was choosing to stay home and raise children was in reality repressed, depressed, oppressed, and in need of enlightenment. But it takes more than unisex clothes, feminist reconstructions of fairy tales, "Take Our Daughters to Work" days, and a lifetime of Barbie deprivation to produce another generation of similarly minded feminists. Most women, whether they consider themselves feminists or not, agree that daughters should have the same access to education and employment opportunities as boys. They agree that laws that take violence toward women seriously should be rigorously enforced. There is still a range of opinions, for those women and men who have the economic luxury to choose, about whether it is best that one of them remain at home with the children or continue to work outside the home. There is no one "feminist" party-line answer on this issue as some of us arrogantly assumed twenty years ago.

But once people decide to have children, future decisions can no longer be based primarily on what's good for the parents. The welfare of children must come first. What children need hasn't changed much over the years, but the ways of addressing those needs have. While a slight majority of families with children have two working parents, millions of women care for their children at home. An increasing number of fathers have taken on the child-care role while their wives bring home the cash. There are combinations that include part-time, working at home, in-home nannies, family day care, day care centers. Despite all of the hot air about working mothers and rotten day care and family values, the extent to which many parents can be at home with their children is driven primarily by economics.

Two things are clear from the research. Good child care is not an impediment to healthy physical, emotional, and social development. But good child care is expensive. Those women who have the least amount of choice as to whether they can leave their children to work usually also have the least amount of choice when it comes to child care. With the withdrawal of welfare, many single mothers are sabotaged in their attempts to find and maintain steady jobs because their child care is unreliable, inadequate, or substandard. Relying on public transportation to take a child to day care and then get to work is always a challenge. The childhood illnesses that upset the precarious balance of an upper-middle-class working parent's life constitute enormous threats to the job security of the working poor.

The issue of a mother's working versus "not working" is contentious. Women still feel the need to defend their choices, whatever they are. There is an amazing lack of empathy in this area, probably because there is so much ambivalence inherent in either choice. This is yet another example of the barrier to empathy that personal distress creates. It's interesting to see how the daughters of feminists look at their mothers' lives and make decisions about following in their footsteps. Daughters formulate their goals less on the basis of their mothers' stated ideologies and more on the whole picture they observe in their mothers' lives. In her book, *Daughters of Feminists: Young Women with Feminist Mothers Talk About Their Lives,* Rose Glickman asked the daughters of feminists whether they would want their mothers' lives. "The question was barely out of my mouth," she writes, "before the majority of daughters answer 'No!' These daughters who so admire their mothers' achievements look on their mothers' lives as an unrelieved obstacle course." There was a common theme they observed in their mothers' lives, one that they did not want for themselves: "struggle." Anne Roiphe, author of *Fruitful: A Real Mother in the Modern World,* describes a similar reaction of upscale high school girls when a high-powered lawyer visited their class to discuss her work. The girls' questions, however, which grew increasingly hostile over time, had nothing to do with the woman's career. Instead they wanted to know what she was like as a mother. How late did she return to her children? Who took care of them? What happened when they got sick? The lawyer became the screen upon which some of these girls projected their own feelings about their accomplished mothers. Would a male lawyer have fared so badly?

Following in Crooked Footsteps

Whenever anyone asked my daughter, even as a young child, if she wanted to grow up and be a psychologist like Mommy, the speed with which she yelled, "No!" took the questioner by surprise. To a person brave enough to ask why, her answer was simple: "Too much work!" I don't have a solid understanding about how my daughter has "turned out" the way she has. However, in the "following in my footsteps"–type career, it's connect-the-dots clear. And it's my own fault. By the time I was finally writing up the results of my dissertation research, my daughter was two. I was touched when she asked Santa to bring her a toy typewriter that Christmas. I took it as proof that I was setting an excellent example in the achievement department and she already wanted to be like me. Santa brought the typewriter. Several days after Christmas, I heard her huffing, puffing, and thumping her way up the stairs. I ran into the hall to see what was wrong. She was dragging the toy typewriter up the stairs, sighing heavily with each step. "Keara," I asked her. "What's the matter?" She shook her head back and forth and repeated a mantra she'd heard too many times before. "I just gotta finish my dish-ertation . . . I just gotta finish my dish-ertation!"

Rules of Disengagement

The harder rules for many other mothers of adult daughters are those of disengagement. When their daughters were children, they had unlimited access to them, their ideas, their fears, their dreams. By early adulthood, it becomes clear that there are many areas in which they don't even know the password to gain access. And sometimes it just kills them that other people do. When a daughter calls home in tears and gives a surface reason for her distress, a mother may find herself wanting to beg, shake, or bribe the whole story out of her. It leaves the mother feeling that she's being asked to set a broken bone without benefit of an X ray. Conversely, there are some young women who have not yet reapportioned the amount of territory they feel comfortable sharing with their mothers. Sometimes it's a mother who is inundated with the specifics of information that she thinks her daughter should be telling someone else.

In either case, the problems with empathy exist not in one person or the other but in their *expectations of each other*. These expectations may have been entirely appropriate for one phase of development but not for young adulthood. Mothers of girls, for example, are often the ones on the social sidelines, hearing the blow-by-blow of every hurt feeling and every rejection in the elementary school blues. Their comfort, often a combination of "Poor baby," "Try this," and "Get back on out there," is the way many girls learn about finessing social relationships. But if a mother tries that with a twenty-year-old, she may find that a lot of the magic has worn off.

Disengagement takes many forms. The daughter's eyes glaze over, the head nods too many times when the mother talks, signaling, "Okay, hurry it up," rather than, "Go on. This is fascinating." There's a great scene in Allegra Goodman's novel *The Family Markowitz,* in which Alma, an ethnographer, is doing an intensive project that involves interviewing old women about their lives, trying to excavate underlying themes in the process of aging. After she visits her parents' house for dinner, her boyfriend pumps her for anything her mother said about him. "What did she say?" he asks eagerly. Alma expresses absolutely no interest in continuing the conversation.

"I don't know." She shrugs. "Nothing much. How am I supposed to register blow by blow?"

"You're supposed to be an oral historian," he points out impatiently.

Her defense is one that's probably shared by many women: "Well, she's my mother, for God's sake. People don't listen to their mother."

Turning Out

In childhood and adolescence, girls are seen as works in progress. As they develop physically, socially, emotionally, and mentally, most observers will delay commenting on the final product until things slow down. Even though we know that early adulthood is not the final product, it's often viewed like those early projections in elections, when TV stations use exit polls to predict the results. There are a number of signs that point to whether a daughter has "turned out" in the ways her mother hoped or expected. In early adulthood, "promise" and "potential" meet the true test in the real world. A daughter's success according to her own perception and that of the outside world can be fairly independent of her mother's assessment. Mothers' gushing or grudging are the extreme outcomes. Either can make a daughter uncomfortable. "Turning out" is an incredibly subjective judgment. A woman could be the youngest Nobel laureate in history, and her mother, when congratulated on her daughter's brilliance, might shrug and say, "Of course, you know, she *still* isn't married." Another mother could have a perfectly happy twenty-year-old daughter, married and stay-at-home mother of one, and wonder, "What is she doing with her life?"

Mothers often have specific criteria for turning out in a variety of areas. Two major issues are marriage and achievement. A daughter's choice of men is a frequent source of a mother's displeasure. Former *New York Times* restaurant critic Ruth Reichl's mother made one of those great indirect complaints about the boys she was bringing home: "Aren't there any boys at your school who don't want to be garage mechanics?" What she said reflected so much more than the content of her "simple" question. Mothers may see their daughters' choices as reflecting upon them. "Mother felt I'd chosen Nathan purposefully as an overall scheme centering on her abandonment," explains a character from Barbara Kingsolver's *Homeland*. For other mothers the question isn't so much the choice of a particular man. Sometimes *no* man is good enough for her daughter, either because she does not want to be replaced as her daughter's primary connection or because she deems no man worthy of her precious jewel. "Admit it," author Dani Shapiro writes to her mother, "you don't think he—anyone—deserves me. . . . You poured enough love and longing for a brood of children into me, your only child, and expected that love to be exponentially returned." Shapiro sums up the frequent lament about mothers' expectations about "paybacks" for love that was always abundant but never free. She develops a flying phobia, because she's afraid not so much of her own death but of what her death would do to her mother. "Later in life," she quipped, "I heard the following definition of what it means to be a co-dependent: You're about to die and somebody else's life flashes before your eyes."

Be Prepared

Many young women, particularly those whose mothers have known the severe limitations of any kind of minority status, are very conscious of being the standard bearers of the next generation. One of the great comforts in oppression is the belief that the road may be easier for one's children. Fatima

Mernissi, author of the memoir *Dreams of Trespass: Tales of a Harem Girlhood,* writes about how her mother's wishes for her daughters' futures were also for her own destiny. "I had to take her revenge," Mernissi says of her mother. Her mother, trying vainly to resist the constriction of a life in which women had very limited options, was determined that her daughters, at least, would know a different life. "This tradition is choking me," she told Fatima. And she actively intervened whenever her daughters even playfully imitated the behavior or garb of the traditional women. Once, when Fatima was playing with a scarf, her mother became furious. "Don't you ever cover your head!" she shouted at her. "Your Grandmother and I have suffered enough of this head-covering business." She imbues her daughter with the sense that what she does with her life concerns more than her generation. It is another level, built upon generations of others, that reach toward something more, something better. I know of few more beautiful wishes than the one she confides to Fatima: "I want my daughters to stand up with their heads erect, and walk on Allah's planet with their eyes on the stars."

African-American mothers have long had to prepare their daughters for a double dose of oppression—for being black and female. In memoir after memoir written by successful African-American women, their mothers are almost always credited with actively preparing them to challenge the status quo. "Each word my mother uttered stood at attention, like a soldier doing battle in the war for improved communication," writes Bebe Moore Campbell about her mother's insistence that impeccable English was a "strategy in the overall battle for human rights." "Bebe, we've got to be prepared" was a fight song of sorts, signaling a challenge that her daughter was going to win. Zora Neale Hurston's mother gave her children the wonderful command to "jump at de sun." Lucille Clifton's mother gave her a directive arising from a belief that the environment she lived in would bring her daughter down, as it had her. "Get away, get away," she told her. "I have not had a normal life. I want you to have a natural life. I want you to get away."

Barriers to Empathy: Competition

Engaging competitively with one's mother or daughter is another common way adult women find to communicate with each other. "Whenever my mother talks to me," complains Pearl in *The Kitchen God's Wife,* "she begins the conversation as if we were already in the middle of an argument." She describes a typical competitive conversation:

> "Tofu, how much do you pay?" asks my mother, and I can tell she's eager to outdo me with a better price, to tell me how I save twenty or thirty cents at her store.
>
> "I've never bought tofu."
>
> "Four rolls of toilet paper, how much?"
>
> "One sixty-nine," I answer right away.
>
> "You see!" she says. "My place, only ninety-nine cents. Good brands, too. Next time, I buy you some. You can pay me back."

These skirmishes or battles can be played out over the most earthshaking and the most unbelievably trivial matters. Who has accomplished more in her work, who is the better mother, who cooks a better turkey, who's in better shape, who's the unhappiest, who *deserves* to be the unhappiest?

Barrier to Empathy: Guilty of Growing Up

Sometimes a mother holds her daughter culpable for something over which the girl has absolutely no control: growing up. It's as if the daughter arbitrarily changes the rules of the game on the mother, who then reacts with thundering or silent rages and rejection at no longer being the one who calls all the shots. This can be particularly difficult in mother-daughter relationships that were exceptionally close during childhood and early adolescence. It occurs with mothers who have imbued themselves and their daughters with the belief that theirs is an exclusive relationship, special and superior to all others in life. In childhood and even adolescence, mother and daughter bathe in the sunlight generated by each other. But when the daughter begins to enjoy the warmth and light of other suns, her mother's world grows cold and dark. When a mother sees her daughter as her singular purpose in life, her one shot at redemption, her yardstick of competence, she sets herself up for a major fall. Eventually she is bound to feel renounced, betrayed, and cut adrift by a daughter who can't perform those functions *and* become an adult at the same time. Like intense affairs, the fifteen- or twenty-year honeymoon in an idealized relationship between mother and daughter can end with as much rage as there was love.

Katie Singer's novel *The Wholeness of a Broken Heart* captures the essence of such a conflict. Celia and her daughter, Hannah, believed that theirs was a relationship of perfect attunement and empathy. It was compromised only when Hannah unknowingly broke the unspoken rules. The book begins with ten-year-old Hannah crawling into her mother's bed in the early-morning hours. Getting into bed with one's mother on a cold dark morning isn't that unusual for a child of her age. But the attributions she makes about it are. "Against her hot body I slide my cold one," she says. "I nestle my back against her breasts; I tuck my feet into her thighs. I weave our fingers and bring her warm hand to my chest. In the cradle of her body my chills subside. I feel warm enough to breathe again." Her hope that she will "melt" in her mother's "heat" is secured by morning. "By dawn, my gown is soaked with our sweat."

As she grows, Hannah begins to demonstrate interest in finding that part of herself that is separate from her mother. When teenaged Hannah discovers that she loves to write and cordons off a private space by using journals, her mother asks to see them. Hannah is not at all sure that she wants her mother to read about things they've never discussed. Her mother then reaches for the journals while simultaneously promising that she won't tease Hannah about things she could *only* have known by *already* having read them. Celia then dismisses Hannah's writing as a sign that she's "too introspective." Even that assault on Hannah's autonomy doesn't rock the boat.

But when Hannah arrives home on a college break and proudly announces that she's going to have a poem published and enthusiastically mentions the woman who is mentoring her, all hell breaks loose. In the space of several heartbeats, Hannah is catapulted from beloved daughter to total stranger—and cast out of her mother's house. "I don't respect you anymore," Celia tells Hannah. "So I no longer respect myself." Her mother cuts her off at the knees, knocks the air out of her, and exiles her to relationship Siberia. Mother and daughter go long periods without speaking. In an attempt at rapprochement, Hannah takes a trip out west to see her mother, stepfather, and cousins. On the way back from a family outing one of the children asks about the many pimples on Hannah's chin, why they are there and whether she can make them go away. Hannah answers the child directly and unself-consciously, until her mother vigorously interrupts to point out a very obvious mountain in the distance. Hannah is once again confused by her mother's anger and demands to know what she's done to deserve it. "What do you want me to say?" Celia explodes, in a tone filled with venom. "That your pimples are offensive? That you're ugly. That that's all anybody notices about you." If this is the price for all those toasty mornings in her mother's bed, I wonder whether it was worth it.

Barrier to Empathy: Sketches or Blueprints?

In her enthusiasm for her daughter's development, a mother can be marching band, roaring crowd, and flashy cheerleader—all lending rousing support on the field. But in her disapproval, she is uniquely capable of sucking all the air out of the Goodyear blimp flying above. Whether she admits it or not, when a mother thinks about her daughter's future, she's not exactly looking at the blank piece of paper upon which her daughter will paint her life. Some mothers are open-ended in their expectations of their daughters, and unconditional in their approval of what they make of their lives. As long as her daughter is happy, financially independent, healthy, free of addictions, and safely outside the criminal justice system, a mother can be reasonably assured that her daughter has "turned out." But many mothers already have a specific landscape sketched in well before their daughters' adult years. Some of these scenes reflect hopes that their daughters' lives will be different from theirs. Other scenes are so similar to the mother's own adulthood that they could be placed one over the other. There are pictures with wide-open spaces for daughters to paint what they want. And there are others so structured and detailed they might as well be paint-by-numbers.

Before their daughters were born, most mothers, when asked about sex preference, insisted that they didn't care, as long as the baby was healthy. With basic health out of the way, mothers quickly imagine and set other goals for their daughters. Mothers of young adults say things like, "Anything my daughter chooses to be is fine with me, as long as she's happy." So, if she's a happy stripper in a seedy bar, would that be okay? If she quits college to follow a music career that goes nowhere for ten years, is that okay? What about if she becomes an ambitious executive who prefers her career over marriage and children? Questions like these often help mothers admit that their initial unqualified acceptance of what their daughters decide to do with their lives actually has a number of restrictions. And these often unspoken restrictions can put serious limitations on a mother's empathy for her daughter's search.

These limits are expressed in subtle and blatant ways. In *The Kitchen God's Wife,* Pearl, a special-education teacher, expresses her delight over getting a good job. Her joy is tempered by her mother's muted reaction. "Right after I announced that I'd been chosen over two other candidates for the same position, she asked, "Two? Only two people wanted that job?" In her memoir, *Tender at the Bone,* food critic Ruth Reichl recalls finding her true calling after years of experimentation. Her mother, an extremely bright woman who had been frustrated in her own career desires, had trouble acknowledging her daughter's success. "When are you going to do something worthwhile with your life?" her mother demanded. This is one of those "what do you want from me?" moments that call for a quick reality check. "I had a respectable job," she had to remind herself. "I was making real money. Every month my name appeared in print. I was even starting to write food articles for magazines in New York." But it wasn't good enough for her mother, who had always fancied herself a great cook, despite the fact that she frequently tested the limits of interesting combinations and freshness. "Food," said her mother disdainfully. "All you do is write about food."

Barrier to Empathy: All or Nothing

Some daughters "turn out" in ways that disappoint or shock their mothers. Any attempts the daughter makes to input new information about herself into her mother's computer can make the whole system crash. The problem is usually not with the data but with the mother's ability to handle it. These scenarios often result in ugly showdowns in which the mother demands that the daughter invalidate the information, take it back, or deny that it ever existed. When the daughter refuses, a door slams shut and time-limited or permanent estrangement sets in. For women, many of these hot zones occur around issues of sexuality and religion. Some mothers have a very difficult time accepting their daughters' sexuality, particularly as they become sexually active. Several decades ago if an adolescent or young-adult unmarried girl became pregnant, it often resulted in her being sent away in shame. Cultural and religious beliefs often codify the bond between a mother and daughter and support mothers' involvement in allowing or inflicting punishment for their daughters' deviation from the "rules." In any culture where women are seen as the possessions of men, or subordinate to men, the consequences for acting like a free agent, especially sexually, are incredibly harsh. For centuries, "turning out" for a woman meant growing into and accepting her prescribed role, then indoctrinating the next generation of daughters in the same tradition.

Barrier to Empathy: Unacceptable Identities

We don't have to look back centuries or to other cultures to find examples of mother-daughter estrangement based on the daughter's developing identity. While the last twenty-five years have brought a loosening of sexual mores, resulting in a less punitive stance toward sexually active young women, sexual orientation is another issue entirely. For many mothers, a daughter's "coming out" is not usually seen as cause for celebration. With the announcement that her daughter is gay, a mother must redraft her expectations about her daughter's life. Conventional dreams of marriage and children are shattered, with mothers initially unable to consider the many alternatives that continue to exist for their daughters. Knowing how stigmatizing it still is to be gay in this culture, a mother may fear for her daughter. Even mothers who consider themselves very modern and open find these beliefs tested when they actually have to confront the realities of their daughters' "lifestyle." There's a difference between having a lesbian daughter in the abstract and having to watch her daughter cuddle with her new girlfriend in the family room. "We expect the generations to detour in some way," admitted a mother who learned that her daughter is gay, "but if we've loved and nurtured, we presuppose something not too far afield. Open-minded as I think I am, a dream dies. I am suffering unfathomed loss, loss of a landscape I took for granted."

Fortunately, many mothers and daughters find ways, over time, to integrate this aspect of the daughter's identity into their relationship in a way that satisfies them both. However, in families whose religious orientation adds the notion of burning in hell to already negative societal beliefs, rapprochement is not always as easily accomplished.

Coming Out In her short story "Only a Phase," Leslie Newman describes Deborah, a young woman who decides to "come out" to her parents in a letter. "I am a lesbian," she writes. "I've known it for a while and now I want you to know it too. . . . I'm tired of hiding. . . . I'm tired of silence. . . . I hope that my taking this risk will bring us closer. I want you to know who I am. I trust that your love for me is real, and that you will accept me as I am, even if that is different from how you want me to be." One week later she is surprised to receive a letter so quickly.

> Dear Deborah,
>
> Thank you for being so honest with us. As you have set such a fine example, I will be honest as well and tell you that you are the most self-centered, self-absorbed, selfish person that I have ever known. I don't understand how two such decent people like your father and I could have raised such a daughter. Don't you ever think about anyone but yourself? How could you do this to us? . . . I have not shown your letter to your father. . . . The least you could have done was think about him. . . . Deborah, where is your head? You never did have any sense.

You Reject My Religion, I Reject You Another divisive issue arises when a member of an observant religious family chooses individual needs over group strictures and standards. Marrying outside one's religion has always been a source of friction within families. In many instances the barriers precluding interfaith marriages have diminished over time. However, the more fundamentalist or orthodox the religion, the greater the likelihood that intermarriage is discouraged or forbidden. It is also the case, in the more orthodox religions, that the roles of women are considerably more restricted.

When Rabbi Miriam Tizrah Firestone fell in love with a minister of the United Church of Christ, the reaction of her family was swift and unyielding. She lived with him for several years, and her relationship with her mother became increasingly distant and hostile. Her mother made it clear that to marry a "goy" automatically meant cutting herself off from the people of Israel—all of them. At one point, from her new home in Israel, her mother called and flatly left the following message: "Tell Miriam her father is dead." Then she hung up. Following her marriage to the minister, Firestone was totally cut off. When she learned that her mother's brother had died, she called to offer condolences. Her mother hung up on her without a word. Several years later, in an incredible coincidence, Firestone bumped into her mother in a Miami airport. She was sure this was the hand of fate, reaching in to bridge the chasm between them. "Mom, hey, Mom! It's me," Firestone yelled, tapping her on the shoulder. Her mother's reaction was devastating. "As she turned around, I looked into her face . . . for the first time in eight years. . . . Then I noticed she was not looking at me, but at the wall behind me, as though I were not there. . . . For the first time, my being dead to her was not just a figure of speech. I actually felt dead, utterly cut off from her in every sense. I could not imagine any experience more devastating than to be ignored by one's own mother."

Curses   Mothers who have been less than empathic with their daughters from childhood through adolescence can be at a loss as to how to control them once they reach early adulthood. Anyone who thinks curses, spells, and hexes are things of the past just has to listen in to some of these attempts in regular conversations. The mother tries, and sometimes succeeds, at knocking the confidence out of a daughter with a simple concept: *her daughter is just like her*. Growing up in difficult relationships with mothers, many daughters often construct and keep a sharply defined mental list of differences between their mothers and themselves. Any girl who reaches young womanhood still believing that she is just like her mother runs the risk of finding herself in, often selecting, situations in which she is always at fault and deserving of abuse. If she identifies strongly with her mother, when she finds herself in a position of power (over employees, friends, men, children), she may reverse roles, make the passive active, and become the perpetrator. After telling her daughter that she was "cold," Ruth Reichl's mother lowered the boom: "Just wait . . . you'll see what it's like. Manic depression is inherited, you know. I wasn't like this when I was your age. You'll probably end up just like me."

DAUGHTERS' EMPATHY WITH MOTHERS
Turning Into

A major concern of many young women is the possibility that they might "turn into" their mothers. This fear always has such a little-girl quality to it, a fairy-tale holdover from *Cinderella,* where the coach "turns into" a pumpkin at midnight, or *Beauty and the Beast,* where Beauty kisses the Beast and "turns him into" a prince. Often when women express their dismay at evidence that they are "turning into" their mothers, it's as if it were a big surprise that there are any adult similarities between the two of them. It's as if some malicious magic descended in the middle of the night and implanted phrases, attitudes, and upper-arm flab that instantly made her more similar to her mother when she woke up.

Women's chagrin when they're caught—by themselves or someone else— talking, looking, or behaving like their mothers suggests that they've never heard of the roles of genetics and environment in shaping a girl into an adult. It reminds me of the Academy Awards, when the announced winners get up and say inane things like what a *total* surprise it is, or how they absolutely *never* expected it. But let's face it, each of them started out with a one-in-five chance of winning. It's not exactly the Publishers Clearing House Sweepstakes.

Early adulthood is often a time when women almost defiantly proclaim their differences from their mothers and assert their goals to do whatever is necessary to prevent themselves from "turning into" them. Turn into them how, exactly? In looks, speech, movement? In the things they say, the way they deal with men and children, the way they take care of themselves? In the esteem they accord themselves and others? The values they deem important? Their phrases, tics, moral lapses? Their vulnerabilities? Their strengths? "I think a lot of us have this need to inoculate ourselves against the maternal virus," writes Doris Fleishman. "The idea being that we would like to be self-invented, self-maintained. For better or worse, our fears are often realized."

Late-adolescent and early-adult women can be quite disdainful of their mothers. They may not know exactly who they want to be when they "grow up," but they know what they *don't* want. If I was rebellious in my teens, then in my twenties I was righteous. I braced against what I perceived to be ineptitude, unenlightened ideas, anything that remotely hinted at conservatism. I took women's studies courses that enabled me to tell my mother how she had basically wasted her life, never considering that one of the things she wasted it on was *me*. I had my own list of commandments, rigidly idealist, liberally dogmatic, and totally uncontaminated by reality—and a lot longer than the ones handed down from Mount Sinai.

Get Away

Some women love their mothers without reservation but know, often from a very early age, that for their own survival they must escape their mothers' lives. They figure it out on their own, or they get it straight from the source— their own mothers. When a girl sees her mother's life so constrained and unhappy, she looks for answers. She can decide that the reasons lie within her mother (mental illness, substance abuse, mean-spirited selfishness) or that her mother exists *within* the reasons (racism, sexism, economics, a poisonous family tree). Witnessing the women of her family who "were measured, manlike, sexless, bearers of babies, burdens, and contempt," Dorothy Allison was convinced that "the women I loved most in the world horrified me, I did not want to grow up to be them. I made myself proud of their pride, their determination, their stubbornness, but every night I prayed a man's prayer: Lord, save me from them. Do not let me become them."

What Doesn't Kill You Can Make You Crazy   Two highly acclaimed plays deal with the pathology of symbiotic and enraged relationships between mothers and the adult daughters who live with them.

Although the outcomes of *'Night, Mother,* by Marsha Norman, and *The Beauty Queen of Leenane,* by Martin McDonagh, are different, the stifling environments, the role reversals, the mutual but not always directly expressed hostility, simmer throughout each, threatening to erupt at any moment. In each play it is clear that the mother has never supported the development of her daughter's identity past the point where she might actually leave and make a go of it on her own. Several minutes into these plays—in which almost 100 percent of the dialogue is between two women—it's clear that by the final curtain both relationships are either going to implode or explode. In *'Night, Mother,* Jessie announces to her mother that she plans to commit suicide later that evening.

> *Jessie:* It doesn't have anything to do with you. [A major understatement.]
> *Mama:* Everything you do has to do with me, Jessie. . . . You can't do anything, wash your face or cut your finger, without doing it to me. . . . You might as well kill me as you, Jessie, it's the same thing. [Boundary problems? This does nothing to melt Jessie's resolve.] You are my child! [And that's just how she sees her.]
> *Jessie:* I am what became of your child. [Read: My development derailed—and it's your fault.]

The mother moves on to guilt, mistakenly thinking that if she reminds her daughter of her responsibilities, she may actually motivate her to stay alive.

> *Mama:* Jessie, how can I live without you? . . . You're supposed to tell me to stand up straight and say how nice I look in my pink dress and drink my milk. You're supposed to go around and lock up so I know we're safe at night, and when I wake up, you're supposed to be out there making coffee and watching me get older every day, and you're supposed to help me die when the time comes. I can't do that by myself, Jessie.

A fusion of identities and a reversal of roles. The daughter is only seen through the lenses of the functions she performs for her mother. There is no recognition of her as a real adult. After a speech like that from my mother, I'd be ready to throw myself in the river.

On the Irish front, always a golden opportunity to view twisted family relationships, *The Beauty Queen of Leenane* exemplifies the type of mother-daughter relationship that, if it doesn't kill you, will definitely make you crazy. Mag and her daughter, Maureen, torment each other in a constant barrage of words, with timing so sharp it can wound. Maureen "shares" with her mother a daydream she enjoys.

> *Maureen:* I have a dream sometimes there of you, dressed all nice and white, in your coffin there, and me all in black looking in on you, and a fella beside me there, comforting me, the smell of after-shave off him, his arm around me waist. And the fella asks if I'll be going for a drink with him at his place after. [A real conversation starter.]
>
> *Mag:* And what do you say? [Read: Let's see how far I can escalate this.]
>
> *Maureen:* I say, "Aye, what's stopping me now?" [Mother has been an impediment to making connections with men. It is only in death that the daughter will be free to pursue a love life.]
>
> *Mag:* You don't! [Deny it.]
>
> *Maureen:* I do! [Affirm it.]
>
> *Mag:* At me funeral? [The ultimate insult.]
>
> *Maureen:* At your bloody wake, sure! Is even sooner! [The penultimate insult.]

No one observing this exchange should be surprised when, at the end of the play, one woman's dead and the other's in a mental hospital.

Curses

Connie May Fowler remembers her enraged mother saying, "No one knows how like me you are. You get everything from me!" Along with brutal beatings and hate-filled looks, she remembers her mother's venomous verbal outbursts. "You are so stupid it makes me sick. I can't believe you came from my womb. You are your father made over—evil and mean. He couldn't stand having a daughter as terrible as you. Yes, it's your fault he's dead. You killed him." And still, even at her mother's death, when her mother's last words are "Go to hell," Fowler longs for the elusive good mother. The one who, at the very last moment, retracts all the hateful words and replaces them with expressions of love.

One of the challenges for a woman who grows up with a volatile or abusive mother is not to internalize everything her mother has thrown at her. Siddalee, from *Divine Secrets of the Ya-Ya Sisterhood* and *Little Altars Everywhere*, had to contend with a mother who perfectly fit the old saying "When she was good she was very, very good, but when she was bad she was horrid." What Sidda learned, through distance and therapy, was that her relationship with her flesh-and-blood mother and her relationship to the mother in her head had to be extricated from each other. She may not be able to change the flesh-and-blood mother, but she could cut the internalized mother down to a more manageable size. Finding a way to resolve the conflict with her mother was a separate task from working to quiet the partly awful mother she carried around in her head. It is a sterling example of how the development of empathy for one's self becomes so crucial for healthy adult development. "I have one main rule for myself these days," Sidda says. "Don't hit the baby. It means: Don't hurt the baby that is me. Don't beat up on the little one I'm learning to hold and comfort, the one I'm trying to love no matter how raggedy she looks. It's sort of a code, a shorthand for the heart."

Truths

Daughters can raise their mothers' ire and upset the family applecart by offering their newly developed versions of "the truth" of their childhood for public consumption. *Divine Secrets of the Ya-Ya Sisterhood,* the saga of four Louisiana girls who form a club called the Ya-Yas, opens with Vivienne, one of the Ya-Yas, furious at her daughter Sidda, who has mounted a very successful semiautobiographical play in New York. Unfortunately for the narcissistic Vivienne, it hits a bit too close to home and would never be considered an ode to her skills as a mother. "My love," she writes in a raging letter to Sidda, "was a privilege that you abused. I have withdrawn that privilege. You are out of my heart. You are banished to the farthest reaches. I wish you nothing but unending guilt." The way a mother and daughter get to that point and the possibilities for any redemption in their relationship are the predominant themes in many women's lives.

Adulthood is the time when we have the freedom to take our own impressions of our families, our own truths, even if they are at significant variance from the family line. Whether those truths are announced at the dinner table, in a novel, or on the radio, they can present a real hurdle in a relationship between a mother and daughter. Accepting that there can be two equally valid experiences of the same event is very hard in emotionally charged situations. There is also a double standard operating in which mothers are fair game for daughters' explorations in conversation, print, comedy monologues, and music, but a mother who reveals her daughter's "truths" in public is seen as much more of a betrayer. A mother, no matter how old her daughter or how lousy their relationship, is constrained in the same ways a therapist or a priest is. A patient can say anything she wants about her therapist, but without consent from the patient, the therapist is prevented from public disclosure, even if it is aimed at correcting misrepresentations or outright lies.

By the time a woman is twenty-one, she has had a very long time to study her mother. Some of her mother's behavior becomes as predictable as if it were scripted. But a mother may also act in ways that her daughter finds incongruous. A mother may disapprove of her daughter's boyfriend because he is irresponsible, while simultaneously dating men who aren't particularly good on the follow-through either. A young woman can love her mother and be an accurate observer of behavior, while at the same time having little understanding or empathy for her. The heady sense of independence and the injection of wisdom that comes with leaving home, meeting new people, and being exposed to different ways of thinking can, at least temporarily, decrease a daughter's empathy.

Although mother and daughter are both technically adults, the mother has years of experience over her daughter, making her *more* of an adult. For example, by her early twenties a young woman has begun to develop attitudes about the kind of long-term relationship she wants with a man. Her mother and father serve as templates, positive and negative, for those decisions. Mothers can be loved as people but not particularly respected in their roles as wives. Young women know a lot more about *falling* in love than *remaining* in it. Their experience in love relationships in the short term bears little resemblance to their mothers' experiences of marriage over the long haul. However, daughters often believe that with their newfound maturity and their careful analysis of their parents' marriages, they can safely say what they will and won't do, how they will and won't allow themselves to be treated, and how their marriages will certainly be more satisfying than their mothers'. The judgments and predictions made on the basis of what they see may not fully reflect the reality of their parents' relationship. "I can't believe how she lets him put her down." "He doesn't love her." "If any man treats me like that, I'll leave him." Maybe there are other things to suggest that he *does* love her, reasons her mother has chosen *not* to leave, that the daughter, for various reasons, doesn't recognize. Women who have identified more with their fathers may have similar observations, with a reversal of the wronged parent.

One True Thing, a novel by Anna Quindlen, begins at such a point. Ellen Gulden, an ambitious writer in her twenties, holds her mother in contempt for being a highly competent homemaker who has accomplished relatively little by Ellen's standards. "All my life," she declares, "I had known one thing for sure about myself, and that was that my life would never be her life." Ellen, who always identified with her distant academic father, begins to see things differently after she moves back home to care for her dying mother. In the day-to-day knowing of her mother, who has always accepted Ellen unconditionally despite her daughter's disdain, Ellen comes to see her mother's enormous strengths and her father's vulnerabilities. As she becomes angrier with her father, she can't understand why her mother has stayed with him as long as she has. Her mother tries to explain marriage in a way that Ellen can't yet grasp. Reflecting a combination of reality, resignation, and the confidence gained from hanging in there over the long haul, mother tells daughter about the concessions of marriage that women never consider when they're young and believe they know precisely what they will and will not tolerate. "You say that love is the most important thing in the world and there's only one kind of love," she tells her daughter, "but time goes by and you've slept together a thousand nights and smelled like spit-up when babies are sick and seen your body droop and get soft. And some nights you say to yourself, it's not enough, I won't put up with another minute. And then the next morning you wake up and the kitchen smells like coffee and the children have their hair all brushed and the birds are eating out of the feeder and you look at your husband and he's not the person you used to think he was but he's your life."

This is a statement that Ellen would have found repugnant for herself and used as another piece of evidence of her mother's passivity. However, in hanging in there with her mother through her illness, Ellen is able to take these words as a reflection of her mother's perspective, not some kind of command to follow in her footsteps. It's so much easier to really listen and be empathic with someone who sees things differently once the issue of control is addressed. For a mother and daughter of very different styles, values, and opinions to be able to let go of their need to control each other is to have a far greater likelihood of empathic connection. Ellen's increased empathy for her mother leads her to question her automatic assumptions about many things. "Being so wrong about her made me wonder how often I am utterly wrong about myself."

Secrets

A family secret in which one parent and child know something that the other parent doesn't produces a dangerous triangle. A child who shares in the secret of her parent's infidelity can have a sense of power and superiority over the wronged parent. Their knowledge can make them feel tremendously guilty about their role in the secrecy and fearful about the future should the other parent find out. One of the major themes in Alice Hoffman's bestseller *Here on Earth* concerns secrets and role reversals between mothers and daughters. Susie Justice, the protagonist's best friend, has known about her father's ongoing infidelity for years. And while it has influenced her relationship with her father, it has been more destructive in her relationship with her mother, whom she sees as a fool for not noticing. Susie has, of course, made the assumption that her mother doesn't "know." Perhaps it's easier to see her mother as a fool than to confront what comes from her idealized father's breach of trust. When Susie was a college freshman, home for the holidays, she was full of herself, "certain of everything a woman could be, all of which, of course, her mother was not." One evening, in anger, she blurted out the secret of her father's affair. Before she could fully expose it, her mother smacked her across the face. "You don't know the first thing about love," her mother screamed. "And you certainly don't know anything about marriage." After Susie left, Mrs. Justice reflected angrily about her daughter's smug certitude and judgments, especially because Susie thought only in terms of "black and white, love or rejection, yes or no," when she knew that love is so much more complicated than that.

To Protect and Defend

Girls who have seen their mothers struggle against adversity can become highly identified with them, often against the person, group, or situation that they perceive to be the cause of their suffering. In loving relationships, girls often develop fantasies of rescuing, curing, or redeeming their mothers. The "bad guy" can be someone or something designated by the mother ("Your father makes my life hell!" or "If we had more money, things would be so much better") or the daughter ("My father is always mouthing off to her. I have to protect her from him"; or "My mother has so much to deal with; I have to help her as much as I can"). A young woman's rescue fantasies can be quite elaborate and focus her goals from an early age. Rosemary Bray, a former editor at *The New York Times Book Review,* was raised by a strong, determined, and resourceful mother who was intent upon getting access to good education and opportunity for her children. An African-American in the Chicago slums, her mother had two forces arrayed against her: poverty and an abusive husband. From an early age Rosemary saw herself in the role of protector. "It was my job to stick up for her," she believed, which led to many unsuccessful attempts to prevent her father from striking her mother. Rosemary was awarded scholarships to private schools and went on to graduate from Yale. By the age of twenty-three she was already an editor at *Essence* magazine. Once she had achieved many goals ahead of her "timetable," and following the death of her father, she set about making all the things she'd ever dreamed for her mother actually come true. "She could certainly go back to school," Bray planned, "the way she'd always wanted to . . . my brother and I could teach her how to drive . . . maybe we could finally take that trip to California. . . . I even imagined that Mama might meet someone who was worthy of her, a man who would treat her well and look after her. I could have a stepfather!"

But just as the most generous wishes of mothers often don't come close to the desires of their daughters, what Rosemary wanted so badly for her mother wasn't really what her mother wanted for *herself*. Rosemary was forced to face this fact while visiting her mother, who worked as a companion to a wealthy white woman. At the woman's penthouse apartment, Rosemary was dismayed when her mother greeted her at the back entrance dressed in a maid's uniform. She couldn't stand the fact that the employer was called Mrs. Taylor, while her mother was called Mary. Everything on the wish list that Rosemary suggested to her mother was turned down. "I wanted more for her; I wanted her to want more," Rosemary wrote in frustration. What she definitely *didn't* want was for her mother to be stuck in what she considered an "Aunt Jemima" role. That dream dies hard, especially when it involves people having to change so that we can give them the gifts we've always wished we could. "I loved my mother fiercely," she writes in her memoir, *Unafraid of the Dark,* "but just as fiercely I knew I could not bear to be her. . . . My fears for her wasted life turned out to be projections into my own future." Rosemary comes to one the most difficult conclusions, the realization that her dreams were separate from her mother's. "I, who knew my mother's love for me all too well, had no excuse for trying to live her life for her." It can take mothers and daughters a lifetime to reach those insights. Some never come close.

Rescue fantasies can be based on childhood constructions of reality that never developed along with the growing child. The core of some of our deepest emotions is unencumbered by the critical thinking that comes with maturity. These feelings are so strong that we accept everything that confirms our viewpoint, and discount anything that doesn't. A daughter can tune in to her mother's unhappiness from a very young age. She will search hard for its cause, and when she thinks she's identified it, she'll stick with it. *Eating Chinese Food Naked* is a sharply funny and touching novel by Mei Ng, about twenty-two-year-old Ruby Lee, who returns to her parents' home in Queens after graduating from Columbia. It doesn't take long for Ruby to fall into the same role she had as a child, operating as a self-appointed guardian over her mother's happiness. "When Ruby was a kid, around the time when other little girls were being dandled on their daddy's knee . . . and thinking about marrying him when they grew up, she was dreaming about marrying her mother and taking her away." At the age of six, "Ruby watched her mother's face; it was a lonesome look," and she concluded that it was all her father's fault. For sixteen years she believed it, without any adjustment. On the surface there was enough evidence to support her point. Her father was grumpy, controlling, and derisive of her mother. But what the child Ruby did not know, and what began to slowly dawn on the adult Ruby, was that it had never been all that simple. Her mother continued to make active choices that kept the conflicted dance with her husband going. She did not need Ruby to save her. She wasn't even as horribly unhappy as Ruby had always imagined. In the end, Ruby learns that her only job is to save herself. It is the only way she will truly grow up.

At the end of her childhood memoir, *The Liars' Club,* an older Mary Karr returns to the scene of her chaotic, often very difficult youth. She takes in some of the same details and stories through adult eyes and sees that some of the horror of her memories was magnified by the powerlessness of childhood. "I never knew," she admits, "that despair could lie." Our perceptions of our mothers are fluid, even in adulthood. Our happy or sad memories are filtered through the lens of our current experience. The meanings of the memories we hold as most important in our formation may not even get picked up on a mother's radar as anything earthshaking. Similarly, when mothers describe events they've been certain would haunt or ruin their children, they may not be able to get an eye blink of recognition. Some of her mother's heroic, selfless moments may be remembered by a child as weak and selfish. Anna Quindlen gives some precious insights on the subjectivity of our memories of parents past and our perceptions of parents present. "Our parents are never people to us, never, they're always character traits, Achilles' heel, dim nightmares, vocal tics, bad noses and hot tears, all handed down and us stuck with them. . . . There is only room in the lifeboat of your life for one, and you always choose yourself, and turn your parents into whatever it takes to keep it afloat."

Let's Get One Thing Straight

In young adulthood, women begin to look at their relationships with their mothers from the enhanced perspective of distance. Without the day-to-day closeness of living together, without the inherent distance whenever one person holds authority over the other, there are new opportunities for insight and empathy. Barbara Kingsolver's story "Islands on the Moon" involves a mother and daughter brought together by a minor car accident. With time to kill in the hospital, they are almost forced to talk to each other. To make things even more interesting, they are both pregnant. With nowhere to go and nothing to distract them, they finally get down to discussing their long-standing differences.

"I never knew what you expected of me, Annemarie," mother Magda confesses. "I could never be the mother you wanted."

Annemarie replies, "I guess I didn't expect anything, and you kept giving it to me anyway. When I was a teenager you were always making me drink barley fiber so I wouldn't have colon cancer when I was fifty. All I wanted was Cokes and Twinkies like the other kids."

Magda and Annemarie discuss other things they've been totally off base about, leading Magda to conclude, "I don't know. Seems like that's just how it is with you and me. We're like islands on the moon."

Annemarie protests, "There's no water on the moon." Her mother's answer contains the recognition that despite years of estrangement, there is still the possibility for change.

"That's what I mean," Magda tells Annemarie. "A person could walk from one to the other if they just decided to do it."

❧ IF YOU'RE A YOUNG WOMAN, WHAT AM I? ❧

Just as a new mother turns her mother into a grandmother, a young-adult daughter is fairly clear evidence that her mother is middle-aged. My daughter was taking a college seminar in girl culture, and since I was writing a book on mothers and daughters, I was invited to speak with her class. I was a bit self-conscious, since I didn't exactly know what girl culture was, even after my daughter explained it to me. I tried to put together a "cutting edge" reading list, with the hope that it might look like I belonged. However, I knew I was doomed from the start, lecturing in a college that was founded by Marxists, for the children of major-league capitalist parents. When I referred to her classmates as "young women," my daughter corrected me with "girls," which "in my day" was a sign of disrespect. I hadn't received notification that it was no longer insulting to call any female over eighteen a girl, but I took her word for it.

I showed up for the seminar wearing the cheap end of Jones New York, with plain gold jewelry and boring shoes. There's no way to describe how unlike everyone else I looked . . . and felt. Just eavesdropping on their discussions before the seminar, I got the sense that a lot of these girls were incredibly bright and confident. I didn't understand much of what they were saying. Terms like "hegemony," "postmodern," and "deconstructionist" make me nervous. I liked these girls. Their hair was strangely colored and haphazardly cut. There was a great deal of facial piercing, and God knows what else was pierced beneath their clothes. At the beginning of the class, I just threw out the concept of mother-daughter relationships to see what they'd do with it. I was surprised and heartened by the ways these girls talked about their mothers, acknowledging clearly positive connections while admitting to specific challenges and conflicts. I asked one student to give me an example of an issue of conflict with her mother.

"My mother's having trouble with my job," she tells me.

I'm thinking her mother thinks maybe she's working too much while she's taking classes, or maybe that the job doesn't pay enough.

"I don't think she understands it," the girl continues.

I nod, thinking, "Okay, there are probably a lot of mothers who don't understand their daughters' jobs."

"I'm writing," she goes on.

"Oh, that's great," I say. I know it's difficult for some people to see that as a job, but I'm certainly sympathetic to the girl's dilemma, already thinking of suggestions for getting her mother with the program.

"It's on the Internet."

"Oh," I say. I'm thinking, "Well, now, the Internet, of course your mother doesn't understand. It takes a while to come around to this technology."

She goes on: "And I'm not getting paid for it yet, but I probably will."

"Okay," I'm thinking. "So her mother doesn't want her to work without getting paid. That makes sense, but if it's on the Internet, it probably has a future." I then ask, "So what are you writing?"

"Pornography."

I try to say, "Oh," as if she just said she was writing the biography of William Howard Taft.

"Lesbian pornography."

My training as a therapist has taught me how to keep my expression impassive, no matter what anyone tells me. A colleague used to describe the moments that catch you by total surprise as "What does my face look like right now?" times. The cool and enlightened identification I'd felt with the girl and my patronizing assumptions about her uncool, misunderstanding mother got a bit shaky with the pornography part. The lesbian component nailed it. At that point, the middle-aged, straight, Catholic-raised mother exploded inside my head. "Holy shit!" I'm thinking. "Lesbian pornography on the Internet? Of *course* your mother is having problems with your job!" The speed of the shift was unnerving because I was so clearly in a minority of one. The class was totally nonplussed, as if her mother's objections were on a par with bitching about a messy room. I wondered what bothered the mother most—that her daughter wrote pornography, that it was on the Internet, that it was lesbian pornography, or that it was being done for free. After all, many decades earlier Anaïs Nin got a dollar a page.

The whole two hours went like that. I found myself wishing I could dislike the girls, but I couldn't. One student asked me what "wave" feminist I was. I didn't know there were waves. I thought there was just the one. "First," I said tentatively. They laughed, not unkindly, but enough to let me know I was really wrong. The first wave, they informed me, was the suffragette movement.

"You're probably more second-wave," one girl said. "Y'know, Friedan, Steinem . . ."

"Actually," my daughter said, "I think she's somewhere between second and third." I felt like a little kid sitting there while a bunch of grown-ups tried to determine my shoe size.

"Third," I'm thinking. "What the hell is third?" The third wave apparently addresses all the faults and failings of the second, particularly in its middle-class, white, heterosexual biases.

I had two reactions to the girls' discussion. The first was, "I agree, and isn't this an interesting discussion, and I wish I was a student again." The second was, "You little pipsqueaks, do you know that some of the things you take for granted, like reproductive choice and Title IX, were accomplished by the disdained second wave? Do you know the crap I took in 1973 when I got married and refused to change my name?" But I was getting dangerously close to the "I walked five miles to school barefoot in the snow" rant that only makes people look old and cranky.

Those two hours actually did more for me than for them. Despite my initial unwillingness to consider their critiques of my feminist perspectives, when I was alone in the quiet of my own office several days later, I found myself integrating their perspectives in my reading and writing. In discussions over the next few weeks I was aware that this initially foreign way of thinking, about which I had felt so defensive, was actually becoming part of me. My initial reaction had been to protect myself from their strange new ideas. It was as if their new and different opinions somehow canceled out mine. Maybe it's an instinct that increases with age. A certain "calcification of concepts" that goes on much earlier than the point at which our intellectual abilities begin to fade. It's hard for mothers to experience themselves in situations where their daughters are visionary and they have become reactionary. It's especially true with many women who have always seen themselves as feminist and liberal, who see one of their missions in life as passing those parts of themselves to their daughters. For years I thought liberal was synonymous with "open," accepting of a myriad of opinions and lifestyles. It wasn't until I heard myself announce to my daughter that if she changes her name when she marries, I will consider myself a failure as a mother that I began to think twice. My daughter has every intention of keeping the name she was born with. That's not the point. Without realizing it, I have developed over time a "success of motherhood" checklist. It has little to do with my enjoyment of motherhood or the fact that I've usually tried my best. It is all based in the way my daughter "turns out," which is determined by so many more influences than our relationship. It was a stupid thing to say (even though a deep, unenlightened part of me still believes it), but it was also an illumination—one that was important to "get" as the mother of a late-adolescent/early-adult "girl." It is possible for people to be simultaneously liberal and rigid. It's also quite probable that I am such a person.

EIGHT

Midlife: Interdependence

No matter how old a mother is she watches her middle-aged
children for signs of improvement.

FLORIDA SCOTT-MAXWELL,
The Measure of My Days

THE DEVELOPMENTAL TASKS OF MIDLIFE

On the face of it, middle age is a stable time, when women basically play out
the hands they were dealt. Old images of middle age were of slowing down,
consolidating gains, and facing empty nests. It's true that in midlife many
women are solidifying the paths they chose in early adulthood—raising the
children born during their twenties, advancing in jobs or careers, and living
in stable marriages. But many other women in their thirties and forties are
having children for the first time (often remaining unmarried). Their career
status may have changed dramatically: women who remained home until
children were school-aged are reentering the workforce, women who have
reevaluated their career choices may be headed back to school or totally different work settings. Women are less likely to marry in their thirties and
forties than their counterparts in their twenties. Since marriage is not a

particularly stable institution, many of those women who married in their twenties won't be married ten or fifteen years later.

Middle age in the twenty-first century is a highly individual experience. Challenges include not being paralyzed by cultural messages that pitch midlife as a dangerous span of time requiring the outlay of pots of money to forestall it or at least cover it up. Getting moved up a notch to "grandmother" is another hallmark for many people. Being the mother of a new mother places that midlife woman in a position in which she can be concretely helpful to her daughter, sometimes wise, and open to what she may learn about herself through this new, often highly satisfying role.

ELUSIVE DEFINITIONS

"Middle age" is a term that most people think they understand, until they're asked to define it. When does it begin? When is it over? What justifies its existence as a separate category? Like the proverbial middle child, it's usually not considered the preferred place in the developmental lineup. Short of finding a "life tape measure" for pinpointing the exact middle of a woman's life, we have only the vaguest sense of what midlife is. Women's longevity has increased dramatically over the last century. A girl born in the United States in 1999 has an average life expectancy of seventy-nine, which translates into a long stretch between adolescence and death.

A quick word-association test: Think about "middle age" in women. What words or images come to mind? Don't censor judgmental or politically incorrect responses. Are the associations primarily positive or negative? What sensory categories do the images reflect? A *visual* image, for example, might include unwelcome features such as gray hair or wrinkles. Another might be a woman's name on the door of a great new office with a window, signifying increased status at her job. *Feeling* images might include the sense of slowing down or aches and pains. In contrast, expansive love for a grandchild or happiness at having more time with a spouse could be more positively charged connections. Smells, sounds, and tastes hold experiences of the past or expectations about the future regarding middle age. If your associations were more negative than positive, you're in the majority. The advertising industry and popular media have launched an all-out assault on middle age, providing us with plenty of negative images in the event that we can't manufacture enough of our own.

IT DEPENDS

The things that pop into my head when *I* think of "middle age" are both decidedly negative—mother-of-the-bride dresses and Depends undergarments. Admittedly strange, but not *totally* out in left field. Recently I attended the wedding of a friend's child. Up until then, whenever a bride's mother was escorted down the aisle, I always entertained "isn't that nice," slightly patronizing thoughts. This was possible because of a major case of denial on my part. Since my own wedding twenty-six years ago, I've continued to identify with the bride. This time, however, after the radiant mother and bridesmaids proceeded down the aisle, it hit me: the guy in the tux with the tears in his eyes was *my* age, and the young woman on his arm used to be our baby-sitter, only a couple of years older than my own daughter. I was not moved. To be honest, I was momentarily horrified. I've always happily considered the possibility of my own daughter's wedding. I can easily cast my husband in the role of the teary beaming father. But in a major omission, I never ever considered myself in the role of the corsage-wearing mother of the bride.

I blame it on the dresses. There must be a special section in department stores where the formless, sexless, pastel "mother of the bride" dresses are segregated from any dresses that suggest the possibility that "middle-aged," "mother," "celebration," "beautiful," and "sexy" can exist together. I once heard that nothing in a wedding should overshadow the bride. Most mother-of-the-bride dresses wouldn't even overshadow the *priest*.

Some things associated with normal aging have come as a big surprise to me, loss of bladder control being one of them. I should have caught on when the ads for adult pads and diapers started to have younger and younger-looking models. But I truly had no idea that anything in my basic abdominal region could go wrong—at least not for another ten years. Then I became wretchedly ill with bronchitis. There are many coming-of-age stories about girls being surprised by menarche, waking up to blood on their sheets. I now have a "coming *of more* age" saga, about wetting the bed at forty-six. "Oh, that's not uncommon with a cough as bad as the one you have," my doctor tried to assure me when I called her one second after the start of office hours. Little did she know that my appointment the next day would test her casual comforting. When I tried to blow into a peak-flow meter I started coughing and choking, and, without realizing it, created a puddle on the chair that then dripped onto the white linoleum floor. I was so sick that my husband was with me, and it wasn't clear whether he was more distressed by the horrible shape of my lungs or the total incompetence of my bladder. I immediately started crying, apologizing, and blubbering to my doctor, who is, fortunately, one of the gentlest physicians I've ever known. She shrugged like I'd just knocked over a little Dixie cup of water, turned to my husband, and instructed him to buy me a box of "junior" Depends, or whatever they're called. His stricken look made it clear he would have preferred being told to go out and score crack cocaine.

My doctor was right. As soon as the bronchitis disappeared, my bladder got a grip. But it's not really over. That was actually just a preview. Now, any time I cough, which is often, since I have asthma, has disaster potential. I always believed that I'd be somewhat cool about the whole aging thing. However, I can't help feeling that it's a bit unfair that I have to carry Tampax and Midol in the same briefcase that now holds several neatly packaged bladder backups.

MIDLIFE IS ALL IN OUR HEADS

Like adolescence, middle age is an idea. It's a concept that implies the existence of unique events that occur midway in the stretch from youth to old age. In many other cultures, and at one time in the history of our own country, these developmental stages didn't "exist." They weren't necessary. People died much earlier, obviating the need for a "middle" section. Apart from puberty, which is its biological anteroom, adolescence too is an abstract concept. But it is so ingrained in our culture that we act like there's total agreement about what it is, when it starts and ends, and its impact on mood, behavior, family, and peer relationships. "Midlife" is a similar idea that carries with it a number of "predictable" attitudes, emotions, and behaviors.

DECLINE: WHAT'S THE STORY?

Margaret Morganroth Gullette, author of *Declining to Decline: Cultural Combat and the Politics of the Mid-Life,* challenges the notion that age and decline are roughly equivalent. She believes that we organize the events of our lives into "narratives," or stories that offer a framework for the vast experience we have on a daily basis. Certain obvious attributes lend themselves as frameworks, such as race or gender. Gullette insists that we are often unaware of the ways these structures limit our attitudes, dreams, and potential. She is most interested in the narratives we tell about age, particularly advancing age.

The typical aging narrative that we apply to ourselves, or others, is the story of "decline." The strong belief that age is synonymous with decline is responsible for many things: our rabid attempts to cover it up or hold it off; assumptions about value that translate into discriminatory behaviors; being "written off" by younger people, patronized by the media, or ignored (stupidly, since the current crop of boomers is entering the general environs) by legislators. Stories we tell ourselves about age are restricted to a very few themes—being over the hill or going downhill. My reaction to mother-of-the-bride dresses and Depends undergarments are examples. When I watched the bride and her father, I immediately launched into my own version of the "story": "Oh my God, he's the father, he's old, he's only a little older than me, that means I'm old, that means the best half of my life is over, that means I'm probably even going to die someday." Although I wasn't aware of it at the time, I had a choice before launching into that scenario. I could have taken my story in a totally different direction. "Oh my God! I've never seen him happier. He looks great. I wonder what it's like not to be paying tuition anymore. They're going to have so much fun touring Greece in a few weeks."

When led to a row of sherbet-colored sacks that a saleswoman designated as "appropriate" for me in my role as "MOB," I might jump to thinking, "Oh, no, how old does this woman think I am? I'm supposed to be frumpy just because my kid decides to get married? That's not my fault. I hate these clothes. Soon it will be time to stop getting haircuts at salons and go to beauty parlors for helmet-head hairdos. It's all over." On the other hand, all I *really* have to say to myself is, "What an absolutely revolting bunch of dresses," and ask the saleswoman to direct me to cooler formal wear. In this way, *I* tell the story, the story doesn't tell *me*. It's a bit harder with Depends, because let's face it, it's as lousy to pee in someone else's chair in your early forties as it was when you were in second grade. I'm heading straight for the deep end on this one: "Oh my God, wetting my pants, next it's diapers, those potty chairs for bedrooms, saggy white underpants and a slip that always hangs too low, that vague smell of urine, and old-lady 'dusting powder', which I still don't know what you're supposed to do with. Bulging veins and chin hair. Bad breath that little kids will make fun of behind my back. Becoming an even worse driver than I am now." I could go on, but the point is clear. So far, I haven't been too successful reworking this particular narrative, other than repeating to myself possible alternatives to each fear: silky underwear, support hose that doesn't look like it, electrolysis, mouthwash, and taxis. These things take time.

Good for the Economy

The more a culture adulates and prizes youth, the more it will marginalize those who don't fall into that category. These days, middle age isn't seen as a stage as much as a "problem." If people are presented with an event as a problem long enough, they are ready and waiting when hordes of experts propose ways to "fix" it. The little "happy faces" pictures that get painted on middle age ("You're not getting older, you're getting better") are just as bad as the messages that say "You're getting older . . . fast. And unless you do something quickly, you're going to get much worse." The truest statement is "You're getting older. And whether you are getting 'better' or 'worse' is largely a matter of perception and choice." The perceptions will depend on which areas are sampled: wisdom, muscular strength, weight, sexuality, wrinkles, comfort living in one's own skin, performance at work, and relationships. Why do commercials for "old-people cars," "silver" vitamins, solutions to the myriad elimination problems, supplements, and preretirement communities show people who look a lot like me? It's not just my imagination. More and more, people in their forties and fifties are being targeted to think of themselves in free fall. And more and more products are proclaimed to be just the things to break, or at least cushion, the crash.

For a woman in her late thirties or forties, this can be very confusing. She finds herself thrust into a new population, somewhere between the minivan and the hearse, that is willing to spend a lot of money to slow that aging process down. How are we supposed to know when to shift from regular brands to "silver"? What the hell do we need the silver kind for, anyway? Why do we, all of a sudden, deserve to drive Lincolns or any other car that promises that now we'll feel like either big-shot old people or very cool middle-aged ones? Will all the biochemical wonders advertised so relentlessly on TV really lead my husband and me to break into a spontaneous dance on a beach or our front lawn? We didn't do that in our twenties. Why would we do it now? And while all of these messages are aimed at pre-middle-aged and middle-aged populations, they are laying down sturdy tracks in the minds of younger generations of women. They will be powerful in influencing a young woman's evaluation of her mother. And they will influence the ways she imagines her own future. There are many realistic and age-appropriate recommendations and guidelines about staying healthy, mobile, and intellectually active. It is in our best interests to remain as healthy as possible. But these are a relatively small proportion of the messages aimed at the aging baby boomers. The "point" of most of the middle-age messages is one of cultivated self-hatred.

The Beginning . . . of the End?

It's hard to define the beginning of midlife for a woman. Scientists might propose the "climacteric" period, also called "perimenopause," in which the ovaries begin to consider the possibility of retirement. For most women, this occurs during the mid- to late forties, as estrogen production declines. It takes about four years for the ovaries to actually hand in their resignation, with menopause typically occurring in the early fifties. Perimenopause and menopause may be *biological* markers of midlife, but *social* definitions have shifted well before that, especially for women.

Women get the message that middle age brings nothing good. Menopause is one biological and psychological minefield after the next. Depression during menopause has often been seen as inevitable. In fact, depression peaks at two points in a woman's life: ages twenty-five to twenty-nine, and the perimenopause period from forty-five to forty-nine, *not* postmenopause. Many women experience temporary changes such as sleep disruption, heart pounding, cloudy thinking, fatigue, and hot flashes. Longer-term changes may include loss of skin elasticity, bone density, and libido. Due to the falling levels of estrogen, postmenopausal women are at increased risk of heart disease. For 10 to 15 percent of women, menopause will be a walk in the park—negligible changes other than cessation of menses. For another 10 to 15 percent, the transition through menopause will be rough enough to interfere with almost all areas of functioning and may require estrogen replacement, additional hormone boosters, vitamins, minerals, behavioral techniques aimed at reducing discomfort (for example, managing the frightening heart pounding that women can mistake for panic, relaxation training, and ways of managing the sleep deprivation that is often at the root of the mood changes women report at this stage), and psychopharmacological interventions.

The majority of women will experience the changes associated with menopause as interferences and discomforts that they can maneuver around. Some of these women will benefit from hormone replacement, others from alternative approaches and herbal supplements. It is somewhat ironic that menopause has been referred to as "the Change." Women's sexual and reproductive development is one change after another. Some are more significant than others, but for women, adjusting to fluctuations is the *norm,* not the *exception.* Women are no strangers to managing the uncomfortable aspects of other developmental changes. Menstrual periods are often preceded by several days of increased irritability, headaches, and depression. Then there are cramps, leakage, birth control and its side effects, infertility hurdles, morning sickness, swollen hands and ankles, back pain, labor, delivery, episiotomies or C-sections, engorged breasts, bitten nipples, and yeast infections. Some fall into the category of "nuisance" complaints. Others are uncomfortable as hell. Some benefit from medical intervention, and some from women's folk remedies.

Gender Differences: Bronze and Rust

Research into the attributes that males and females say they would look for in a mate reveal distressing but not entirely surprising results. The female attributes deemed most attractive by men are those qualities that are the most temporary: a very limited, youthful version of beauty. Females, on the other hand, list more enduring characteristics that have a higher likelihood of remaining stable over a lifetime: personality, sense of humor, integrity—things that are not nearly as youth-dependent. Most women go into marriage without thinking of themselves as products under warranty. The concepts of wear and tear, trading in, and trading up don't occur to them when they say, "I do." Unfortunately, many men act like they were given a choice on the altar: richer/poorer, sickness/health, better/worse, *or* ten years, whichever comes first.

At a relatively early point in our lives, our culture operates on the belief that age bronzes a man and rusts a woman. At a certain number of miles, the odometer for men gets turned back to zero, while the odometer for women continues to measure every single mile they cover. For example, a generation of wonderful actresses, now in their forties and early fifties, are being replaced by much younger actresses, while actors in their fifties and sixties are continuing to win the same kinds of parts they've had throughout their careers. Many of the roles that are being taken by younger women aren't necessarily ingenue parts, in which being a twenty-four-year-old is truly called for. The past year in film witnessed countless romantic pairings of young actresses and men old enough to be their fathers or even their grandfathers. The women in their forties and early fifties have established impressive credentials in acting. It's not like Meryl Streep, Jessica Lange, Holly Hunter, and Susan Sarandon are getting ugly and out of shape, either. But their stock is going down anyway. They will play maternal roles, pathetic women, crazy women, peripheral women. They still look terrific, stylish, and sexy, but it matters less and less. It's the same story that actress Lillian Gish wryly commented upon years ago: "You know, when I first went into the movies Lionel Barrymore played my grandfather. Later he played my father, and finally he played my husband. If he had lived, I'm sure I would have played his mother. That's the way it is in Hollywood. The men get younger and the women get older." With the exception of some grandes dames in the news media, age (regardless of the wisdom gained through experience) for women is a liability. I always know a respected newswoman is on the way out when she moves from the six o'clock news, to five o'clock, to four, ending up at some hardship outpost like 5 A.M. The only difference between the impact of the message on a mother and on a daughter is that for the mother these losses are obvious; for the daughter, they are being filed away in the "time bomb" section of their memories, ready to come out of retirement at the developmental stage when they can do the most damage.

One Size Does Not Fit All

Even with the propaganda that tries to make midlife some one-size-fits-all phenomenon, the lives of women in their late thirties, forties, and fifties are so diverse that there are fewer and fewer baseline experiences that unite them all. With the many advances in fertility treatments, as well as women's freedom to pursue careers by delaying children, even the choice and timing of motherhood isn't a common denominator. On one maternity ward, for example, could be a married twenty-one-year-old with a newborn in her arms, who has just made the smiling forty-two-year-old woman standing next to her a grandma. In the next bed, a forty-two-year-old single woman nurses her child as she talks on the phone with the infant's sixty-five-year-old grandmother. An unmarried fifteen-year-old makes her thirty-five-year-old mother a grandmother, her fifty-three-year-old grandmother a great-grandmother, and her seventy-five-year-old great-grandmother into a great-great-grandmother. And even though the thirty-five-year-old is technically a grandmother, the odds are high that she will function as a mother to both the fifteen-year-old and the newborn. Down the hall, a thirty-five-year-old woman is laboring with triplets, most likely the result of harvesting multiple eggs in fertility treatments. A brother and sister in their late twenties tap on the nursery window to see their new half sister, the product of their forty-four-year-old mother's second marriage.

These are not outlandish scenarios. The birthrate for women in their thirties and forties increased dramatically over the past decade. It has leveled off over the past several years, but the number of women having babies in "middle age" is significantly higher than it was two decades ago. Teen birthrates are continuing to decrease, with rates for African-American and white girls at a forty-year low. Births to unmarried women of all ages constituted almost 33 percent of all births in 1996. One of the most dramatic shifts for women in midlife is the availability of fertility-enhancing treatments that leave the childbearing window open longer. How long the window *should* be open is a controversial issue. Just because a fifty-three-year-old woman can sustain a pregnancy, should she? Apart from the biological implications, what are the psychological and cultural implications of having such dramatic age differences between parent and child?

Perhaps the most striking recent finding is that, as the Centers for Disease Control put it, the "multiple birthrate for older women is skyrocketing." Since so many babies of older mothers are conceived through various fertility treatments, the likelihood of multiple births is higher than usual. From 1980 to 1997, the twin birthrate increased 63 percent for women forty to forty-four and almost 1,000 percent for forty-five- to forty-nine-year-olds. The triplet-plus rates are equally astounding. There's been a 400 percent increase of triplets-plus for women in their thirties, and a 1,000 percent rise for women in their forties. On the surface, this may look like good news for women who wished to delay children till later in their lives. One pregnancy equals instant family. The bad news is that multiple births are associated with higher risks to infants. CDC reports indicate that low birthweight, very low birthweight, and infant mortality were four to thirty-three times higher for twin and triplet-plus births than for singles.

Unfortunately, the problems associated with multiple births also appear to increase with age, suggesting that maternal age and multiple births interact in some way to increase infant risk. Many complications of multiple births have permanent consequences. Although women who have waited until middle age to have children may be better able to bear the financial burden of caring for infants with complications, in terms of health, energy, and life expectancy there may be problems, especially since it's likely that there's at the very least another twin or triplet, who may or may not also have impairments. The older the woman is, the less likely she is to have a parent who is in a position to provide substantial assistance. In fact, a middle-aged mother may have a newborn at the same time she is caring for her own mother, whose health or independence is becoming increasingly compromised.

A forty-year-old mother contending with newborn twins is in a very different situation from a woman of the same age who's packing her youngest child off to college. The forty-year-old grandmother who has three generations living under her roof has a very different life from a single forty-year-old with no plans for children. The accumulation of forty years in a woman's life tells us very little about the territory she currently inhabits, and places significant limits about how much we can generalize about the "typical" middle-aged woman, her mother, and her daughter. However, respecting the inherent variations, certain themes in mother-daughter relationships do become more salient when a woman hits midlife.

Reflection

For many women middle age is a time of reflection. This doesn't mean leisurely walks down memory lane but rather active attempts to apply new insights both to understand the past and to direct the future. It's a crucial point at which a woman must grapple with the differences between *societal* definitions of her status, which capitalize on what she is not, compared with other approaches that underscore who she *is* and what she can *become*. If midlife women actually swallowed all the garbage about how they should feel at this point in their lives, they'd flush themselves down the toilet. They are no longer young; they are unattractive and asexual. Those whose children are beginning their adult lives are minus one "legitimate" role; those who never had children have lost even that. Some women exert twice the effort just trying to "maintain." They are perfect targets for the commercialization of middle age and endorse the notion that the goal of middle age is not to *appear* middle-aged. Others, like author Jacquelyn Mitchard, receive the same advice from almost everyone: "The key to maturity is to risk less and settle more."

Elizabeth Kaye, author of *Mid-life,* made no bones about her initial distress at leaving young adulthood. But slowly she began making positive associations between her memories of her mother at her age and her own experience. "Just prior to my thirty-fifth birthday," she writes, "I began to notice that my friends and I were conversing less about frivolous matters like love and work and more about the true essentials like medical insurance and desk chairs with added support for the lower back. I enjoyed these dialogues. There was a sweetness to indulging in the same concerns and complaints I'd heard my mother and her friends express."

This perception, and the increased comfort level that comes with it, can follow a period of feeling resigned and resentful, angry about being kicked out of the "girls' club," wondering if all the stereotypes about "dried-up" women are true. Most women find they aren't. "Like so many women my age, at about forty," writes Margaret Morganroth Gullette, "I started feeling better. It was a convalescence, a slow mid-life cure—as if we were taking tiny homeopathic pills marked Energy, Enlightenment, Self-Delight." Midlife can also offer welcome relief from the constraining expectations of the past. There is something freeing in the "Oh, the hell with it" approach to life. It's like saying no to one more day of wriggling, shimmying, and sucking it up to the daily imprisonment of relentlessly confining underwear with the word *control* somewhere on the label. Everyone knows what Gullette means. But "letting go" can be much more positive than giving up.

In middle age, many of the burdensome expectations and "rules" that women once believed were so important lose their value. "All one's life as a young woman is show," wrote Doris Lessing, "a focus of attention, people notice you. You set yourself up to be noticed and admired. And then, not expecting it, you become middle-aged and anonymous. No one notices you. You achieve a wonderful freedom. It's a positive thing. You can move about, unnoticed and invisible." Gullette takes it a step further. She gets mad. In response to the book title, *How Did I Get to Be Forty and Other Atrocities,* she quips, "I got to be forty by not dying beforehand, and damn it if I'm going to consider that as an atrocity."

The Lost Years

A mother at midlife and her daughter in early adulthood are both in fertile periods for reflecting, rediscovering, and reinventing their relationship. Daughters begin to venture into the territories of work, independent living, romantic relationships, marriage, and children—familiar terrain to their mothers. Despite the fact that the category headings have remained the same, the explosion of cultural, medical, and technological changes in the twentieth century have guaranteed that each generation of women grows up in a different "world." For each, her world will color her goals, her freedom of movement within society, her power, and her control over her health and reproductive life. For women born in the late 1940s, expectations about marriage, work, and motherhood differed dramatically from those of women born in the late 1960s. A 1940s mother may have had a combination of career and motherhood but, unlike her sixties-generation daughter, not simultaneously. Regardless of decade, a mother whose economic world gave her no choice but to juggle a low-paying job with tending children and keeping house may have trouble understanding her financially comfortable daughter's decision to return to work as quickly as possible following the birth of her child.

Birthrate statistics indicate major changes over the past twenty years. Beneath the numbers are stories that describe shifts in women's reproductive lives that will dramatically impact their empathy with another generation. The birthrate was higher for women born in the 1940s, and the ages at marriage and the birth of their first child were younger than they are now. The divorce rate, as well as the percentage of unmarried mothers, has increased over the past four decades. Among women married during the 1940s, the divorce rate was 15 percent for whites and 18 percent for African-Americans. It's a dramatically different picture for women married in the late 1960s and early 1970s, where the rate is 50 percent for whites and 60 percent for African-Americans. Unlike their mothers, women are much more likely to live with their potential spouse *before* marriage. The divorce rate among these couples is higher than average. And it's no small difference that a majority of mothers, whether by choice, necessity, or both, work outside the home.

Chances of adopting an American infant are very limited. The "relinquishment rate" for newborns has gone from 40 to 50 percent in the 1950s and '60s to 9 percent in 1973, to 4 percent in 1981, to a negligible 1 percent in 1995. The falling rate of adoption appears due to changes in choices among white teenagers, who constitute 70 percent of adolescents giving birth.

We never give up the ideal of the perfect mother. Unlike Santa Claus, the Easter Bunny, and the Tooth Fairy, who are discarded when fantasy succumbs to reality, we are more willing to suspend rational thought when it comes to mothers. When a child "gets" the lies that, with good intentions, have been perpetrated upon her, she usually doesn't lash out at Santa, bad-mouth the Tooth Fairy, or trash the Easter Bunny to younger believers. But the myth of the perfect mother persists despite the millions of pieces of evidence to the contrary. Thirty and forty years after we've retired Santa, we're still looking for that magic in our mothers and are as disappointed as little kids when we don't get it.

After a difficult period in her thirties, Elizabeth Kaye felt that she really needed her mother. "I called her in New York," she writes, "and a day later she flew out to Los Angeles and we took a room overlooking the Pacific in the old Miramar Hotel. The next morning, I woke before she did and lay in bed, listening to her breathe as she slept in a narrow bed on the other side of the night table. My mother had come three thousand miles. Now she was five feet from me. Yet the wish to commune with parents can be so sharp, so profound, that however close we venture, it still may not be near enough."

In many ways, the struggle to reconcile the gap between what we wish and what is humanly possible is the same from a mother's perspective. At some point her daughter was a dream child, constructed by her out of wishes, needs, projections, and vestiges of generations past. And at another point her daughter naturally veered or steered off course. How mother and daughter handle the inevitable differences between dream and reality, hunger and satisfaction, pain and comfort is the task of a lifetime, one that is never finished, even when one of them dies.

These unchallenged ideals of perfection stand in the way of the chance mother and daughter ever have to be together as adults, equally. It is always a challenge to equalize a relationship in which power and dependence were once so heavily weighted on one side. Gullette reminds us that it's often a possibility we only see with regret, once our mothers have died. Reconnection, at least by early middle age, has the obvious benefits for both participants that come with a deep enduring equal relationship. Just as daughters turn to their mothers as models, historians, and teachers, Gullette believes, the opportunity for a daughter to accompany her mother as she moves through middle and old age is of benefit to both.

If a daughter can see her mother in midlife as falling outside the traditional rigid and self-fulfilling "decline" perspective, her expectations about her own middle years may shift. She doesn't have to deny the primarily physical changes that occur in midlife. What she has to fight is the immediate association to all of the negative consequences associated with those changes. The leaps are automatic but almost always "off." How does the fact that I now have to wear a knee brace when I play racquetball suggest that I am ready to be traded in and sold for parts? Of the thousands of things I do in a day, there are numerous examples of age-related changes. It takes me a good five to ten seconds longer to find my keys in my forties than it did in my twenties. Of course in my forties I also have a whole lot more keys than I had twenty years ago, suggesting a full life despite the memory "deficit." In listing the things I might do in a day—sitting at a computer and writing steadily for three hours; lifting and lugging bags of fertilizer and mulch up the long steps to my house; retrieving a little boy from preschool to spell his mother; crawling around on the floor; running in the park; reading something in preparation for writing a magazine article; talking with a friend for an hour about a movie we interpret completely differently; packing for a business trip the next day—I will filter out the power and energy required for those tasks. I will deemphasize the intellectual sophistication I couldn't have had at age twenty-five. I certainly won't credit the amount of control I have over my days. Stuck in the "decline mode," I will give a "weighting" to anything remotely suggesting "over the hill," so that it contributes ten times more to the overall perception of age than the many other things I do.

MOTHERS' EMPATHY WITH DAUGHTERS
Familiar Territory

Mothers have considerable experience with issues (love, marriage, children, work) that become focal in the lives of young adults. Whether or not daughters agree with the conclusions their mothers have made on the basis of their experience, one thing can't be denied: mothers are "experts." They may know a lot more about broken hearts, shaky marriages, jobs, and the all-consuming nature of motherhood than their daughters think. Their empathic connection with their daughters is not just the sum of all of their experiences. It's the wisdom they're able to extract from it. The immediacy of pain, of need, of anger, of failure is ever-present in youth. What we feel in the moment is how *it will always be.* But by middle age, mothers have a longer-range perspective. The tentative, clinging child they worried about is now out there tackling the world with success and abandon. The child who seemed to have "born to win" tattooed on her forehead has taken underachievement to new lows and is relatively content in her early twenties to act like she's fifteen. Things the mother thought would surely kill her (being left by a husband, losing a child, having next to no money) don't.

It is easy to get so stuck in our perceptions of those closest to us that we accept only the new information that confirms the impression we already have, and discount any that doesn't. A totally demonized or idealized mother or daughter is a direct result of such rigid perspectives. We can get stuck because we don't look hard enough or long enough. We aren't curious. We don't ask questions. We are perfectly content to grow old with perspectives that have served us well in the past, and often it doesn't matter if we're missing important information.

It's All Relative

The very same things that drive a mother and daughter apart in childhood or adolescence may draw them together in adulthood. I spoke at a conference recently, where a gregarious fifty-one-year-old woman who had survived breast cancer described to me her two "easy" daughters and her *difficult* one. Given my business, when I hear the word "difficult," I jump quickly to school troubles, conduct problems, lousy peer relationships. The difficult daughter, now twenty-five, had always been "independent," never wanting to have anything done for her. Like Rayona, in Michael Dorris's *A Yellow Raft in Blue Water,* she probably "would have learned to change her own diaper until she saw that it was easier just to train herself." She was "stubborn" and "distant." I could think of more positive renderings of each of these traits, but I kept my mouth shut. Unfortunately for the girl, she was the firstborn, so all of her mother's fantasies of what being a "good daughter" meant weighed heavily on her. The second and third daughters were exactly what the mother had in mind, making the firstborn even more of an exception. The firstborn was a "successful" child in the outside world, but she was never the touchy-feely girl her mother expected and wanted.

Years later, the widowed mother was devastated with a breast cancer diagnosis discovered during a routine mammogram. She required immediate surgery and chemotherapy. Daughters two and three matched her emotional fear and distress. They were emotive, empathic, and supportive of their mother. But the firstborn took care of business. Because she was temperamentally more self-contained, she was able to use all those well-honed independence skills to help her mother. She dealt with the insurance company and the hospital. She made the arrangements for follow-up care. She had a higher tolerance than her sisters for dealing with the nitty-gritty elements of her mother's treatment, such as dealing with the considerable nausea and changing surgical dressings. Her assertive approach sometimes ruffled a few hospital feathers, but since it was in the service of her mother, the family saw it in a very positive light. Her mother realized that this daughter loved her no less than her other daughters, and that those aspects of her daughter's personality that she had undervalued earlier had to be considered in an entirely different light.

Regrets

Part of growing up involves learning how to recognize and deal with our mistakes. There are few areas in which errors loom so large as in motherhood. The stakes seem impossibly high and the probability of falling short even higher. It often feels particularly cruel that we can't have second chances, "do-overs," opportunities as mothers or daughters to get it right in another life. The closest mothers get to a do-over is having another child. The rest of life is so much more forgiving. We get second, third, or billionth chances at something. We have additional shots at jobs, at marriages. Advances in technology are allowing us to replace parts (biologically engineered or donated). We can undo so many awful habits. But we get only one shot at our mothers and one shot at our daughters. After that we have only memories and the wisdom or torture of reflection to keep us company.

Empathy in Retrospect

Tillie Olsen, author of the short story "I Stand Here Ironing" (a sure bet to make me cry at every reading), describes a relationship in which the embroidery of regrets and sorrow, love and compassion, insight and the passage of time yields a growing empathy for the daughter and the mother. The mother's reflections about her eldest daughter, nineteen-year-old Emily, are prompted by a teacher's note home asking that she "manage the time" to come in to discuss Emily, "a young woman who needs help." In a minimum of words the teacher communicates a lack of empathy (not to mention respect) for the mother. She implies that the mother is stingy when it comes to devoting time to her daughter; something is wrong with the daughter, the teacher has a sense of what it is, and it's probably the mother's fault.

Being summoned to a child's school for a conference outside the regularly scheduled ones can reduce even a confident parent to a second-guessing jellyfish. A summons is even more difficult when the teachers are closer in age to the child than to the parent and are free from the constraints or humility that arises from actually having children of one's own. "Even if I came," muses the mother, in a silent conversation with the letter-writing teacher, "what good would it do? You think because I am her mother I have a key, or that in some way you could use me as a key? She has lived for nineteen years. There is all that has happened outside of me, beyond me."

Only from the particular vantage point of being midlife women with young adult daughters can we see the things we wish we'd done differently or recognize things we'd totally overlooked. We use the present to understand the past, with the knowledge that who and how our daughters are at this very moment is only one of many yardsticks we can use to understand more about ourselves as mothers. As they sort through their relationships with their own mothers, our mothers watch as we make our way in the world, and they see themselves as women through the one daughter or another. Often they are surprised to hear the voices of their own mothers in their daughters and granddaughters.

These perceptions are far more complex than the reflexive "Oh my God, I'm turning out like my mother!" self-accusations. Like Tillie Olsen's character, mothers look at themselves in earlier times—their strengths and their frailties. They consider the situations that couldn't be helped. There are the responses so automatic they can't be recalled. They pore over the knowledge they have accumulated about each child. The things they knew then and the things they only see now. They see how the world looks at their children, and how their children look back. They see the setbacks and small victories. They mesh their dreams with their realities, and their emotional connections to their children persist long past the time when they are the primary influences in their lives.

In her ironing-board reflections about Emily, the mother covers a broad range of influences (severe illness and early separation, substandard child care, single parenthood, no money, the second-born sister "who was everything

Emily was not," and other children who were "pushing up, demanding"). Despite the pain of remembering, she continues, realizing that much of what she now knows about Emily, she knows with the passage of time and the experience of other children. What came automatically with the younger children was more difficult with Emily, partially because of her temperament and partially because the mother was anxious and overwhelmed most of the time. She wonders about one particular dance between them—Emily hated school and tried vainly to find ways of staying at home with her mother. But there was "never direct protest, never rebellion." She uses the experience with her other children as a new template upon which to understand Emily. "I think of the others in three-, four-year-oldness—the explosions, the tempers, the denunciations. . . . What in me demanded that goodness in her? And what was the cost, the cost, the cost to her of so much goodness?" She remembers the advice of an old man in the neighborhood that she should smile at Emily more when she looked at her. "What was on my face," she wonders, "when I looked at her? I loved her. There were all the acts of love. It was only with the others I remembered what he had said, and it was the face of joy, and not of care or tightness or worry I turned to them—too late for Emily." But her mother also realizes that some things aren't too late for Emily—that she has found a comfortable niche, one in which she feels like "somebody." Despite the sorrows and regrets about Emily's childhood, her mother is optimistic for her future because she believes that she "will find her way."

A Peanut Butter Sandwich: Smooth or Extra Chunky?

The concerns of the middle-age woman run far deeper than vanities about getting "old." Even more significant to her day-to-day life is her position in the generational lineup. Mothers at midlife are the peanut butter between two slices of bread. The late-adolescent and early-adult daughters are becoming more independent, but many are still in need of a great deal of support. Their attempts to create a new generation will often require a mother's guidance, wisdom, and plain old help. This reflects the natural progression of a relationship between women of these ages. The difference is with the other slice of bread—the mother's mother, who, because of illness, altered finances, widowhood, or just the fading capacities for some aspects of independent living (like driving), needs more from her daughter. As a culture we are tolerant of the dependence of children on their parents, teachers, and societal structures, secure in the knowledge that they will "outgrow" childhood and attain independence. Middle-age women find that there is much less tolerance or support for their aging mothers. Unlike other cultural groups, we equate physical decline with intellectual, social, and emotional stagnation or regression. Elder women, once considered the repositories of wisdom and authority, the keepers of family and community history, are measured only by their neediness.

DAUGHTERS' EMPATHY WITH MOTHERS

As a woman takes on roles that she once associated with her mother, she is bound to reinterpret her past through these new experiences. Her thinking has to "stretch," so that she can reinterpret her mother as a person. She must take a two-dimensional person labeled Mom, and actively set out to discover the dimensions of the woman who exists within, and *beyond,* her role as mother. Mothers often have an easier time recognizing their daughters' personhood. As her daughter grows, a mother has the day-to-day opportunity of seeing her in a variety of contexts, not only in her role as daughter. To recognize the humanity of one's mother is to confront a painful reality—that she is as flawed as she is gifted, that some of her behavior has directly contradicted other words or actions, that her availability, strength, and affection have always been variable. For someone who was in control of children's lives, she may have lacked control over her own. Every one of us is inherently contradictory, but with mothers it's tough to get past that piece of humanity. Something in how we think about mothers makes their inconsistencies so glaring, so difficult to accept.

A daughter has to have a certain level of maturity before she can deal with some of her mother's attempts to talk about herself. Now that mother and daughter are on a more level playing field, it can appear to the mother that she has a confidante in her daughter. Since her daughter is now a member of the "club," she is deemed old enough for some of her mother's more revealing disclosures. These confidences may be about events in the past (affairs by either partner in the marriage, lost children, dissatisfaction, childhood history, mental illness) or ongoing concerns. Timing is crucial here, because as much as daughters say they want to be treated like adults, they may prefer not to know some of what their mothers wish to tell them.

S. Jhoanna Robledo writes about a relationship with her mother that was plagued by frequent separations in childhood, and conflict and distance as she became an adult. During one of her mother's visits, Robledo had a painful insight about their interactions: "We are usually good at picking emotional scabs until they bleed. Sometimes I think it is the only way we know how to be with each other." As Robledo began to take on more adult roles, her mother began to confide in her daughter details of the difficulty of being a single, poor mother. She recounts stories of her daughter's illnesses, of her own miscarriages and a traumatizing stillbirth. "Each time she spoke I wanted to run out of the apartment," recalls Robledo. *Then she had a daughter.* "Years later I realized she offered these stories as a way of sharing herself. I didn't fully understand that my mother shows her love through stories. Each tale she tells is meant as a gift, even if it's the kind you don't want." She links the development of her own identity with the capacity to see her mother as an individual. "As I struggle to define myself," she writes, "my mother has come into focus. Since having my own child I've begun to think less about what my mother didn't give me and more of what she did." Robledo comes to a realization that is a prerequisite for stepping into an adult relationship with one's mother: "there is more to my mother than motherhood."

Sometimes no amount of "maturity" can make a woman ready to see her mother as a real person. In Margaret Atwood's short story "Significant Moments in the Life of My Mother," the narrator is "startled" by her mother's comment as they sat on a childhood bed sorting clothes from an old trunk. "In my next incarnation," said her mother, "I'm going to be an archaeologist and go around digging things up." The narrator is totally taken aback by this revelation. "It was the first time," she said, "I'd ever heard my mother say that she might have wanted to be something other than what she was. I must have been thirty-five at the time, but it was still shocking and slightly offensive to me to learn that my mother might not have been totally contented fulfilling the role in which fate had cast her: that of being my mother." I can envision Atwood's character smacking herself on the head as she later uttered this wonderful insight: "What thumbsuckers we all are . . . when it comes to mothers."

To see her mother as a person, a daughter has to be able to see herself as a person too. It sounds simplistic, but many women never get there. We are more than our mothers' daughters, *and* they are more than their daughters' mothers. So much of the misunderstanding in this relationship is rooted in the inability to hold those two concepts simultaneously. As we grow, we develop an understanding that people do not exist in vacuums, that no behavior can be explained without examining its context. The way we think about and respond to an act of murder, for example, depends on the circumstances around it.

No Wonder You . . .

As daughters edit and amend their versions of their mothers' biographies, new pieces of information will often jump-start their empathy. Sometimes it's a lightbulb-going-on-over-a-head kind of reckoning. A young woman takes the same mother she's been dealing with for twenty-five years, then sharpens the contrast, adjusts the color, and elaborates the degree of detail. Two adult friends, both distressed over their mothers' angry, verbally abusive outbursts through childhood and adolescence, may come to view the behaviors somewhat differently when they know more about their mothers' backgrounds. The daughter who learns several pieces of information about her mother's childhood—for example, that she was brutally beaten at seemingly random intervals by her own mother—may develop greater empathy for her mother than the daughter whose mother's history was fairly benign. A mother who suffered savage beatings as a child may have trouble understanding *why* her daughter is angry at her for yelling all the time, since she has never once raised a hand to her. Filling in the blanks about a mother does not make everything okay. Insight is great, but it doesn't change the past or even the feelings about the past. But knowledge is a power that can help a woman become unstuck and move on in her life. A letter written by sculptor Meg Belichick to her mother is an example of an empathic understanding of her mother, combined with the wish to heal her. "I wish I could have been your big sister or your mother. I would have protected you, sent your grandfather to a hospital or jail. You could have colored pictures at the kitchen table until lunchtime."

Threads of Generations

A frequent theme in women's fiction, biography, and memoir is the impact of a young woman's perception of her grandmother, and how that alters her perception of her mother. Grandmother-grandchild relationships are often significant for their mutual warmth, support, and unconditional acceptance. Commenting on the way a skipped generation greases the wheels of family relationships, Judith Viorst marveled at the differences between her relationship with her mother and her children's experience of the very same woman. "I had lived with my mother in anger and love—I suppose most daughters do—but my children only knew her in one way: as the lady who thought they were smarter than Albert Einstein, as the lady who thought they wrote like William Shakespeare, as the lady who thought every picture they drew was a Rembrandt, as the lady who thought that whatever they were and whatever they wanted to be was . . . completely great." The grandmother is often a source of wisdom, a mediator, giver of gifts for no reason, lavish with love and low on the expectations.

It's been said that one of the joys of grandparenthood is the ability to enjoy children in the present moment. With their own children, the focus was always on the future, on responsibility and consequences. It's hard for a mother to revel in the moment with a three-year-old who has just splattered the kitchen with her macaroni and cheese, refuses to get her shoes on, is tormenting the dog, and screaming at the top of her lungs. It's not easy to live in the present with a fourteen-year-old whose most expressive acknowledgment of her mother's existence is a sneer, whose grades have plummeted from A's to C's, who's sneaking around with a suspicious-looking eighteen-year-old boy, who trashes every room in the house and treats her family members as if they were no more than coresidents in a penitentiary. Someone's got to deal with the tough stuff, the mess, the anger. It's great to have another person who is removed from the day-to-day, who has a totally different experience of the child. It is often strange for a woman who has a very conflicted relationship with her mother to observe the unconditional love zone that her mother has built around her grandchildren. "Mothers and daughters," writes Erica Jong, "it's a comedy, but also a tragedy. We fill our daughters with all the chutzpah we wish for ourselves. We want them to be free as we were not. And then we resent them for being what we have made. With granddaughters, it's so much easier. And great-granddaughters."

Intergenerational Insights

Helen MacFarquhar, the main character in Cathleen Schine's novel *The Love Letter,* has a wonderful epiphany about her place in the loopy, multithread matriarchy of her own family when her mother, Lillian, and grandmother Eleanor arrive for a visit of indeterminate length. Her grandmother hops out of the old Jaguar she refuses to drive or sell and grandly announces, "I'm here!" Emerging from the driver's side, Lillian quips to Helen, "She's here and she's all yours. What you choose to do with her is your business. But may I suggest strangulation as a most satisfying option." Eleanor confides to her granddaughter, "She dislikes having an aged parent. . . . Imagine how I feel. With an aged daughter." Following this small but charged exchange, Helen realizes, "No wonder I'm such a bitch. Third-generation bitch. Nature and nurture, a conspiracy, a confederacy." She wonders if *her* daughter will become the fourth generation, and secretly hopes so, because she is "so proud of her grandmother, her mother, herself." I love this interaction because it's an example of how the very same behaviors of mothers and grandmothers that drive a daughter crazy at one point in time can later be sources of pride and identification.

When we're in the midst of a relationship, particularly if there are problems, we can't know which behaviors will be "redeemed" someday and which will be as lousy in the future as they are in the present. Others are issues more of quantity than quality, as evidenced in another scene from *The Love Letter*. As Helen watches her grandmother unpack and settle in, she becomes acutely aware, once again, of her eccentricity and vanity. She "thanked the Fates that Eleanor was her grandmother and not her mother. A generation's distance muted Grandma Eleanor's effect, like the artful lighting of a photograph."

In a letter written for an anthology on mothers and daughters, writer

Carolyn See is more than generous in acknowledging her mother's good points. How she survived the bad points is what makes her memoir, *Dreaming,* so riveting. See recognizes that by acting in opposition to her mother's destructive directives and feelings, she saved herself. There are probably few things as satisfying as becoming a good mother without the benefit of having had one. See's relationship with her own daughters helped her gain even greater appreciation of the childhood minefield she somehow survived. Through her daughters' shared perceptions of their impossible grandmother, See received important validation. In the letter she writes, "You detested my children; I was crazy about them. And your meanness has had a bracing effect. My daughter Lisa was bullied over the phone by some East-Coast-bitch-editor used to reducing writers to tears, just for the fun of it. Lisa met her bullying with cutting contempt and later flew into a rhetorical rage. . . . 'Who does she think she's pushing *around*? Doesn't she know I grew up with GRANDMA KATE?' "

Fifty Ways to Lose Your Mother

Following the death of her mother, fifteen-year-old Gráinne in Lisa Carey's *The Mermaids Singing* discovers that Clíona, the grandmother she hasn't seen since she was three and from whom her dead mother was estranged, is coming to take her back to Ireland. She hates the idea. Having been extremely close to her single mother, she has automatically internalized without question all of her mother's antagonisms, especially about the family. Recognizing that it will be an adjustment, not only to go on living without her mother but to move to a country she doesn't remember, everyone advises her to "give it time." But Gráinne, remembering her mother's silence about her own mother, will have none of it. " 'I don't want to give it any time,' she protests, 'I don't want to give her anything. If she really is my grandmother she must be a horrible person because Mom obviously couldn't stand her. She wanted her dead.' "

The focus of *The Mermaids Singing* is how the stories of Gráinne's mother, grandmother, and great-grandmother are woven tightly together in some places and dangerously frayed in others, and how all of it comes to bear on Gráinne. The repetition of abandonment and rejection is almost compulsively reenacted over the generations, and threatens to do so in Gráinne's case as well. Grieving for her estranged daughter while having to care for her rather strange and hostile grandchild launches Clíona into a painful examination of the past. Why was the relationship with her daughter, Grace, so different from Grace's close relationship with *her* daughter, Gráinne? This question brings Clíona to memories of the fractious, barren relationship with her own mother, so totally different from what Grace and Gráinne enjoyed and lost prematurely. When we think about the history of families, we often emphasize the view from top to bottom, asking what was the impact of the first generation on the second, the first and second on the third, and so on. A bottom-to-top approach initially seems counterintuitive as a way of making sense of anything, but in family relationships, it can be quite illuminating. It is only in coming to know Gráinne that Clíona becomes able to feel and think differently about the generations on either side of her. When she thinks about her daughter, her insights coexist alongside her regrets. "I sometimes think," she reflects, "God planned our lives all wrong. What's the use in learning the truth so long after the opportunity to use it has gone by?"

For Clíona, reflection is a torture. As she thinks about the many battles she had with her daughter, each unwilling to share in the responsibility for their mutual unhappiness, she realizes the waste of those moments, and the long silent stretches that followed. "I'd take the blame," she swears, "all of it, heaped like coals on my head, if I could just have her back awhile. Back for the beginning. Newborn and flat-faced, rashy and wailing with colic. I'd cherish every scream. She'd be the best-loved baby since Jesus Christ Himself."

At least with her daughter, Clíona finally has some sense of what went wrong. But it's the relationship over which she had the least control that still most confuses her. Her wish for her own mother is at once childlike and knowing. It recognizes her childhood conception of her mother as an angry witch, from whom she became estranged, and adds a growing appreciation for her mother's vulnerability—something so hard to see with hostility in the picture. "Bronach—the Irish word for sorrowful—was my mother's Christian name. It is only after my own life as a mother that I can see how the name suited her. If I could have just one moment back, one time when she was screaming at me in rage, then I could say: 'I'm sorry you're lonely, Mum.' Maybe it would have made a difference; we might have ended up the best of friends, like Grace and Gráinne."

As we get better at picking up the nuances of relationships and conversations, we connect the dots and assemble a framework to order our confusion. Understanding mother-daughter relationships usually involves the gradual buildup of evidence, and then interpretation and reinterpretation of it over time. The evolution of a daughter's insights about her mother is greatly advanced by having many chances to observe herself and her mother together.

Road Song, a gripping memoir by Natalie Kusz, is the story of a family who moves to Alaska. The relationship between Natalie and her mother across the span of childhood to adulthood is a salad in which the main ingredient clearly is love. Other ingredients include anger, rebellion, distrust, steadfastness, and respect. A traumatic event intervened early and gave the salad a mighty toss, forever altering the relationship. Young Natalie was attacked by a pack of huskies who tore her face apart so badly that she lost an eye and had to undergo many surgeries and grafts. Her mother was profoundly affected by that horror and went into "a black time . . . where fear filled her chest like a black wind blowing." She became preoccupied with her children's safety. "She said that mothers had a thousand thoughts to get through within a day, and that most of these thoughts were about avoiding disaster." But her mother's most gnawing concern was not her children's safety but her *obsession* with it.

Obsession, to her, meant only one thing—that she was on her way to the thing she feared most in life: becoming her mother. As a child Natalie noticed a strain between her mother and grandmother. She recalls wondering why her mother spoke so differently to her mother on the phone from the way she spoke to anyone else. How could she be on the phone for a long time and say so very little? And "when she rang off," why would her mother lean against her father and sigh, "Julius, she makes me so tired"? It's easy to imagine a little girl wondering how a mother could get tired just from talking on the phone, especially since she had no idea what was being said. It was only much later that Natalie's mother confided that her mother had always seemed "bent." She was intensely and unpredictably moody, paranoid, and intrusive. She always pitted people against each other and behaved totally inappropriately with her daughter's friends and suitors. When Natalie's mother finally demanded that her father tell her the truth about her mother, he admitted that she had been diagnosed as paranoid schizophrenic with the recommendation that she remain hospitalized. He could not do it, and instead moved his family far west "to a place with new air, knowing as his daughters grew older that they would breathe their mother's breath for the rest of their lives." He sacrificed his daughters for his wife, and they grew up without the most important information children in a distressed environment can have—a framework in which to understand what's going on around them and what's being done to help and protect them.

As Natalie's mother acquired more information about her mother's condition, it was a relief to know that there was nothing she could do to make her better. However, when she read about the genetics of schizophrenia, she had a whole new set of fears and became committed to watching herself like an "enemy" in a concern for the well-being of her own children that shadowed her for a lifetime. Early on, children learn about their parents' soft spots, even if they don't understand them. You don't have to be able to name the particular bone you plan to break when you throw a stone, you just have to know that it will be a surprise and it will do damage. When, in anger, Natalie once accused her mother of being just like her grandmother, she knew precisely the trajectory of that flying object, even though she didn't understand how hard it would hit. When a woman's worst fear is that she may turn out like her mother, she is usually very sensitive to cues that suggest it is so. Given the degree to which her mother's mental illness had so negatively impacted her life, and given the way she'd been kept in the dark for so long, it's no wonder that Natalie might as well have drawn a bull's-eye on her mother's body that said "Hit me here."

Forgiveness

Forgiveness of one kind or another often becomes more possible after a change in perspective. When someone hurts us badly, the old adage about forgiving and forgetting seems ridiculous. What could possibly change the *fact* of the hurt? Aside from total amnesia, not much. It's only when the victim can view the perpetrator or the hurtful behavior within a new context that a shift is possible. It's not necessarily a conscious process. The passage of time, for example, sometimes changes the way we think about how we've been hurt. Pain that is in the past may be easier to put to rest than pain that continues to be inflicted in the present, or pain that lingers long after the initial injury. One mother intermittently assaulted her daughter during childhood, only when she was stinking drunk, and never again after she got clean and sober. Another mother continued to drink, made no effort to stop, and switched from physical to verbal abuse only when her daughter equaled her in size. As these daughters struggle to understand, they may come up against a truth many people hate to acknowledge—that the cruelty inflicted upon us by people who are supposed to love us makes absolutely no sense at all. Some young women enter psychotherapy preferring to blame themselves for the actions of their parents, just so they can have the illusion that the puzzle fits together. "My mother loves me. I tried her patience by being difficult, by not understanding how hard her life was, by never helping when she needed me. She had no choice but to act in the way she did."

The wounded party tries to put herself in the spike heels of the one who kicked her. She tries to take into account those factors that might have motivated the behavior. At the heart of the wounded person's examination is the hope that over time, intellectual understanding will offer one way to minimize the intensity, duration, and intrusiveness of the pain. That understanding can come from a variety of sources—psychotherapy, reading and learning about specific conditions or problems that may have influenced the mother. It can be the product of alliances with other siblings, who can say, "Yes, that's how it happened. You got it the worst. Remember . . . ?" Such perspectives are extremely helpful in this regard.

Writer Donna Baier Stein recalls the mutual hurt and distance she felt with her mother and articulates the tremendous paradox of two women who want each other to change for the better and will wound the hell out of each other in the process of wanting. "You and I are the two who most want to heal each other and the least able to do so," she writes to her mother. Revealing a piece of childhood history that could keep a shrink captivated for months, Stein describes her unique childhood sleepwalking habits. Asleep, she would walk to the refrigerator, open it, and ask, "Mom, are you in there?" She and her mother laughed about it for years, but the motivation behind those midnight searches haunted her. Had her mother really been cold? She could only face that question and its answer when she looked beyond herself and her mother. In a letter to her mother she admitted that she had, indeed, found her mother "cold . . . until finally, finally, I knew you were your mother's child."

Just as changes in stage lighting can influence a scene's mood, rhythm, and highlights, applying different lenses to family dramas can influence thoughts, feelings, and reactions. Most of our lives are lived in color. Color conveys emotion and intensity, distance, approachability. Our memories are color-coded, some in bold, proud primary colors, others muted and ambiguous, still others foreboding and dark. We can change the intensity of sections of our life stories by thinking or feeling about them differently. A jagged bloodred may be tempered into a more tolerable persimmon.

Lorrie Moore, a tremendously gifted observer of the frailties and strengths of human relationships, writes often about the process whereby new insight tells old ideas to hit the road. In that instant, a major shift occurs, invisible to the outside world. A woman sees her mother in a different light. She may reconsider *herself,* and perhaps even their relationship, in that light. Without words, the daughter's new perspective is likely to inspire new behavior, to which her mother might respond. The daughter in one of Moore's short stories comes to a realization that frees her from years of suffocation and anger that she and her mother inflicted upon each other. Mother and daughter were always in opposition, until the daughter's sudden insight: "It was really the world that was one's brutal mother, the one that nursed you and neglected you, and your own mother was only your sibling in that world." Such an entirely different perspective can turn a long history of antagonism toward a new empathy and connection.

❧ HOLDING UP THE SKY ❧

Dear Mom,

It's the middle of October, one of those days with enough edge in the air that it catches me pleasantly off guard each time I leave the house. The trees are barely holding on to their last, best leaves. Or is it the leaves that are hanging on? I'm never quite sure. Already two or three days past peak, they are stunning, but also sad. In the space of days, they will litter the ground, colorless and brittle, without a hint of how spectacular they've been. In childhood, fall was always the beginning of things. School with the scratchy uniforms and straight lines. New pencils and notebooks. The smell of burning leaves. The contagious enthusiasm of Halloween. The countdown from one kid holiday to the next. Now fall means being cheated of light. Now it is Keara who begins school, several hundred miles away. The view from every window offers a preview of winter, as the gorgeous full trees that circle my house turn naked and their branches grotesque. I don't think about beginnings much anymore. I'm too preoccupied with endings.

Nine years ago today you made the forty-five-minute drive to my house. It probably looked so regular on the outside—Keara's carved pumpkin on the steps, a patchwork of fallen leaves blanketing the lawn, the pine needles so thick on the walk that you always warn me about, where someone could take a spill. The green shutter, partially unhinged, neglected for six months. We kept saying it would look better if we either put it back where it was or took it down altogether, but somehow its precarious attachment to the exterior of our house fit the general tone inside. For months the house had been my fortress, my prison, my tomb. The only place I could shed the exhausting masquerade of normalcy, like a pair of shoes, the second I walked through the door. It was a house I poisoned with my presence, muting lively conversation, stifling all humor. I made the air heavy and the light fade. I made it impossible to love out loud. The usual constant music in our house gradually became too loud for me, at any volume. Lyrics tripped up my shaky concentration. Laughter was a cruel joke, with a punch line I could never remember, even though I tried. I was a ghost in my home. A stranger in my family.

Every moment of that horrible depression was even worse because of Keara. An eleven-year-old girl who watched her mother evaporate before her eyes. She couldn't comprehend why love, no matter how strong, couldn't heal. She didn't understand the reason so much of our relationship had gone from being a delight to feeling like a chore. She wondered what she had done to make it happen or what she might do to make it better. And as I got worse, she discovered a new darkness to fear, one that no cracked door or nightlight could help. As a psychologist I'd been well schooled in mother bashing, and I became the recipient of my harshest criticism. I know I complain about my childhood, the injustices, the slights, the judgments not in my favor. We all tease you in those "And remember when you . . . ?" and "How could you have . . . ?" litanies of accusations. But yours were the misdemeanors of motherhood; mine felt like capital crimes.

You were never weak with us. In fact, you were and are the strongest person I know. It is the quality I most value and sometimes most resent. Even as a child, I knew I didn't have your confidence, your ease with new situations, your generous enthusiasms. When I saw Grandmother's moods and inconsistencies, the way she manipulated you and your sister and brothers, I felt such relief that you didn't pull that stuff with us. Sometimes your strength makes you think you're right about things you aren't. Sometimes your way is the only way. But the bottom line is that I've always envied your confidence and strength. I was never particularly manipulative, but in so many other ways I've turned out to be Grandmother's girl, the mother you reacted against. What does that mean for Keara? What does it mean for me?

Nine years ago you arrived as I was going through the motions of packing. Keara was gathering her things for school. Brian was as sorrowful as I've ever seen him as he headed off to work to listen for hours to people recounting their versions of pain. We needed the money, but I think he was also relieved not to be the one checking me in. He looked so tired. Tired of me. I had to say good-bye to the two people whose presence in my life had kept me alive, long past my first thoughts of suicide. Brian was grim. Keara was confused, with a forced cheerfulness. You were organized and as upbeat as possible under the circumstances.

When the door closed behind them, I was convinced that I had just died, with no hope of resurrection. With them gone, I could let you be my mother, not the one who drove me to the hospital and waded through the interminable admission to a psychiatric unit, but the mother soothing the fears of my scared-stiff self, who wanted to run away, who felt cornered and panicked. In my escalating agitation, you said over and over, "You have tried everything. You made a decision. You need to see it through," always following quickly with a question like "Did you pack socks?" You knew—in a way I know with Keara—that in the face of a child's all-out panic, rational discussions are of little value. As I faced getting my tonsils out, you knew not to give me the medical litany of why the surgery "made sense." You coached me, baby step to baby step, with the most important of all assurances: "It will be all right."

As adults, we often disparage or diminish the importance of that kind of comfort. Perhaps we fear it's a lie. Some kids die getting their tonsils out. And, there's no getting around it: it's going to hurt like hell afterward. It's still scary. It's really not going to be all right. But comfort isn't really about outcomes. When someone says, "It will be all right," it means, "Hang on, you won't suffer this horrible, jagged-edged, terrifying, agonizing panic or despair or pain forever." I stood there while you zipped my suitcase and carried it *downstairs. I stood there while you checked the house for things I'd forgotten. You led the way out the door, down the long steps, to the car. You reminded me to use my seat belt and helped me as I fumbled with it. We drove a silent two miles to the hospital. You followed colored arrows that made no sense to me, but landed us at Admitting.*

You kept up the most meaningless, one-sided conversation as we waited there. In the haze of your words, I was making second-to-second decisions about whether to stay or bolt. Without making it obvious, you placed your hand on my arm as you read from a book of silly and little-known facts and trivia. At a different point, your method of passing time, given the context, would have been major material for the next family get-together—"Can you believe she actually read me a trivia book minutes before I would be locked up on a psychiatric unit?" Everyone would laugh and rib you, as always. But that moment would never become the stuff of family fable. Those little-known facts you kept reading were the glue that kept me in place. I was like a baby who can't yet speak the language and can only understand a little of it. But one of the surest ways of quieting that baby's distress is saying anything in the tone of love and protection—even if it's just a list of names from the phone book.

What was it like when the nurse opened my suitcase and purse and carefully searched the contents for things I wouldn't be allowed to keep? You and she kept the conversation going while I watched, wondering about the many ways of hurting myself that I'd never considered before. You had to do all of this with me, for me, knowing that in your purse you had a plane ticket to Boston, where you'd be heading the next day to be with your mother. How bad could our intergenerational timing get? Grandmother was becoming less and less able to cope alone in that big house. She was generally anxious and had begun to have panic attacks. We all knew that this was not a situation that would get much better without some drastic changes. And it was time for you and your siblings to hash things out.

I didn't want you to go. That's not true. I knew you had to go. I just didn't want you to leave me. My depression and hospitalization were so painful for Dad, all-time hater of hospitals, who would feel compelled to take over as a daily visitor. Dad, who immediately upon entering any hospital room looks ready to leave. With his pens and paper and chocolate-covered cherries, John Philip Sousa tapes, and brisk walks around and around the hospital, he gave me so much. But he and I are so alike; he had less distance from the pain. I could lean against him safely, but if I collapsed into him, we would both have fallen. And Brian, who'd always been so solid and unflappable, was exhausted and frightened. Still, he continued to give more love than most people ever expect or receive. For him to hear the full force of my fear, my terror at being alone, my belief that my brain was disintegrating, that nothing, not even electroconvulsive therapy, would help, would be unbearable. I needed you.

I needed the woman who milked, and burped, and walked me for miles of screaming, gas, and boredom. Who nursed me through countless high fevers and long illnesses, tolerated my cutting disdain, somehow maintained hope through my consistent underachievement, unfortunate contacts with alcohol, store security forces, and police. I needed a mother who could accept my certainty that the boy I loved at sixteen was the one I would marry, but who would make me hold off as long as possible. You've stood at the bedside of your seriously ill and comatose children. I have no idea what the broken-bone and orthopedic-surgery count is up to now, but I know it's well into double digits. You rushed more than one of us to emergency rooms for ingesting awful things. You heard school principals threaten and carry out suspensions and expulsions. You have managed children running through glass they didn't see, and children whose fists made contact with walls they definitely did. You have watched helplessly while your children did hand-to-hand combat with dangerous addictions. You've seen us marry and divorce. You were there for the birth of our children and loss of our pregnancies. You still grieve the sudden death of a young son-in-law and the long imprint of that loss on your daughter and granddaughter.

Keara, upon hearing about only half of this, turned to me when she was twenty, shook her head in disbelief, and declared, "Boy, did you get off easy!" And so far, at least on the big-ticket items, she's right. But Keara's long-distance pain is so hard for me to bear. I want to spare her what I've known of suffering. It's irrational. But I don't want her heart to break any more than it already has. I want her to slip into work she loves and float up the ladder of success. I hope she has childbirth with no pain and gets a perfectly healthy child who sleeps eight straight hours. I pray every night that she will be spared what you and I know is one of the family curses—depression, or as you might call it, my "cross to bear." I can't bear that she may brush up against the thing that makes me feel like I'm trapped underground, alive but alone.

The things I want most for her are the things I can't give. The things I most fear for her I can't protect against. Twenty-two years ago, everything

*Keara needed was wrapped up in one neat package: me. I was food, skin, a
steady heartbeat, a soothing voice. I effortlessly picked up her frequencies and
knew her rhythms. It was an inexpressible kind of power. Mothers have it with
their babies just long enough to be simultaneously awesome and awestruck. But
it doesn't last. It's not supposed to. For the rest of our lives we will mourn something we'll never fully remember or understand—that a mother and a daughter will never again be to each other all that they were in the beginning. How
did you do it, Mom? How did you see the fires burning, the boats sinking, the
time bombs that sometimes had your children's names on them, and know that
a mother is not always able to run into the fire, raise the boat, or defuse the
bomb? What she has to do is in some ways harder. She has to help heal the
burns, allay the fears of the water, plug up the leaks, and give instructions on
detecting potential explosions. How did you check your oldest daughter into a
psychiatric unit for suicidal depression? How did you make it through those
minutes without having to escape to the bathroom to splash cold water on your
face and tell yourself just to hold on? That you had to take things one at a
time. First me. Then Grandmother. How did you sit on that plane to Boston,
soaked in the sorrow of your daughter, anticipating the expanse of your mother's
neediness?*

*Because of the ECT, I don't remember much of the time you were in Boston.
But I remember the day you returned. You visited me in the hospital. We went
out to the courtyard, and I was aware for the first time in a long while of the
word* beautiful. *The rainy and cloudy days that had persisted since my
admission had taken the weekend off, and the autumn sun was making up for
lost time. I could feel the strong rays on my face, almost blessing me with light.
You pulled a small package of clay from your bag and initiated your own version of art therapy. You weren't aware that since my admission I'd already
had art therapy inflicted upon me on a daily basis. You also didn't know that
my basic assessment of it was that it was neither art nor therapy. But you persisted as you always do, making your own sculpture, pushing it into my palm,
instructing me what to do with it, and not taking no for an answer.*

*We did a couple of rounds of push/pull, the issue always being who would
give in first.*

"Go ahead and try it."

"I don't want to."

"You haven't even tried it yet."

"I don't want to."

"Look at how easy it is to work with."

"I really don't want to."

In those seemingly fruitless rounds, I began to feel something that had been gone for a long time. I was becoming annoyed. And it felt so good. Whatever happened to the damn clay was far less important than the audible murmurs of my lost self. I had an opinion, at least for a moment, and the desire to stand my ground. My hair was limp, my clothes were hanging off me from such fast weight loss, my skin was gray. I shuffled around like an old lady, my memory was shot to hell from the treatments, but you could tell me to do something and I could say no. I actually felt something. It was like those defiant stands I took at two or twelve or twenty, when it was only by bumping up against you that I learned about myself. I don't remember whether I finally sculpted something with you or not. It doesn't matter. I didn't know it then, but that small struggle about clay was a sign that I was getting well. And in the nine years since that October I have learned how those echoes of childhood—constancy, structure, love, faith, rebellion, autonomy, regression, fear, and empathy—reverberate between a mother and daughter as much in adulthood as they do in childhood. And that they have the very same potential for causing pain or comfort now that they did then. I never knew that. Did you?

Martha

Dear #1 Daughter,

One of the immutable, incontrovertible, and inexorable truths about living is that there will be good days and bad days—and hellishly worse days. That situation—your going into a psychiatric unit for ECT at the same time that my mother was falling apart with panic attacks and begging me through other family members to come to Boston and make it all better—was right down there in the pits of the inferno. You seemed somewhat the easier of the two because I really believed I was leaving you in a place that could help you, no matter how painful the process.

Most of it is a dark blue blur in my mind, which was on heavy overload. I remember the trip to the hospital and the mindless chatter you mentioned. When in doubt, I talk! Leaving you and flying to Boston had an unreality about it. I had to worry in sequence. First I would concentrate on you, trying to imagine what the treatment was like, checking the clock to see where you were in your day—*and praying like mad that the whole process would remove your depression like a clean eraser across a blackboard. Then I would try to plan for your grandmother's future when I knew that there was no solution that would ever make her happy, and that I must do this without the moral support of my sister, who was in Oxford for almost a year.*

How do I get through these times? I don't think of myself having strength so much as the ability to step into a mind-set where I operate in a different way—and accomplish what must be done. Numbness helps. It is for me a shutting down of feelings—and a narrowing of focus to a minute-by-minute basis. I turn very still inside, as though all emotion, feeling, and general thought drains away. It is doing anything that needs to be done with only the moment and the task at hand being of any importance. As long as there is something I can think of to do, I function. There is no past and no future. It is in the quiet times—and in bed—that the horrors loom. Usually exhaustion finally gives me some surcease in a comalike sleep, with weird and frightening dreams. Your memory of the clay is true—but we did make something, which I took home and baked (it was plastic clay) and brought back to you when you were home. You looked at it blankly with no memory of having made it. That was okay. It had fulfilled its function.

We sat in the sun on an unseasonably warm October afternoon, you and I. I saw you recovering and saw you a bit more feisty than when I went to Boston. We played with clay, shaping and reshaping it while we chatted as though we were on a coffee break. It was a beautiful hour. We had found help for my mother, and had settled for a time her life's situation. I knew it was only a temporary fix, fraught with problems, but for the time being things on both fronts were better than they had been. I was relieved. The problems were ebbing. Life was a bit easier, and I think that really is all one can ask. Isn't it?

I love you

Mom

NINE

∾

Later Years: Shifting Needs

I had grown big, but my mother was bigger, and that would
always remain so.

JAMAICA KINCAID

THE DEVELOPMENTAL TASKS OF OLD AGE

In the elder years a woman is faced with challenges in physical health specifically due to aging (such as hearing loss) and the advancement of long-term
problems that are particularly exacerbated in old age (such as diabetes). The
experience of loss is common and requires one adjustment after another.
Decisions about the continuation and direction of career arise at this time and
often lead to unanticipated changes. For example, the much-longed-for
retirement of a husband may lead to greater freedom for him but more constraints on his wife's life. "He's always *there,*" complained a family friend. "He
expects me to make him lunch. I haven't had to fix someone's lunch for thirty
years!" Efforts to avoid isolation and loneliness, two of the unsung risks for
health problems and mortality, become integral developmental tasks. To be
able to look at one's ultimate death without turning it into an immediate
death *sentence* is a major task for women in their elder years.

HOW OLD IS OLD?

As we continue to develop, the labels we've used to describe stages of life become increasingly arbitrary and useless. With infancy, childhood, adolescence, and somewhat with young adulthood, knowing a person's age will provide some framework for making some basic predictions about physical development. Most people, regardless of culture, don't walk at six months. Menarche is unusual in six-year-old girls. By eighteen, most males have outgrown bedwetting. Acne is common in adolescent males and females. Although physical changes occur across the life span, they vary considerably. I will be much more accurate describing the physical, social, emotional, and cognitive status of the "typical" three-year-old girl than I will the "typical" seventy-year-old woman.

AGE TAKES THE BLAME

What goes into making it over the long haul? Women, at least as far as longevity is concerned, have the edge over men. Genes appear to have some hand in determining the length of life, as well as the susceptibility to specific conditions that, in and of themselves, are life-threatening. With more public education about illness, women's knowledge has increased in specific areas. Due to aggressive public-awareness campaigns, women are far more informed about prevention and early detection of breast cancer and osteoporosis than were their counterparts several decades ago.

Many of the conditions women complain of as part of "getting old" or "declining" do not actually begin in older age. In fact, a number of our vulnerabilities and complaints are the *accumulation* of abuses we have inflicted on our bodies from adolescence onward. After forty years, smoking will take your breath away, whether you're old or not. Sun worship is a one-sided affair, which lines the face far more than the passage of years. Playing a sport on a bad knee or with chronic back problems without effective treatment contributes to deterioration that becomes more evident when Social Security kicks in.

A midlife daughter can look to her mother's health as a predictor of her own, resulting in many different reactions. She may choose to see her mother's osteoporosis or Type II diabetes as a "done deal" for herself in the future. With that sense of futility, a woman is likely to neglect early diagnostic procedures and unlikely to adopt behaviors that are influential in preventing or controlling the illness (nutrition, exercise, and medical interventions that can make a significant difference). When she assesses herself as being fated for lung cancer when she watches her mother reach for breath after breath, she fails to consider what *behaviors* she shares with her mother that are known culprits in the illness.

ROLE CHANGES

As she enters middle age, a woman confronts changes associated with aging in her mother as well as herself. Regardless of the quality of their relationship, with the exception of the occasional emergency, many women in early midlife have had few reasons to worry about their mothers' functioning on a day-to-day basis. But gradually, or with a scary late-night phone call from a hospital hundreds of miles away, an entire picture can change. Many mothers become less able to care for themselves and, whether they like it or not, need the help of others to accomplish what was once second nature. Depending on her prior relationship with her daughter, a mother in need of support, supervision, or care can feel anywhere along the continuum from neutral to agonized; the worse the relationship, the more difficult the dependency. The mother-daughter relationship shifts over and over again to accommodate the fluctuating needs of the mother, midlife daughter, and granddaughter. Middle-aged mothers who are still not "finished" with their daughters and granddaughters must stretch to care for their aging parents. Women constitute 71 percent of family caretakers. With longevity increasing, it is not only middle-aged women but also elder women who are caring for even older mothers.

The "oldest old," those aged eighty-five and over, are a rapidly growing population, one that the baby boomer generation is not equipped, mentally or financially, to handle at present. At eighty-five and older, it's estimated that women outnumber men by a ratio of five to two. Elderly women are more than three times more likely than elderly men to have lost a spouse to death and therefore to be living alone. Consistent with their economic status at other ages, elderly women are nearly twice as likely as elderly men to live in poverty. African-American and Hispanic women are even more likely to go through their older years under conditions of financial hardship. Whoever applied the term "golden years" to this time of life was a bit out of touch about its hardships.

MOTHERS' EMPATHY FOR DAUGHTERS/DAUGHTERS' EMPATHY FOR MOTHERS

Elder mothers and daughters experience each other very differently. There is no exact way to define the list of things that annoy mothers and daughters about each other at this stage, no list delineating the variety and intensity of *the emotions they feel about each other*. Some of the stress on relationships is rooted in biology; for example, reduced physical strength compromises total self-sufficiency, and a recently failed eye exam at the Department of Motor Vehicles severely restricts freedom. A mother may need help carrying out tasks she used to do alone. Despite the fact that she knows she needs help and is, in the abstract, grateful to her daughter for providing it, there can be tremendous resentment. Sometimes this leads to a struggle, as in the huffy "No, I'll shovel the snow off my own sidewalk, thank you very much," to the urgent entitled call at 6:30 A.M. reporting that she's down to four rolls of toilet paper, they'd better get to the store early and what time should she expect her daughter to pick her up?

Karen Fingerman, a leading researcher in the area of elder-mother relationships with their daughters, emphasizes the very different worldviews each brings to the table. These differences are often a product of their generations, guaranteeing what Fingerman calls a "developmental schism" between mother and daughter. In one study she compared middle-aged mothers' and young-adult daughters' enjoyment of visits with each other with the enjoyment of midlife women's visits with their elder mothers. Middle-aged mothers and young-adult daughters reported that a major subject of their enjoyable visits was the daughter's entry into adult life, while elder mothers and their middle-aged daughters tend to focus on the extended family. Mothers in both age groups were more invested in the relationship than their daughters.

Similar patterns are observed when elder mothers and their midlife daughters are asked about how they handle conflict in their relationships with each other. There are significant differences in content and style, with elder mothers putting a more positive spin on conflicts with their daughters. "It wasn't a fight," a mother might say about a disagreement with her adult daughter. "We had 'words.' " Mothers also tend to underestimate the intensity of their daughters' anger, even when their daughters think they're giving strong signals about how mad they are. Mother and daughter could probably agree that there was some heat in their unpleasant interactions. But what to an adult daughter constitutes total meltdown may to her mother be nothing more than "blowing off a little steam." Daughters get particularly angry when mothers use passive-aggressive methods (stop calling or in other ways let the relationship lapse) as the expression of anger. Not surprisingly, different things annoy mothers and their adult daughters in their relationship. Daughters particularly resent their mothers' intrusiveness and any lapses in taking care of themselves. Mothers' complaints often focus on their grandchildren and their daughters' husbands.

How do adult daughters and their mothers view themselves as "family"? When a daughter thinks "family," the constellation of spouse, children, and herself comes to mind. Her mother, on the other hand, has a much more extended view of family, which includes many more people, among them the daughter's children and spouse. These perceptions are likely to explain at least one kind of conflict. If a mother "shares" some wisdom with her daughter about how she should be handling her granddaughter, the daughter might think to herself, "I wish she would mind her own business!" The problem is that from her mother's perspective, she *is* minding her business. If it's *her* family, then it's *her* business. A woman who is able to view her mother's annoying behavior in the context of the person her mother is, rather than as an intentional attempt to drive her up the wall, is less likely to be stressed by the relationship.

Conflict also intensifies around positive transition times for either mother and/or daughter (a mother's retirement, mothers becoming grandmothers, grandmothers becoming great-grandmothers). These are times of multilayered emotions. The suitcase each woman brings to the event is full of a lot more than clothes. When the scene shifts to the adult daughter, mother, and grandmother, the dynamic changes again. New alliances are formed. The grandmother translates to the mother (wanted or not) observations about the granddaughter, perhaps drawing important similarities or obvious differences she sees between the two of them.

The grandmother can also reach farther back into familial history and draw connections all the way from physical attributes (she has her great-aunt Ruby's nose) to emotional interactions (Honey, you and your mother are having the same fights that she and I used to have). "My daughter now rails at me as I once railed at my mother," writes Erica Jong. "When Molly monologues, sparing no one with her barbed wit, my mother and I look at each other and smile. 'Tell her you're sorry you were such a dreadful mother,' my mother says, her voice dripping with irony. 'And *apologize*.'" After Jong follows up with her own teasing apology, she gets that great kiss-off from her adolescent daughter, "Yeah, yeah, yeah."

At Cross-Purposes

In her book *Another Country,* psychologist Mary Pipher marks a subset of elders for consideration—the "old old." Conflict and misunderstanding between elderly mothers and their daughters result from the fact that they are members of different *family* generations but also different generations of *time and culture.* They are, by virtue of our placement in the century, at cross-purposes.

Pipher recounts a therapy session with a sixty-eight-year-old woman and her thirty-five-year-old daughter; when they entered her office she could quickly tell that she was going to have to deal with different generational "time zones." "They had different memories, comfort levels about self-disclosure, and ideas about how to deal with pain," she comments. This meant that they defined the conflict between them very differently, had different approaches to expressing emotion and managing conflict, especially when it's "aired" in front of a stranger, and different goals for settling disagreements.

The Friendly Skies   To demonstrate a common generational time-zone foul-up, Pipher asked attendees at a conference to imagine getting on a plane or a train and watching as a small elderly woman gets on and seems headed in their direction. There is a small groan in the audience, suggesting what I always feel: "Oh, *please* don't let her sit next to me." Of course, probably by virtue of my making that wish, she always *does* end up beside me. And she seems like a perfectly nice woman, but I know she's going to do the absolute worst thing. *She is going to try to talk to me.*

Even little kids can pick up hostile vibes, dirty looks, and total disinterest when I establish the fact that there will be no friendship from me on a particular flight. But an elderly woman is totally immune. I could throw drinks at her and spit an entire bag of peanuts onto her pastel cardigan, and she'd probably find some way to forgive me. It's important to establish the parameters early, because sharing one word with her will be the equivalent of feeding a stray cat. We will have formed a relationship, one that lasts throughout the flight and sometimes extends to meeting her family waiting at the gate. I don't want a relationship. At my age I'm already into divestiture. But I seem condemned to fly the really friendly skies. I have never once remained silent beyond takeoff with any woman over seventy sitting next to me. Why? Because women in my generation see getting on a plane all by themselves, apart from the discomfort and the possibility of crashing, as a time of relative peace and quiet. There are no cell phones, the tone is hushed, and the code of conduct emphasizes anonymity. But women of my grandmother's and great-grandmother's generations would find this behavior rude. To approach someone, sit next to her, not acknowledge her presence, and not ask some polite questions would be treating her as if she were invisible.

Once I remind myself that she and her placement in history are potential sources of interest and stories, then I don't have to feel that she's *inflicting* herself on me. I can actively participate in a midair conversation, as a partner rather than as a stranger. Sometimes we are so threatened by age, and so conditioned to relegate our elders to the dustbin because we assume that age has erased their vital engagement with the world. We believe that stories about the past are inherently unproductive and boring, that their perceptions of the current state of the world are irrelevant, that they are and have always been asexual. These assumptions are part of the stories we tell ourselves about aging, and unless we begin to challenge those assumptions now—and insist that others change theirs—*we* will become the women walking down aisles of planes, the subject of younger women's seat assignment prayers. I wouldn't have wanted this for my grandmother, certainly don't want it for my mother, dread it for myself, and get really depressed when I imagine that avoidance still strong with my daughter. Respecting our elders means much more than tolerating them. If we are ever to restore the strength of connection between generations of women, something that is sorely lacking, we must make concerted efforts to restore the respect due our elders. Elder women of today are no less deserving of it than they were a century ago, but our attitudes, so much a function of cultural values, have changed enormously, enlarging the gap that separates one generation of women from the next.

Abuse

Abuse of elders is becoming more recognized as a very real problem within family settings. It is estimated that 10 percent of the elderly population suffer from abuse or neglect, ranging from financial manipulation to outright physical abuse. A 1998 Cornell study reported the dangerous impact of being a victim of abuse, apart from the effects of the abuse itself. Mortality rates indicated that "only 9 percent of those with a reported incident of abuse and 17 percent of those suffering from self-neglect survived during a thirteen-year follow-up period." These rates are startling compared with those for a group of same-aged, nonabused elders. There were "no direct-injury-related, injury-related" deaths in the group that was mistreated, suggesting that maltreatment has a more "insidious" threat to life. Mark Lachs, M.D., in the *Journal of the American Medical Association,* reported that "even when adjustments were made to account for chronic diseases, social factors, and other conditions associated with increased death rates among the elderly, mistreated older people were three times more likely to die than older people who were not mistreated."

Abuse is most likely to happen in situations of intense dependency in which it's the abuser who is dependent on the victim. In many cases, victims of elder abuse have an adult child who needs them for housing and financial support. Victims often feel trapped by their family obligations and have a strong sense of powerlessness that makes them less likely to register a complaint. The examples of *The Beauty Queen of Leenane* and *'Night, Mother* described in chapter 7 typify that kind of poisonous relationship.

Squeeze

For other women, the squeeze is more pronounced than that of one needy generation on another. Many an older woman has her children *and* her children's children living with her. And it's not unusual for her elderly mother to reside with her as well. The "golden years" don't look all that great when increasing age just means increasing responsibility with decreasing resources. As a result of sweeping changes in the welfare system, the number of "child only" cases—in which only the child receives benefits—has skyrocketed. These are kids whose parents may be in rehab or jail. Their parents may have lost custody due to neglect or abuse. Or their mothers may be part of the growing population of women who succumb to AIDS. "Child only" cases usually involve residence with a grandmother, and the monthly benefits for a child are lower than adult benefits, providing elder women with the most minimal of resources to raise these children, and little support, assistance, and training to prepare adolescents to transfer out of welfare when they reach the benefit-cutoff point. It's estimated that there are 1.8 million children in this position, which means that many, many grandmothers and even great-grand-mothers function as the custodial "parents."

A recent *Washington Post* feature detailed the story of Katie Bell Oliver, a fifty-seven-year-old resident of Craven County, North Carolina. A former cook who was disabled by a fall, she lives in a battered trailer with four grandchildren, ages two, three, five, and eight; the eight-year-old is profoundly mentally disabled. Of her twenty-nine-year-old daughter, who sometimes looks for work and housing and sometimes just "takes off," Oliver says, "These young girls have these babies, and they just don't think." Many women are in similar positions and would probably echo Oliver's frustration. "It's like you're living in Vietnam. Something has to give before I have a nervous breakdown." If she could be designated as a foster parent, she could receive four times the amount of support she currently receives, enabling her and her grandchildren to move into more suitable housing. But under the current catch-22 system, she would be rejected because her trailer would never pass inspection. While many people are beginning to realize some of the unforeseen consequences of welfare "reform" and the need to make adjustments, others cite the many reasons for keeping things the way they are. Just as the best way to blaspheme the positively perceived word *mother* is to put the word *welfare* in front of it, the best way to restrict benefits to grandmothers is to highlight the ones who are "benefiting" from the system.

I'd be interested in hearing Katie Oliver's response to the conservative reasons for not "reforming" welfare reform: mothers are trying to evade work requirements, and grandparents are getting money they don't need. In the empathic words of one official, "If you go back thirty years to my childhood, grandparents did not get compensated for taking care of grandchildren. It's not something we want to perpetuate. I believe that government should only do those things for us that we cannot reasonably do for ourselves." My guess is that Katie Oliver would welcome him over, and be glad to enlighten him.

At the other end of the spectrum are legislative battles over grandparents' rights. The hotly contested U.S. Supreme Court case of *Troxel* v. *Granville* (June 5, 2000) was decided in favor of parents (provided they qualified as "fit"), against the wishes of grandparents. It affirmed that grandparents' rights and decisions about child contact and visitation were under the discretion of the parents. As shifts in family constellations continue, issues of custody and visitation among "nonparents" are going to become increasingly heated and complicated, requiring states to exercise the wisdom of Solomon in future explorations of legal rights and "blood rights." As it stands at this writing, regardless of previous involvement and attachment to their grandchildren, grandparents' access is controlled totally by the child's parent.

Vulnerability

One of the most striking refrains of midlife women is that having an aging and increasingly vulnerable mother makes *them* feel more vulnerable. As long as a woman's mother is alive there is a protective fence between her and oblivion. At this point women who spent so much time waiting to be treated like an adult want to retract the wish. Their mothers have driven them up the wall for forty years, and only now do they come to appreciate the value of that particular wall. The very real fact is that from their sixties on, many women are dealing more frequently with loss. Given the differences in male and female life expectancies, women are more likely to become widows. They are losing their husbands and friends to illness and death. If they have developed illnesses associated with aging, they may suffer the loss of mobility and freedom. The loss of autonomy is painful in any adult, no matter how old. Adult daughters can easily become frustrated with what they see as their aging mothers' morbid or negative outlooks. Elizabeth Kaye describes a common way this is expressed: "When my mother reached mid-life, she took to marking time in terms of other people's disasters—before Bob was diagnosed with cancer, when Jill was in the hospital, after Eleanor died."

Observing an aging mother, one who's now pulling up the rear when she used to lead the pack, one who is no longer as careful with her appearance as she once was, or who fits any of the other indicators that we use in our personal definitions of aging or "decline," is always difficult. Even a woman who spent most of her life fantasizing about that one swift kick that will land her mother on her ass realizes that when it comes right down to it, she prefers or needs to have her mother vertical. The recognition that her mother is changing, and needing more and more care, almost always involves ambivalence for her daughter. On the one hand, a daughter has some concept of "payback" and an awareness that she must contribute something to make her mother's life easier. On the other hand, she may also feel like a four-year-old stomping her foot at being told she has to switch costumes with a playmate. "It's not fair!" we can almost hear her say. "I'm the beautiful princess! I don't want to be the stupid queen!"

The wish for more time with her mother, for the luxury of being two old ladies together, is something that daughters often experience as they age. This can be a passive regret, or an active attempt to maximize the moment. There's a beautiful letter by writer and English professor Feenie Ziner to her dead mother, in which she expresses the need to release the many obstacles common to mothers and daughters and share a role that is so important to her: "Now it is I with my blue-veined hands. I am the grandmother. It is I who await the ringing of the doorbell. . . . Couldn't we be grandmothers together? I don't care if you win, I'll let you win. By now everything's been deplored, defined, belittled, understood, predicted. . . . Yes, everything's been said a thousand times. Only one word has never been said, nor will I speak it now because you are alive in me: my irritant, my critic, my goad. My venerable, beloved imperishable mother."

Barrier to Empathy: Resentment and Fear

A woman's need to see her mother as functional, healthy, and eternal is, regardless of a lifetime of ambivalence, very strong. As mothers lose some of their physical speed or agility, as memory becomes spottier, as they lose interest in things that were once central to them, daughters often can't quite believe it. In *Traveling Mercies,* a collection of essays about spirituality, sanity, and family (not necessarily in that order), Anne Lamott watches with "enormous gentleness and annoyance" as her midseventies mother struggles to gain her balance while walking along a beach. Lamott is impatient with the increasingly clumsy ways her mother moves, dresses, and applies makeup. In her more paranoid moments she considers the possibility that her mother is faking the whole thing. "I secretly believed she could do better if she tried, that . . . she acts this way to torture and control me. In my worst moments, I imagine her at home just before I pick her up, wearing a telephone headset and berating some commodities trader. Then when she hears me knock, she dashes to her bedroom, stashes the headset, pulls on her Ruth Buzzi cardigan, applies lipstick to her teeth, and totters to the front door to let me in."

Barrier to Empathy: I'm Fine, You're Not

It's difficult to deal with a mother who refuses to admit her vulnerability, *especially* to her daughter. The mother feels safe only when she is in control—of herself and the relationship. Even if it's partially a façade, sucking it up and being fiercely independent are sometimes good ways to navigate in deep and freezing waters. To have a daughter who was once totally dependent now be the one pointing out her mother's slippage can be a humiliating experience. Many women will push even harder and deny even louder that anything has changed; they are in no more need of help than they were at forty. The daughter can't win. As long as her mother holds to her invulnerability, her daughter can't be much more than a worried onlooker. It keeps the daughter in the role of child and refuses her the chance to test the next step in her relationship with her mother. Unfortunately, many of these situations aren't resolved by some natural adjustment to each other's needs over time. Due to some pivotal experience, a mother is forced to cry "uncle" from a position of defeat—whether it's due to a fall, a minor stroke, a car accident and license revocation, financial collapse, or illness.

In her short story "Which Is More Than I Can Say About Some People," Lorrie Moore follows these themes in the misadventures of a mother and daughter on vacation in Ireland. The daughter, Abby, who's wrestling with fearfulness in general and a public-speaking phobia in particular, has attempted every method of getting "the cure." The idea of kissing the Blarney Stone, with its promise of the "gift of gab," finally draws her, in desperation, to Ireland. And an unlikely pairing—between her and her mother—is made solely on a practical basis; Mrs. Mallon can drive a stick shift, and Abby never learned to drive at all. Throughout the trip, Mrs. Mallon pushes and provokes her resistant daughter along. She proposes adventures that are always a bit too risky for Abby, then shames her daughter by doing them herself.

When Abby admits she finds it scary crossing the border into Northern Ireland, her mother dismisses her with "If you get scared easily." Abby realizes that this was "becoming the theme of their trip—that Abby had no courage and her mother did. And that it had forever been that way." At every stop her mother blusters her way through the things Abby refuses to do. At the Blarney Stone she prompts, coaches, and bullies Abby into the precarious and unnatural posture that the kiss requires. ("You came all this way! Don't be a ninny!") Abby finally does what she came to do: kisses the slimy stone. When her mother's turn comes, and Abby watches her unsteadily lowering herself into position, she realizes that her long-held perception of her mother was just that—long held, and perhaps a wee bit rigid. As she watches her mother struggle, she sees that the "fierce bonfire of a woman had gone twitchy and melancholic—it was a ruse, all her formidable display." Her mother is suddenly and completely terrified.

Instantly it becomes Abby's turn to coach her vulnerable, unsteady mother and retrieve her safely from the stone. That pivotal moment marks a change in the entire balance of their relationship. Because Mrs. Mallon is no longer all-brave, Abby no longer has to be all-scared. They retire to a local pub, and Abby, the public-speaking phobic, "feels a toast coming on." In spite of the long-held belief that her mother never showed her much affection, Abby is now able to give her mother credit for one of the traits she has always valued most about herself—her "knack for solitude." Now, raising her glass, Abby constructs a bridge of words to her mother. "May the worst always be behind you," she improvises, using the standard Irish bullshit way of starting out by saying anything and hoping to God that wiser words will eventually roll off the tongue. "May your car always start . . ." She falters, but continues her quips, wishing her mother a "holding roof, healthy children and good cabbages." Finally, with her voice growing "gallant, public and loud," Abby finishes: "and may you be with me in my heart, Mother, as you are now, in this place; always and forever—like a flaming light." And her mother, the one who was never before at a loss for words, the one who "had never been courted before, not once in her entire life," blushed and answered reverently, "Right."

Mourning a Mother Who's Still Here

When a daughter shifts into the role of caretaker, she also mourns a tremendous loss—that of being someone's child. In her novel *The Autobiography of My Mother,* Jamaica Kincaid captures the loneliness of giving up that role, whether it is snatched away suddenly or erodes over time. Her narrator, Xuela, describes herself, the motherless child, as having "nothing standing between myself and eternity; at my back was always a bleak, black wind. . . . I only came to know this in the middle of my life, just at the time when I was no longer young and realized that I had less of some of the things I used to have in abundance and more of some of the things I had scarcely had at all." Poet Wanda Coleman, recognizing her mother's powerful role in helping her transition from a girl who felt ugly, big, and black, underlines the smaller things her mother did to that end, like making sure her daughter had the confidence that comes from being well dressed. But in the process, she gave her daughter much more than nice clothes. As Coleman writes, "Oh mama, when I lose you, I'll lose my only true witness."

What Is a Self Without Memory?   Lacking memory, we lose our ties to the people we love. The daughter can't receive validation—for the

ways things were, or for her mother's experience of the relationship now. It's like being cast in a play and being told that there's no rehearsal, no script, and the other cast member has no idea why she's even there. In her essay "My Mother Is Speaking from the Desert," Mary Gordon recounts the erasure of her mother's memory and self over an agonizingly long time. As she describes the growing distance between them, she struggles to understand. "She seems to be speaking from the desert," writes Gordon. "Everything she says now is spoken from the desert, a desert she has in part created. But only in part. Mostly, I suppose, the desert was created because she is eighty-six, and something has hardened, or broken, or worn out. The part she made came about through a dark will and sense of worthlessness. Believing she deserves nothing, she surrounds herself with empty air." Despite everything she does to find the right care for her mother, attend to her health, try to coax from her enjoyment of things she used to love, Gordon fails to change the fact that her mother is evaporating. And with a litany of limits, she gives in to her basic powerlessness. "I cannot keep a living spirit in her body," she laments. "I cannot make her remember. I cannot keep her from a living death, a rock-like existence, almost without consciousness. I cannot keep her from a life in which death would make very little difference."

It is at this point that many women mourn their mothers, long before their actual deaths. The reality that, on some level, their essence is already buried or obliterated is a grief these daughters face on a daily basis. Gordon adds her voice to that grieving: "Where has your memory gone, my mother? It was not an object, it was spirit, and the spirit, like the flesh, it seems, can be entirely consumed."

Commuter Caretaking

Journalist Tracy Thompson wrote about being the mother of a young daughter and, in the blink of an eye, the long-distance commuting caretaker after her mother's stroke. What strikes me so clearly about this and other women's accounts is their honesty—the frustration, the despair, the grief, the mess, the mutual antagonisms, the family turned upside down, and the inevitable losses. But in the midst of it all, memories return, and are shared, clarified, and disputed by siblings and parents. Age and infirmity advance, but insights, reflections, and discussions often fall backward, effortlessly. Connections between the present and the past are illuminated. In the face of loss, even in strained relationships, there is the frequent need to treasure. As Thompson and her sister worked to sell their mother's house so that she could be relocated to an assisted-living community, all around them they faced memories of their childhood and the strong associations they had with their home and their mother. After seeing an old family friend, still vibrant and healthy, Thompson writes, "I suddenly missed my own mother in a way I hadn't since childhood . . . when she succeeded for a time in creating for my sister and me the illusion that the world was a bubble of perfect love and safety. Now that her hair is white and her days are an unremitting regimen of pills and physical indignity, I wish I could return the favor. I wish I could make her old age as easy for her as she made childhood for me."

Mother Loss

The death of a mother is one of the most powerful events in a woman's life. So many women have insights into their mothers only after they've died, like Lillian Hellman, who realized, "My mother was dead for five years before I knew that I had loved her very much." The story of a mother and daughter continues to write itself past the death of one or the other. While both are alive, even the most empathic, strongly bonded relationship still has the lag imposed by each being at different "places" over time. "I was a mother myself," remarks Anne Bernays about her mother, Doris Fleishman, "before I began to see that she possessed some habits of mind, some attitudes I positively admired. Let's say her influence on me started when I was quite young but, like one of those capsules that releases tiny beads of a drug over an extended period, it didn't kick in until I was past my prime."

A mother leaves her daughter in the lurch when she dies. Regardless of the quality of the relationship, the daughter is now the one holding the bag. And for many women, that is a frightening prospect. Even for women who lost their mothers very young, the sense of loss is profound. There is the first loss, when a mother actually dies. And then there's the rest of her life spent without a mother. The experience of being "motherless" is one that leaves many women feeling off balance for a long time.

Links in a Chain

The impending loss of a mother often makes women more acutely aware of their place in the generations, as well as the extent to which all the wisdom of the matriarchy is preserved. There is major variation among families of women, with some having a clear sense of the larger picture of which they are a part. The sense of a tradition that serves as a framework for belonging is often a source of great comfort. In the words of Gayl Jones, "My great-grand-mama told my grandmama the part she lived through that my grandmama didn't live through and my grandmama told my mama what they both lived through and my mama told me what they all lived through and we suppose to pass it down like that from generation to generation so we'd never forget." Other daughters find comfort in the narrative their mothers have told them many times—that they will carry with them parts of the generations, and that those parts will remain alive and always available in times of challenge or sorrow. "If you are ever in a bad moment in your life and you feel that you cannot go on," writes Salome to her daughter Sally in Erica Jong's *Inventing Memory,* "remember that you are the daughter of a woman who was the daughter of a woman who believed that strength came from accepting the contradictions of life rather than pretending that life had no contradictions."

✌ DÉJÀ VU ALL ✌ OVER AGAIN

I asked my mother to write about the threads of influence across the generations of women in her own life. She replied in a letter:

Often I wonder what made me the person I am. I know that, like you, I am much more like my father—and not at all like my mother. You asked me about the empathy I felt for my mother and what applied to my family from our rela-tionship. The mother I had from birth to adolescence was not the same person I had from then till marriage—and was not the same mother I had from mar-riage until she died.

   Your great-great-grandmother died in a fall when your great-grand-

mother, Mary Cunningham (Mamie), was a baby. Her Aunt Liza stepped in as a mother figure. They lived in a large household of married and unmarried Cunninghams where there were two other young girls, a little older than Mamie. Mamie always felt that she was the Cinderella in this situation and was at odds with her two cousins to some degree or another all of her life. Perhaps this explains her dark view of life, her very suspicious nature and her determined attempts in her own family to control her children's lives.

Your grandmother spoke about her childhood in very glowing terms, except for the fact that her mother tried to keep them all from making close friends. This worked when they were young—but as your grandmother matured— graduated from Salem Normal and taught school, she made many friends. Her mother resented this bitterly and would give your grandmother the silent treatment when she had the temerity to go away for the weekend with her very active group. Your grandmother spoke of an occasion when her mother would not look at or speak to her for a full two-week period. Your great-grandmother would have done well with the Amish and their shunning.

After your grandmother's marriage, her mother continued to keep up her attempts at control. She would write long letters chastising your grandmother for supposed transgressions. They were often written on many different slips of paper, and included newspaper clippings. I can remember my mother leaving a letter from her mother unopened on the hall table for several days until she could summon the courage to read it. I remember her tearing the letters up in tiny pieces and her mood would be very subdued. After a visit there was always a list of sins sent. They really did a number on your grandmother.

Your great-grandmother had trouble with your grandmother's two sisters as well. Margaret, the youngest, handled it by allowing her mother to run her life completely. When Margaret found a suitor it is said that your great-grandmother threatened to divorce your great-grandfather if the relationship continued. This, as you know, left an awful legacy for my mother when her mother died and with great resentment your grandmother took Margaret in. Margaret totally shifted her dependence from her mother to her sister. I remember my mother exploding one year when Margaret gave her a Mother's Day card. Margaret had absolutely no idea what the whole upset was about. My mother's sister Ruth solved her relationship problems by eloping and moving away after a couple of years. She visited Salem once a year and later only filled her children with glowing reports about her mother—so that their view of the whole situation was utterly unrealistic. Your great-grandmother always told us how wonderful Ruth's kids were—and probably told them the same about us. The result was resentment on both sides—which might have been her purpose.

My "first" mother gave me a very happy family life. I felt loved, cared for and cherished. I was encouraged and also taught by what she said (and unfortunately could not put into play later in her own life), that I could do or become anything I was willing to work for and that I was as good as anyone else. I had a very happy childhood. I owe my mother a great debt, which I tried to repay throughout my life by doing many of the things I thought would please her. They always did—for a day or two—and then intermittently (when I visited for those long summer visits that were vacations to you). But there was enough stubbornness in me that I would not do everything her way— and she was very angry at me for that. She really wanted Nancy and me to be different people. And that was the problem. We rather liked ourselves the way we were.

She was especially caring when one of us was ill, a trait I admired and emulated. When I was bedridden at the age of eleven in a body cast in a hospital bed in the dining room, she was expecting your Uncle David. She tried to make my life as comfortable as possible—and she allowed me to listen to soap operas on the radio—all day long—which meant that she heard them too, as that house was compact and sound carried. I think of what a penance that would be for me, who thrives on silence—to be exposed to that drivel all day— every day. Yet not only did she never complain, she asked each morning when she could vacuum, and I would choose the fifteen-minute time slot that looked to be the least interesting in my day's roster. I can still recite the openings of many of those programs: "Our Gal Sunday"—which asks the question, "Can a girl from a little mining town in Colorado find happiness as the wife of a wealthy and titled Englishman?" The answer, of course, was only once in a while and thereby hung many improbable adventures. There was Helen Trent, Lorenzo Jones, Ma Perkins, and more, subjected constantly to unbelievable (and very slow) happenings. I remember one Helen Trent scenario where it took a person who was shot five episodes to crawl up a staircase. Oh, agony! Oh, ecstasy!

We moved to Jason Street when I was thirteen, and it was right after this that my mother began to show the signs that were so difficult to live with during her life. This was around the time I began to do more and more of the household work. I guess I felt that if I could relieve her of some of the stress of *having a larger house to manage, it would make her better. At the same time she was praising me for this she was denigrating my sister, Nancy, for not helping more. When Nancy was young she wouldn't stay overnight at anyone's house, and I think my mother extrapolated from this that Nancy would be her Margaret. (She alluded to it often, even cruelly making fun of her for her lack of independence.) When Nancy found her confidence, which she did in high school, it threatened your grandmother, and as a result Nancy could do no right. Somehow I knew this was an unfair view, and Nancy and I—while leading parallel lives and not great friends (though not enemies either)—managed to ignore my mother's good daughter/bad daughter scenario. We were able to be open enough to the possibility of closeness, and the opportunity presented itself after my marriage, and we did finally connect, and remain very close.*

My marriage led to strengthening the bond with my sister, but things took a downward step with my mother when I married and moved away. The key words are "moved away." There was a lot of your great-grandmother in your grandmother, and she really wanted us all living right around her. I think she saw shopping trips and lunches and dropping in on each other as a perfect way to live with her children. When that didn't happen she felt cheated. From then on, she was unhappy and angry much of the time. I think life never met her expectations for very long. She could not be happy with all the wonderful things she had because they did not fulfill her expectations. Nancy and I have always thought that to be such a sad situation. My mother had so much going for her. She was attractive (when she tried), charming, interesting, could entertain, paint, you know the list. She had each of her many grandchildren convinced— even through adulthood—that they shared a secret bond, a special friendship.

But she was like a child whose birthday presents are many and wonderful but do not include some outrageously expensive gift she wished for desperately and goes into a screaming fit or a silent sulk. She could not give up her wishes. The problem really was that none of us knew what they really were. We came to realize in our forties, I think, that we could never ever please her more than briefly, and in certain ways that insight led us to stop trying.

I have always been sad that her difficult personality prevented me (and I think wisely) from asking her to come live with your father and me when it became evident that she could no longer live alone. I came very close—but I knew that it would not work. She was never going to be content—and your father and I were not willing in the final analysis to risk what could happen.

I could have easily lived with your Grandmother Manning. In fact, when she became forgetful and the family was making plans, I offered to have her come to Maryland, but they didn't want her so far away. And that is perhaps the saddest thing of all—that I could invite my mother-in-law and not my own mother.

I loved my mother, but she certainly did not make it easy to do so. I am, I think, so different from her because I was born with a different temperament from hers—but also, and perhaps more of an influence, I watched how she suffered and how much of it was willful and needless. I promised I would never ever do the same—especially to my daughters.

AFTERWORD

※

Elephants and Other Big Mothers

Wildlife is not a particular interest of mine—with one major exception: elephants. Despite obvious differences in color, size, and the general tusk/trunk business, female humans and female elephants have a great deal in common. They live in fairly stable family units usually comprising five or six members; these units form strong bonds with other families and create larger communities. For a long time, observers of elephant group behavior have marveled at the ways in which members of one family seem to know, from a great distance, when other families are in the general area. Researchers discovered that the sophistication of elephants' rumbling communications was too subtle for human ears to discriminate. In contrast to the high-frequency sounds emitted by other animals, elephant "talk" occurs in a range of lower frequencies that humans can't detect.

When elephants identify related groups from a distance, they get very excited, "screaming and trumpeting, greeting each other by raising heads in the air and clicking tusks, intertwining trunks and rumbling loudly, flapping ears. . . . They whirl around and rub one another." Their temporal glands (tear ducts) go into high gear, leaving trails along their faces. When they get *very* happy, they really let go—urinating, defecating, rumbling, and trumpeting, which is a lot like what goes on at my family reunions, minus the ear flapping.

Both elephants and people form intense attachments to their offspring, devoting enormous time and energy to their development. Childhood is an extended period for humans and elephants, in which kids and calves are vigilantly protected, instructed, and given "feedback" about acceptable and unacceptable behaviors. Human children and elephant children both go through a period of "displacement," when their mothers give birth again and must invest significant attention to insuring the survival and development of the newborn. In adolescence, males and females are treated quite differently. By the time a male calf has been hanging with his family for about fourteen or fifteen years, his mother has gotten pissed off enough by his increasing aggression and sexual energy that she boots him out. It's time for him to leave home and join the Big Boys. Females, on the other hand, stay with their mothers, often assisting in the care of younger offspring, having children of their own, and taking in their mother's world wisdom as their key to survival.

Bulls may associate with one another, but they are too competitive to live in the spirit of cooperation that sustains the females in family and community life. Unlike the females, who observe a more subtle succession of the maternal line, bulls will attempt to reshuffle the hierarchy with a few good slams or a sharp smack with a tusk. Imagine a bunch of male elephants in a bar. They swap stories and buy one another beers, but if a hot cow lumbers in, it will be every bull for himself . . . for her. Contact with females occurs in brief but intense flings. Male hierarchies are based primarily on size, strength, and guts. Top Bull always gets to go first in the mating order.

An elephant cow's fertility is similar to a human female's, peaking at age eighteen or nineteen and extending to the age of forty, after which it drops off dramatically. Like humans, elephant females live long after their reproductive capabilities decline. This makes them different from almost every other species. What do they do when high maintenance motherhood is behind them? They keep on "keeping on." They become matriarchs, or matriarchs-in-waiting. Like the grandmothers who are essential to the Hadza and similar hunter-gatherer tribes, the matriarchs are primarily responsible for gathering food that supports a lactating daughter. They may also be instrumental in the care of the child who's been banished from the nipple. With an estimated four million U.S. children in the primary care of their grandparents, a similar pattern may emerge for humans.

MATRIARCHS

A matriarchy is not necessarily a traditional male hierarchy that happens to have a temporary female CEO. These aren't the same lame-duck lineages as the House of Windsor, where Queen Elizabeth II reigns, essentially a figurehead, and due to the absence of male heirs, a figurehead by default.

The matriarch of an elephant family is typically the oldest and largest of the group. She is joined by other cows, male and female calves, and females who have yet to produce offspring, and often serve as "aunties" to young calves who are gaining more independence from their mothers. Power and leadership in the family is not determined by aggressive contests of swagger and strength. The hierarchy with females is not a vertical lineage of who can beat up whom. A cow, by virtue of her maturity, steps into the role of matriarch usually in her forties. When she becomes too old or infirm to lead, the next-oldest cow will gradually take on more and more of her role. The precipitous death of the matriarch (by hunters, for example) is a disaster for the entire family, since the group's memory goes with her. This memory is more than a series of sentimental elephant photos or films. It is *survival* memory— the way to raise children, the best places to forage in wet and dry seasons, the closest watering hole, how to detect impending threats, when to charge or flee from danger. Matriarchs aren't just wise, they're gutsy. During a charge, the matriarch is always in front. In retreat, she brings up the rear. Since elephants spend, on average, sixteen hours a day eating, the matriarch is constantly on the lookout for the "range equivalent" of the next Safeway or 7-Eleven, which her "uncanny knowledge of habitat" helps her locate.

CONNECTION AND LOSS

What is so striking about elephants is their empathic behavior when a family member is wounded, sick, dying, or dead. They will gently stroke a fallen elephant, or prod it with their trunks. Older females try bravely to lift the ailing ones with their tusks. A calf might prod its mother by trying to suckle. Others will try to stuff grass or branches into its mouth. Feisty young males may try to revive a dying female by mounting her, which, as we know from human experience, has never been a particularly effective cure for death. When it is clear that the elephant is dead, family members stand around in silent commemoration. They gather branches to cover the body, then slowly move on. Often the mother or child of the fallen elephant will have the most difficulty leaving, mourning openly and lingering until all the others have gone. Clive Spinage, an expert on elephant behavior, recalls the surge of emotion he felt when he accompanied a ranger in Africa to deal with a young calf caught in a fence, way beyond saving. Unfortunately, the first shot, an attempt to end the elephant's misery, did not provide a painless death. Spinage watched, transfixed, as the mother tried to raise the failing calf with her tusks. "Just after it died," Spinage writes, "she raised her trunk high into the air and gave vent to a penetrating wail of anguish. And it was a wail, not a trumpet, which echoed forlornly over the countryside. My flesh tingled. I had never heard anything like that before, pitiful in its desperate intensity and poignant with sorrow. After standing over the dead body for about half an hour the grief-stricken cow then turned and slowly followed her departed comrades."

Cynthia Moss, another observer of African elephant families, describes the way long-term attachments and close knowledge of family members intensifies their reaction to death, well beyond what is typical of many species. While she admits that elephants probably don't have the rumored "graveyards," they do have a strong concept of death, and an emotional reaction to it. "Elephants," she writes, "recognize their own carcasses or skeletons. When they come upon an elephant carcass they become quiet and yet tense in a different way from anything I have seen in other situations. First they reach their trunks toward the body to smell it, and then they approach slowly and cautiously and begin to touch the bones, sometimes lifting them with the feet and trunks. They seem particularly interested in the head and the tusks. They run their trunk tips along the tusks and lower jaws to feel the crevices and hollows in the skull. I would guess they are trying to recognize the individual." She cites an example of a calf who had the strongest and longest reaction of any of his group when they came upon an elephant jawbone. It turned out to be the remains of his mother.

ARE WOMEN MATRIARCHS?

The difference between a matriarchal elephant and an elder woman is striking. The matriarchal elephant amasses knowledge and transmits it to her daughters over the course of their entire lives together. She leads, directs, models, protects; she knows when to fight and when to stand back. Her value to the group has nothing to do with fertility or keeping her youthful figure. Her family survives on her wisdom, and they all know it. Elder women may be central to a matrilineage, meaning that women trace themselves back through their maternal line. However, in terms of matriarchy, elder women *lose* their power over time, either because it's taken away, they let it go voluntarily, or they never had much in the first place. As she ages, a woman becomes more peripheral to the functioning of her family, the workplace, and society in general. Her wisdom, which is also rooted in memory and many years of experience, doesn't stand a chance in an information-age culture, where knowledge is valued only when it's new. Memory is taken care of by machines that can intake incredible amounts of information and call it back in a fraction of the time it takes regular people, and with greater efficiency. The only problem is that wisdom is often confused with a combination of accuracy and speed. Imagine an eight-year-old girl typing a description of her family into a computer. Thirty years later in computer memory, that description will be exactly as it was, uncontaminated by experience. But in *human* memory, images, thoughts, and emotions about her family will have changed thousands of times from that original eight-year-old version. Like the elephant matriarch, it is a cumulative memory, which is a direct function of age and the willingness to learn from experience. An elder woman can contribute many things, sometimes at all-time peak-performance levels, to the continuing care and survival of her family, community, and culture, yet few look to her for guidance and true leadership.

KILL THE MATRIARCH

A long time ago hunters discovered something about elephants that also applies to people, especially women, right here and right now: if you want to maximize the vulnerability of a family, disable the matriarch. Losing her without warning panics the family. They are crippled without memory, the road map to survival. In their confusion they become easy prey for hunters. The entire organization that served them so well collapses with the matriarch, and in situations where there isn't an elder cow who "knows the territory," their functioning disintegrates.

Elephant families offer a worthwhile model for human mothers and daughters to consider. It includes the basic belief that it is *possible* to exist without males being in charge. This is not at all an endorsement of putting men on the periphery. But as long as women, consciously or unconsciously, hold the attitude that males, by birthright, have the deep-down power and always will, we paralyze ourselves and our daughters. Power, as defined by women, may be very different from the male model, which combines competition, control, and individual achievement. Elephant matriarchs are incredibly powerful, but they operate on more cooperative principles, in which interdependence is the norm. There's nothing wrong with competition. In fact, as we've seen in the surge of girls' and women's participation in sports, it can be terrific, an antidote to passivity and a reminder that the body can be valued for what it does, rather than how it looks.

Advances in science, math, computer technology, and business, among other fields, are fueled by competition—with other countries, universities, research teams, companies—or even by trying to top one's "personal best." But power based in competition and control is a model that works well in some situations and is totally inadequate in others. To the degree that women don't have nearly as much of it as men, everyone is at a disadvantage. This is not a slam against men. However, looking at the bottom line, men continue to retain the traditional seats of power in the financial, political, educational, media, and religious realms. The priorities of some of these groups have served agendas that are not in the best interests of women and children, in this country and globally.

BIG LIES

If I had a dime for every time over her twenty-two years that I've told my daughter, "You can be anything," I wouldn't still be worrying about covering my mortgage from month to month. Before her birth, my husband and I affirmed our commitment to raising a Keara the exact same way we would raise a Colin. But that changed the instant she was born. Gender-based attributions were made immediately. She was "dainty," "petite," and destined "to break a lot of guys' hearts." Didn't my husband look "cute" holding her? No one said how I looked, which in retrospect was probably a good thing. Standing at the nursery window, I always knew that if someone was pointing out a baby as a "bruiser," he was either referring to a boy or about to freak out the parents of a girl.

Once we got her home, our feminist beliefs didn't meet any major obstacles for the first year. We were the architects of her environment. At twelve months she was getting all the right input; we emphasized toys that would stimulate her achievement in male-oriented activities and downplayed traditional female ones. By the time she was eighteen months, however, the fantasy that the two of us could raise a child without gender bias began to look like a major crock. Our first error was in confusing gender bias with *genderlessness*. We were at cross-purposes with some aspects of our daughter's development, believing that she could be "corrected" if she veered too far off course. She hit two and it was all over. She moved into Pink Land, lock, stock, and barrel. Now it was play makeup and high heels, dresses instead of overalls, flirting with her father, playing tea party and house. Suddenly her sturdy toy truck was useful only to shuttle her dolls from place to place. *And then came Barbie.* She bugged me from the age of two, to my breaking point somewhere during three, at which time I threw up my hands, slunk into a store, and bought the cheapest Barbie (in many ways) I could find. Barbie didn't fit into my "You can be anything" mentality, no matter how they dressed her up.

As my daughter was more and more exposed to the "real world," my firm *belief* that she could do or be anything faded into a *wish*. I realized that the unspoken part of my message to her was "You can be anything *I* want you to be." "You can be anything I couldn't be." The inference was, of course, that all of her "wants" would be vertical and upwardly mobile. The real world made me a liar. And in the eighties, the lies were subtle and destructive. Often a mother doesn't even recognize the incongruence between what she's told her daughter and what her daughter actually sees. But suddenly, as she experiences events through her daughter's eyes, her own perceptions are forced to shift dramatically.

I remember watching a State of the Union Address with my daughter when she was about nine or ten. As the camera swept back and forth over the imposing assembly—Supreme Court justices, cabinet, House of Representatives, Senate—and I watched my daughter taking in the scene, I had a painful insight: "My God, *it's still a bunch of white guys!*" My daughter's comment, which sounded innocent but cut to the bone, was, "Do you think they ask the women to wear those bright-colored suits so they stand out?" Ten years later, there's no appreciable difference. Of the 100 members of the U.S. Senate, 9 are women. Of the 435 representatives in the House, only 56 are women. How do we explain this to our daughters? How does it fit with our exhortations that they can be anything?

We encounter the same conundrum in many traditional religions where the deity is male and, therefore, his representatives are male. As my daughter prepared for her confirmation in the Catholic church, how did I explain why, as she put it, "God was a guy," and why women couldn't be priests? I could give her the litany about how incredibly arbitrary, rigid, and unfair it all was. What puzzled her was my ability to draw boxes of tolerance around many of these "facts of life" for myself. What I said about the equality of women with years of words, I undid as soon as she recognized my inaction and angry resignation.

On her daughter's second birthday, Anna Quindlen struggled with a similar shift in the way she viewed the status of women in this country. Focused on the clear differences between the rights and opportunities of men and women, Quindlen had always been able to see "the glass half full," emphasizing the progress, however slow, toward change. However, two years of being the mother of a girl gave her an entirely different understanding of "progress." The very same glass was now "half empty." This realization hit a depth of anger on behalf of her daughter that she hadn't registered for herself. As she projected herself and her two-year-old into the future, she wondered how she would explain and encourage her daughter. "Do I say, 'You'll get used to it'?" she asks. "No," she answers, "today is her second birthday and she has made me see fresh this two-tiered world that, despite all our nonsense about post-feminism, continues to offer less respect and less opportunity for women than it does for men. My friends and I have learned to live with it, but my little girl deserves better. She has given me my anger back and I intend to use it well. That is her gift to me today. Some birthday I will return it to her, because she is going to need it."

DO WHAT I SAY, NOT WHAT I *DON'T* DO

Mothers often profess one thing, then invalidate it with their own behavior. It's a universal human foible. A mother tells her daughter not to drink, while she's getting sauced every night. Hypocrisy is so much easier to determine when words and their opposing actions can be *specified*. It's much harder to identify a disconnect between words and *inaction*. If we verbally express our horror over children killing one another in schools or on street corners, yet do nothing but register our own powerlessness, we offer our daughters the contagious sense that women's strong convictions are nice, but they go nowhere. Going back to examples from earlier chapters, it's like holding a screaming infant and having tremendous empathy for her hunger but not translating it into any kind of useful care. The mother of the child who just lost her ice cream to the floor is clearly compassionate in her attempts to get her to talk about it. But the value of conversation melts as quickly as the lost ice cream. Without an action component, empathy, in most situations, is little more than a nicety.

BEYOND ONE MOTHER, ONE DAUGHTER

This is especially true when we move beyond considering mother-daughter dyads as if these relationships exist independently. It is hard to write a book about empathy, as it applies within a mother-daughter relationship, without exploring the extension of that empathy *beyond* the boundaries of the two women. While it's very possible to be a great parent and a lousy citizen, as well as a lousy parent and a great citizen, an integration of the two is urgently needed to transform conditions that range from unacceptable to wretched for a majority of the world's women and children. Our discussion of the many barriers to empathy has focused on the way that getting up close and personal to another's pain may be so threatening that the need to withdraw is overwhelming. Why is it so threatening?

On a global level, there is a tremendous sense of powerlessness when it comes to taking on complex problems like starvation or unremitting violence. Think back to one of the major barriers to empathy—personal distress. These shoes are very uncomfortable to wear. We hear about women in Afghanistan whose lives have been so totally constricted by the Taliban. About woman after woman dead from AIDS in Kenya, often not even knowing how they became infected and how they infected the children they leave behind. We see images of terrified girls being subjected to the centuries-old practice of female circumcision, often being held down by their own mothers. We hear the brothers and fathers of young women in Jordan who unapologetically admit that they had to kill a sister or a daughter suspected of dishonoring the family. We read that the United Nations estimates that up to half of all women and girls in some countries have experienced physical violence at the hands of a partner or family member and more than sixty million females are missing from popular statistics, killed deliberately or neglected because of gender. We hear about the kidnapping of young girls for rampant international sex-slave business, or see the haunted eyes of young girls, multiply raped as spoils of war. We see our own girls, babies holding babies, who consider their future as nothing but a life sentence. We see girls who believe that their greatest physical accomplishment is to become so insubstantial as to almost disappear. And if we can manage to fix our eyes and ears on these cruel images, we will probably feel bad, really bad. The sheer history or power that creates and maintains those haunting images overwhelms us and makes us feel impotent to affect change. It is so much easier to turn the newspaper page or click on another station.

Closer to home for many mothers is the issue of how they are going to stand against the current cultural standards that have moved so far beyond taste and style that they threaten the health and safety of their daughters. The sexualization of girls in childhood, the continual emphasis on female attractiveness as a performance criterion for almost anything, and the dismantling of whatever accord an adolescent girl can make with her body are recognized by politically liberal and conservative women. They may come at the issues from different directions and offer different solutions, but the majority can agree on the *problem*.

What do we do about it? We do what we have always done when things go wrong: we blame the mother. It's not the outright mother bashing of old. Now the euphemism is "the family." The genesis of children's problems is in the family, the specific family of which she is a member. Often "family" fault translates into "mother" fault—either because she's a single parent, or she has a job, or she doesn't, or her children are in day care ten hours a week or forty.

On and on. The bottom line, and the one usually missed, is that young children are fertile in every area of development, and that an active nurturing environment is what advances those areas. Kids aren't getting it. And they're not getting it because it's not a big priority. We know that other people in addition to or instead of a parent can help boost a child's sense of self, control, confidence, social skills, intellectual development, and visual motor skills. But that costs money. When day care is good, it's fine. When day care is less than good, it's not.

Many look with disdain at the idea that two parents have no choice but to work. In contrast, we accept that single mothers have to work and that the care of their already vulnerable children is up for grabs.

THERE ARE CHOICES

The process of developing empathy between and among women can be a daunting task, especially when it seems that we have nothing in common (with a woman in Bangladesh, or the fifteen-year-old banging around in her bedroom), no universal way of communication, and such a limited range of choices. There's a passage from Amy Tan's *The Joy Luck Club* in which An-Mei Hsu, the mother of Rose, one of the younger women in the book, looks at the shambles of her daughter's marriage and registers how, despite her efforts, she and her daughter share the very last thing she ever wanted for her: "I was raised the Chinese way: I was taught to desire nothing, to swallow other people's misery, to eat my own bitterness. And even though I taught my daughter the opposite, she still came out the same way! Maybe it is because she was born to me and she was born a girl and I was born to my mother and I was born a girl. All of us are like stairs, one step after another, going up and down, but all going the same way." But through understanding the stories of her mother, An-Mei finds she has learned a great deal about herself, and about Rose, who feels she has absolutely no choice in her troubles. She knows she needs to counteract those up-and-down stairs, all going the same way. "If she doesn't speak, she is making a choice. If she doesn't try, she can lose her chance forever."

Consensus and Its Failings

For all of the "cooperative" spirit women are supposed to bring to interactions with other women, there is an incredible amount of intolerance and righteousness. On some level, it has a "kill the matriarch" component to it. As long as we fight among ourselves, we will be disabled from effective action. Most women lack a sense of the matriarch within themselves—a certain comfort with whatever level their wisdom, experience, courage, and capacity to lead is now, combined with the conviction that those skills will only increase with time. I'm not talking here about resurrecting the concept of "sisterhood," which many women unfortunately consider the sole province of feminism. The sense of connection to other women can be gratifying and powerful. That connection too is often subverted, however, when conflict and disagreement (differentiation) arise. For some reason, women *love* consensus. It is a wonderful way to give equal time to everyone, to attend empathically to people's feelings, and to compromise. But it's also really hard to make timely decisions through consensus. Everyone dies a slow death by politeness. If women focus on differences and conflicts, they fear that the discord, the bruised egos and hurt feelings, will undermine the strength of the relationship. With those concerns, women see the risks to group cohesion as not worth whatever progress they might make. Men are much better at separating out relationships from clashes about ideas, goals, and opinions. They can be like elephant bulls ramming up against each other, and following the outcome of the conflict, they still enjoy a good roll in the mud together.

It is ironic that "healthy" relationships of many biological sisterhoods are highly ambivalent—fraught with conflict, full of love. Whenever I think of my three sisters, I think of fighting. Not just little wars with words. All-out mean-talking, toy-breaking, badmouthing, clothes-stealing, screaming, seething fights. But no one, no one, could threaten my sisters in any way and not have to deal with me. In adulthood, the four of us have a different take on almost every topic we raise. We debate one another openly or whisper behind one another's backs. We love our own worldviews and one another. So how do we plan even a birthday party without killing one another? More and more, I see that we have come to the realization that it is not our mission in life to change the views of the other women we love. Somehow it was always easier to know that about men. We can disagree about our parents, our childhoods, our brothers, our children, politics, and values, without the goal of conversion. Consensus comes in very low in the hierarchy of love.

Erica Jong's novel *Inventing Memory* is the story of several generations of women and the threads that connected them over a century of amazing changes in the world. Much of the story is told in the form of letters between mothers and daughters. The following excerpt of one of the letters reflects a matriarch's insight into how mothers and daughters (and, I would add, women in general) feel themselves powerless to effect real change. "Every daughter is taught to blame the mama and exonerate the papa! This is how the papas stay in power. If mamas and daughters ever formed a union—that would change everything! But instead we fight each other, and the papas go free like the capitalistic bosses. Perhaps you will understand when you have a daughter of your own. Darling, what I understand now is that we are all part of a chain. We are ripples in a river. As on a rosebush, the single rose does not matter, but the stumpy root with its stubborn life. Like a vine, not the grape itself, but the gnarled, pruned stalk."

When empathy is confused with niceness, passivity, or agreement, it loses its power. It is possible, for example, to differ on issues of reproductive rights and still exercise collective power to demand more funding for research and treatment of breast cancer. We've seen it in the success of MADD (Mothers Against Drunk Driving), where women, tired of the lax monitoring and punishing of offenders, mobilized to define the problem, increase public awareness, offer alternatives, and promote legislation and community practices that cut down on the alarming number of people killed and seriously hurt in alcohol-related accidents. Polls in the wake of the string of school shootings demonstrate that women are more in favor of gun control than men. Despite women's statistical majority, that viewpoint shows up nowhere in law. Women can reasonably differ in their interpretation of the Second Amendment—about who really has the right to bear arms. That's a given. But if the issue is narrowed to concern the access of children and adolescents to guns, there would probably be even more agreement. Looking down the barrel of the NRA and its money and power is enough to make anyone want to pack up their toys and head home. That's what they and other special-interest groups are counting on as they steamroll legislators whom we have elected, so that reform is shut down.

The Million Mom March on Washington on Mother's Day 2000 resulted in the construction of many bridges among women who wouldn't ordinarily know one another. Sometimes it's only when things go wrong that outrageous practices become exposed and changed. For example, almost every woman I know who's ever given birth, or plans to in the future, shudders at the prospect of "drive-by childbirths," where women are limited to twenty-four hours of hospitalization insurance benefits. This is an area in which women mobilized with physicians against a major special-interest group, and succeeded in changing the law. While it sounds delusional, I often fantasize about women forming their own issue-oriented "lobbies," with things like a national bake sale or an American craft fair, in which participation isn't totally rooted in cash, and women within communities work together in whatever ways they feel comfortable. It's going to take a major paradigm shift for women to see themselves at "matriarchs" and communicate to their daughters that they are matriarchs-in-the-making.

OF COURSE I UNDERSTAND

Another threat to empathy is the assumption that we understand someone or something—when we don't. It's amazing to me how much I can be like the little girl who thinks that by putting her hands over her eyes she cannot be seen or that whatever was in her field of vision has ceased to exist. For most of my life, I never counted myself among the "prejudiced," or later, "racists." When it came to "understanding" poverty, cultural diversity, and sexual orientation, I was enlightened. It was the most narcissistic of positions. It took an involuntary membership in a very stigmatized group—people who suffer from serious psychiatric illnesses—to be on the other side of outright cruelty, along with helpful, solicitous reactions that had their own kind of cruelty. For the first time I was consciously aware of being treated differently—through a single lens: my diagnosis. Now when I hear or see amusing references to "mental patients" and "loony bins," I wonder how anyone could see these things as funny. I have a dark and perverse sense of humor, but there are certain forms of human suffering that are out of bounds. It was only by being treated differently on the basis of one piece of information that I "got it." As I experienced people who totally misunderstood me, I realized how wrong I'd been about any of the groups of people I thought I understood.

The only way to bridge these seemingly impenetrable boundaries is by *intentional stretching*. This is not an intellectual exercise. The formation of new and different connections requires an active, emotional, and persistent investment in making it work. And we can include our mothers and our daughters in the process. A wonderful example of an intentional bridge built between mothers and their adolescent girls is offered by Shireen Dodson and Teresa Parker, authors of *The Mother-Daughter Book Club: How Ten Busy Mothers and Daughters Came Together to Talk, Laugh, and Learn Through Their Love of Reading*. They organized a group of mothers and their teenage daughters to meet monthly for a book discussion followed by a meal. Few situations offer such an opportunity for mothers and daughters to hear other mothers' and daughters' reactions to things. The potential for cross-pollination is wonderful. A girl who totally disagrees with her mother about a book may find that a couple of the other mothers actually agree with *her*. When the lines fall along a typical mother-daughter split, there is a certain reassurance: "Okay, I'm not alone in thinking this way." Girls don't get many chances to see their mothers in conversation with other mothers and daughters. It's an important vehicle for the communication, exploration, and transmission of values and traditions that women have lost over the century. For her oldest daughter, Dodson decided that she wanted the group to be composed entirely of African-Americans. When her second daughter, who knew a good thing when she saw it, wanted her own book group, hers evolved into an interracial group, presenting new bridges to cross and offering more gold to mine.

I read recently about a group of Washington, D.C., women, led by superior-court judge Mary Gooden Terrell, who reinstituted the practice of high tea and invited at-risk girls to join them on a regular basis. High tea involves the obvious demands of dressing up and learning the rules of etiquette. But it is about so much more than white gloves and broad-brimmed hats. The older women are mentors to the younger women invited into the group. The young women find themselves welcomed into regular conversation with adults who find them interesting, who invite them to share a ritual that had been important to them as they grew up. In asking the girls to commit to the group on such issues as attendance, school grades, and staying out of legal trouble, these women are telling them that they are important to them, that they will hang in there with them long after the cucumber sandwiches have disappeared. High tea, in this context, is an interdependent sport.

This model has also been attempted in church groups where women from different religions, economic levels, ages, and races commit to get-togethers for prayer, conversation, and food. In an article about one such program, women described the many positive aspects of repeated contact, especially as they met in different churches. They also emphasized the awkwardness involved in the early phase but in retrospect saw it as inevitable, unavoidable, and in many ways necessary. It is normal and natural to feel awkward in new situations. Feeling awkward can be a good sign. It often signals a *beginning*, not a reason to quit. It means we're exposing enough of our vulnerability so that it's possible to connect. It is a gift we give to ourselves and to our daughters. Over time, these and other bridges will broaden our base of experience and understanding; we'll be like the elephant matriarch.

Expanding our capacity for empathy will encourage us to extend ourselves even more to others and allow us to receive from them gifts we never realized we wanted or needed. It's as true for imperfect mothers and daughters as it is for perfect strangers. At a recent U.N. conference on women and violence, a young voice of great authority spoke. Grace, at thirteen, was kidnapped by the Lord's Resistance Army of Uganda and trained to fight, steal, kill, and teach younger children to kill. She saw many peers used sexually as temporary "wives" of the soldiers. After two years she escaped. Five years after being kidnapped, she testified about the progress in worldwide issues regarding the maltreatment of women and children. "But ninety minutes, or even one whole day, speaking at the U.N. is still not enough," said Grace. "It is not enough until every girl in every country is safe, can express her views and is heard." Grace is calling all of us matriarchs, installed or in waiting, to step into our power. Like female elephants, human mothers and daughters already know how to flee. Now it's time to take another page from our elephant counterparts, the matriarchs. *It's time we learn to charge.*

NOTES

ONE: MOTHERS AND DAUGHTERS: THE BIG DEAL

10   *"My wife"*   Letter to "Mr. Blue," Garrison Keillor, *Salon*, 17 October 2000.

11   *"A mother is always"*   Talmud cited in Erica Jong, *Inventing Memory: A Novel of Mothers and Daughters* (New York: HarperCollins, 1997).

12   *"I'll hail my mother"*   Courtney Love, in Amy Raphael, ed., *Grrrls: Viva Rock Divas* (New York: St. Martin's Griffin, 1995).

13   *Gloria Steinem recalls*   Gloria Steinem, "Ruth's Song (Because She Could Not Sing It)," *Outrageous Acts and Everyday Rebellions* (New York: Holt, Rinehart & Winston, 1983). This is one of the best accounts I've read about what it means to grow up with a parent who suffers from a severe psychiatric illness.

13   *"Why do you have to use me"*   Amy Tan, *The Joy Luck Club* (New York: Ivy Books, 1989).

14   *Mothers scarred by their own abuse*   J. Milner, L. Halsey, and J. Fultz, "Empathic Responsiveness and Affective Reactivity to Infant Stimuli in High and Low Risk for Physical Child Abuse Mothers, *Child Abuse and Neglect* 19, no. 5 (1995): 767–80; P. Rosenstein, "Parental Levels of Empathy as Related to Risk Assessment in Child Protective Services," *Child Abuse and Neglect* 19, no. 5 (1995): 1349–60.

15   *Insulting the mother of a rival*   "Mamma!" *Colors* 35 (1999): 96–101.

16   *"Names were called"*   N. Tucker, "Jurors Near Fisticuffs in D.C. Hit-Run Trial," *Washington Post*, 24 May 2000.

16   *"Islands on the Moon"*   Barbara Kingsolver, "Islands on the Moon," *Homeland* (New York: Harper & Row, 1989).

17   *Anne Frank reflected*   Anne Frank, *The Diary of a Young Girl: The Definitive Edition* (New York: Bantam, 1995).

17   A *similar censorship*   Sylvia Plath, "Journals," *The New Yorker,* 27 March 2000. For a more complex approach see M. Rutter et al., "Integrating Nature and Nurture: Implications of Person-Environment Correlations and Interactions for Developmental Psychopathology," *Development and Psychopathology* 9 (1997): 335–61.

20   *"As is the mother"*   Ezek. 16:44 New Revised Standard Version.

20   *another biological contribution*   Winifred Gallagher, *ID: How Heredity and Environment Shape the Way You Are* (New York: Random House, 1996); Jerome Kagan, *Galen's Prophecy: Temperament in Human Nature* (New York: Basic Books, 1996).

20   *Gender differences*   G. M. de Courten-Myers, "The Human Cerebral Cortex: Gender Differences in Structure and Function," *Journal of Neuropathology and Experimental Neurology* 58 (1999): 217–26; A. Kastrup et al., "Gender Differences in Cerebral Blood Flow and Oxygenation Response During Focal Physiologic Neural Activity," *Journal of Cerebral Blood Flow Metabolism 19* (1999): 1066–71; H. Davidson, K. Cave, and D. Sellner, "Differences in Visual Attention and Task Interference Between Males and Females Reflect Differences in Brain Laterality," *Neuropsychologia* 38 (2000): 508–19; S. Orozco and C. Ehlers, "Gender Differences in Electrophysiological Responses to Facial Stimuli," *Biological Psychiatry* 44 (1998): 281–89; J. Oliver-Rodriguez, Z. Guan, and V. Johnson, "Gender Differences in Late Positive Components Evoked by Human Faces," *Psychophysiology* 36 (1999): 176–85; J. Ragland et al., "Sex Differences in Brain-Behavior Relationships Between Verbal Episodic Memory and Resting Regional Cerebral Blood Flow," *Neuropsychologia* 38 (2000): 451–61; T. A. Kimbrell et. al., "Regional Brain Activity During Transient Self-Induced Anxiety," *Biological Psychiatry* 46 (1999): 454–65; F. Schneider et al., "Gender Differences in Regional Cerebral Activity During Sadness," *Human Brain Mapping* 9 (2000): 226–38; M. George et al., "Brain Regions Involved in Recognizing Facial Emotion or Identity: An Oxygen-15 PET Study," *Journal of Neuropsychiatry and Clinical Neuroscience* 5 (1993): 384–94; R. Gur et al., "Sex Differences in Regional Cerebral Glucose Metabolism During a Resting State," *Science* 267 (1995): 528–31; J. Haller et al., "Defeat Is a Major Stressor in Males While Social Instability Is Stressful Mainly in Females:

Towards the Development of a Social Stress Model in Female Rats," *Brain Research Bulletin* 50 (1999): 33–39.

22   *father absence in the timing of early menarche*   B. Ellis and J. Garber, "Psychological Antecedents of Variation in Girls' Pubertal Timing: Maternal Depression, Stepfather Presence, and Marital and Family Stress," *Child Development* 71 (2000): 485–501.

22   *They also stress autonomy*   M. Rastogi and K. Wampler, "Adult Daughters' Perceptions of the Mother-Daughter Relationship: A Cross-Cultural Comparison," *Family Relations,* July 1999.

23   *This is poignantly portrayed*   Gish Jen, "Who's Irish?" *The New Yorker,* 14 September 1998.

23   *In a scene*   Amy Tan, *The Joy Luck Club.*

25   *Conflict between mothers and daughters*   R. Larson et al., "Changes in Adolescents' Daily Interactions with Their Families from Ages 10 to 18: Disengagement and Transformation," *Developmental Psychology* 32 (1996): 744–54.

26   *"collective" versus the "relational"*   S. Gabriel and W. Gardner, "Are There 'His' and 'Hers' Types of Interdependence? The Implications of Gender Differences in Collective vs. Relational Interdependence for Affect, Behavior, and Cognition," *Journal of Personality and Social Psychology* 77 (1999): 642–55.

27   *"blues of the American woman"*   Beth Gutcheon, *The Perfect Patchwork Primer* (Baltimore: Penguin Books, 1978). For an interesting look at the quilting culture, see *America Quilts,* produced by Diane Kostecke for Wisconsin Public Television, 1999. It is available from PBS Home Video.

TWO: EMPATHY: THE STRONGEST BRIDGE

33   *calling a medical student "empathic"*   Harold Morowitz, "The Pre-Med as a Metaphor of Antipathy," in *Empathy and the Practice of Medicine: Beyond Pills and the Scalpel,* ed. Howard M. Spiro (New Haven: Yale University Press, 1993).

34   *Irish journalist Nuala O'Faolain*   Nuala O'Faolain, *Are You Somebody? The Accidental Memoir of a Dublin Woman* (New York: Henry Holt, 1996).

34   *When Alice McDermott*   D. Streitfeld, "Bethesda Novelist Tops Book Awards," *Washington Post,* 11 November 1998.

35   *Gretel Ehrlich's memoir*   Gretel Ehrlich, *A Match to the Heart: One Woman's Story of Being Struck by Lightning* (New York: Pantheon, 1994).

36 *Psychologist Judith Jordan dismisses* Judith Jordan, ed., "A Relational Perspective for Understanding Women's Development," *Women's Growth in Diversity: More Writings from the Stone Center* (New York: Guilford, 1997).

37 *Without consciously trying* T. Chartrand and J. Bargh, "The Chameleon Effect: The Perception-Behavior Link and Social Interaction," *Journal of Personality and Social Psychology* 76 (1999): 893–910.

38 *neglectful teenage mothers* C. Cooper, "The Effect of Social Support on Adolescent Mothers' Styles of Parent-Child Interaction as Measured on Three Separate Occasions," *Adolescence* 25 (1990): 49–57; D. Koniak-Griffin, I. Verzemnieks, and D. Cahill, "Using Videotape Instruction and Feedback to Improve Adolescents' Mothering Behaviors," *Journal of Adolescent Health* 13 (1992): 570–75.

38 *Child molesters* Y. M. Fernandez et al., "The Child Molester Empathy Measure: Description and Examination of Its Reliability and Validity," *Sex Abuse* 11 (1999): 17–31.

39 *children's perspective-taking skills increase* N. Eisenberg et al., "Consistency and Development of Prosocial Dispositions: A Longitudinal Study," *Child Development* 70 (1999): 1360–72.

42 *Empathy can also be seen* Jean Baker Miller and Irene Stivers, *The Healing Connection: How Women Form Relationships in Therapy and in Life* (Boston: Beacon Press, 1997).

43 *"tend and befriend" style* S. E. Taylor et al., "Biobehavioral Responses to Stress in Females: Tend-and-Befriend, Not Fight-or-Flight," *Psychological Review* 107 (2000): 411–29.

43 *Oxytocin* R. Turner et al., "Preliminary Research on Plasma Oxytocin in Normal-Cycling Women: Investigating Emotion and Interpersonal Distress," *Psychiatry* 62 (1999): 97–111.

45 *The children of Holocaust survivors* F. Hogman, "Trauma and Identity Through Two Generations of the Holocaust," *Psychoanalytic Review* 85 (1998): 551–78.

47 *When people actually projected themselves* C. B. Batson, S. Early, and G. Salvarani, "Perspective Taking: Imagining How Another Feels Versus How You Would Feel," *Personality and Social Psychology Bulletin* (1997): 751.

57 *Researchers have applied the distinction* H. Fritz and V. Hegelson, "Distinctions of Unmitigated *Communion from Communion*: Self-Neglect and Overinvolvement with Others," *Journal of Personality and Social Psychology* 75 (1998): 121–40.

59   *Conversations between early-adolescent girls*   E. Monck, "Confiding Relationships Among Adolescent Girls," *Journal of Child Psychology and Psychiatry* 32 (1992): 37–45.

THREE: PREGNANCY AND CHILDBIRTH: RAW MATERIALS

63   *In one study*   F. Pedersen et al., "Prenatal Maternal Reactivity to Infant Cries Predicts Postnatal Perceptions of Infant Temperament and Marriage Appraisal," *Child Development* 67 (1996): 2541–52.

64   *"feet propped up"*   Rebecca Wells, *Little Altars Everywhere* (New York: Harper Perennial, 1992).

65   *In Amy Tan's* The Kitchen God's Wife   Amy Tan, *The Kitchen God's Wife* (New York: Putnam, 1991).

68   *Naomi Wolf*   Naomi Wolf, "Life Within Life," in *Child of Mine,* ed. Christina Baker Kline (New York: Delta, 1997).

68   *Writer Rita Ciresi*   Rita Ciresi, "Spittin' Image," in Kline, *Child of Mine.*

68   *Johns Hopkins researchers*   D. Perry, J. DiPietro, and K. Costigan, "Are Women Carrying 'Basketballs' Really Having Boys? Testing Pregnancy Folklore," *Birth* 26 (1999): 172–77.

68   *"I have never since felt so closely accompanied"*   Isabel Allende, *Paula* (New York: HarperCollins, 1994).

69   *Daniel Stern, M.D.*   Daniel Stern and N. Bruschweiler-Stern, *The Birth of a Mother* (New York: Basic Books, 1998).

69   *Christina Baker Kline*   Kline, *Child of Mine.*

71   *Novelist Carolyn See*   Carolyn See, in *From Daughters to Mothers: I've Always Meant to Tell You,* ed. Constance Warloe (New York: Pocket, 1997).

71   *In her memoir*   Jan Waldron, *Giving Away Simone: A Memoir* (New York: Times Books, 1995).

72   *In Frank McCourt's stirring memoir*   Frank McCourt, *Angela's Ashes* (New York: Scribner, 1996).

72   *From the moment of her birth*   McCourt, *Angela's Ashes.*

74   *This is definitely the case*   Wells, *Little Altars Everywhere.*

76   *This can introduce an unintentional burden*   Elissa Schappell, "In Search of the Maternal Instinct," in Kline, *Child of Mine.*

80   *The likelihood is that the daughter's pregnancy*   J. Pearson et al., "Grandmother

Involvement in Child-Care Giving in an Urban Community," *Gerontologist* 37 (1997): 650–57; S. Pope et al., "Low-Birth-Weight Infants Born to Adolescent Mothers: Effects of Coresidency with Grandmother on Child Development," *Journal of the American Medical Association* 269 (1993): 1396–4000; P. East, "The Younger Sisters of Childbearing Adolescents: Their Attitudes, Expectations and Behaviors," *Child Development* 67 (1996): 267–82.

81   *When young Maya Angelou*   Maya Angelou, *I Know Why the Caged Bird Sings* (New York: Random House, 1996).

82   *Responding to women*   Chris Rock, *Bigger and Blacker,* HBO 1999.

84   *Novelist Barbara Kingsolver recalls*   Barbara Kingsolver, in Warloe, *From Daughters to Mothers.*

87   *Writer Marge Piercy*   Marge Piercy, "Voices After Dark," in Warloe, *From Daughters to Mothers.*

89   *Unlike the timing of other roles*   K. Somary and G. Stricker, "Becoming a Grandparent: A Longitudinal Study of Expectations and Early Experiences as a Function of Sex and Lineage," *Gerontologist* 38 (1998): 53–61; A. Douglas, "Grander Than Thou Baby Boomers Ready to Put Their Stamp on Grandparenting," *Chicago Tribune,* 2 June 1999.

FOUR: INFANCY: MUTUAL ATTACHMENT AND SYNCHRONY

95   *In a study provocatively titled*   E. Johnson and T. Huston, "The Perils of Love, or Why Wives Adapt to Husbands During the Transition to Parenthood," *Journal of Marriage and the Family* 60 (1998): 195–204.

96   *Anne Lamott*   Anne Lamott, "Sleeping In," *Salon,* 7 January 1999.

97   *"Motherhood"*   Janet Maloney Franze, "A Creation Story," in Christina Baker Kline, *Child of Mine* (New York: Delta, 1997).

97   *But I'm much more impressed*   For engaging overviews of child and parent development using evolutionary, biological, and cultural lenses, Meredith Small's *Our Babies, Ourselves: How Biology and Culture Shape the Way We Parent* (New York: Anchor Books, 1998) and Sarah Blaffer Hrdy's *Mother Nature: A History of Mothers, Infants and Natural Selection* (New York: Pantheon, 1999) are excellent resources.

98   *Role of vocalization in maternal-infant relatedness*   C. Ward and R. Cooper, "A

Lack of Evidence in 4-Month-Old Human Infants for Paternal Voice Preference," *Developmental Psychobiology* 35 (1999): 49–59; J. Lobermand et al., "Feasibility of Using fMRI to Study Mothers Responding to Infant Cries," *Depression and Anxiety* 10 (1999): 99–104.

98   *Role of vision in maternal-infant relatedness*   M. Chung and D. Thomson, "Development of Facial Recognition," *British Journal of Developmental Psychology* 86 (1995): 55–87.

98   *Role of smell in maternal-infant relatedness*   H. Varendi, R. Porter, and J. Winberg, "Does the Newborn Baby Find the Nipple by Smell?" *Lancet* 344 (1994): 989–90; J. Winberg and R. Porter, "Olfaction and Human Neonatal Behavior: Clinical Implications," *Acta Paediatrica* 87 (1998): 6–10; H. Varendi et al., "Soothing Effect of Amniotic Fluid Smell in Newborn Infants," *Early Human Development* 51 (1998): 47–55; A. Fleming, M. Steiner, and C. Corter, "Cortisol, Hedonics and Maternal Responsiveness in Human Mothers," *Hormonal Behavior* 32 (1997): 85–98; R. Sullivan and P. Toubas, "Clinical Usefulness of Maternal Odor in Newborns: Soothing and Feeding Preparatory Responses," *Biological Neonate* 74 (1998): 402–8.

98   *Role of touch in maternal-infant relatedness*   T. Field, "Early Interventions for Infants of Depressed Mothers," *Pediatrics* 102 (1998): 1305–10.

99   *In her hilarious and moving essay*   Elissa Schappell, "In Search of the Maternal Instinct," in Kline, *Child of Mine*.

100   *"I'm in the milk"*   Maurice Sendak, *In the Night Kitchen* (New York: HarperCollins, 1995).

101   *A mother's early interaction*   R. Feldman, C. Greenbaum, and N. Yirmiya, "Mother-Infant Synchrony as an Antecedent of the Emergence of Self-Control," *Developmental Psychology* 35 (1999): 223–31; C. Stifter, T. Spinrad, and J. Braungart, "Toward a Developmental Model of Child Compliance: The Role of Emotion Regulation in Infancy," *Child Development* 70 (1999): 21–32.

101   *Mary Catherine Bateson*   Mary Catherine Bateson, *Composing a Life* (New York: Plume, 1990).

102   *But if that was all a mother did*   J. Cassidy, "Emotion Regulation: Influences of Attachment Relationships," *Monograph Society for Research in Child Development* 59 (1994): 228–49; G. Kochanska et al., "Individual Differences in Emotionality in Infancy," *Child Development* 69 (1998): 375–90; G. Kochanska, K. T. Murray, and K. T. Harlan, "Effortful Control in Early Childhood: Continuity and Change, Antecedents and Implications for Social

Development," *Developmental Psychology* 36 (2000): 220–32; E. Buchholz and H. Marben, "Neonatal Temperament, Maternal Interaction, and the Need for 'Alonetime,' " *American Journal of Orthopsychiatry* 69 (1999): 9–18.

105   *Nearly half a million unmarried girls*   Paula Span, "Be My Baby: An Unwed Teen, an Infertile Couple, and the Adoption Quandary—Parallel Lives," *Washington Post Magazine,* 18 June 2000.

106   *Jan Waldron gave up*   Jan Waldron, *Giving Away Simone: A Memoir* (New York: Times Books, 1995).

107   *According to Deborah Sichel*   Deborah Sichel and Jeanne Watson Driscoll, *Women's Moods: What Every Woman Must Know About Hormones, the Brain and Emotional Health* (New York: William Morrow, 1999). Fiona Shaw's *Composing Myself: A Journey Through Postpartum Depression* (South Royalton, Vt.: Steerforth Press, 1998) and Susan Kushner Resnick's *Sleepless Days: One Woman's Journey Through Postpartum Depression* (New York: St. Martin's Press, 2000) present contrasting portraits of British approaches and U.S. approaches toward treating postpartum depression. See also Karen Kleiman and Valerie Davis Raskin's book, *This Isn't What I Expected: Overcoming Post-Partum Depression* (New York: Bantam, 1994).

107   *The incidence of postpartum*   D. Blazer et al., "The Prevalence and Distribution of Major Depression in a National Community Sample: The National Comorbidity Survey," *American Journal of Psychiatry* 151 (1994): 979–86.

108   *Maternal depression has far-reaching*   For an overview of the impact of maternal depression on child and adolescent development, I suggest Anne Sheffield's *Web of Sorrow: Overcoming the Legacy of Maternal Depression* (New York: Free Press, 2000). In addition the following studies demonstrate the ways in which maternal depression undermines the scaffolding of the maternal infant bond: T. Field et al., "Right Relative Frontal EEG Activation in 3-to-6-Month-Old Infants of Depressed Mothers," *Developmental Psychology* 31 (1995): 358–63; J. Braungart-Rieker et al., "Infant Affect Regulation During the Still-Face Paradigm with Mothers and Fathers: The Role of Infant Characteristics and Parental Sensitivity," *Developmental Psychology* 34 (1998): 1428–37; M. Radke-Yarrow et al., "Depressed and Well Mothers," *Child Development* 65 (1994): 1405–14.

110   *"a hurricane in its perfect power"*   Maya Angelou, *Wouldn't Take Nothing for My Journey Now* (New York: Random House, 1993).

113 *There's a great moment*   Julia Alvarez, *How the Garcia Girls Lost Their Accents* (New York: Algonquin Books, 1991).

Sarah Bird   Sarah Bird, "Baby Blues: A Journal," in Kline, *Child of Mine.*

114 *Beverly Donofrio describes*   Beverly Donofrio, *Riding in Cars with Boys: Confessions of a Bad Girl Who Makes Good* (New York: William Morrow, 1988).

FIVE: CHILDHOOD: LEARNING THE LANGUAGE OF FEELING; "I CAN, THEREFORE I AM"

128 *Mothers of socially skilled*   G. Pettit et al., "Mothers' and Fathers' Socialization Behaviors in Three Contexts: Links with Children's Peer Competence," *Merrill-Palmer Quarterly* 44 (1998): 173–93; K. Kerns, L. Klepac, and A. Cole, "Peer Relationships and Preadolescents' Perceptions of Security in the Child-Mother Relationship," *Developmental Psychology* 22 (1996): 457–66.

130 *Boys usually face cruelty*   N. Crick, J. Casas, and H. Ku, "Relational and Physical Forms of Peer Victimization in Preschool," *Developmental Psychology* 35 (1999): 376–85; N. Crick and M. Bigbee, "Relational and Overt Forms of Peer Victimization: A Multiinformant Approach," *Journal of Consulting and Clinical Psychology* 66 (1998): 337–47.

130 *The evidence is fairly clear*   E. Hodges et al., "The Power of Friendship: Protection Against an Escalating Cycle of Peer Victimization," *Developmental Psychology* 35 (1999): 94–101.

130 *Empathic girls have mothers*   N. Eisenberg et al., "The Relation of Empathy-Related Emotions and Maternal Practices to Children's Comforting Behavior," *Journal of Experimental Child Psychology* 55 (1993): 131–50; C. Herrera and J. Dunn, "Early Experiences with Family Conflict: Implications for Arguments with a Close Friend," *Developmental Psychology* 33 (1997): 869–81; T. Field et al., "Adolescents' Intimacy and Friends," *Adolescence* 30 (1995): 133–40; G. Kochanska, "Mutually Responsive Orientation Between Mothers and Their Young Children: Implications for Early Socialization," *Child Development* 68 (1997): 94–112; N. Eisenberg et al., "The Relations of Empathy-Related Emotions and Maternal Practices to Children's Comforting Behavior," *Journal of Experimental Child Psychology* 55 (1993): 131–50; J. Krevans and

J. Gibbs, "Parents' Use of Inductive Discipline: Relations to Children's Empathy and Prosocial Behavior," *Child Development* 67 (1996): 3263–77.

142 *Women are ruminators*   S. Nolen-Hoeksema, "Explaining the Gender Differences in Depressive Symptoms," *Journal of Personality and Social Psychology* 77 (1999): 1061–72; S. Nolen-Hoeksema and C. G. Davis, " 'Thanks for Sharing That': Ruminators and Their Social Support Networks," *Journal of Personality and Social Psychology* 77 (1999): 801–14.

143 Ramona and Her Mother   Beverly Cleary, *Ramona and Her Mother* (New York: William Morrow, 1998).

145 *"Whether or not one wants to change"*   Carol Bly, "My Dear Republican Mother," in *From Daughters to Mothers: I've Always Meant to Tell You*, ed. Constance Warloe (New York: Pocket, 1997).

145 *In her refreshingly honest article*   Mona Gable, "Girly Girl," *Salon,* 12 January 1999.

148 *Lois Gould*   Lois Gould, *Mommy Dressing: A Love Story After a Fashion* (New York: Anchor, 1998).

149 *Ellen Glasgow wrote*   Ellen Glasgow, *The Woman Within: An Autobiography* (New York: Harcourt Brace Jovanovich, 1954).

151 *Poet Carol Bly*   Carol Bly, "My Dear Republican Mother," in Warloe, *From Daughters to Mothers*.

152 *One of the best examples*   Dorothy Allison, *Two or Three Things I Know for Sure* (New York: Dutton, 1995).

153 *M. Elaine Mar*   M. Elaine Mar, *Paper Daughter: A Memoir* (New York: HarperCollins, 1999).

153 *One of the most excruciating recountings*   Dorothy Allison, *Bastard Out of Carolina* (New York: Dutton, 1992).

154 *Maxine Clair describes*   Maxine Clair, "October Brown," in *Rattlebone* (New York: Penguin, 1994).

155 *Eliza Minot's novel*   Eliza Minot, *The Tiny One* (New York: Knopf, 1999).

156 *Carolyn See*   Carolyn See, in Warloe, *From Daughters to Mothers*.

156 *Poet and novelist*   Alice Walker, *In Search of Our Mothers' Gardens* (New York: Harcourt Brace Jovanovich, 1983).

SIX: ADOLESCENCE: IDENTITY, DIFFERENTIATION, AND THE DOOR THAT SWINGS BOTH WAYS

167   *"proliferation of selves"*   Susan Harter et al., "The Development of Multiple Role-Related Selves During Adolescence," *Developmental Psychopathology* 9 (1997): 835–53; S. Harter, P. Waters, and N. Whitesell, "Relational Self-Worth: Differences in Perceived Worth as a Person Across Interpersonal Contexts Among Adolescents," *Child Development* 69 (1998): 756–66.

174   *In Elizabeth Strout's novel*   Elizabeth Strout, *Amy and Isabelle* (New York: Random House, 1999).

174   *In her epic novel*   Sandra Jackson-Opoku, *The River Where Blood Is Born* (New York: Ballantine, 1997).

175   *"When I was sixteen"*   Barbara Kingsolver, "Stone Dreams," in *Homeland* (New York: Harper & Row, 1989).

175   *When adolescent girls*   E. Koff and J. Rierdan, "Preparing Girls for Menstruation: Recommendations from Adolescent Girls," *Adolescence* 30 (1995): 795–811; E. Koff and J. Rierdan, "Premenarcheal Expectations and Postmenarcheal Experiences of Positive and Negative Menstrual-Related Changes," *Journal of Adolescent Health* 18 (1996): 286–91.

175   *Mothers are anxious*   N. McElroy, "Looking Back in Wonder," in *From Daughters to Mothers: I've Always Meant to Tell You,* ed. Constance Warloe (New York: Pocket, 1997).

176   *In Maxine Clair's* Rattlebone   Maxine Clair, "Secret Love," in *Rattlebone* (New York: Penguin, 1994).

176   *And in* Amy and Isabelle   Strout, *Amy and Isabelle.*

176   *"A major issue"*   bell hooks, "Girls Together," in *Sister to Sister: Women Write About the Unbreakable Bond,* ed. Patricia Foster (New York: Anchor Books, 1995).

177   *In* Dreaming in Cuban   Cristina Garcia, *Dreaming in Cuban* (New York: Ballantine, 1992).

177   *Early puberty starts a girl off*   B. Ellis and J. Graber, "Psychological Antecedents of Variation in Girls' Pubertal Timing: Maternal Depression, Stepfather Presence, and Marital and Family Stress," *Child Development* 71 (2000): 485–501; G. Xiaojia, R. Conger, and G. Elder, "Coming of Age Too Early: Pubertal Influences on Girls' Vulnerability to Psychological Distress,"

Child Development 67 (1996): 3386–4000; J. Graber et al., "Is Psychopathology Associated with the Timing of Pubertal Development?" *Journal of the American Academy of Child and Adolescent Psychiatry* 36 (1997): 1768–76; G. Slap et al., "Evolving Self-Image, Pubertal Manifestations, and Pubertal Hormones: Preliminary Findings in Young Adolescent Girls," *Journal of Adolescent Health* 15 (1994): 327–35.

178 *During childhood, the rates of depression* S. Nolen-Hoeksema and J. Girgus, "The Emergence of Gender Differences in Depression During Adolescence," *Psychological Bulletin* 115 (1994): 424–43.

In Amy and Isabelle Strout, *Amy and Isabelle.*

179 *"What Is Victoria's Secret?"* C. Hubbard, "What Is Victoria's Secret?" *Salon,* 23 July 1999.

179 *Berie Carr* Lorrie Moore, *Who Will Run the Frog Hospital?* (New York: Knopf, 1994).

180 *In Rebecca Wells's novel* Rebecca Wells, *Little Altars Everywhere* (New York: HarperPerennial, 1992).

181 *Ethnic differences in body image* J. Siegel et al., "Body Image, Perceived Pubertal Timing, and Adolescent Mental Health," *Journal of Adolescent Health* 25 (1999): 155–65; K. Brown et al., "Changes in Self-Esteem in Black and White Girls Between the Ages of 9 and 14 Years: The NHLBI Growth and Health Study," *Journal of Adolescent Health* 23 (1998): 7–19; A. Hill and J. Franklin, "Mothers, Daughters and Dieting: Investigating the Transmission of Weight Control," *British Journal of Clinical Psychology* 37 (1998): 3–13; J. Ogden and C. Elder, "The Role of Family Status and Ethnic Group on Body Image and Eating Behavior," *International Journal of Eating Disorders* 23 (1998): 309–15; D. Schwartz et al., "Body Image, Psychological Functioning, and Parental Feedback Regarding Physical Appearance," *International Journal of Eating Disorders* 25 (1999): 339–43.

181 *Lois Gould's memoir* Lois Gould, *Mommy Dressing: A Love Story After a Fashion* (New York: Anchor, 1998).

183 *In Mei Ng's* Mei Ng, *Eating Chinese Food Naked* (New York: Washington Square Press, 1998).

184 *Given the number of women who are abused* C. Heim et al., "Pituitary-Adrenal and Autonomic Responses to Stress in Women After Sexual and Physical Abuse in Childhood," *Journal of the American Medical Association* 284 (2000): 592–97; C. Heim and C. Nemeroff, "The Impact of Early Adverse Experi-

ences on Brain Systems Involved in the Pathophysiology of Anxiety and Affective Disorders," *Biological Psychiatry* 46 (1999): 1509–22. This is one article in a compilation of evidence that childhood abuse is the hurt that keeps on harming. When a woman leaves childhood, the history of abuse comes with her, influencing her emotional, physiological, and social responses to routine stressors as well as traumatic events.

184 *There's a wonderful passage* Kaye Gibbons, *A Cure for Dreams* (New York: Vintage Books, 1991).

184 *Dorothy Allison recalls* Dorothy Allison, *Two or Three Things I Know for Sure* (New York: Plume, 1995).

187 *The mother in Fae Myenne Ng's novel* Fae Myenne Ng, *Bone* (New York: Hyperion, 1993).

188 *For writer Joanne Meschery* Joanne Meschery, in Warloe, *From Daughters to Mothers*.

191 *There's a moving passage* Amy Tan, *The Kitchen God's Wife* (New York: Putnam, 1991).

193 *Lois Gould's memoir* Gould, *Mommy Dressing*.

194 *Mary Mebane describes* Mary Mebane, "Mary," in *Writing Women's Lives: An Anthology of Autobiographical Narratives by Twentieth-Century Women Writers*, ed. Susan Cahill (New York: HarperPerennial, 1994).

194 *Ellen Gilchrist's wonderful character* Ellen Gilchrist, *Net of Jewels* (New York: Little, Brown, 1992).

195 *Sidda* Wells, *Little Altars Everywhere*.

195 *PBS special on mothers* L. Alvarez and A. Kolker, *Moms*, Corporation for Public Broadcasting, 2 May 1999.

196 *The novel* Amy and Isabelle Strout, *Amy and Isabelle*.

198 *In a haunting memoir* Helen Epstein, *Where She Came From: A Daughter's Search for Her Mother's History* (New York: Little, Brown, 1997).

199 *Novelist Barbara Kingsolver* Barbara Kingsolver, in Warloe, *From Daughters to Mothers*.

200 *Gloria Steinem writes movingly* Gloria Steinem, "Ruth's Song (Because She Could Not Sing It)," in *Outrageous Acts and Everyday Rebellions* (New York: Holt, Rinehart & Winston, 1983).

201 *As her mother was literally making a bonfire* Mary Karr, *The Liars' Club* (New York: Penguin, 1995).

201 *Carolyn See* Carolyn See, *Dreaming: Hard Luck and Good Times in America* (New York: Random House, 1995).

SEVEN: YOUNG ADULTHOOD:
TURNING OUT AND TURNING INTO

210   *Jacquelyn Mitchard*   Jacquelyn Mitchard, *The Rest of Us: Dispatches from the Mother Ship* (New York: Viking, 1997).

214   *"My relationship with my mother"*   Helen Epstein, *Where She Came From: A Daughter's Search for Her Mother's History* (New York: Little, Brown, 1997).

214   *Meg Wolitzer's novel*   Meg Wolitzer, *Surrender, Dorothy* (New York: Scribner, 1999).

215   *the concepts of separate and attached*   Katie Granjo, Betsy   Kennedy, and William Sears, *Attachment Parenting: Instinctive Care for Your Baby and Young Child* (New York: Pocket Books, 1999); William Sears and Martha Sears, *The Baby Book: Everything You Need to Know About Your Baby* (New York: Little, Brown, 1993). Both books propose that rapid response to baby's cries, breast-feeding on demand, carrying as much as possible, delayed weaning, gentle discipline, and the "family bed" will enhance the bond between parent and child. In many respects attachment parenting encourages practices that are automatic within other cultures. The difference is that these are typically not cultures in which individual autonomy is valued over the collective's needs.

220   *Writer June Bingham*   June Bingham, "Should Mother's Day Be Matriarch's Day?" in *The Source of the Spring: Mothers Through the Eyes of Women Writers*, ed. Judith Shapiro (Berkeley, Calif.: Conari Press, 1998).

220   *"I am never so full"*   Katie Singer, *The Wholeness of a Broken Heart* (New York: Riverhead, 1999).

224   *In* The Bean Trees   Barbara Kingsolver, *The Bean Trees* (New York: Harper & Row, 1988).

224   *In a subsequent novel*   Barbara Kingsolver, *Pigs in Heaven* (New York: HarperCollins, 1993).

226   *One of the unfortunate byproducts*   Anne Roiphe, *Fruitful: A Real Mother in the Modern World* (New York: Houghton Mifflin, 1996).

226   *Good child care*   Child Care Bureau and the Head Start Bureau of the Administration for Children and Families, *Quality Care for Infants and Children*, report, U.S. Department of Health and Human Services, September 1998. Three good resources on the topic are E. Galinsky, *Ask the Chil-*

dren: What America's Children Really Think About Working Parents (New York: William Morrow, 1999); Susan Chira, *A Mother's Place: Taking the Debate About Working Mothers Beyond Guilt and Blame* (New York: Harper-Collins, 1998); and James Levine and T. Pittinsky, *Working Fathers: New Strategies for Balancing Work and Family* (Reading, Mass.: Addison-Wesley, 1997).

227   *Daughters formulate*   Rose Glickman, *Daughters of Feminists: Young Women with Feminist Mothers Talk About Their Lives* (New York: St. Martin's Press, 1993).

227   *Anne Roiphe*   Roiphe, *Fruitful.*

229   *There's a great scene*   Allegra Goodman, *The Family Markowitz* (New York: Washington Square Press, 1997).

230   *"Aren't there any boys"*   Ruth Reichl, *Tender at the Bone: Growing Up at the Table* (New York: Random House, 1998).

230   *"Mother felt I'd chosen Nathan"*   Barbara Kingsolver, "Stone Dreams," in *Homeland and Other Stories* (New York: Harper & Row, 1989).

230   *"Admit it"*   Dani Shapiro, "Mother I Am Listening," in *From Daughters to Mothers: I've Always Meant to Tell You*, ed. Constance Warloe (New York: Pocket, 1997).

231   *"I had to take her revenge"*   Fatima Mernissi, *Dreams of Trespass: Tales of a Harem Girlhood* (Reading, Mass.: Addison-Wesley, 1994).

231   *"Each word"*   Bebe Moore Campbell, *Sweet Summer: Growing Up with and Without My Dad* (New York: Putnam, 1989).

231   *"jump at de sun"*   Zora Neale Hurston, "My Mother Was One to Dare All," in Shapiro, ed., *The Source of the Spring.*

231   *"Get away, get away"*   Lucille Clifton, "Generations," in *Writing Women's Lives: An Anthology of Autobiographical Narratives by Twentieth-Century Women Writers,* ed. Susan Cahill (New York: HarperPerennial, 1994).

231   *"Whenever my mother talks"*   Amy Tan, *The Kitchen God's Wife* (New York: Putnam, 1991).

233   *Katie Singer's novel*   Singer, *The Wholeness of a Broken Heart.*

235   *Ruth Reichl*   Reichl, *Tender at the Bone.*

237   *In her short story*   Leslie Newman, "Only a Phase," in *Her Face in the Mirror: Jewish Mothers and Daughters,* ed. Faye Moscowitz (Boston: Beacon Press, 1994).

238   *When Rabbi Miriam Tizrah Firestone*   Miriam Tizrah Firestone, *With Roots in Heaven: One Woman's Passionate Journey into the Heart of Her Faith* (New York: Dutton, 1998).

239 *After telling her daughter* Reichl, *Tender at the Bone.*

240 *"I think a lot of us"* Anne Bernays, "Doris E. Fleishman," in Shapiro, *The Source of the Spring.*

240 *"the women I loved most"* Dorothy Allison, *Two or Three Things I Know for Sure* (New York: Plume, 1996).

240 *Two highly acclaimed plays* Marsha Norman, *'Night, Mother* (New York: Hill & Mann, 1983); and Martin McDonagh, *The Beauty Queen of Leenane* (New York: Vintage, 1996).

242 *Connie May Fowler* Connie May Fowler, "If Only," in Warloe, *From Daughters to Mothers.*

243 *"I have one main rule for myself"* Rebecca Wells, *Divine Secrets of the Ya-Ya Sisterhood* (New York: HarperCollins, 1996).

245 One True Thing Anna Quindlen, *One True Thing* (New York: Random House, 1994).

246 *Alice Hoffman's bestseller* Alice Hoffman, *Here on Earth* (New York: Putnam, 1997).

247 *Rosemary Bray* Rosemary Bray, *Unafraid of the Dark: A Memoir* (New York: Random House, 1998).

248 Eating Chinese Food Naked Mei Ng, *Eating Chinese Food Naked* (New York: Washington Square Press, 1998).

249 *At the end of her childhood memoir* Mary Karr, *The Liars' Club* (New York: Penguin, 1995).

249 *Some of her mother's heroic, selfless moments* Quindlen, *One True Thing.*

250 *Barbara Kingsolver's story* Kingsolver, "Islands on the Moon," in *Homeland.*

EIGHT: MIDLIFE: INTERDEPENDENCE

259 *Margaret Morganroth Gullette* Margaret Morganroth Gullette, *Declining to Decline: Cultural Combat and the Politics of the Mid-Life* (Charlottesville: University Press of Virginia, 1997).

263 *attributes deemed most attractive by men* S. Sprecher, Q. Sullivan, and E. Hatfield, "Mate Selection Preferences: Gender Differences Examined in a National Sample," *Journal of Personality and Social Psychology* 66 (1994): 1074–80.

263 *Lillian Gish* Lillian Gish, in *An Uncommon Scold: Words to Live By,* ed. Abby Adams (New York: Simon & Schuster, 1989).

264   *birthrate for women*   Department of Health and Human Services News, 5 October 1999.

265   *Perhaps the most striking recent finding*   Centers for Disease Control, "Multiple Birthrate in Older Women Is Skyrocketing," bulletin 14 September 1999.

266   *"The key to maturity"*   Jacquelyn Mitchard, *The Rest of Us: Dispatches from the Mother Ship* (New York: Viking, 1997).

266   *Elizabeth Kaye*   Elizabeth Kaye, *Mid-life: Notes from the Halfway Mark* (Reading, Mass.: Addison-Wesley, 1995).

267   *"All one's life"*   Doris Lessing, in Adams, *Uncommon Scold*.

268   *The birthrate was higher for women*   A. Bachu, *Fertility of American Women* (Washington, D.C.: Bureau of the Census, September 1995).

271   *Like Rayona*   Michael Dorris, *A Yellow Raft in Blue Water* (New York: Warner, 1998).

272   *"I Stand Here Ironing"*   Tillie Olsen, "I Stand Here Ironing," in *Tell Me a Riddle* (New York: Dell, 1956).

273   *"Even if I came"*   Olsen, "I Stand Here Ironing."

273   *"who was everything"*   Olsen, "I Stand Here Ironing."

274   *Even more significant*   Two books that address the implications of increased longevity and the growing elderly population on the lives of women are Patricia Beard, *Good Daughters: Loving Our Mothers as They Age* (New York: Warner, 1999); and Mary Pipher, *Another Country: Navigating the Emotional Terrain of Our Elders* (New York: Riverhead, 1999).

276   *S. Jhoanna Robledo*   S. Jhoanna Robledo, "Visits with My Mother," www.babycenter.com.

276   *In Margaret Atwood's short story*   Margaret Atwood, "Significant Moments in the Life of My Mother," in *Bluebeard's Egg* (New York: Fawcett Crest, 1983).

277   *A letter written*   Meg Belichick, "As If I Am You," in *From Daughters to Mothers: I've Always Meant to Tell You,* ed. Constance Warloe (New York: Pocket, 1997).

278   *Judith Viorst*   Judith Viorst, "Family Feelings," in *Her Face in the Mirror: Jewish Mothers and Daughters,* ed. Faye Moscowitz (Boston: Beacon Press, 1994).

279   *"Mothers and daughters"*   Erica Jong, *Inventing Memory: A Novel of Mothers and Daughters* (New York: HarperCollins, 1997).

279   *Helen MacFarquhar*   Cathleen Schine, *The Love Letter* (New York: Houghton Mifflin, 1995).

279   *She "thanked the Fates"*   Schine, *The Love Letter*.

280   *Carolyn See*   See, in Warloe, *From Daughters to Mothers*.

280   *Following the death of her mother*   Lisa Carey, *The Mermaids Singing* (New York: Avon, 1998).

282   Road Song   Natalie Kusz, *Road Song: A Memoir* (New York: Farrar, Straus & Giroux, 1990).

284   *Writer Donna Baier Stein*   Donna Baier Stein, "My Vocation," in Warloe, *From Daughters to Mothers*.

285   *Lorrie Moore*   Lorrie Moore, "Which Is More Than I Can Say About Some People," in *Birds of America* (New York: Picador, 1998).

NINE: LATER YEARS: SHIFTING NEEDS

295   *Women constitute 71 percent*   Administration on Aging. U.S. Department of Health and Human Services, *Older Women: A Diverse and Growing Population,* fact sheet.

295   *At eighty-five and older*   U.S. Census Bureau, *The Aging of the U.S. Population,* 4 May 1995.

296   *Karen Fingerman*   Karen Fingerman, "Sources of Tension in the Aging Mother and Adult Daughter Relationship," *Psychology of Aging* 11 (1996): 591–606; and " 'We Had a Nice Little Chat': Age and Generational Differences in Mothers' and Daughters' Descriptions of Enjoyable Visits," *Journals of Gerontology: Psychological Sciences and Social Science*s 55 (2000): 95–106.

298   *"When Molly monologues"*   Erica Jong, "My Mother, My Daughter, and Me," in *The Source of the Spring: Mothers Through the Eyes of Women Writers,* ed. Judith Shapiro (Berkeley, Calif.: Conari Press, 1998).

298   *In her book* Another Country   Mary Pipher, *Another Country: Navigating the Emotional Terrain of Our Elders* (New York: Riverhead, 1999).

298   *different generational "time zones"*   Pipher, *Another Country*.

300   *Abuse of elders*   Lachs et al., "The Mortality of Elder Mistreatment," *Journal of the American Medical Association* 280 (1998): 428–32.

300   *Abuse is most likely*   Lachs et al., "Risk Factors for Reported Elder Abuse and Neglect: A Nine-Year Observational Cohort Study," *Gerontologist* 37 (1997): 469–74; K. Pillemer, "The Dangers of Dependency: New Findings on Domestic Violence Against the Elderly," *Social Problems* 33 (1995): 146–58.

301 *A recent* Washington Post *feature* Barbara Vobejda and Judith Havemann, " 'Child-Only' Cases Rise on Welfare Rolls: Parents Ineligible or Absent," *Washington Post,* 2 January 1999.

302 Troxel *v.* Granville Edward Walsh, "Court Limits Visitation Rights of Grandparents; State Can't Override Decision of a Fit Parent, Justices Say," *Washington Post,* 6 June 2000.

303 *"When my mother reached mid-life"* Elizabeth Kaye, *Mid-life: Notes from the Halfway Mark* (Reading, Mass.: Addison-Wesley, 1995).

303 *a beautiful letter* Feenie Ziner, "For the Time Being," in *From Daughters to Mothers: I've Always Meant to Tell You,* ed. Constance Warloe (New York: Pocket, 1997).

304 *In* Traveling Mercies Anne Lamott, *Traveling Mercies: Some Thoughts on Faith* (New York: Pantheon, 1999).

305 *Lorrie Moore* Lorrie Moore, *Birds of America* (New York: Picador, 1998).

306 *Jamaica Kincaid* Jamaica Kincaid, *The Autobiography of My Mother* (New York: Farrar, Straus & Giroux, 1996).

306 *Poet Wanda Coleman* Wanda Coleman, "Dear Mama: Words Having Failed," in Warloe, *From Daughters to Mothers.*

307 *Mary Gordon recounts* Mary Gordon, "My Mother Is Speaking from the Desert," in Shapiro, *Source of the Spring.*

307 *"Where has your memory gone"* Gordon, "My Mother Is Speaking."

307 *Journalist Tracy Thompson* Tracy Thompson, "Change of Place," *Washington Post Magazine,* 20 June 1998.

308 *"My mother was dead"* Lillian Hellman, *An Unfinished Woman: A Memoir* (New York: Little, Brown, 1969).

308 *"I was a mother myself"* Anne Bernays, in Warloe, *From Daughters to Mothers.*

309 *In the words of Gayl Jones* Gayl Jones, *Corregidora* (Boston: Beacon Press, 1987).

309 *Other daughters find comfort* C. Reese and R. Murray, "Transcendence: The Meaning of Great-Grandmothering," *Archives of Psychiatric Nursing* 10 (1996): 245–51.

309 *"If you are ever in a bad moment"* Erica Jong, *Inventing Memory: A Novel of Mothers and Daughters* (New York: HarperCollins, 1997).

AFTERWORD: ELEPHANTS AND OTHER BIG MOTHERS

314   *"screaming and trumpeting"*   Richard Estes, *The Behavior Guide to African Mammals* (Los Angeles: University of California Press, 1991).

316   *"uncanny knowledge of habitat"*   Cynthia Moss, *Elephant Memories: Thirteen Years in the Life of an Elephant Family* (Chicago: University of Chicago Press, 2000).

317   *Unfortunately, the first shot*   Clive Spinage, *Elephants* (London: Academic Press, 1997).

317   *Cynthia Moss*   Cynthia Moss, *Thirteen Years in the Life of an Elephant Family* (New York: William Morrow, 1988).

321   *On her daughter's second birthday*   Anna Quindlen, "The Glass Half Empty," in *Thinking Out Loud: On the Personal, the Political, the Public and the Private* (New York: Fawcett, 1994).

323   *We hear about women in Afghanistan*   Z. Rasekh et al., "Women's Health and Human Rights in Afghanistan," *Journal of the American Medical Association* 280 (1998): 449–45.

323   *We see images of terrified girls*   Fauziya Kassindja and Layli Miller Bashir, *Do They Hear You When You Cry* (New York: Dial Press, 1999).

323   *We hear the brothers and fathers*   *Crimes of Honor,* a documentary, aired originally on Cinemax, 28 February 2000. Narrated by Olympia Dukakis, this often horrifying program focuses on three women murdered by male family members over such issues as refusal to marry a cousin, running away, presumed sexual behavior. Such men have historically not been punished at all, or have suffered relatively benign consequences for killing their own sisters, daughters, and wives. The writings of Islam and Christianity are used to support the practice, despite the fact that documentation of its religious legitimacy is totally lacking. The efforts of three Jordanian women to change the laws, and the lax enforcement of the existing laws to protect vulnerable women, offer a ray of hope in an otherwise devastating film. See also Donna Abu-Nasr, "The Shame of Honor Killings," *Seattle Times,* 6 July 2000.

323   *We read that the United Nations*   United Nations Fourth World Conference on Women, Beijing, 1995, and Beijing+5; *The World's Women 2000: Trends and Statistics,* United Nations Statistical Division, May 2000.

324   The Joy Luck Club   Amy Tan, *The Joy Luck Club* (New York: Ivy Books, 1989).

326   *Erica Jong's novel*   Erica Jong, *Inventing Memory: A Novel of Mothers and Daughters* (New York: HarperCollins, 1997).

328   *A wonderful example of an intentional bridge*   Shireen Dodson and Teresa Parker, *The Mother-Daughter Book Club: How Ten Busy Mothers and Daughters Came Together to Talk, Laugh, and Learn Through Their Love of Reading* (New York: HarperCollins, 1997).

328   *superior-court judge Mary Gooden Terrell*   Patrice Gaines, "Hats on for High Tea: Society Inducts Inner-City Girls into Mentoring Program," *Washington Post,* 8 July 2000.

329   *Grace, at thirteen, was kidnapped*   "Grace," speaker at the United Nations Beijing+5 Conference, "Gender Equality, Development and Peace for the Twenty-first Century," New York, June 2000.

ACKNOWLEDGMENTS

Thanks to my editor, Jennifer Brehl, who patiently guided me and this project through to its completion. Her interest in and enthusiasm for the subject matter was particularly important during those times when I never wanted to hear the words *mother* or *daughter* again. My agent, Arielle Eckstut, extends herself well beyond her contractual duties. She is a trusted literary sounding board, a constant friend, and provides a firm kick in the ass when necessary. I am grateful to Rachel Klayman who was responsible for breathing this book into life. Copyeditor Margaret Wimberger provided the manuscript with a much-needed going-over. I picture at least ten nuns turning over in their graves.

John, Mary, Brian, Brett, Julie, and Riley Depenbrock introduced me to the beauty of the Chesapeake Bay and allowed me to reside there in complete silence for blessed stretches of time. My parents, John and Mary Louise Manning, remain the source of limitless love and encouragement. The older I get, the more grateful I am for their active involvement as heads of the family. My sisters, Sarah, Priscilla, and Rachel, and brothers, Mark and Chip, along with partners and progeny are an open and endless source of support and material. My mother-in-law, Jane Depenbrock, will be greatly missed. Nancy Ryan, David Cooney, and Peter Cooney regaled me with mother-daughter stories from generations past. My nieces, Chelsea, Christie, Tori, and Grace, were excellent examples and sometimes challengers of my psychological understanding of development. Nephews Tom and Sean provided interesting contrasts.

My sister-in-law Janet Weschler and niece Karen have also been wonderful models. Raina Graves and her children, Jade, Deven, and Darren, have become a second family—a great gift for a woman who misses her grown-up girl.

Pat Dalton has been my true companion in motherhood. Our friendship began as partners in pregnancy and continues as our daughters move into adulthood. Writers Andrew Solomon, Meri Nana-Ama Danquah, and Rich Simon are more recent treasures. I thank Kay Jamison for long lovely lunches, elephants, patchwork quilts, and so much more. Rosie O'Donnell's encouragement of my writing means a great deal to me. I am honored to have *her* writing at the beginning of this book.

When I become too aware of the dark random cruelty in the world, my daughter, Keara Manning Depenbrock, reminds me, by her very existence, of a parallel world full of light, possibility, and compassion. I have been blessed. And if I forget it from time to time, I can count on her to remind me. My husband, Brian Depenbrock, risked banishment with his frank assessment of my first draft, which, distilled to its essence would boil down to the word *sucks*. Little did he know that my request for him to critique the book fell into the "Does my butt look big in this?" line of inquiry in which there is no possible way for the respondent to win. The fact that he was correct ultimately sank in, and now I thank him for his rock-solid honesty. My butt does look big. The first draft did suck. He loves me anyway. And it's more than enough.

♨ HarperSanFrancisco Quill

Books by Martha Manning:

THE COMMON THREAD
Mothers and Daughters: The Bond We Never Outgrow
ISBN 0-380-80379-8 (paperback)

Drawing on her personal and professional experiences, Manning casts a fascinating new light on what can—and should—be a dynamic, fluid, and mutually empowering relationship.

"For women whose automatic response to the word 'mother' is a groan. . . clinical psychologist Manning offers a new view on a relationship that begins at conception and can continue long after the other's death." —*Publishers Weekly*

CHASING GRACE
Reflections of a Catholic Girl, Grown Up
ISBN 0-06-251312-5 (paperback)

"I used to think that grace is what happens when your toast falls butter-side-up. But that's not grace, it's good fortune. Grace is what helps you celebrate the joy of a good landing and tolerate the disappointment of a bad one." —Martha Manning

"Poignant, witty, often caustic . . . Manning's meditations will appeal to thoughtful readers of every persuasion." —*Library Journal*

UNDERCURRENTS
A Life Beneath the Surface
ISBN 0-06-251184-X (paperback)

This riveting memoir traces the devastating path of clinical depression through the diaries of Martha Manning—a psychotherapist who became a patient and underwent electroshock therapy.

"A convincing testament to the inexorable cruelty of depression and a frightening reminder of its unprejudiced choice of victims." —*New York Times Book Review*